C000132929

Advance Praise for **Movements on the Streets and in Schools**

"What does counter-pedagogy mean today? Within the framework of governmentality studies, *Movements on the Streets and in Schools* provides some answers as it takes us through critical ethnographic narratives on school life and life in the streets of Oaxaca and Mexico City. The author describes counter-pedagogy as 'an action within the normative frameworks of state-funded public education where the actors enact their education in a different way,' to then conclude that 'government, the conduct of conducts, leads to chances for counter-pedagogies, not in spite of the state that drafts educational reforms and deploys repressive force but rather through these measures.' Detailed ethnographic research carried out over years and lucid analysis allows us to understand the complexity of everyday struggles for public education waged by teachers not only in school but also in the street. The book winds between struggles in Mexico that date back to the beginning of the twentieth century and meticulous current fieldwork that gathers multiple voices. It sheds light on the tragedies—like the forty-three teachers in Ayotzinapa killed by government forces—that continue to ravish Mexico and the region in general. Talking about governmentality and resistance the book, then, has a lot to say about critical pedagogical practices and the everyday struggles for public education, not only in Mexico and Latin America but—most likely—in other regions as well."

Silvia Grinberg, Universidad Nacional de San Martín, Argentina

Movements on the
Streets and in Schools

This book is part of the Peter Lang Education list.
Every volume is peer reviewed and meets
the highest quality standards for content and production.

PETER LANG
New York • Bern • Berlin
Brussels • Vienna • Oxford • Warsaw

Stephen T. Sadlier

Movements on the
Streets and in Schools

State Repression, Neoliberal Reforms,
and Oaxaca Teacher Counter-pedagogies

PETER LANG
New York • Bern • Berlin
Brussels • Vienna • Oxford • Warsaw

Library of Congress Cataloging-in-Publication Data

Names: Sadlier, Stephen T., author.
Title: Movements on the streets and in schools: state repression, neoliberal reforms,
and Oaxaca teacher counter-pedagogies / Stephen T. Sadlier.
Description: New York: Peter Lang Publishing, 2019.
Includes bibliographical references and index.
Identifiers: LCCN 2018028671 | ISBN 978-1-4331-5381-5 (hardcover: alk. paper)
ISBN 978-1-4331-5382-2 (paperback) | ISBN 978-1-4331-5383-9 (ebook pdf)
ISBN 978-1-4331-5384-6 (epub) | ISBN 978-1-4331-5385-3 (mobi)
Subjects: LCSH: Teachers—Political activity—Mexico—Oaxaca (State)
Teachers' unions—Mexico—Oaxaca (State)
Educational change—Mexico—Oaxaca (State)
Education and state—Mexico—Oaxaca (State)
Classification: LCC LB2844.53.M62 O257 2019 | DDC 371.109727—dc23
LC record available at https://lccn.loc.gov/2018028671
DOI 10.3726/b13269

Bibliographic information published by **Die Deutsche Nationalbibliothek**.
Die Deutsche Nationalbibliothek lists this publication in the "Deutsche
Nationalbibliografie"; detailed bibliographic data are available
on the Internet at http://dnb.d-nb.de/.

Cover image: "Sadne$s, Halt, No, Fear, Violence."
Street art, Oaxaca City, Mexico, June 2010.
Photograph by Stephen T. Sadlier.

The paper in this book meets the guidelines for permanence and durability
of the Committee on Production Guidelines for Book Longevity
of the Council of Library Resources.

Table of Contents

Figures

Foreword

Not so long ago, a centralized education system in Mexico started to mold national consciousness through an educational strategy in a nation with diverse *pueblos*.[1] However, in recent decades, policy and official textbooks in Mexico have shifted away from trying to unite everyone and toward a project of standardization and accountability. Teachers in rural Oaxaca are fighting to maintain professional dignity and safeguard teaching from a collapse into training exercises, where human beings become human resources. This book presents a series of semi-related stories about how political and economic forces—from the business sector, the federal government, international free trade agreements, international banks, the United Nations, and the police—have a hand in the workings of rural public education. This book also tells stories about how parents, schoolchildren, teachers, and many others struggle for a better life through education, by accepting some elements of what the executive stakeholders mandate, rejecting others, and working in the gaps between the official and unofficial.

Today, families, students, and teachers in Mexico and across the globe are weighing in on their public education. In recent years in Chile, students themselves have organized against how school vouchers have eviscerated the quality of public schools. High school students, called the *pingüinos* for the appearance of their school uniforms, have succeeded at getting an audience with President Bachelet after riot police used excessive force against them, a visual that stole the thunder away from the new president, a one-time political prisoner in the infamous Villa Grimaldi detention center. In Mexico, forty-three preservice teachers at the Ayotzinapa Normal School were recently *disappeared*.[2] Decision makers in the Mexican government and the National Educators' Union (SNTE)[3] have attempted to defund rural normal schools, institutions that have been producing socially committed activists for a century.[4] Public schooling has factored into other public struggles, suggesting that the value of publicly funded schooling, and the conduct[5] of the actors who participate in it, is contentious.

Considering the local specificities and universal trends that weave into public schooling, this book explores how teachers carry out their practice through the channels of ongoing public debates, conversations, and what Tsing (2005) has called "friction of global connection" (p. x). In the chapters that follow, teachers from Oaxaca, Mexico, factor their public and pedagogical work through friction, through *quality, patrimony,* and *governability.* Thus, I provide examples of teacher struggles over the present and future of public education when privatization, standardized measurements counting as the sole indicator of quality, and the metrics of the marketplace now guide policy makers, administrators, teachers' unions, teachers, pupils, and parents.

This book is about pedagogies, both in spaces where teacher activists face police and paramilitary violence and across contexts where market-based reforms prevail. The story might just as well discuss educational actors facing free market trends in schooling anywhere across the globe; though, the location in Mexico is not coincidental. One country's educational apparatuses, historical struggles over knowledge, and citizen formation through education tend to follow a local path. Yet today, education has been saddled onto economic productivity in Mexico as much as in the United States; teachers the world over face analogous pressures for accountability and outcomes-based learning and experience surveillance and reforms that attempt to remake teaching and learning into marketable, manageable, and comparable units of productivity.

Our story here plays out in southeastern and central Mexico, in part because that is where I became a teacher and researcher. I first taught and studied teaching practices at the University of Guadalajara, Mexico, where professional artists and intellectuals volunteered their expertise to the university. Juan José Arreola, who had just won the *Premio de Literatura Latinoamericana y del Caribe Juan Rulfo*, a major literary prize in Latin America, would lecture to packed rooms a few doors away from my classroom. I would visit the university library downtown and observe Fernando del Paso, serving as head librarian, and attend film festivals at Cineforo Universidad de Guadalajara, where the directors and actors would turn from their front row seats and greet an applauding public. Decades later, when I started my doctorate at the University of Massachusetts (UMass), I felt a similar sense of collective service. Though UMass had become less accessible to the middle and working classes and less supported by the state legislature, inside the university I saw solidarity and activism that reminded me of two decades earlier when I taught in Mexico and observed teaching as a public commitment. At UMass, I first met Julie Graham, a political economist who theorized about how theft and gift giving were economic activities. At Julie's rethinking economy class, professors sat in because of Julie's immense reputation, while social science and humanities graduate students shared as much about community-supported agriculture and antiracism as straight-up political economic theory. When I met Julie, I had been supervising preservice teacher candidates who were seeking state licensure. At first, I doubted if I belonged in the class until Julie began to talk about planting vegetables in urban gardens. Everyone belonged in the conversations, perhaps less because of the inclusivity of the topic than from Julie's manner of drawing everyone in to rethinking economic practices.

Julie was not well then, though her eyes had a smolder of mischief, and learning with her lacked any prescribed routine. She would assign her own books and make no apology about it, and yet even as our class discussed ideas she had propagated, she let us talk them out, remain silent, or express elliptical or scattered concepts without trying to varnish over the conversation with her truth. When I took my turn to speak, Julie just listened and avoided entering the discussion until I had finished. She approached me later to say that she was glad I was in the class. I was in awe of Julie as a teacher more than as an expert in political economy.

Three years after studying with her, I was completing the fieldwork in Oaxaca City that would produce this book. Julie had died earlier that year, yet I only came to feel her absence when I ran into her equal in Oaxaca. I had been reading the work of Gustavo Esteva and sought him out by following the trail of topics and events that interested him. A day after knocking on doors for his contact info, this public intellectual sent me his first of many email responses. If Julie was renowned, Gustavo was legendary. To me, Gustavo also resembled the civic-minded artist intellectuals I had observed twenty years earlier in Guadalajara, though he showed greater commitment to political economic justice. Like Julie, he spoke with effervescence, gesturing through his whole body in the way Julie would glow through her eyes. Further, Gustavo treated students much like Julie had done. Concepts and interventions belonged in conversation rather than in dusty books or coherent philosophies; thus, these two scholars, Julie in the north and Gustavo in the south, scaffolded intellectual, activist, and affective pedagogies that led me to the public intellectual of Oaxacan schoolteachers featured in this book. Out of gratitude for this, I dedicate this book on teachers and teaching to Julie Graham and Gustavo Esteva.

I would also like to acknowledge the manifold means of support that enrich this book. First, Chapter Five includes material previously published in *Global Studies of Childhood*, volume 8, issue 1, and Chapter Seven is a reworking of an article in *Journal of Latinos and Education*, volume 15, issue 4. I am grateful for the example of parents, students, and teachers who strive toward public education for everyone. I cite the example of Barbara Madeloni, who buoyed the efforts of her students to reject a preservice assessment that outsourced teacher education to a for-profit regime. I also recall Maricela López Ayora and Dalia Guzmán Vásquez, who have shown me how to believe in public education and to approach research over tea and coffee before data recorders and notepads. I extend admiration-filled thanks to teachers José Luis, Nancy, Rocio, Angie, Toñis, Sergio, Mariluz, Lulu, Oscar, Pablo, Bernardo, Freddi, and Sara. Mexico City- and Oaxaca City-based scholars and activists showed prodigious generosity with their time and knowledge. Hugo Aboites, Eduardo Bautista, and Bulmaro Vásquez Romero took time out of their schedules to discuss Mexican social movements and education. Salomón Nahmad Sittón engaged with me over email while Gloria Zafra and Francisco Verástegui offered pages of narrative responses to my questions.

At UMass, my dissertation committee, Maria José Botelho, Sangeeta Kamat, Barbara Cruikshank, and Laura Valdiviezo, first recommended I write this book. I attentively observed how each one taught. Maria José Botelho proved key in my linking pedagogies of the streets with critical and emergent literacies in schools. My first connection with her was when she introduced herself at a conference and talked with me for an hour on affect in critical pedagogy, the sets of views on teaching and learning as unavoidably political. Sangeeta Kamat became the first professor to show me how teaching and learning depended on rigorous social theory and on a student's willingness to dig into theory without seeking immediate application. I met Barbara Cruikshank at a keynote presentation she made at a conference on theorist Michel Foucault, and it was she who recommended both the friction format for this book and proposed that writing it might help me conduct myself as a teacher differently. Laura Valdiviezo turned my gaze to ethnographic storytelling, providing books from her personal library to encourage an appreciation for this mode of observing and representing. The present book would have remained unwritten if not for the backing of these four masters. Additionally, professors Sonia Álvarez and Meg Gebhard allowed me to draw my ongoing research into UMass course papers.

I am indebted to other practitioners and scholars outside those in Oaxaca, Mexico City, and Amherst. From the School for International Training (SIT), Alvino Fantini and Beatriz Fantini embodied the joys of teaching dinner table *tertulia*. At SIT, Paula Green and John Ungerleider modeled how to relate post-conflict with education. Similarly, Silvia Grinberg at the Universidad Nacional de San Martín and María Elena García and José Antonio Lucero at the University of Washington (UW) shared personal contacts and insightful readings on Latin American social movements, introducing me to the Dangerous Subjects works-in-progress group where Filiberto Barajas-López and Cynthia Steel provided insightful comments on my book prospectus. Additionally, geographers Sarah Mills and Peter Kraftl helped me explore spaces of education while Paul Carr and Brad Porfilio facilitated my knowledge of education and militarism. Kara Dellacioppa, Judy Hellman, Rebecca Tarlau, and Ruth Trinidad Galván engaged with me electronically on issues of culture and power in Latin America, and an anonymous reviewer with *Journal of Latinos and Education* offered resources for linking humor to classroom teaching.

Among my researcher peers, I have benefited from check-ins, chats, messages, editorial glances, and funding support. I thank Olga Acosta, César Antonio Aguilar, Cristina Arancibia, Martha Balaguera, Gloria Barragán, Rukmini Becera, Thelma Belmonte Alcántara, Adriana Bustamente, Julieta Chaparro, Roxana Chiappa Baros, Farida Flemming, Flor García, Erin Goldstein, Avertano Guzmán, Jennifer Johnson, Marky Jean-Pierre, Larry Geri, Jeff Kelly-Lowenstein, Rebecca Lisi, Kathy McDonough, Marcia de Mello, Clara Meza, Nacho Morales, Alice Nelson, Lee O'Donnell, Fabiola Orozco-Mendoza, Marcela Romero, Rafael Rogers, Luis Antonio Silva, Luis Octavio Silva, Carmen Villagómez, and Elsa Wiehe. Michelle Sadlier provided indispensable editorial assistance.

Logistically, I thank the UMass School of Education and Undergraduate Advising and Learning Communities for funding during my studies as well as the university's Center for Latin American, Caribbean and Latino Studies for their 2010 predissertation grant. 2013–2014 William J. Fulbright Teaching and Research Core Scholar funding enabled this project to extend from individual articles to a single text. The Interlibrary Loan departments of UMass, UW, and South Puget Sound Community College graciously dug up books and articles that feature throughout. The CEDES 22 office of Oaxaca's Sección 22 generously shared documents, and the leaders of Mexico City's Sección 9 permitted me to enter trade union conferences. A special thanks to Guadaloupe Alcántara for her hospitality in Mexico City as well as the teachers, parents, and students in San Sebastián Abasolo, Oaxaca City, and Huajuapan de León. The words here are mine; I assume responsibility for lapses and inaccuracies as well as moments of joy within.

Notes

1. *Pueblos* signifies *people* in a more personalized *you-and-I* sense than people as *la gente*. *Pueblos* also means towns or communities of people with similar ethnicity or language.
2. One teacher expressed to me how the state wages a "low-intensity" war against teachers. Teachers in Oaxaca discuss disappearances and other repression to eliminate a political rival, evident in the unresolved case of the forty-three missing preservice teachers from Ayotzinapa, Guerrero, just west of Oaxaca.
3. The Mexican state created the SNTE trade union apparatus in 1943 to incorporate the teachers into a governable syndicate (Torres, 1991, p. 165).
4. See Castellanos and Jiménez (2007) for a background on rural normal school radicalism across Mexico and Concha Malo (2015) for the Ayotzinapa preservice teachers in 2014.
5. Though I may consider *conduct* as a synonym of *behavior*, I use it with a double meaning. *Conduct*, as a noun, becomes the way we choose to think, feel, and act in the institutional and interpersonal landscapes in which we go about our business. As a verb, *to conduct* is the manifold ways that institutions (public radio funding drives, corporate advertising, and recycling canisters) appeal to our sense of truth, goodness, and responsibility. We conduct ourselves and we are conducted by others (see Dean, 2010; Lemke, 2011; Li, 2007; Popkewitz, 2009; Rose, 1999).

References

Castellanos, L., & Jiménez, M. C. A. (2007). *México armado 1943–1981*. Mexico City: Ediciones Era.

Concha Malo, M. (2015). Ayotzinapa: Preocupaciones abiertas. *Cotidiano, 189*, 45–49.

Dean, M. (2010). *Governmentality: Power and rule in modern society*. Los Angeles, CA: SAGE.

Lemke, T. (2011). *Foucault, governmentality, and critique*. Boulder, CO: Paradigm Publishers.

Li, T. (2007). *The will to improve: Governmentality, development, and the practice of politics*. Durham, NC: Duke University Press.

Popkewitz, T. (2009). Why the desire for university-school collaboration and the promise of pedagogical content knowledge may not matter as much as we think. In M. A. Peters, A.C. Besley, M. Olssen, S. Maurer, & S. Weber (Eds.), *Governmentality studies in education* (pp. 217–234). Rotterdam: Sense Publishers.

Rose, N. (1999). *Powers of freedom: Reframing political thought.* New York, NY: Cambridge University Press.

Torres, C. A. (1991). El corporativismo estatal, las políticas educativas y los movimientos estudiantiles y magisteriales en México. *Revista Mexicana de Sociología, 53*(2), 159–183.

Tsing, A. L. (2005). *Friction: An ethnography of global connection.* Princeton, NJ: Princeton University Press.

Movements of Diverse Inquiries

In April 2011, toward the end of my second of two field visits to research the political projects in public elementary schools in southeastern Mexico, I entered a café in the touristic part of Oaxaca City, the state of Oaxaca's principal urban area. From a magazine rack I pulled down *Noticias*, a local newspaper sympathetic to the public elementary school teachers whom I had been shadowing for a year in their protest and classroom teaching activities, and a perceived "enemy" of the ruling party, the Partido Revolucionario Institucional (PRI) (Velásquez, 2010, p. 180). Reading *Noticias* at the café, which sold whole grain muffins and organic lettuce, I took a short break from writing up my field notes.

At this café I would often run into others doing Oaxaca-based research and activism projects, including Oaxacan public school teachers from out of town. One rural *telesecundaria*[1] teacher, whose laptop keystroke rhythm I had interrupted when I saw a book on pedagogy beside her on the table, became a participant in the present critical ethnography, a loose assembly of qualitative research methodologies that maintain that social research does not just capture what happens in the world but is a force in the social world, too. This teacher would ride eleven hours by bus to her state's capital every weekend, work at cafés like this one, then travel Sunday night another eleven hours to be present for Monday morning teaching. This day, sitting with my *Noticias*, I read that a small subsection of the unionized Oaxacan teachers of the Sección 22, the teachers' trade union local in Oaxaca who spearhead the Coordinadora Nacional de Trabajadores de la Educación (CNTE) dissident movement,[2] would be passing in protest nearby. Marching, a public pedagogical practice (Biesta, 2012; Sandlin, Schultz, & Burdick, 2009), has become customary among unionized Oaxacan teachers both to critique the Mexican state and private educational initiatives and to call for the democratization of the Sindicato Nacional de Trabajadores de la Educación (SNTE) within which the Sección 22 operates. Eager to catch up with these teacher campaigners, I folded up the newspaper, stepped out, and walked northwest to intersect them in the piercing midday sun.

Without further details of the teachers' march, I estimated where they might be at that hour: trudging the avenues from the Oaxaca state's institutional unit, the Instituto Estatal de Educación Pública de Oaxaca (IEEPO),[3] of the national Secretariat of Education, the SEP, northwest of downtown, heading toward the *zócalo*, the shady central square of the venerable provincial capital. As a state institution, the IEEPO opened its doors in 1992 and modernized educational reforms that disconnected select administrative activities from the educational administration apparatuses in Mexico City in favor of local entities (Martínez Vásquez, 2004).[4] Oaxacan teachers have since used the IEEPO building to orient protests. The practice of gathering before the gaze of an institutional adversary is common, just as the façade of the SEP office in the historic center of Mexico City has been the location of teacher protests in the nation's capital, soliciting responses from allies and adversaries.[5] For the pedagogies of the teachers governed by what goes on inside these edifices of state authority, protesting in the streets formed part of their teaching.

In the early afternoon I caught up with the teachers, walking with children in groups of twos and threes and toting umbrellas as they marched past Llano Park, just north of downtown. When I saw them, they had started to issue taunts at a hushed, gazing collection of members of the 95th Infantry Battalion, in helmets and fatigues, who sat in a green troop transporter parked at the curb. The soldiers never stirred, and the teachers passed without major incident.[6] I stood reading marchers' signs and scanning their faces but recognized none of them, as they toted the insignias of delegations, union subsections of at least forty teachers, from diverse parts of Oaxaca state.[7] When the chanting marchers passed the placidly seated soldiers, I turned toward the park behind me, which was also filled with teachers.

As I walked toward Llano Park, I heard my name. A group of children came running to meet me. I had not seen these faces in the several weeks that had lapsed since my visit to their elementary school in the village of Tecotitlán.[8] I paused to greet them in the heart of their state's capital city and decided to follow them to their destination, a collection of white tarpaulin pavilions recently erected for an open-air educational festival. The students had come to read aloud from their favorite books, an established literacy practice in the school,[9] and I wondered if their teacher lingered nearby. By a cluster of the stretched vinyl sun shelters, I recognized several mothers from my fieldwork in Tecotitlán, but with no teachers around, I wandered by the scores of booths that temporarily filled the center of the park by the statue of former President Benito Juárez,[10] another rural Oaxacan who came as a child to Oaxaca City.

As I ambled, the teachers at the pavilions who were running the educational festival projected none of the contrarian opinions of the marchers; for indeed, the IEEPO had sponsored the event. I wondered how a wing of the same dissident teachers' union could engage in an anti-state protest while their comrades beside me worked side by side with the targets of the protest. This juxtaposition captured my attention, and wishing to learn about how a teacher saw the contours between the state and the predominantly primary-school-level public educators, I paused to ask a mid-career teacher about this connection. I had met this educator in Tecotitlán a year before at a school book festival where some of the same students I encountered in the park had performed and read. I asked her how teachers' union loyalists and state education officials collaborated at the reading event and if the marchers' antipathy to the state drowned out her work at the pavilions. It was kind of a moot question, as beside us, dancing student shoes click-clacked on the wooden stage by banners of the "We Learn Together" festival that bore IEEPO crests and was supervised by Sección 22 members.[11] Mid-event, my inter-locutor indicated that attention to reading was booming in Oaxacan education. This involved the participation of many educational stakeholders, including a pedagogical wing of the Sección 22 that through in-service training manuals and workshops (CEDES 22, 2010; CNTE, 2010a, 2010b) promotes the instructional viability of *alternative education,*[12] the pedagogies of *Indigenous*[13] worldviews, anti-classism and well-framed learning for students of all backgrounds (Hernán-dez, 2009, p. 337). She specified that IEEPO officials hold meetings with "them," meaning those in the union; hence, for all the radical politics, adversaries collab-orated.

I realized that I could not depend on clear ideological divisions if I was going to approach the critical literacies of Oaxacan educators. Indeed, affiliation supple-ness shapes the pedagogies of Oaxacan educators: sometimes they dissent as mem-bers of the Sección 22; sometimes they embrace the officialdom of the IEEPO;

and sometimes they navigate between the cracks of these two. For example, a zone supervisor[14] revealed that "change" should and does take place in the classroom, not the marches. And when she marched, as all Sección 22 members do, she strode in mute protestation against the peer pressure to verbalize rebellious claims.[15] I emphasize here that critical educators resist state-sponsored repression and refuse misguided educational reforms,[16] though critical educators at times obtain state and private sector funding for their projects, carry out the projects below tarpaulins and tree canopies alongside rivals and neutral observers, impose a sense of being present (Sassen, 2002, p. 11) in buildings and on streets where they lack any authority, and neither offer nor believe in promises that the future will be better than this.

This story is about the critical movements undertaken by politically and pedagogically active teachers who at times operate as state-funded public servants, at times as activists in a trade union, and at times in the crevasses between or within the two. The story focuses on how elementary school teachers returned to their villages after November of 2006. This came after a police raid against a teacher encampment in mid-June had spurred what teachers called *el Movimiento*,[17] the Movement of 2006,[18] a phase of the multidecade dissident teachers' movement in Oaxaca.[19] The social upheaval involved hundreds of organizations and hundreds of thousands of individuals asking for the resignation of the Oaxaca governor, though the call did not come from a single interest group.[20] Educators paint a complex portrait of a dissident union active in these protests and in school-based teaching. This set of associations and undertakings offers a captivating and worthy opening toward noticing actually existing critical pedagogies in a larger activist movement, conducted through movements of diverse inquiries rather than a unified strategy.

Spacing Pedagogy

I herein use the term *pedagogy* to describe the process of how social relationships work when people are developing knowledge, sharing meaning, or participating in institutions. This is not just about a teacher teaching or a student studying, nor is it a dynamic that is easily captured and categorized by observing the nitty-gritty of family, peer group, or teacher-student relations. Pedagogy, as I describe it in this story, is not only analysis of best practices for addressing student needs but also how we come to understand what a best practice is and why it is important in the first place. Pedagogy is in part teaching students how to handle words and information, and in part how politics, economics, and history operate outside of the classroom. Borrowing from Carmen Luke (2010), I recognize that "pedagogy" is not "an isolated intersubjective event" but instead is "fundamentally defined by and a product of a network of historical, political, sociocultural, and knowledge relations[21]" (p. 130). A pedagogical practice thus begins not with teaching and learning, but rather with inquiring into how social networks sustain students, parents and teachers both in and out of schools. The ways a teacher or researcher links intersubjective events of knowledge relations to culture, history, and political economy is what I call *spacing* pedagogy.

Spacing pedagogy in this story, which is primarily set in Oaxaca and Mexico City, presents us with a problem of scale. There is friction between the local and the global that interacts in spacing pedagogy. Oaxacan educators work under locally specific cultural, artistic, linguistic, and historical conditions, demonstrated by resistance movements drawing on local artistic motifs (Albertani, 2009; Rubin, 1994), speech (Campbell, 2001), and alternative education (Hernández Castillo, 2001; Maldonado, 2010). But the local is only part of the story. Unlike the United States, however like Brazil, Colombia, and Chile, Mexico has a legacy of centralized educational policy, though modernization projects in education have taken root in communities in an incomplete and uneven manner (García Canclini, 2001).

The 1910–1917 Mexican Revolution, led by teacher anarchists (Cockcroft, 1967) and rural intellectuals (Knight & Urquidi, 1989) toppled a dictatorship. Two decades later, in the 1930s, public educators went to rural communities and helped forge the modern secular nation through universal schooling (Raby, 1974; Vaughan, 1982, 1997). A socially committed teaching praxis has a long history in Mexico.[22] Lucio Cabañas, who led an insurrection among the destitute in the early 1970s (Hodges, 1995, p. 95) and nonviolent pedagogues across Oaxaca, who served as the primary village links to the outside world (Howell, 1997, p. 266), however, grew out of nonlocal occurrences like the 1968 Mexico City student uprising (Hodges, 1995, p. 112) and the Cuban Revolution (p. 95). Teachers see their work in local, regional, and international terms, so a question of scale that makes carrying out an ethnography of critical teaching problematic in terms of where to set boundaries.

The problem of scale furthermore clashes with a moral commitment among teachers that makes it challenging for them to separate teaching from their communal, familial, and spiritual roles. In some cases, teachers have taken on pastoral roles in a social commitment to local conditions. Becoming a godparent, a Mexican tradition for establishing mutual aid and widening the extended family, has fallen to rural teachers.[23] One teacher I interviewed, for example, reported cases of parents taking their newborns to the teacher for baptism, as recently as the 1970s. Another teacher, even more recently found himself playing a godfather role by advocating before a court of law for a student who was wrongly accused of participating in a massacre. The teacher told the judge that the student couldn't have carried out the crime because the student was in class at the time.

"Who is going to stand up for the students if I don't?" the teacher explained to me when we talked about his commitment to advocating for students and their families in the court of law. Oaxacan teachers, when coming to the city to protest, come as civil servants and trade unionists who bear a historical burden for helping the needy. Teaching for many becomes as moral as it is occupational, for it involves taking up "intellectuals of the poor" (Foweraker, 1993, p. 19) and community advocate (Bautista Martínez, 2010a) positions which are galvanized when politicians and the business elite attempt to turn education from a "social right" to a "commodity (*mercancia*)" (Arriaga Lemus, 2015, p. 2). Oaxacan public teachers engage in their communities, as salaried civil servants for the Mexican state and as activists for public education in general.

It would be reductionist, however, to label village teachers as rural or confine their practice to their schools and communities when they campaign in Oaxaca City and Mexico City and act against free-market reforms that have shaped education worldwide.[24] I often opted to leave the state of Oaxaca to research Oaxacan teachers. When it was in full protest mode, in late May 2010, I walked around the Mexico City[25] zócalo, a leafless concrete square with a central flagpole unlike its sylvan counterpart in Oaxaca. In those early weeks of my fieldwork, I remained in the capital city because of the prominence of Oaxacan teacher activism. In my first day of fieldwork, I talked with a Oaxacan teacher at the Mexico City zócalo *plantón* (see figure 1.1) at a makeshift booth with electricity and several cellphones plugged into chargers. Then, leaving for Oaxaca on a first-class bus a week later, I sat beside a young woman who worked as an administrative assistant in a rural Oaxacan school and who was returning home after her week of duty at the plantón urban open-air protest encampment, sleeping on flattened cardboard boxes below tarpaulins and attending social and political gatherings. Mexico City is a Oaxacan city, pedagogically speaking (see figures 1.2 and 1.3).

As much as the pedagogies go beyond the local, they also step outside of formal teaching and learning. Concluding my fieldwork in May 2011, again on the Mexico City zócalo, I observed assorted groups such as the Mexican Electrical Workers Union (SME) organizing against the privatization of their trade, and the promoters of justice for the murderers of Oaxacan public intellectual, Bety Cariño and Finnish aid worker, Jyri Jaakkola, who were gunned down by paramilitaries in the village of San Juan Copala, Oaxaca. During the year since my arrival, someone had painted the gray zócalo stone red and added poetic ruminations and political statements in white. One message, in full view of the presidential balcony, suggested that if Mubarak[26] got ousted in Egypt, why not the Mexican leadership today? Elsewhere on this central square, a rectangular vinyl banner with a printed image of Mexican President Felipe Calderón[27] stood taut like volleyball net with piles of old shoes on the ground before it. A man speaking through a loudspeaker invited bystanders to step up and throw shoes at the president, as this was a tried and true form of social protest from the Middle East, an apparent reference to an Iraqi journalist who hurled shoes at President George W. Bush at a press conference, two and a half years earlier. More overtly serious placards and pasted signs

Figure 1.1: Mexico City zócalo, May 2010. Source: Author.

Protest plantón tarpaulins in the foreground, the Municipal Cathedral behind left and the Federal Palace far right. One of the scarlet awnings on the Palace façade is the ceremonial presidential balcony. The tricolor Mexican flag is held by the central flagpole, the base of which bore notices for missing people. Behind that, in the gap between the two edifices of clerical and state power, each of which is open to the public, is the site of Templo Mayor, an excavated pyramid that dates from the time this spot formed the center of Tenochtitlan, the capital of the Aztec civilization. Notice a pedestrian passageway connecting the sidewalks of commercial streets with the zócalo, opening the square to passersby with no necessary role to play in the protests, interest in politics, religion, or history. Its public accessibility turns these multipurpose openings into fields of vibrant public pedagogies.

of missing people on the central flagpole lingered beside the Calderón shoe-toss booth. As much as the Mexico City plantón becomes a Oaxacan pedagogical space, its sonic and visual landscape tells stories of other people's politics.

Oaxacan schoolteachers stand out across the protest-space pedagogies on the Mexico City zócalo in part because the teachers take on struggles broader than best practices in the classroom. One day, near the Mexico City zócalo, I attended a teacher conference run by the Sección 9, the Mexico City counterpart to Oaxaca's Sección 22. Outside the venue, busses lined up on the narrow colonial streets. At the curb, one passenger bus read, "Democratic Conquest Oaxaca Sección 22," while another bore the insignia of the Escuela Normal Rural Vanguardia, a women's residential teacher training facility in Oaxaca. The three-day event, the "Fourth National CNTE Congress on Alternative Education: In Defense of Public, Secular and Free Education! United and Organized We Shall be Victorious,[28]" revolved around education proposals to cast aside official textbooks of limited cultural relevance and stop standardized tests like the Programme for International Student Assessment (PISA),[29] run by the Organisation for Economic Co-operation and Development (OECD).[30] These measures, according to the conference *convocatoria*, the call for participation in the event, have reduced Mexican public education into training for "capitalist domination and exploitation" (CNTE, 2010b, p. 1).[31] Instrumentalizing teaching and learning creates friction with the intellectuals of the poor who work as rural public schoolteachers across Mexico, particularly in Oaxaca. Events like this education conference reveal how teachers consider that recent educational reforms have sterilized teaching and learning, and alternative educational proposals need to recover their scientific and political rigor.[32]

When I entered the conference venue at the main building of the Sección 9, it became clear that many attendees and presenters were not teachers from the twenty-one locals in the CNTE[33] and that the teaching and learning scope of the event wove into political protests. Press photographers circulated, climbing up on the auditorium stage to place their long lenses into presenters' faces. Many presenters voiced opinions on how to theorize and scaffold culturally relevant teaching and learning to supplant the state-centered one. Delegates from across eighteen Mexican states affiliated with CNTE were in attendance, and Oaxacan members of the Sección 22 took on visible roles as dialog facilitators. Others, like university professors from National Pedagogical University, National Autonomous University of Mexico, Metropolitan Autonomous University–Xochimilco, and the Bolivian ambassador to Mexico, spoke on emancipatory education.

Figure 1.2: A sign for teacher bus tickets from the Mexico City plantón. "[Bus] tickets to Oaxaca. 200 Mexican Pesos. The teacher, Belén," with a Oaxaca City telephone number. Source: Author.

Figure 1.3: A sign for teacher bus tickets on the side of the Sección 22 main building, Oaxaca City. "Tickets to the Mexico City plantón. Leaving today. 240 [Pesos] one way, 500 [Pesos] round trip," with a Oaxaca City telephone number. Source: Author.

Organizational aspects stood out such as the *mesas*, work tables, whose outcomes were detailed in the conference proceedings (CNTE, 2010a) and the *tallers*, workshops, which dealt with ways teachers could transform Mexican education (CNTE). Astonishingly, when a group of teachers who had spearheaded a midday Mexico City teacher protest march arrived at the Sección 9 building in the late afternoon, the delegates poured out onto the street. The head of the Sección 22, Azael Santaigo Chepi, with his coequal in the Sección 9 standing beside him, lectured on the nature of the alternative education struggle. Chepi's street speech made the first page of the official conference proceedings as a "message of installation" (p. 2), suggesting that these open-air words were as germane to the alternative education conference as the mesas and *talleres*. As the teacher protest at the plantón several blocks away blended with other zócalo activities, the teachers' work at the alternative education conference interlaced the auditorium sessions on classroom teaching with the impromptu street speeches by union political leaders. While union events, responses to economic inequity and cultural politics, weave into teaching, lines blur between the topography of conferences, protests, and the streetscape. Spacing rural pedagogies in Oaxaca calls for knowing the linkages with marches and conferences in Mexico City; as teaching involves delivery of classroom content. This practice forms part of wider social movement activity, theorized by Thayer (2010) as "bundles of relationships" like the individuals and groups operating at these downtown Mexico City events, "charged nodes in larger political arenas" (p. 204).[34]

To proceed with spacing pedagogy in this story, I seek an alternative geography of cultural practice. That is, addressing teaching and learning transcends student-teacher interactions and extends beyond village and family life. Banks (2008) advocates for engaged citizenship and Street (1996) describes democracy struggles taken up by school teachers from Chiapas state; still, most curriculum and instruction research tends to conflate critical teaching and learning into what happens in school or the family, ignoring the pedagogies of street protests and conferences that we see here. Elementary school teaching becomes synonymous with the four walls, roof, chairs, and desks of formal schooling. Curriculum and instruction scholars also tend to credit schooling in United States and Western Europe as more pertinent or authentic. This school-centered and global north emphasis[35] becomes apparent in how the research on Mexican teachers is cast as comparative (see Johnson, 2013; Street, 2001), not as germane to the wider question of what it means to teach in today's era of free-market capitalism and knowledge economy policies. Giving privilege to the global north classroom disregards how the benchmarks of educational excellence have long gone global, how pedagogical and activist responses from the global peripheries resonate beyond national boundaries, and how the rural landscape of Oaxaca maintains living sociocultural connections with urban Mexican and transborder migrant communities.[36] The Alianza por la Calidad de la Educación (ACE) legislation, for instance, channeled teaching and learning in Mexico into quality maximization terms parallel to those of No Child Left Behind in the United States. Teachers in Mexico have made transnational interconnections with their counterparts in Canada and the United States (Arriaga Lemus, 1999, 2016). Still, methodologically, critical literacy studies theorize meaning-making as local (Gee, 2005; Pennycook, 2010), a microanalytic hold insufficient to explain how zócalo protesters in Mexico City cite Tahrir Square protesters in Cairo, how a Oaxacan teacher stops Mexico City traffic to address union leaders from across the country or how as a global city like Moscow or Hong Kong (Sassen, 2005, p. 34) Mexico City patches into worldwide networks.[37] A more-than-local squint and set of conceptual tools is indispensable for spacing the pedagogies we will see here.[38]

Friction

Looking at the circumstances that enable and shape teaching and protesting, in village or city, helps this study approach critical teaching and gives grounding for counter-pedagogies, which will be addressed later. Geographer Cindi Katz (2001) offers insight that resonates with the way Oaxacan teachers speak about their work. Katz suggests that political-economic events unfold topographically (p. 719). On a topographical map, for instance, a mountain range maintains the same elevation hundreds of miles along a ridgeline. In higher altitudes, human, animal, and plant life changes, while topographical lines of a similar altitude a continent away mark out the same summer wildflowers. Topographies of Oaxaca reveal how Zapotec-speaking towns at 1,500 meters in the water-scarce Central Valleys differ from villages in the Mixteca Alta, at 2,200 meters in pine forests where distinct languages and cultural practices predominate.[39] Someone from the Central Valleys may never meet or share common interests with someone from the Mixteca Alta until they work together in Sonora, Northern Mexico, as Martínez Novo (2006) has reported. The zócalo in downtown Mexico City factors into rural Oaxacan topographic lines, especially with rural educators coming and going between the main cities for union activities at protest encampments (see figures 1.2 and 1.3) that advertise cheap interurban transportation. There is topography at work even on the zócalo: a protester asked me for my identification card to ensure I was not sent by the Mexican state to surveil them, as he gestured toward the presidential balcony across the street, on the opposite corner from the Municipal Cathedral. When the teacher checks to see if I am the Palacio's eyes, he juxtaposes protests carried out by people who may never meet in their home states with the security forces of the stone facades of the power elite. Lines of sight from the presidential balcony upon teachers mean presidential lines of sight to the carnival of flying shoes and signs of a deposed President Mubarak. The Mexico City zócalo topographies go further afield than Oaxaca, translating[40] from struggles in Iraq and Egypt. If only framed as situated practices in schools and trade unions, and not as topographical, the committed public intellectual work of rural Oaxacan schoolteachers might slip past unnoticed.

In addition to topographies, "friction of global connection" (Tsing, 2005, p. x) helps this study explain the local practices within broader geographies of power. Friction aids the researching of what people do, think, and say in different settings, the "awkward, unequal, unstable, and creative qualities of interconnection across difference" (p. 4). To illustrate, protesters in Mexico City addressed President Calderón in the public space below the presidential balcony, not only through plainly stated critiques against his handling of Mexico but by throwing shoes at his likeness, recalling the Iraqi journalist tossing his shoes to protest the policies of U.S. President George W. Bush. It is as if President Bush's press conference in a war-ravaged Iraq and Calderón's hold on the executive office in a free-market-driven, neoliberal,[41] Mexico lack legitimacy in similar measure, and the two heads of state are not leading their nations toward the progress, security, and growth they promise. The shoe-toss booth is a flashpoint where the friction of governability becomes palpable. An abundance of bad governance drives the teachers into political action with a focus on collective decision making at protests and conferences like the ones described here, so friction of global connection, the movement of projects within civil service spaces of rural public schools and within trade union topographies of urban protests, will guide us in the coming pages.

This story coalesces through such frictions. From *below* (Street, 1996; Trinidad Galván, 2005), researchers have helped expand the spaces and practices of teaching, learning, and policy. However, political and pedagogical action *within* (Sadlier & Arancibia, 2015) formal spaces of learning and protesting is what concerns us here. The critical pedagogies within the normative domains of public schooling and nationwide trade union organizing, for decades theorized as *ideological state apparatuses* of consent-formation through cultural and nonviolent means (Wolff, 2005), situate critical teaching and organizing that has evaded the detailed attention I give it here. Friction of global connection enables an approach toward the thoughts and deeds as conceived and carried out by actors on the inside who work within institutional boundaries. To illustrate how actors inside school and union spaces engage through contested frictions, let us consider how opposing views of democracy develop in this study. Though it tackled specific teachers' union issues, the alternative education conference in Mexico City showcased above saw at least three competing readings of democracy.

Democracy is understood and carried out by friction. First, at the conference work tables, the friction of democracy involved the advocacy for individual and group rights.[42] Conference work table one (CNTE, 2010a) demanded the Mexican state "recognize *niños y niñas*[43] as endowed with rights, including to an education" (p. 7) and "respect of rhythms and conditions" of the nationwide teachers' movement (pp. 8–9). Conference work table two made similar pleas, designing teaching and learning to "recognize linguistic diversity, the salvaging of identity and the appreciation of...ancestral cultures..." (p. 11). At one point in the work table two discussion, a teacher from the state of Michoacán laid out his project on teaching rural children with lessons on local plants and harvest practices. His eco-pedagogical work echoed the conference theme of culturally relevant teaching but argued against the restriction of knowledge as distinctly Indigenous,[44] preferring instead to teach children of all backgrounds to think and act in line with nature and manual labor. Be it a group-specific or cosmopolitan framing for alternative education, the debate, the friction, revolves around proposals for grounding democratic education.

Second, democracy as friction surfaced in the conference with a breakdown in rules of order. In one *mesa* discussion, I sat in an auditorium beside two Oaxacan delegates, one who had explained to me that she had become more active in the teachers' movement after 2006, when opponents of the teachers assaulted her on the streets of Oaxaca City. In our initial conversation, she mused on how the CNTE came to decisions from the bottom up. In that same session, after the facilitator at a rectangular table on the raised dais closed the meeting to audience comments, an older man introducing himself as "*padre de familia* (parent)" requested the session microphone. When the lead facilitator granted the man the microphone, the Oaxacan delegate beside me rolled her eyes in exasperation, given that a disruption in agreed upon protocol is a disruption in a democratic meeting. The CNTE dissident caucus differentiates itself from the mainstream SNTE for the latter's history of union bosses sitting in their positions for decades. CNTE events like this conference follow procedures, like not yielding the floor to an out-of-turn speaker by facilitator digression. Respecting the voices of the rank and file, even in the smallest decisions, is foundational for the CNTE (Street, 2001, p. 150). No one voice gets to obstruct the voices of others.[45]

Third, by aptly identifying democracy as a cornerstone for alternative education at the conference, parents pinpointed a democratic shortfall. Later in the conference, an older man and woman from a parents' group, the Unidad Popular[46] de Madres y Padres de Familia (2010), distributed a handout against the "abuses" committed by school directors and teachers who charge fees (*cuotas*) from public school parents:

> You teachers are not alien to this [payment]. This is why we are [at the conference]. Because we know that this [teachers'] movement that has come to be called democratic has in fact ignored the needs of parents. Just the same, on occasions it is the classroom teachers (*maestros de grupo*) themselves that are falling into the trap, making quota payment the condition of enrollment. You know very well that educational law[47] establishes that that is not fair consideration (*contraprestación*). (p. 1)

The parents reveal the unconstitutionality of demanding payment for enrollment in public schools, and they juxtapose this impropriety with the dissident teachers' professed democracy. In other words, practice the democracy you preach, teachers, and don't charge us money for public schools. By favoring inclusive schooling, allowing (and eye rolling at) speaking out of turn, and criticizing public school fees, competing versions of democracy helped me understand the social life of the conference. This episode of democracy at the conference is a snapshot of how to research by friction: The Unidad Popular de Madres y Padres de Familia indexes democracy not as an abstract ideal but as an "engaged universal" (Tsing, 2005, p. 8), a contestable and lived rendition of democracy in public elementary education. The methodological device of friction that plants democracy into practical and localized terms will help us in the following three sections which are organized around the movements of quality, patrimony, and governability.

Stories

The pursuit of the spaces and relationships of the movements on the streets and in schools brings me to storytelling as the fiber that keeps this story together. In the following pages, I elaborate movements on the streets and in schools via three frictions: quality, patrimony, and governability. In these three, I position this work as pieces of storytelling, modes of analysis and recall that breathe life into the lived histories that have gotten neglected or rendered into the oblivion of chronological factuality. Stories are not so much expressive of prior experience as formative of new ones (de Certeau, 1988, p. 81). The telling forms part of the story, and what is told in dream-like fashion reveals transformative possibilities to the teller and listener that a truth told directly may not (Simpson, 2012, p. 114). For some researchers, the telling may lead to realistic portraits (Lawrence-Lightfoot, 2005), solidarity (Delgado Bernal, Burciaga, & Flores Carmona, 2012), or storied contingency rather than voiced authenticity[48] (Kamler, 2001). I wrote up field notes mindful of what García Canclini (2001) called a transdisciplinary, social-world *nomadic* approach that contemporary cultural studies in Latin America requires (p. 2) and narrated those notes following St. Pierre (2011) who viewed that a storied approach yields richer data than an orderly process of qualitative coding.

By building the present stories about teaching, it occurred to me how I began teaching through stories. I come from a lengthy line of teachers and chroniclers out of New Orleans, Louisiana, having arrived generations earlier from Havana, Santo Domingo, and Tamaulipas. These slave-owning Creole ancestors delved into business ventures until they faced ruin after the Civil War, one ending up running off to New York with a lover and working as a Spanish and French translator. When meeting hundreds of my extended family members during visits to New Orleans as a child, I would hear accounts of an aunt serving as school principal during desegregation, an uncle lecturing at Tulane about the Louisiana marshland, and a star athlete at school assaulting my music teacher father in the hallway. Accounts of these events came to me during mealtimes, where ten people eating meant ten people talking at once, and getting through these conversations resembled ethnographic research, where what the listener knows can depend on whom they sit next to. For me, these food-mediated, storied networks endured until August 2005, when I evacuated New Orleans ahead of Hurricane Katrina.

When I came back to New Orleans six weeks after the hurricane, conversations picked up right where they left off before evacuation; everybody wanted to know how everyone else endured the rains and levee breaks. On one occasion Sister Theresa, a Carmelite nun, greeted me in the foyer of an event hall with a story about her retreat center where a group had ridden out Katrina. As she recalled the story, she gazed at a photographic montage of spring flowers. Several months before Katrina, I had taken the photographs as a favor to the sisters for their retreat center promotion brochures. Given how neither the photographic negatives nor the camera had survived Katrina, Sister Theresa's memory of those photographs recalled my hurricane experience too, as I remembered Seda who had spent the afternoon with me the day I took the pictures, and whose contact information I had lost. Surely, Hurricane Katrina disrupted pedagogical connections, though just the same, I might recognize that Katrina has engendered storytelling, too. My teacher colleagues in New Orleans became chatty about their post-Katrina journeys, my department head presented at a conference on the paths each of us had undertaken. I never saw Seda again or returned, except to visit.

I took up my doctoral study at UMass, and I continued to teach, where I noticed my classes became a magnet for other involuntary migrants. Among my students were survivors of the 2004 Indian Ocean tsunami, who described being away from their seaside communities in Sumatra during the fateful day of the big wave and coming home to ruin. There was also a Palestinian student who longed for his ancestral home so much that he drew a key from a shirt pocket, revealing that it unlocked a door to a family home razed by paramilitaries in 1948. Through these disaster and conflict associations, I saw teaching as far more than instruction, relating it instead to narratives that people share of what has not quite finished happening. With these disaster and conflict storylines, I took to researching *emergent* (Botelho & Rudman, 2009) and *powerful* (Gee, 2001) literacies, which to me have become nomadic disclosure strategies to postpone the likelihood of forgetfulness.[49] Studying literacies, I ended up reconnecting with my former Oaxacan colleagues, students, and friends, as the 2006 Movimiento erupted, and I began to worry about their safety just as so many a year before had worried about mine. Reactivating those Oaxacan contacts set me on the research path that culminates in this book.[50]

I suggest here that stories are not just voiced or scripted nostalgia, for they have political effects too. As I mentioned, teachers who endure disaster or conflict gravitate toward storied relationships; teaching stories come out of the quietness of witnessing much of our practice without peers and wanting our peers to hear us, so if we forget, we forget gradually and through social contact. Stories entail a kind of alertness, an oftentimes overstated pledge we make so that we keep from falling into self-neglect.[51] This self-care can also be collective, especially in Oaxaca, as the teachers and their allies in the plantones encounter repression and surveillance, and congregating in larger numbers can promote safety. In 2006, Oaxaca City erupted when a teacher protest met with police violence, and police violence met with neighbors coming out of their houses to offer teachers sticks and stones to push back at the police. The months of protest in 2006 led to a profusion of video (Freidberg et al., 2007; Law, 2008; Mal de Ojo TV & Comité de Liberación 25 de Noviembre, 2007), print (Dalton, 2007; Esteva, 2007b; Martínez Vásquez, 2007; Osorno & Meyer, 2007), and multimodal (Stephen, 2013) stories and analyses. Among the foremost intellectuals in Oaxacan politics over the years have been painters (Albertani, 2009), who show art as a public mechanism for street-level

Figure 1.4: Graffiti, Independencia Avenue, Oaxaca, Summer 2010. Source: Author.

The mocking stencil on the left is Ruiz Ortiz with his bludgeoning club and a swastika belt buckle. Painted in red is "Eviel =" URO, comparing 2010 PRI gubernatorial candidate, Eviel Pérez Magaña, with URO. Other graffiti: *Viva el Partido Comunista de Mexico (M–L),* Long live the (Marxist-Leninist) Communist Party of Mexico. UABJO, the Benito Juárez Autonomous University of Oaxaca. *Libertad a los detenidos ¡Libertad a Yolanda Martinez!* (sic), Freedom for those who have been detailed. Free Yolanda Martinez!

politics (De La Rosa & Schadl, 2014; Porras Ferreyra, 2009; Reed, 2005). Street artists using terse and crisp metaphors, graphics, and double meanings have also provided some of the most dazzling records of 2006 (Nevaer & Sendyk, 2009), such as a reiterated image of the governor of Oaxaca, Ulises Ruiz Ortiz, known as URO, bearing a bloody cave man's stick (figure 1.4). Those accounts are often presented to the outside eye as narrative rather than calculation, being that the telling of a thing strikes harder than the factual reporting of it.

Discourses

One of the building blocks of storytelling, at least in the formal research world of curriculum and instruction, is understood as a *discourse*. The encounters that drive this story would be impossible to capture in print without drawing on the social theory device of discourses. Let me exemplify one and detail how they help us here. In the village of Tecotitlán, I interviewed one of the elementary school mothers on the question of reading practices. She revealed that her son had become a more autonomous reader recently, bringing books to the bathroom and reading for hours, a process that started when he heard a storyteller perform at school. The storyteller, María Antonia, often recounted with gestures and animal noises, a *genre move*[52] that excited her son to keep reading. After his experience with storytelling at school, one day his mother found herself reading to him when he told her to stop. She had acted out the characters in voice and gesticulation, following the storyteller, but he said that she did not need to do that. A storyteller was a storyteller, and his mother reading to him was his mother reading to him. As a novice book reader in the early grades of a rural elementary school, he captured the nuances related to the right kind of delivery of fables, oral narration, and his mother's read-along practice. How he possessed and fulfilled this knowledge draws from what are known as *discourses*.

What are discourses? Just as two reasonable witnesses may retell an event with differing details, discourses, through forces that help explain the world, explain through complexity, even contradiction. To Michel Foucault (1980), a discourse works as "a series of discontinuous segments" (p. 100), suggesting that a discourse possesses recognizable material form, though the form may not cohere if we sit down and analyze it for its intrinsic structure. For example, consider the contradictory reasons for the multibillion-dollar United States/Mexico border wall built during a time when countries economically integrate with free-market vigor. Proposed for excluding, monitoring, and confining the lives of the undocumented, whose labor is necessary for economic growth (Nail, 2013), and evoked as populist campaign strategy of a business magnet in a presidential campaign, the wall seems at odds with the in-vogue predominant beliefs of globalization and cosmopolitanism. How does this contradiction coexist? People come to think what they think and do what they do more out of common sense of what is right and good than out of a result of reasonable, objective inquiry. This is where discourses stoke the fires of thought and action. Delany (1994) suggested that a discourse "assigns import," indexes the "non-serious," (p. 239) and is "not a set of criteria met or missed by a text," but rather, a discourse opens the ways in which we come to understand a text (p. 234). I might also add that discourses help us grapple with nontexts, silences, and contexts too. This is not a mere question of logic or reason, for sometimes discourses persist because incongruities coexist or because one's knowledge of, say, storybooks and storytelling, is peripheral to directed efforts to sit down and learn the basics about storybooks;[53] nevertheless, discourses remain clear to the person operating within them. For the story-loving elementary student, something about the theatrical presence of a storyteller—a person invited through applause, who crosses the stage before an audience of many—diverged from his mother reading to him in a smaller space, sitting with a book on her lap, with an audience of one,. No single component demarcated *storyteller* from *mother reading*, so to look at discursive elements of a social practice like reading with his mother might best be understood in terms of what the event rubs up against, like listening along with a storyteller or reading in silence. A seven-year-old story aficionado may never know for sure what a storyteller is, but he is not fooled when somebody who is not a storyteller tries to act like one.

A key to unlock discourses is also not found within the discursive events themselves. Storytellers, for example, do things that mothers who read stories do not. If we want to capture the discursive elements of a storyteller, we cannot do so by staring too directly at what we see as the essences of a storyteller. I observed this in Mexico City spending a day with María Antonia, the storyteller who visited the Tecotitlán Book Fair and whom I will call upon in Chapter Three. Our errand during my visit involved María Antonia hunting for a bamboo birdcage for a forthcoming performance, and none of the cages we had seen sufficed. We strode through the market by her house, and without permission, she approached the fruit stalls and squeezed the pith out of fruit after fruit. I could almost see her start to perform as she carefully grasped fruit and deepened her voice. As several other vendors noticed us, she described each fruit and asked about the farm delivery timetables, she fed the juicy bits to me without offering money, all before the vendors' beaming grins. But then, when we made it to the birdcage area of the market, and in her husky voice, María Antonia became bothered and demanded a cage of bamboo or palm reed instead of the metal and plastic ones we saw there. She envisioned what a birdcage needed to look like for her intended performance, and she was going to find exactly that kind of cage. María Antonia, who happens to be a mother, differs from the reading mother over how María Antonia the storyteller lives her life when talking about fruit, asking for birdcages, or otherwise not telling stories. I saw this in the eyes of people whom she met. A discourse works like this: no one can say for sure what makes a storyteller a *storyteller*, but children, fruit vendors, and birdcage sellers are put at ease by a performer who comes by for a visit and can distinguish a storyteller from a mother, teacher, customer, or neighbor.

Critique

It would be hasty to expect the reader to accept frictions, storytelling, and discourses as chosen tools for this story without describing what I mean by the term *critique*. *Critique* for educators is often couched in ways of examining, say, the self during and after the practice of teaching (Schön, 1987). It is difficult to imagine teaching today without the belief that knowledge is under construction. However, constructivism is not the kind of critique the teachers in this story primarily call upon. In my research, several teachers asked if I had read the book *La vida en las escuelas* by Peter McLaren (2005), a text on race and critical pedagogy in an urban New Jersey school. Raquel, a teacher in a highland region of northeastern Oaxaca, noticed that the injustice she read about in McLaren's New Jersey school occurs across her region in Oaxaca. The teachers' movement events like the alternative education conference discussed earlier come from McLaren's anti-capitalist standpoints, for even the term *alternative* suggests that critical education needs to sidestep the capitalist state and foment critical consciousness[54] outside those repressive relationships. Critiquing and supplanting state education through alternative education are main objectives for the Centro de Estudios y Desarrollo Educativo de la Sección 22 (CEDES 22), the pedagogical wing of the Sección 22 responsible for alternative education. One teacher reported that a CEDES 22 operative had rejected her use of learner-centered games and pasta pieces for teaching mathematics to village children because her work was not *alternative* enough. When I went to the same CEDES 22 office to request documents, the front desk attendant asked if I was "from the state?" When I said no, he let me pass. Hence, a main view of criticality in Oaxaca, especially through the teachers' union, is that public school teaching and learning have become subverted by state-endorsed textbooks and evaluations of the marketplace, which is unjust by its very nature; therefore, to critique is to understand how dominant systems work and change systems that reproduce the unjust system. This *conflict theory* critique appears often in Sección 22 and their CEDES 22 pedagogical division.[55]

In addition to conflict theory, *cultural relevance* shapes critique. At Tecotitlán Elementary, the school of the children I met in Llano Park and where María Antonia told stories, I met a woman serving tacos during morning recess. Hearing she had studied at the school, one day I asked her about her school days. In her time, beside the school was a stream the pupils played in. But the school experience was not joyous, she said, as the *Mestizo*[56] teachers from Oaxaca City would hit the children who spoke in Zapotec instead of Spanish. Hitting affects the one being hit and also strikes at the observers who witness from a distance, giving the "potentially guilty" (Foucault, 1995, p. 108) a sample of what awaits them if they act out.[57] The taco vendor never mentioned if she experienced corporal punishment, but she said she never finished elementary school. During my months of visiting the school, I only heard Spanish spoken, though teachers discussed efforts to make learning more accessible and nonpunitive.

Cultural relevance, beyond outlawing corporal punishment for speaking Zapotec, is based on communal practices in Oaxacan villages. A person from one of the *pueblos originarios*[58] in the Central Valleys by Tecotitlán, according to Esteva (2010), finds it challenging to go on to university and keep their membership in their community (p. 116). This cultural estrangement has led teachers in Tecotitlán to engage in teaching and learning to foster a "sense of belonging," in the words of one teacher. Across Oaxaca, fomenting a sense of belonging comes about through the pedagogical techniques of French socialist pedagogue, Célestin Freinet, and from communalist ways of integrating work, decision making, and social festivities (Meyer & Maldonado, 2004, 2010). Unlike conflict theory critique, cultural relevance focuses less on replacing the official pedagogies and more on fomenting autonomy and teaching and learning based on local ways of seeing the world. Specifically, cultural relevance has drawn from what public intellectual Martínez Luna (2007) has called the "*communalocratic*" cultural and political lifeways (p. 96), the placing of pueblo governance into localized and socially negotiated parameters rather than political party-based constraints. Cultural relevance recognizes that even in societies with equal rights under the law, historically nondominant groups have what Kymlicka and Norman (1994) call "differentiated" needs (p. 340) that the schools must address. Making schools less corrective and more embodied and playful has figured into the culturally relevant pedagogies we get in Chapter Three.[59] Like conflict theory, cultural relevance is widely discussed in Oaxaca by teachers like those at the alternative education conference noted previously.

Conflict theory and cultural relevance provide critical frameworks for teachers in many villages like Tecotitlán, though a third mode of critique, the *counter-pedagogy*, will concern us most in this story. The CNTE union apparatus, for its part, conducts democracy as germinal to thinking and acting as a dissident teacher, though pamphleteers from the parents' organization at the CNTE conference framed democracy differently, linking public schools, where parents need not pay fees, with the professed democracy of the dissident teachers. The moral or ideological authority of a union apparatus, as strong-arming and exhorting as it may be, sets up the possibility for individual freedom through the same systems that indoctrinate and regulate. Every effort spent to discuss alternative education and democratic governance at the conference aided the parents in their counter-pedagogy, their call for a democratic and inclusive school where teachers respected the free public mandates of the Constitution. Asking for a different kind of education, one conducted democratically, is an example of a counter-pedagogy, the mode of critique emphasized in this story.

A counter-pedagogy comes in a version of political and ethical action known as *counter-conduct*,[60] which itself depends on a theory of power as *government*. Power is sometimes carried out through acts of violence or formal regulations, and sometimes power, visible through its "breakdowns, conflicts, and instabilities" (Nail, 2013, p. 112), works through social and institutional interactions that do not appear dangerous or official.[61] Government, the "conduct of conduct" to Mitchell Dean (2010), encompasses the range of strategies deployed to bring us toward certain thoughts and behaviors; to conduct the conduct of others is the shaping of their thoughts and actions. But because shaping thoughts and actions is not primarily exercised by force, command, or manipulation, we can choose to conduct ourselves differently (p. 21).[62] A counter-conduct, as a rejoinder to practices of government, comes when as individuals or groups, in "somewhat unpredicted acts of freedom" (Pyykkönen, 2015, p. 11), we recognize how we are being governed and choose to participate in a different way. When our thoughts and actions are governed, we can also choose to act otherwise, and a how a person chooses to act otherwise reveals how counter-conducts differ from conflict theory modes of critique.

This distinction may seem excessively theoretical, but counter-conducts emerge in the flesh and blood and provide hope for greater social participation in the public sphere (Peters, 2016, p. 31) and expand what is meant by *resistance* (Binkley & Cruikshank, 2016, p. 5). To *resist* in conflict theory means negation, a refusal to participate. Counter-conducts start with the ways our thoughts and actions are governed, but instead of refusing power, a counter-conduct occurs through participation. To put it another way, a counter-conduct breaks with the long-standing notion of power as the powerful using power against the powerless. This traditional, conflict theory view of power is like an archer shooting an arrow at a target. Power is the arrow, and empowerment is stopping the projectile from penetrating the target's defenses. In this conflictive way of seeing power, A acting over B, the archer maintains singular possession of power, and the target, enjoying a limited range of options, either lives in the struggle against piercing arrows or colludes with the archers. A counter-conduct, to be sure, may occur even when arrows are flung, and archers remain alert on bulwarks; however, for us to recognize the movements on the streets and in schools in a broader, hopeful, and participative sense, we might start seeing the individual beyond the archer/ target binary and as an agent capable of "undecidable openness" (Tazzioli, 2016, p. 100). Archers may always take their aim, but bows and arrows are not the only game that people can play. Counter-conducts describe those other games played, though they are often discarded as inconsequential elements of social and cultural life and not given their due as veritable pedagogical and political practices.

The counter-conduct's educational correlate, the counter-pedagogy, is what most concerns us here.[63] A counter-pedagogy at Tecotitlán Elementary, for instance, relates to ringing bells to alert students and teachers to change classes, explained in Chapter Three. In my visit, the bell rang daily on a standardized schedule to indicate the start and stop of class time. One day, as the first period bell sounded, a sixth-grade teacher stood on the esplanade by the director's office and continued to talk with a parent, with the director within earshot. Minutes passed with the teacher still ignoring the bell, while the school director was standing by. The teacher on duty will ring the bell every day like this, though teachers and students start and stop class periods at will. Timetables may seem like untouchable products of power, until the actors involved ring the bells and then choose to ignore them. The still-rung but disregarded bells reveal a counter-pedagogy, an acceptance of a timekeeping regime but not in the ways that officials expect.[64]

Tlacuache Güero

I framed and carried out ethnographic research,[65] observing and participating as both insider and outsider. After living in Guadalajara from 1991 to 1995, I came to Oaxaca in 1997 to teach English at an institute. On campus, I found myself invited to the *cantinas* to drink beer and eat spicy peanuts and to play *frontón* on the public courts. After spending time with this group, faculty members told me I had become an identified as member of the group of local male teachers known as the *tlacuaches*, the Maya language word for a dark-furred opossum-like rodent. I was teasingly dubbed *el tlacuache güero* (the white rodent), a moniker I carried for years.

I have carried out the fieldwork with all the recognition and disregard that participation as white rodent would allow. Naming someone *rodent* might sound derisive, as attributing animal traits to people is considered uncomplimentary in Mexico; however, *güero* carries positive connotations. A *tlacuache* is known as especially unattractive, with its dark pelt and the habit of lurking in shadowy fissures of rocks and forests, and güero is a term used for a male with fair complexion.[66] The other tlacuaches were primarily *moreno* (dark-skinned) Oaxacans of low social economic status. The fairer-skinned *mestizo/a* and metropolitan faculty members at our institute hailed mostly from Mexico City, Puebla, and Xalapa and seemed to resist Oaxaca. One such teacher on campus would send his laundry back to Mexico City each Friday while many others would take the red-eye bus to and from their home cities each weekend. In the ways that racialization and social class have played out across Mexico, the more urbanized, northern, upper middle class, and fairer-skinned a person is, the closer they resemble what has been eugenically fashioned as an evolved *cosmic race*,[67] a term of integration where *mestizo/as* represent racial harmony (Stavans, 2011, p. xi) and becoming a mestizo downgrades non-mestizo rural Oaxacans to "primitivizing temporalization" (Norget, 2006, p. 65). Being rural and darker, even with nationalist myths that praise the Indigenous past, denotes social and economic backwardness in today's terms, a topic I take up further in Chapter Two. Calling a group of male teachers by a folksy and Indigenous-origin name, tlacuaches, involves raced and classed inflections. Generally, the rest of the teachers on campus viewed the tlacuaches as crude, vulgar, and boozy, all stereotypes of Indigenous Oaxacans. I would note that the tlacuaches embraced the name, and tlacuache güero felt to me like a term of endearment. Spending time with this group as I did, and getting lightheartedly dubbed the white rodent, hinted at my white masculine privilege, even as the sobriquet was issued with sarcasm.

Despite their racialized and lower-class standing at the institute, the tlacuaches stood out as a complex association, whose political presence on campus reveals the importance of incorporated groups in Mexican education. My friend and co-tlacuache Esteban, a graduate in philosophy from the National Autonomous University of Mexico (UNAM), explained to me that the tlacuaches functioned as more than a group of low-brow, dark-skinned pranksters teased by the fair-skinned urbanites who send their laundry home on weekends. Instead, the leaders of the group served in a campus political network in the backdoor service of the directors, a dynamic that corresponds to the ways informal political networks govern many institutional spheres like schools, trade unions, and peasant organizations. Esteban, in personal communication, pointed out that the tlacuaches, "given their cultural, social, political, and economic identity, represented a simple handling of power, and that is what distinguished them from the bulk of the teachers." For generations, Mexican academic institutions have depended on what Esteban called *grupos de contención* (containment groups) to keep an eye on the political views of newcomers. Interconnected with their meeting regularly with the dean of the faculty to report on other teachers, Esteban clarified that

> the tlacuaches are just a sample of what occurs so much in this *pinche*[68] country as in so many others: the bureaucratization of the teacher which at the same time is the fetishization of his or her being, and therefore labor. What you cannot forget is the fact that [the tlacuaches] stand as intervening forces for fulfilling of very specific objectives that have nothing to do with education in the strictest sense…[but instead they represent] power contestations in order for everything to rotate around the three points of conservation, reproduction and endorsement of power.

Esteban calls the tlacuaches individuals guided toward political participation where *tlacuachism* helps school leaders maintain their hegemony. Such peer-focused intelligence gathering occurred across the system; the exchange of information between dean and tlacuache meant promises of money and promotion. People on campus knew this. I recall a moment when, passing a teacher whose spouse had gotten a new position running the campus bookstore, Esteban whispered to me, "*cuidadísimo con ese cabrón, güey*[69] (be super careful with that one, man.)" A teacher hanging around with the guys one day and his partner landing a new job the next seemed shady to Esteban, though in his everyday affect, Esteban remained equally jovial with all colleagues.[70]

My days working and socializing with the tlacuaches at the pedagogical institute in the late 1990s differed from my 2010–2011 investigation across the Oaxacan and Mexico City sites where unionized teachers taught, organized, and socialized. In contrast to my research, the pedagogical institute, a product of the 1990s institutional push toward developing human capital for the North American Free Trade Agreement (NAFTA), departed from the older incorporated politics of schooling. Corporatism (*corporativismo*),[71] and its version found in Mexico, *caciquismo*,[72] the integrating of groups and individuals like the tlacuaches, became vital for our deans. Correspondingly, teachers have opposed the top-down school-centered power by rolling their eyes at conferences when rules of order break down, deciding by consensus (Bautista Martínez, 2010b, pp. 230–231) and maintaining affective bonds with peers, parents, and students, as we will see in subsequent chapters. But unlike other public universities and primary and secondary schools, our institute lacked any independent student federation or trade union mechanism surveillable by institute authorities. What is more, as I recall, academic deans one day cautioned a group of five teachers seated together at the school café that unsupervised large groups were not allowed.

As a *grupo de contención* tasked to cover the rest of us and assess the degree of political danger each one might represent, the tlacuaches helped in school governance. Some outspoken teachers at the institute faced hard consequences when stepping out of line. As Esteban criticized the head of the institute in an interview with a local newspaper, he found himself an object of interest. He ended up on a moment's notice leaving the institute, urged to resign by one of the tlacuaches, who suggested Esteban might face grave consequences for his public arguments. Esteban reported that all this happened literally overnight. When driving out of town after his dismissal, Esteban recalled a Chevy Suburban SUV with tinted windows escorting him for several miles on the curving, narrow highway, "judicial police," he insisted, there to show him that his way out of town was a one-way trip. In response to this, to learn more on how the incorporated political intermediaries operated at the institute, I inquired why I had avoided the dangers of tlacuache surveillance. "*Eras un gringo inofensivo, güey* (you were a harmless gringo, man)," he responded, meaning that I was a sort of a mascot, outside the monitoring function of the containment group, and unlikely to spread ideas to outsiders as Esteban had done with speaking to the press.[73] Being tlacuache güero suggests that in Oaxaca I enjoy social and professional legitimacy as a teacher and benefit from white male privilege, but I lack major political influence or threat potential. Between these positions I carried out this research as insider and outsider.

Movements on the Streets and in Schools

Working at the pedagogical institute and interacting in the social and political sphere of the tlacuaches, I met a rural elementary teacher named Lourdes who introduced me to a group of other rural Oaxacan public elementary and secondary school teachers. It would be through Lourdes and her peers that I eventually learned about the CNTE teachers' movement and the Oaxacan Sección 22 protests and assemblies in part because the teachers would miss my English classes for their activism. Lourdes, eight years later, would update me on the progress of the 2006 Movimiento and corresponding fear and danger that encircled the teachers. Then in 2010, Lourdes would invite me down, promising to help me research post-Movimiento critical pedagogies. Because they come from my prior teaching and personal experience, the stories on the political projects of teachers like Lourdes have become part of my own story. Indeed, though not *autoethnographic* (Mitra, 2010) or *performative* (Denzin, 2003), my own embodied experiences of dispossession and teaching in rural public schools are inseparable from the post-conflict teaching, learning, and cultural politics narrated in these pages.

In the critical ethnographic inquiry, even as helicopter snipers shot at teachers, an objective fact, I do not lay claims on truth or draw upon a defined set of methodological gear boxes that help me accurately capture the counter-pedagogies carried out on the streets and in schools by Lourdes and her contemporaries. Rather, through frictions, I build on the stories on Oaxacan instruction and activism in recent Movimiento testimonials and analyses (Bautista Martínez, 2010b; Clemente, 2007; Comisión Civil Internacional de Observación por los Derechos Humanos (CCIODH), 2007; Dalton, 2007; Esteva, 2007b; Law, 2008; Martínez Vásquez 2007, 2009; Osorno & Meyer, 2007; Sotelo Marbán, 2008; Stephen, 2013). These authors have addressed teacher activism, though teacher efforts, the latitudes (Ong, 2006) and topographies (Katz, 2001) of social movements and classroom pedagogies have not been traced out in terms of an embodied practice of critical teaching.

The storied inquiries that have resulted in this book ask what this embodied practice of critical teaching might look like for teachers who face state repression and neoliberal reforms. This book started in the fall of 1997 as a conversation between Lourdes and me on what it meant for each of us to teach critically. As my student, she would remind me how empire and privilege worked through my North American white male observations of Oaxaca and affected my empathy and understanding with the life in Oaxaca. Years later, she and I would discuss the question of being freer people through learning how to critique, as taught by Paulo Freire (1994). Then, when the 2006 conflict affected Oaxacans, our conversation shifted away from theoretically abstract notions of liberation and onto grounded experience of safety when physical danger menaced the protesters. As I began fieldwork four years after that, I found Lourdes and her colleagues were passing around a copy of a book on the ethics of self-care (*cuidado de sí mismo*) (Foucault, 1990) from Lourdes's father's library, even quipping once, before sipping a beverage, that they were "*cuidando de sí mismo* (taking care of the self)." The stories on teaching that I relate here become critical insofar as claims for social justice on the streets and in schools coincide with teachers gathering together with no stated political aim but to delight in one another's presence. Indeed, critical pedagogical responses to repression and reform in this story resemble the protest march and reading event at Llano Park introduced at the start of chapter: where dissident teachers protest state reforms and repression dissident teachers take their students, to read and perform under tarpaulins with logos and crests of state agencies. In direct terms, this book addresses the question of how the pedagogies of the streets and schools confront and coincide with the physical danger of repression and the epistemic violence of market-based reforms. In the next chapters, three movements of critique move, weaving through three frictions: quality (Chapters Two and Three), patrimony (Chapters Four and Five) and governability (Chapters Six and Seven).

Notes

1. Since 1967, *telesecundarias* have provided satellite-fed lessons to remote areas of Mexico to expand secondary school coverage (Durán, 2001).
2. The Coordinadora Nacional de Trabajadores de la Educación, la CNTE, is not a breakaway teacher organization. It remains within the larger Sindicato Nacional de Trabajadores de la Educación, el SNTE, Latin America's largest trade union. CNTE members oftentimes maintain ties within the very agencies that they oppose. Sección 22 of Oaxaca, along with teachers of neighboring Chiapas, have militated within the CNTE for decades (Street, 1992; Yescas Martínez & Zafra, 1985). This militancy expanded during the 2013–2014 mobilization, in which the CNTE served as a linchpin nationwide for the labor and wider sociopolitical movement in favor of education as a public good, the constitutional rights of teachers as state workers, and the democratization of the union (Arriaga Lemus, 2014).
3. The Instituto Estatal de Educación Pública de Oaxaca.
4. The 1992 law de-federalized some of the functions of Mexico's public education system to the individual states like Oaxaca (Martínez Vásquez, 2004). The central state's oversight of public education, which in rural areas like Oaxaca had impacted in village life since the 1930s, would retreat, minimize the public role of the public schoolteacher, and engender a teacher critical response.
5. Public disturbances before symbolic façades elicit responses. During the summer of 2010, reports circulated of teachers from the state of Michoacán who in protest had gouged a hole in the 18th-century *castellano* craftwork in the door of the SEP building in Mexico City. In response, damage assessors appeared from Instituto Nacional de Antropología e Historia and fingers were pointed in terms of which group was holding up the dialog process between the teachers and the state (Poy & Martínez, 2010, p. 12).
6. The jeered-at soldiers on this day faced the marchers' *consignas*, chants to rally support, which served as *frames*, open declarations of a political struggle presented in a convincing and support-incenting way (Olesen, 2007, p. 23).
7. The political entity of Oaxaca State becomes significant, though not singular, in framing this study on teaching and political projects. The State becomes one unit in the ways that agencies like the IEEPO and the Sección 22 become nodes of mobilization and socialization. The World Bank has also reinforced the state boundaries through "subnational" loans (Rojas & The World Bank, 2002) and setting the parameters of improvement: "[Mexico] is country of contrasts-between rich states and states still

struggling with poverty; between thriving urban centers and destitute rural areas; between those members of the economy seeking to compete with OECD countries and the majority of the population for whom the promise of globalization has not materialized" (de Ferranti, 2001, p. xxiii).

8. Village and institute names that might identify people are pseudonyms throughout.

9. *Venture philanthropy* foundations (Lipman, 2011, p. 100) in Oaxaca have begun to fund projects on reading for pleasure to promote general reading habits.

10. Juárez remains an esteemed member of the Mexican political pantheon. His political stature often underwrites a cultural or political project, though, as he also stands as an example of Indigenous assimilation into mainstream Mexican society, his legacy remains contentious (see Esteva, 2007a).

11. Since the 1992 educational reforms, the Sección 22 has enjoyed privileges, including the right to nominate department heads in the IEEPO (Cortés, 2006, p. 74).

12. Called *educación alternativa* in Spanish, it has embraced teaching and learning proposals to supplant the official, mainstream curriculum since 1979 (Hernández, 2009) until now (CEDES 22, 2010; CNTE, 2010a, 2010b) and has considered the mainstream curriculum culturally irrelevant and colonizing.

13. The lines between Indigenous, *Mestizo/a*, and *campesina/o* across Mexico remain contested. Different regions hold differing views on ethnicity (Stephen, 2002, p. 87). One teacher I spoke with described her parents as Zapotec. She neither spoke a variety of the language nor was accepted by a community, so she indicated that she could not call herself Zapotec.

14. The supervisor is an IEEPO-employed coordinator of a territory of twelve schools, the immediate boss of school principals, and a member of the Sección 22.

15. Sección 22 *consignas* are not exclusively a choral recitation or graffiti of an orthodox position during protests and union activities, for the chants and painted statements can deploy clever metaphors and humor (see Chapter Seven).

16. Resisting repression is a stated goal of alternative education, which becomes pedagogical when teachers interrogate the history of domination in schools (CEDES 22, 2009). In their own words, to the Sección 22, "critical pedagogy, despite not constituting a unified discourse, has been able to point out many of the contradictions in the discourses of positivism, ahistoricism and depoliticization" of "liberal and conservative analytical modalities" of teaching which predominate in most teacher education academic departments (p. 17). To the radical teachers in Oaxaca, you have to become a knower before you can be a resister.

17. I will call the 2006 Movement, as Oaxacans do, the *Movimiento* to distinguish it from the nationwide dissident and democratic teachers' movement through CNTE, which also began in the Mexican Southeastern states (Yescas Martínez & Zafra, 1985).

18. See Martínez Vásquez's (2009) reading of the 2006 Movimiento as a "movement of movements" which emerged in a massive antiauthoritarian expression of pent-up public exasperation (p. 330).

19. Yescas Martínez (2006) has observed the Oaxacan teachers' movement progressing in phases, starting in 1980 with the teachers confronting the hegemony of the teachers' union bosses (p. 19).

20. Consider the barricades (see Chapter Six), which served as defense mechanisms around Oaxaca City during the 2006 Movimiento. One testimony (el Alebrije, 2007) describes barricades as neighborly and social more than radical-consciousness-laden outposts of the street-level struggle.

21. The term *knowledge relations* refers to the ways that individuals, institutions, scientific methodologies, and beliefs in what is real, identifiable, and valid already are at play before us. Though we can't just decide what something means, we walk into knowledge relations and play a creative and communicative role in helping shape them. The word *relations* further suggests that knowledge relations are not secured by lock and key but instead are available for us to participate in, even if unequally.

22. *Praxis* is what you do to comprehend how power works and to intervene with direct action; it means learning plus transformative political action. *Practice* is a set of meaningful activities, but to practice something does not necessarily mean to set about changing the world. The movements on the streets and in schools at times call for direct action for concrete change and at times call for the politics of chatting with friends, eating and joking to preserve social networks.

23. Judith Friedlander (1975) illustrates how taking on the role of a godparent means an extended commitment: "Doña Jacoba had asked a school teacher who was working in the village at the time to officiate at the baptism of little Zeferina. The teacher soon left Hueyapan, married and settled down in her native Mexico City. Then during the Revolution, when the hardships of everyday life made each mouth to feed an enormous burden, Doña Jacoba called on Zeferina's godmother to keep the child for a period of time" (p. 33).

24. The stated position of the dissident teachers' union in Mexico is that current-day educational reforms are derived from the state, businesses and international organizations like the The Organisation for Economic Co-operation and Development (OCDE), whose objective is to privatize public education. Yet reforms to Mexican education bear a definitive transnational tint, guided by demands for "quality" for cheap *maquiladora* labor, inside Mexico, and for migrant labor outside (CNTE, 2013, p. 15).

25. Called by locals *el D.F.* or the Federal District, Mexico City enjoys centrality in Mexico. Even in the current age of decentralization of some functions of the federal government, like Oaxaca's IEEPO, all of Mexico depends on decisions, ideas, styles, and trends that circulate in Mexico City.

26. Faced with widespread opposition, Egyptian President Hosni Mubarak was deposed three months prior, after thirty years in power.

27. President from 2006 to 2012, Calderón was of the conservative political party, the PAN, which held the executive branch from 2000 to 2012. During writing, the

Partido Revolucionario Institucional (PRI) has returned to *Los Pinos* with President Enrique Peña Nieto.

28. Words spoken or written originally in Spanish and presented here in English or bilingually are my translations, unless otherwise noted.

29. An educational quality test used by OECD to calculate and rank math and reading. Oaxacan teachers often critique it as a technique to raise human capital, guide knowledge toward individuality, and promote efficiency and self-sufficiency.

30. The OECD is an intergovernmental organization of the thirty-four largest economies in the world. It has no mandate and membership is voluntary, but as their metrics stand for international quality standards, the agency becomes arbiter of the ways the so-called free market should influence social life arenas like education. As such, the OECD is as much a social policy agency as it is about economics.

31. The logic of economic development turns into a strategy of governance when the social welfare the state used to provide (i.e., teaching as a cultural missionary project) has less influence, while the training of self-starting and flexible labor becomes gains greater force. For the neoliberal politics of *devolution* and *responsabilization*, see Brown (2015, p. 131).

32. The first alternative education Oaxaca State conference, seven years prior in 2003, resolved to "put an end to traditionalism, switching our teaching (*docente*) practice with innovative programs" (Hernández, 2009, p. 331). Alternative education focused "on making a critical, analytical and reflexive school" [and] "include[d] an educational model in the service of Indigenous education, considering...preschool, primary, secondary and adult education grounded in the reality and surroundings of individuals" (p. 332).

33. In the fall of 2013, with the austerity measures instituted by President Enrique Peña Nieto, the teachers' movement mobilized across Mexico once again, and more union locals of the SNTE turned toward the CNTE dissidence in opposition to the cutbacks.

34. Social movement and classroom practices link up in primary and secondary schooling (Hagopian, 2014). In Oaxaca, social movements and teaching are correlated. At a conference in 1982, the nascent Oaxacan teachers' dissident movement organized to foment the "conscientization" of the unionists (Cortés, 2006, p. 44) and the "fight for the democratization of teaching at every level [via] scientific, philosophical and grassroots (*popular*) principals" (p. 48).

35. A major publisher, who chose not to publish this book, explained to me that they do not publish books on education from non-US settings, while my colleagues have reported that coworkers and potential employers find their transnational curriculum and pedagogy research and experience exotic or irrelevant.

36. From the village of Yalálag, Oaxaca to Los Angeles, California, a practice of *chusca* dances parodies tourists and outsiders (Cruz-Manjarrez, 2013, p. 186).

37. Art historian Selma Holo (2004) reports that understanding activities in Mexico City were key for her Oaxaca research (p. 15).

38. *Local* education is best understood translocally. Sierra Norte activist Jaime Martínez Luna (1982) notices that Spanish has also been used in Indigenous resistance practices (p. 77), and Guillermo Bonfil Batalla (1996) concurs that the exploration of the deep roots of rural Mexico is not possible by detachment from the "west" (p. 167). Teacher and activist Miguel Linares explains that the 2006 Movimiento across Oaxaca benefited from transnational activist networks (Albertani, 2009, p. 65).

39. Views of personhood via citizenship and nationhood via the territorial integrity of the state have changed in the face of free-market socioeconomic and law-and-order security reforms (Ong, 2006). The changes in citizenship and national sovereignty have played out *latitudinally* (p. 21).

40. Ideas and practices *translate* (Tsing, 2005) from one social movement to another, though the translation process can privilege the notions and practices of the more powerful (de Lima Costa, 2014). The asymmetries of power involved in translation also make it interesting, for "[t]ranslation, or its refusal, is a strategic political act in the hands of social movements, whether it involves the sharing of knowledge to foster an alliance or the interruption of a dominant discourse to defend autonomy" (Thayer, 2010, p. 224).

41. Neoliberalism is often seen as the shift from a nation-state that takes care of citizens through entitlements to a nation-state that expects individuals to take care of themselves. The neoliberal state will still support public schools by framing teaching and learning more in terms of a commodity that parents and pupils select for personal gain than as a public good. Pedagogies of neoliberalism work through a recognition of historically excluded cultural groups (Hale, 2005), the respect and protection of women (Phipps, 2014), and a quest for skills-based flexibility (Ong, 1999). This shift, according to Bernstein (2001), has turned every part of our social world into a society completely permeated by pedagogical commodity exchanges (p. 365).

42. Street (1996, 2001) describes teacher democratic processes after 1979 in their participative origins in Chiapas, while Cortina (1990) approaches union democracy in terms of women's participation and exclusion.

43. *Niños y niñas*—literally "boys and girls"—is also used for "children." Specifying both genders rather than defaulting to the male collective *niños* is an intentional mode of speech inclusiveness. Here we can read it as a discursive device giving equal female-gendered weight to the masculine noun.

44. Oaxaca is known for establishing bilingual and multicultural education around the local ways of knowing, becoming, and governing. Through the intersectionality (Hancock, 2007) or solidarity with other movements, teachers and other activists also attempt to cultivate discussion and action. Teachers, in particular, have a radical tradition that is rooted in anti-capitalism and anti-statism. Antonio Gramsci (Forgacs, 2000), a radical thinker widely read in Mexico, provides a useful starting point.

Gramsci favored the collaboration across linguistic and cultural difference rather than overly provincializing the work at hand (pp. 326–327).

45. Many of the teachers in this study are women with advanced training in pedagogy and social theory. Like the delegate rolling her eyes at the older male facilitator who broke the democratic rules of order, Lourdes and Wendy have critiqued how men with lower levels of training and experience become school directors despite the predominance of women. For gender and teaching in Mexico, see Cortina (1989, 1990, 2006), Howell (1997), López (2001), and Street (1996).

46. *Popular* meaning of the *people*. See Bartlett (2005) for the term's use in Latin American social movements (p. 344).

47. This is a reference to Article Three of the 1917 Constitution that guarantees secular, free, and universal public education for all Mexicans.

48. What's authentic is not always what is local or ancestral. Bonfil Batalla (1996) explained that "cultural elements of foreign origin do not in themselves indicate weakness or loss of authenticity within Indian cultures. The problem does not consist of the proportion of 'original' traits as opposed to 'foreign' traits …" (p. 137).

49. Regarding Chile after Pinochet, Nelly Richard (2010) discusses memory politics in the arts, museums, and the confessional genre and Graciela Rubio Soto (2013) theorizes and critiques the pedagogies of memory in public spaces and in schools.

50. Though activism will color the horizon of this story, I do not position this as activist educational anthropology, as undertaken in the compelling work of Dyrness (2011). Most of the teachers in this study carry out both research and activism whether I research them or not, and most teachers and parents took the more radical efforts to enact social change as less crucial than the need to transform communities through high-quality classroom instruction. For teacher activism, see Denham and C.A.S.A. Collective (2008), Gibler (2009) and the articles in the November–December 2007 issue of *Cuadernos del Sur* (Arellanes Meixueiro, 2007; Dalton, 2007; Esteva, 2007b).

51. Narratives yield greater alertness (Clandinin, Pushor, & Murray Orr, 2007, p. 21), help practitioners rethink their craft (Clandinin, Connelly, & Chan 2002), and "think with" the mutilated landscape (Tsing, 2015, p. 38).

52. A *genre move* is a communicative device deployed to anticipate a response from an interlocutor (see Bakhtin, 1986). Genres are so nuanced that almost every utterance represents a new genre. Here, the mother's presentation of animals becomes a move that a storyteller might use to an audience to show animals are animals, not humans. But a mother reading to her son should include genre moves that are not animal noises, in the son's view.

53. A contradiction becomes *contradiction* only when two elements of a single thought or action go side-by-side in ways that defy prior understanding. Across rural Mexico, things that should go separate often go together. Bonfil Batalla (1996) suggests that what's rural defies all logical explanation (p. 29); across such landscapes like Oaxaca, economic activity cannot be divided from social activity (p. 26) any better than belief

can be separated from reason (p. 27). Bonfil Batalla in *Mexico Profundo* has given us a literal and metaphorical term for appreciating cultural contradictions, the *milpa* (p. 25), the cornfield. As it combines corn, beans, squash, and *chile* on the same plot, a milpa is not just a cornfield. Contradictions are worthy analytical watermarks. In his study of the U.S. anti-migration wall with Mexico, Nail (2013) observes contradictory ideas in coexistence; though, to clarify a contradiction is not to resolve it (p. 128) but rather to capture the possibilities that the contradictions enable. What is more, Tsing (2015) shows how life thrives on "contaminated diversity" (pp. 32–33).

54. Critical consciousness also includes commitment to the teachers' movement, as this has become *"desvirtuado"* (removed of its integrity) due to trade union practices of corruption and authoritarianism (Cortés, 2006, pp. 60–61).

55. It may seem overreaching to translate political economy into teaching and learning techniques undertaken in public schools where no apparent entrepreneurial transfers take place. However, CEDES 22 views that the state uses schooling to develop human resources, not active citizens (CEDES 22, 2007, 2009, 2010).

56. Being Mestizo implies a learned identity, part of federal "de-Indianization" strategies for Mexico (Knight, 1990, p. 73) and drawn from the "liberal longing" in Mexican cultural politics after 1857, when constructs of Mexican citizenship distanced itself from being Creole or Indigenous (Bonfil Batalla, 1996, pp. 110–111).

57. Post-Revolutionary schooling (1920s and 1930s) assimilated Indigenous groups into the mainstream. This had occurred decades before the teachers slapped students in the mid-twentieth century, as Indigenous communities had faced the dispossession of their lands to create a wage labor force (Knight, 1990, p. 79).

58. Though *Indigenous* is widely used, according to one teacher, Pueblos Originarios is a preferred identifier for the dozens of communities in Oaxaca with pre-Hispanic claims.

59. Differentiated pedagogies have followed political rights Indigenous pueblos earned in Oaxaca, such as a community's right to elect leaders and remain politically autonomous of the Oaxaca State government and the official political parties (Hernández Díaz, 2007). Collectivist political participation in rural Oaxaca has struggled against the Mexican Constitution promoting individualism (Durand Ponte, 2007, p. 12) and the "hyper-individualism" of the present neoliberal policy turn (p. 36).

60. Graffiti writers reclaiming derelict urban spaces (Christen, 2009) and the use of the term *counter sciences* in Lather (2006) might be considered counter-conducts.

61. Qualitative methodologies become motor force of critique. Throughout, I take critique as a "movement" (Foucault, 1998a, p. 278) and "a labor of diverse inquiries" (1998c, p. 56). Critique is a *movement of diverse inquiries.*

62. It is argued that "power is only exercised over free subjects" (Foucault, 1998b, p. 139). But this does not mean we enjoy total freedom, for it is "essential to governmentality to produce discourses that 'neutralize' this freedom, thus giving [people] the impression that there is no real choice to be made" (Lorenzini, 2016, p. 18).

63. The 2006 Movimiento involved violent repression, which teacher activists did not choose. The Oaxaca state government also deployed discursive strategies such as calling the Movimiento an urban guerrilla offensive and labeling teachers as irresponsible. So, even authoritarianism depended on a conduct of conducts. See Lemke (2011) for a short and insightful overview of government through state systems of security (pp. 50–51).

64. McGinn and Street (1984) remind that the officials who mandate school bell ringing need teachers and students to endorse their leadership. "The expansion of educational opportunity necessary to re-establish legitimacy of the government created conditions that favoured the organisation of opposition to the government" (p. 332). When participation is summoned, look for counter-conducts. In schools and on streets, look for counter-pedagogies.

65. My guiding research question has been on how classroom teachers have undertaken critiques of neoliberal policy shifts and repressive violent practices while working as civil servants in a state apparatus. For my first field visit, May 2010–August 2010, I shadowed three former students of mine who were active in the Sección 22 of the SNTE teachers' union. In a second field visit, January 2011–May 2011, I collaborated with a sixth-grade teacher on a school reading project, visiting his school each day and attending weekend in-service teacher trainings and teacher protest events.

66. With an established European and Middle Eastern descendent population in urban Mexico, the use of *güero/a* does not call someone an outsider the way *gringo/a* would. Güero/a does, however, indicate elevated social class status, as whiteness is often associated with the elite. This class distinction is illustrated by a disparaging comment to situate one fellow tlacuache with fair skin: "He's a *güero de rancho* (a country-style whitey)" someone once called him, meaning, he was less sophisticated and classy than one would expect from a güero.

67. Marentes (2000) offers more on the cosmic race and Mexican modernist reforms.

68. *Pinche* is an offensive term used as an adjective to discredit a noun; here it's "wretched" or "messed up."

69. *Güey*, a pejorative term for "person" is used here to identify male friends. Many curse words such as *cabrón* (big goat) are frequently used with positive connotations to denote the speaker and listener are part of an inside group.

70. For more on the state, political activism and higher education in Oaxaca, see Shepherd (2015).

71. Cook (1996) considers corporatism a system of exchanging loyalty for the promise of future political goods, while Arnove and Torres (1995) locate it as "form of the capitalist state that, being the result of a popular revolution, has a broad mass base of popular support despite its capitalist class character" (p. 315). To understand the political role of the tlacuaches and the corporatist relationships in Mexico, we need to look back a little further, to the 1910 Mexican Revolution and aftermath. For elementary schools, corporatism might involve providing teachers the incentives to spy

on others, pamphleteer for a candidate, or collect school fees from parents. Throughout the twentieth century, such exchanges of information and deeds for money or promotion became operationalized in schools. Haber (2007), in examining Mexican social movements, has considered twentieth-century Mexico an "inclusionary authoritarian regime" unlike the military dictatorial ones throughout Latin America (p. 53). Corporatism is partly how such authority became inclusive.

72. In Mexico, *caciques*, as bosses, historically operate in the unions and peasant organizations. The roles of political groups within institutions and their practices of *caciquismo* have been explored by Knight and Pansters (2006). Cook (1996) and Foweraker (1993) have noticed that bosses with extensive powers in the periphery have taken power in the center. This happened with SNTE president Elba Ester Gordillo, a teacher from Chiapas, who became the union president (see Chapter Seven). Caciquismo in schools affects teachers' lives and bodies, as Street (1996) reported principals abusing teachers for house cleaning and sexual favors. Even so, as Street added, the caciquismo would never constitute a final word, as reactions to the hegemonic practices in the late 1970s engendered the CNTE, the democratic and dissident caucus within the SNTE.

73. Bautista Martínez (2010b, pp. 48–55) outlines caciquismo in Oaxaca, and Smith (2008) shows how this governance draws on cultural politics.

References

Albertani, C. (2009). *Espejo de México: (Crónicas de barbarie y resistencia)*. San Pedro Cholula, Mexico: Altres Costa-Amic.

Arellanes Meixueiro, A. (2007). Un zócalo destruido, pueblo enfurecido, *Cuadernos del Sur, 11*(24–25), 139–148.

Arnove, R., & Torres, C. (1995). Adult education and state policy in Latin America: The contrasting cases of Mexico and Nicaragua. *Comparative Education, 31*(3), 311–326.

Arriaga Lemus, M. L. (1999). NAFTA and the Trinational Coalition to Defend Public Education. *Social Justice, 26*(3), 145–155. Retrieved from http://www.socialjusticejournal.org/archive/77_26_3/77_09ArriagaLemus.pdf.

Arriaga Lemus, M. L. (2014, Fall). The struggle to democratize education in Mexico. *NACLA Report on the Americas, 47*(3), 30–33.

Arriaga Lemus, M. L. (2015). Insurrección magisterial: México 2013. *Revista Intercambio, 7*, 2–4. Retrieved from http://revistaintercambio.org/index.php/INTERCAMBIO/article/view/1.

Arriaga Lemus, M. L. (2016). The Mexican teachers' movement: Thirty years of struggle for union democracy and the defense of public education. *Social Justice, 42*(3), 104–117. Retrieved from https://ezproxy.spscc.edu/login?url=http://search.proquest.com/docview/1802183693?accountid=1172.

Bakhtin, M. M. (1986). *Speech genres and other late essays*. Austin, TX: University of Texas Press.

Banks, J. A. (2008). Diversity, group identity, and citizenship education in a global age. *Educational Researcher, 37*(3), 129–139.

Bartlett, L. (2005). Dialogue, knowledge, and teacher-student relations: Freirean pedagogy in theory and practice. *Comparative Education Review, 49*(3), 344–364.

Bautista Martínez, E. (2010a). La lucha por el reconocimiento: Maestros indígenas de Oaxaca. *El Cotidiano, 25*(159), 101–107. Retrieved from http://search.proquest.com/docview/748401506?accountid=14784.

Bautista Martínez, E. (2010b). *Los nudos del régimen autoritario: Ajustes y continuidades de la dominación en dos ciudades de Oaxaca.* Oaxaca, Mexico: IISUABJO.

Bernstein, B. (2001). From pedagogies to knowledges. In A. Morais, I. Neves, B. Davies, & H. Daniels (Eds.), *Towards a sociology of pedagogy: The contribution of Basil Bernstein to research.* New York, NY: Peter Lang.

Biesta, G. (2012). Becoming public: Public pedagogy, citizenship and the public sphere. *Social & Cultural Geography, 13*(7), 683–697.

Binkley, S., & Cruikshank, B. (2016). Introduction: counter-conduct. *Foucault Studies,* 3–6.

Bonfil Batalla, G. (1996). *México profundo: Reclaiming a civilization.* Austin, TX: University of Texas Press.

Botelho, M. J., & Rudman, M. K. (2009). *Critical multicultural analysis of children's literature: Mirrors, windows, and doors.* New York, NY: Routledge.

Brown, W. (2015). *Undoing the demos: Neoliberalism's stealth revolution.* New York, NY: Zone Books.

Campbell, H. (2001). *Mexican Memoir: A personal account of anthropology and radical politics in Oaxaca.* Westport, CT: Bergin & Garvey.

CCIODH. (2007). *Informe sobre los hechos de Oaxaca. Quinta visita del 16 de diciembre de 2006 al 20 de enero de 2007* (Report). Barcelona: CCIODH. Retrieved from http://cciodh.pangea.org/.

CEDES 22. (2007). *Taller estatal de educación alternativa: TEEA 2007–2008: La complejidad de la práctica educativa desde la perspectiva de la investigación acción* (instructional material). Oaxaca, Mexico.

CEDES 22. (2009). *Taller estatal de educación alternativa: TEEA 2009–2010* (instructional material). Oaxaca, Mexico.

CEDES 22. (2010). *2010 Resolutivos del III congreso estatal de educación alternativa, 20–21 de mayo.* Oaxaca, Mexico: Sección 22, SNTE.

Christen, R. S. (2009). Graffiti as public educator of urban teenagers. In J. A. Sandlin, B. D. Schultz, & J. Burdick (Eds.), *Handbook of public pedagogy: Education and learning beyond schooling* (pp. 233–243). New York, NY: Routledge.

Clandinin, D. J., Connelly, F. M., & Chan, E. (2002). Three narrative teaching practices—One narrative teaching exercise. In N. Lyons, & V. K. LaBoskey (Eds.), *Narrative inquiry in practice: Advancing the knowledge of teaching* (pp. 133–145). New York, NY: Teachers College Press.

Clandinin, D. J., Pushor, D., & Murray Orr, A. (2007). Navigating sites for narrative inquiry. *Journal of Teacher Education, 58*(1), 21–35.

Clemente, A. (2007, June 1). English as cultural capital in the Oaxacan community of Mexico. *Tesol Quarterly, 41*(2), 421–425.

CNTE. (2010a, May). *Resolutivos, IV Congreso Nacional de Educación Alternativa, 28–30 de Mayo* (Conference Proceedings). Mexico City.

CNTE. (2010b). *Convocatoria, IV Congreso Nacional de Educación Alternativa.* (Ephemeral material). Mexico City.

CNTE. (2013). *Resolutivos, V Congreso Nacional de Educación Alternativa, 25–27 de abril de 2013* (Conference Proceedings). Mexico City.

Cockcroft, J. D. (1967). El maestro de primaria en la Revolución Mexicana. *Historia Mexicana, 16*(4), 565–587.

Cook, M. L. (1996). *Organizing dissent: Unions, the state and the democratic teachers' movement in Mexico.* University Park, PA: The Pennsylvania State University Press.

Cortés, J. V. (2006). El movimiento magisterial Oaxaqueño: Una aproximación a sus orígenes, periodización, funcionamiento y grupos político–sindicales. In J. V. Cortés (Ed.), *Educación, sindicalismo y gobernabilidad en Oaxaca* (pp. 33–86). Oaxaca, Mexico: Editorial del Magisterio Benito Juárez/ SNTE.

Cortina, R. (1989). Women as leaders in Mexican education. *Comparative Education Review, 33*(3), 357–376. Retrieved from ERIC database.

Cortina, R. (1990). Gender and power in the teacher's union of Mexico. *Mexican Studies/Estudios Mexicanos, 6*(2), 241–262.

Cortina, R. (2006). Women teachers in Mexico: Asymmetries of power in public education. In R. Cortina & S. San Román (Eds.), *Women and teaching: Global perspectives on the feminization of a profession* (pp. 107–128). New York, NY: Palgrave Macmillan.

Cruz-Manjarrez, A. (2013). *Zapotecs on the move: Cultural, social, and political processes in transnational perspective.* New Brunswick, NJ: Rutgers University Press. Retrieved from http://www.ebrary.com.

Dalton, M. (2007). Los organismos civiles en Oaxaca y el movimiento ciudadano: Causas y consecuencias. *Cuadernos del Sur, 12*(24/25), 63–80.

Dean, M. (2010). *Governmentality: Power and rule in modern society.* Los Angeles, CA: SAGE.

de Certeau, M. (1988). *The practice of everyday life.* Berkeley, CA: University of California Press.

De Ferranti, D. (2001). Introduction. In M. Giugale, O. Lafourcade, V. H. Nguyen, & World Bank (Eds.), *Mexico, a comprehensive development agenda for the new era* (pp. xxiii–xxiv). Washington, DC: The World Bank.

De La Rosa, M. G., & Schadl, S. M. (2014). *Getting up for the people: The visual revolution of ASAR-Oaxaca.* Oakland, CA: PM Press.

Delany, S. R. (1994). The rhetoric of sex, the discourse of desire. In T. Siebers (Ed.), *Heterotopia: Postmodern utopia and the body politic* (pp. 229–272). Ann Arbor, MI: University of Michigan Press.

Delgado Bernal, D., Burciaga, R., & Flores Carmona, J. (2012). Chicana/Latina testimonios: Mapping the methodological, pedagogical, and political. *Equity & Excellence in Education, 45*(3), 363–372.

de Lima Costa, C. (2014). Introduction to debates about translation: Lost (and found?) in translation/feminisms in hemispheric dialogue. In S. E. Álvarez, C. de Lima Costa, V. Feliu, R. Hester, N. Klahn, & M. Thayer (Eds.). *Translocalities/translocalidades: Feminist politics of translation in the Latin/a Américas* (pp. 19–36). Durham, NC: Duke University Press.

Denham, D., & C.A.S.A. Collective. (2008). *Teaching rebellion: Stories from the grassroots mobilization in Oaxaca.* Oakland, CA: PM Press.

Denzin, N. K. (2003). *Performance ethnography: Critical pedagogy and the politics of culture.* Thousand Oaks, CA: Sage.

Durán, J. (2001). The Mexican telesecundaria: Diversification, internationalization, change, and update. *Open Learning, 16*(2), 169–177.

Durand Ponte, V. M. (2007). Prólogo. In J. Hernández Díaz (Ed.), *Ciudadanías diferenciadas en un estado multicultural: Los usos y costumbres en Oaxaca* (pp. 11–34). Mexico City: Siglo XXI Editores/Universidad Autónoma Benito Juárez de Oaxaca.

Dyrness, A. (2011). *Mothers united: An immigrant struggle for socially just education.* Minneapolis, MN: University of Minnesota Press.

el Alebrije. (2007). Las noches en la Ciudad de la Resistencia: Entrevista a "El Alebrije." In. C. Beas Torres (Ed.), *La batalla por Oaxaca* (pp. 197–202). Oaxaca, Mexico: Ediciones Yope Power.

Esteva, G. (2007a). Líbranos del peso juarista. In G. Esteva, F. Gargallo, J. Martínez Luna, & J. Pech Casanova (Eds.), *Señor Juárez* (pp. 17–49). Oaxaca, Mexico: Archipiélago.

Esteva, G. (2007b, November). La otra campaña, la APPO y la izquierda: Revindicar una alternativa. *Cuadernos del Sur, 12*(24/25), 5–37.

Esteva, G. (2010). Beyond education. In L. Meyer & B. Maldonado (Eds.), *New world of Indigenous resistance: Noam Chomsky and voices from North, South and Central America.* San Francisco, CA: City Lights Books.

Forgacs, D. (Ed.). (2000). *The Antonio Gramsci reader: Selected writings 1916–1935.* New York, NY: New York University Press.

Foucault, M. (1980). *The history of sexuality,* Vol. I. New York, NY: Vintage.

Foucault, M. (1990). *The care of the self: The history of sexuality,* Vol. III. London: Penguin.

Foucault, M. (1995). *Discipline and punish: The birth of the prison* (2nd ed.). New York, NY: Vintage.

Foucault, M. (1998a). What is critique? In P. Rabinow & N. Rose (Eds.), *The essential Foucault: Selections from the essential works of Foucault 1954–1984* (pp. 263–278). New York, NY: The New Press.

Foucault, M. (1998b). The subject and power. In P. Rabinow & N. Rose (Eds.), *The essential Foucault: Selections from the essential works of Foucault 1954–1984* (pp. 126–144). New York, NY: The New Press.

Foucault, M. (1998c). What is enlightenment? In P. Rabinow & N. Rose (Eds.), *The essential Foucault: Selections from the essential works of Foucault 1954–1984* (pp. 43–57). New York, NY: The New Press.

Foweraker, J. (1993). *Popular mobilization in Mexico: The teachers' movement 1977–87.* New York, NY: Cambridge University Press.

Freidberg, J., Van, L. J., Patterson, L., Alvarez, Q. F., Corrugated Films, & Mal de Ojo TV. (2007). *Un poquito de tanta verdad.* Seattle: Corrugated Films.

Freire, P. (1994). *Pedagogy of the oppressed.* New Revised 20th anniversary edition. New York, NY: Continuum.

Friedlander, J. (1975). *Being Indian in Hueyapan: A study of forced identity in contemporary Mexico.* New York, NY: St. Martin's Press.

García Canclini, N. (2001). *Hybrid cultures: Strategies for entering and leaving modernity.* Fourth Printing. Minneapolis, MN: University of Minnesota Press.

Gee, J. P. (2001). What is literacy? In P. Shannon (Ed.), *Becoming political, too: New readings and writings on the politics of literacy education* (pp. 1–9). Portsmouth, NH: Heinemann.

Gee, J, P. (2005). *An introduction to discourse analysis: Theory and method.* New York, NY: Routledge.

Gibler, J. (2009). *Mexico unconquered: Chronicles of power and revolt.* San Francisco, CA: City Lights.

Haber, P. L. (2007). *Power from experience: Urban popular movements in late twentieth-century Mexico.* University Park, PA: Pennsylvania State University Press.

Hagopian, J. (Ed.). (2014). *More than a score: The new uprising against high-stakes testing.* Chicago, IL: Haymarket Books.

Hale, C. (2005). Neoliberal multiculturalism: The remaking of cultural rights and racial dominance in Central America. *PoLAR: Political and Legal Anthropology Review, 28*(1), 10–28.

Hancock, A. M. (2007). When multiplication doesn't equal quick addition: Examining intersectionality as a research paradigm. *Perspectives on Politics, 5,* 63–79.

Hernández, F. G. (2009). La educación alternativa y el movimiento pedagógico en el discurso de los maestros democráticos de Oaxaca, como contexto de la educación bilingüe e intercultural. In M. J. Bailón Corres (Ed.), *Ensayos sobre historia, política, educación y literatura de Oaxaca* (pp. 288–340). Oaxaca, Mexico: IIHUABJO.

Hernández Castillo, R. A. (2001). *Histories and stories from Chiapas: Border identities in southern Mexico.* Austin, TX: University of Texas Press.

Hernández Díaz, J. (2007). Presentación. In J. Hernández Díaz (Ed.), *Ciudadanías diferenciadas en un estado multicultural: Los usos y costumbres en Oaxaca* (pp. 7–10). Mexico City: Siglo XXI Editores/Universidad Autónoma Benito Juárez de Oaxaca.

Hodges, D. C. (1995). *Mexican anarchism after the revolution.* Austin, TX: University of Texas Press.

Holo, S. (2004). *Oaxaca at the crossroads: Managing memory, negotiating change.* Washington, DC: Smithsonian Books.

Howell, J. (1997). 'This job is harder than it looks': Rural Oaxacan women explain why they became teachers. *Anthropology & Education Quarterly, 28*(2), 251. Retrieved from Bibliography of Native North Americans database.

Johnson, J. M. (2013). Teachers as agents of change within Indigenous education programs in Guatemala and Mexico. In C. J. Benson & K. Kosonen (Eds.), *Language issues in comparative education: Inclusive teaching and learning in non-dominant languages and cultures* (pp. 153–170). Rotterdam: Sense Publishers.

Kamler, B. (2001). *Relocating the personal: A critical writing pedagogy.* Albany, NY: State University of New York Press.

Katz, C. (2001). Vagabond capitalism and the necessity of social reproduction. *Antipode, 33*(4), 709–728.

Knight, A. (1990). Racism, revolution and indigenismo: Mexico, 1910–1940. In R. Graham (Ed.), *The idea of race in Latin America 1870–1940* (pp. 71–113). Austin, TX: The University of Texas Press.

Knight, A., & Pansters, W. G. (Eds.). (2006). *Caciquismo in twentieth-century Mexico.* London: Institute for the Study of the Americas.

Knight, A., & Urquidi, M. (1989). Los intelectuales en la Revolución Mexicana. *Revista mexicana de sociología, 51*(2), 25–65.

Kymlicka, W., & Norman, W. (1994). Return of the citizen: A survey of recent work on citizenship theory. *Ethics, 104*(2), 352–381.

Lather, P. (2006). Foucaultian scientificity: Rethinking the nexus of qualitative research and educational policy analysis. *International Journal of Qualitative Studies in Education, 19*(6), 783–791.

Law, Y. (2008). (DVD) *Sígueme cantando: Sonidos de la lucha oaxaqueña.* Mal de Ojo Producciones.

Lawrence-Lightfoot, S. (2005). Reflections on portraiture: A dialogue between art and science. *Qualitative Inquiry, 11*(1), 3–15.

Lemke, T. (2011). *Foucault, governmentality, and critique.* Boulder, CO: Paradigm Publishers.

Lipman, P. (2011). *The new political economy of urban education: Neoliberalism, race, and the right to the city.* New York, NY: Routledge.

López, O. (2001). *Alfabeto y enseñanzas domesticas: El arte de ser maestro rural en el Valle de Mezquital.* Mexico City: CIESAS.

Lorenzini, D. (2016). From counter-conduct to critical attitude: Michel Foucault and the art of not being governed quite so much. *Foucault Studies, 21*, 7–21.

Luke, C. (2010). Introduction: Feminisms and pedagogies of everyday life. In. J. A. Sandlin, B. D. Schultz, & J. Burdick. (Eds.), *Handbook of public pedagogy: Education and learning beyond schooling* (pp. 130–138). New York, NY: Routledge.

Mal de Ojo TV, & Comité de Liberación 25 de Noviembre. (2007). (DVD). *Compromiso cumplido.* Oaxaca, Mexico: Mal de Ojo TV.

Maldonado, B. (2010). *Comunidad, comunalidad y colonialismo en Oaxaca, México: La nueva educación comunitaria y su contexto* (Doctoral dissertation). Department of Mesoamerican and Andean Cultures, Faculty of Archaeology, Leiden University.

Marentes, L. A. (2000). *Jose Vasconcelos and the writing of the Mexican revolution.* New York, NY: Twane Publishers.

Martínez Luna, J. (1982). Resistencia comunitaria y cultura popular. In G. Bonfil Batalla (Ed.), *Culturas Populares y Poliitica Cultural* (pp. 65–78). Mexico City: Museo Nacional de Culturas Populares/SEP.

Martínez Luna, J. (2007). De Juárez a García. In G. Esteva, F. Gargallo, J. Martínez Luna, & J. Pech Casanova (Eds.), *Señor Juárez* (pp. 73–99). Oaxaca, Mexico: Archipiélago.

Martínez Novo, C. (2006). *Who defines Indigenous? Identities, development, intellectuals, and the state in northern Mexico.* New Brunswick, NJ: Rutgers University Press.

Martínez Vásquez, V. R. (2004). *La educación en Oaxaca.* Oaxaca, Mexico: IISUABJO.

Martínez Vásquez, V. R. (2007). *Autoritarismo, movimiento popular y crisis política: Oaxaca 2006.* Oaxaca, Mexico: UABJO.

Martínez Vásquez, V. R. (2009). Antinomias y perspectivas del movimiento popular en Oaxaca. In V. R. Martínez Vásquez (Ed.), *La APPO: ¿Rebelión o movimiento social?: Nuevas formas de expresión ante la crisis* (pp. 329–347). Oaxaca, Mexico: IISUABJO.

McGinn, N., & Street, S. (1984). Has Mexican education generated human or political capital? *Comparative Education, 20*(3), 323–338.

McLaren, P. (2005). *La vida en las escuelas: una introducción a la pedagogía crítica en los fundamentos de la educación.* Mexico City: Siglo XXI.

Meyer, L. M., & Maldonado, B. (Eds.). (2004). *Entre la normatividad y la comunalidad: Experiencias innovadoras del Oaxaca indígena actual*. Oaxaca, Mexico: IEEPO/Colección Voces del Fondo; Serie Molinos de viento.

Meyer, L. M., & Maldonado, B. (Eds.). (2010). *New world of Indigenous resistance: Noam Chomsky and voices from North, South, and Central America*. San Francisco, CA: City Lights Books.

Mitra, R. (2010). Doing ethnography, being an ethnographer: The autoethnographic research Process and I. *Journal of Research Practice, 6*(1), 1–21.

Nail, T. (2013). The crossroads of power: Michel Foucault and the US/Mexico border wall. *Foucault Studies, 15*, 110–128.

Nevaer, L. E. V., & Sendyk, E. (2009). *Protest graffiti—Mexico: Oaxaca*. New York, NY: Mark Batty.

Norget, K. (2006). *Days of death, days of life: Ritual in the popular culture of Oaxaca*. New York, NY: Columbia University Press.

Olesen, T. (2007). The funny side of globalization: Humour and humanity in Zapatista framing. *International Review of Social History, 52*(15), 21–34.

Ong, A. (1999). *Flexible citizenship: The cultural logics of transnationality*. Durham, NC: Duke University Press.

Ong, A. (2006). *Neoliberalism as exception: Mutations in citizenship and sovereignty*. Durham, NC: Duke University Press.

Osorno, D. E., & Meyer, L. (2007). *Oaxaca sitiada: La primera Insurrección del siglo XXI*. Mexico City: Random House Mondadori.

Pennycook, A. (2010). *Language as a local practice*. New York, NY: Routledge.

Peters, M. A. (2016). Dissident thought: Systems of repression, networks of hope. *Contemporary Readings in Law and Social Justice, 8*(1), 20–36.

Phipps, A. (2014). *The politics of the body: Gender in a neoliberal and neoconservative age*. Malden, MA: Polity Press.

Porras Ferreyra, J. (2009). Las expresiones artísticas y la participación política: El conflicto oaxaqueño de 2006. In V. R. Martínez Vásquez (Ed.), *La APPO: ¿Rebelión o movimiento social?: Nuevas formas de expresión ante la crisis* (pp. 219–245). Oaxaca, Mexico: IISUABJO.

Poy, L., & Martínez, E. (2010, July 14). Exigen liberación de maestro detenido por daños en la SEP. *La Jornada*. Retrieved from http://www.jornada.unam.mx/2010/07/14/politica/012n2pol.

Pyykkönen, M. (2015). Liberalism, governmentality and counter-conduct; An introduction to Foucauldian analytics of liberal civil society notions. *Foucault Studies, 20*, 8–35.

Raby, D. L. (1974). *Educación y revolución social en México*. Mexico City: Sep-Setentas.

Reed, T. V. (2005). *The art of protest: Culture and activism from the civil rights movement to the streets of Seattle*. Minneapolis, MN: University of Minnesota Press.

Richard, N. (2010). *Crítica de la memoria (1990–2010)*. Santiago, Chile: Ediciones Universidad Diego Portales.

Rojas, F., & The World Bank. (2002). *Chiapas programmatic economic development Loan (PEDL) Project* (Report No. PID11530). Washington, DC: The World Bank. Retrieved from http://web.worldbank.org/external/projects/main?pagePK=64283627&piPK=73230&theSiteP K=40941&menuPK=228424&Projectid=P074751.

Rubin, J. W. (1994). COCEI in Juchitán: Grassroots radicalism and regional history. *Journal of Latin American Studies, 26*(1), 109–136.

Rubio Soto, G. (2013). *Memoria, política y pedagogía: Los caminos hacia la enseñanza del pasado reciente en Chile.* Santiago, Chile: LOM ediciones/UMCE.

Sadlier, S. T., & Arancibia, M. C. (2015). Toward a society where everyone is always studying: Access at an elite Chilean research university. *International Journal of Qualitative Studies in Education, 28*(9), 1049–1064.

Sandlin, J. A. Schultz, B. D., & Burdick J. (Eds.). (2009). *Handbook of public pedagogy: Education and learning beyond schooling.* New York, NY: Routledge.

Sassen, S. (2002). The repositioning of citizenship: Emergent subjects and spaces for politics. *Berkeley Journal of Sociology, 46*, 4–26.

Sassen, S. (2005). The global city: Introducing a concept. *Brown Journal of World Affairs, 11*(2), 27–43.

Schön, D. A. (1987). *Educating the reflective practitioner: Toward a new design for teaching and learning in the professions.* San Francisco, CA: Jossey-Bass.

Shepherd, A. V. (2015). Government versus teachers: The challenges of educational progress in Oaxaca, Mexico. *Current Issues in Comparative Education, 17*(1), 27–35.

Simpson, Z. (2012). The truths we tell ourselves: Foucault on parrhesia. *Foucault Studies, 13*, 99–115.

Smith, B. (2008, April 1). Inventing tradition at gunpoint: Culture, caciquismo and state formation in the Region Mixe, Oaxaca (1930–1959). *Bulletin of Latin American Research, 27*(2), 215–234.

Sotelo Marbán, J. (2008). *Oaxaca: Insurgencia civil y terrorismo de estado.* Mexico City: Era.

Stavans, I. (2011). *José Vasconcelos: The prophet of race.* New Brunswick, NJ: Rutgers University Press.

Stephen, L. (2002). *¡Zapata Lives!: Histories and cultural politics in Southern Mexico.* Berkeley, CA: University of California Press.

Stephen, L. (2013). *We are the face of Oaxaca: Testimony and social movements.* Durham, NC: Duke University Press.

St. Pierre, E. A. (2011). Post qualitative research: The critique and the coming after. In N. Denzin, & Y. S. Lincoln (Eds.), *Sage handbook of qualitative research* (4th ed., pp. 611–625). Thousand Oaks, CA: Sage.

Street, S. (1992). El SNTE y la política educativa, 1970–1990. *Revista Mexicana de Sociología, 54*(2), 45–72.

Street, S. (2001). When politics becomes pedagogy: Oppositional discourse as policy in Mexican teachers' struggles for union democracy. In M. Sutton & B. A. Levinson (Eds.), *Policy as practice: Toward a comparative sociocultural analysis of educational policy* (pp. 145–166). Stamford, CT: Ablex Publisher.

Street, S. L. (1996, January 1). Democratization "from below" and popular culture: Teachers from Chiapas, Mexico. *Studies in Latin American Popular Culture, 15*, 261–278.

Tazzioli, M. (2016). Revisiting the omnes et singulatim bond: The production of irregular conducts and the biopolitics of the governed. *Foucault Studies, 21*, 98–116.

Thayer, M. (2010). Translations and refusals: Resignifying meanings as feminist political practice. *Feminist Studies, 36*(1), 200–230.

Trinidad Galván, R. (2005). Transnational communities en la lucha: Campesinas and grassroots organizations "Globalizing from below." *Journal of Latinos & Education, 4*(1), 3–20. Retrieved from ERIC database.

Tsing, A. L. (2005). *Friction: An ethnography of global connection.* Princeton, NJ: Princeton University Press.

Tsing, A. L. (2015). *The mushroom at the end of the world: On the possibility of life in capitalist ruins.* Princeton, NJ: Princeton University Press.

Unidad Popular de Madres y Padres de Familia. (2010, May 29). *A los asistentes al congreso nacional de educación alternativa* (Letter).

Vaughan, M. K. (1982). *The state, education and social class in Mexico 1880–1928.* DeKalb, IL: Northern Illinois University Press.

Vaughan, M. K. (1997). *Cultural politics in revolution: Teachers, peasants, and schools in Mexico, 1930–1940.* Tucson, AZ: University of Arizona Press.

Velásquez, L. I. (2010). *Noticias,* el embate del gobierno autoritario. In I. Yescas Martínez & C. Sánchez Islas (Eds.), *Oaxaca 2010: Voces de la transición* (pp. 176–182). Oaxaca, Mexico: Carteles editores.

Wolff, R. D. (2005). Ideological state apparatuses, consumerism, and U.S. capitalism: Lessons for the left. *Rethinking Marxism, 17*(2), 223–235, 333. Retrieved from https://ezproxy.spscc.edu/login?url=http://search.proquest.com/docview/212147805?accountid=1172.

Yescas Martínez, I. (2006). *Al cielo por asalto: (Notas sobre el movimiento magisterial de Oaxaca).* In J. V. Cortés (Ed.), *Educación, sindicalismo y gobernabilidad en Oaxaca* (pp. 19–31). Oaxaca, Mexico: SNTE/ Editorial del Magisterio Benito Juárez.

Yescas Martínez, I., & Zafra, G. (1985). *La insurgencia magisterial en Oaxaca 1980.* Oaxaca, Mexico: IISUABJO.

Movement I: Quality

2

Quality Rendered Pedagogical

In education, a focus on outcomes and good evaluation and accountability systems are key to enhance the efficiency of the system and are a necessary condition for an efficient devolution of responsibilities.

—From *The education challenge in Mexico* (Guichard, 2005, p. 17)

El objetivo de la educación comunitaria es lograr una atención de calidad a los estudiantes miembros de pueblos originarios con el fin de que tengan una formación sólida y amplia, basada en su identidad.

The objective of communitarian education is to achieve a careful commitment to high quality for student members of the *pueblos originarios*. The end result is for them to get concrete, wide-ranging and identity-based educational formation.

—Benjamín Maldonado (2010, p. 17)

Telenovelas Educating the Millions

Quality education moves in conflictive ways. March 2011, Mexico City. A spat circulated when the country's top educator, Secretaría de Educación Pública (SEP) secretary Alonso Lujambio from the National Action Party (PAN), stated at an educational award event before agents of the mass media that *telenovelas* were an "important instrument for the education of millions" (Román, 2011, para. 2) to promote citizenship and higher literacy rates. "We are advancing in the fight against educational *rezago* (backwardness/drag); there are many years of accumulated rezago, so it is a task requiring persistence, stubbornness and years of effort," Lujambio added (para. 7). *Telenovelas*, Mexican soap operas, are widespread and accessible, but they are often associated with lower-brow and less serious forms of entertainment than those that one might expect from Lujambio, who was then seeking his party's nomination for the 2012 presidency.[1]

The telenovela comment met with an immediate backlash from Lujambio's critics. Narro Robles, *rector* of Universidad Nacional Autónoma de México (UNAM), Mexico's premier research university, disparaged Lujambio's cavalier views, responding that in Mexico "education must be seen as a matter where the bigger intention is not only to teach something or transfer information. Education implies forming citizens so that every Mexican recognizes and follows through with his or her obligations" (Olivares & Morelos, 2011, para. 4). Thus, education to the *rector* becomes a matter of nation-building through forming skills and mindsets for that imposing challenge. Similarly, Lourdes Barbosa, president of a gender advocacy group, stated that telenovelas do not promote citizenship[2] but instead model antiquated gender roles (Poy, 2011, para. 3). Finally, a spokesperson for the Coordinadora Nacional de Trabajadores de la Educación (CNTE) dissenting faction inside the Sindicato Nacional de Trabajadores de la Educación (SNTE)[3] pointed out that telenovela-type programming serves as a corporate "smoke screen" (para. 2). The CNTE administrator considered that Lujambio's comment made sense only "if we believe that [Lujambio] was seeking to appease the television duopolies[4] to cement support for a presidential run; otherwise it can only be qualified as one more of his incoherencies" (para. 3). This is to say that for the radical movement in the trade union, telenovelas epitomize the media's plan to stupefy and commodify, and so Lujambio is either shrewdly corporate or fumblingly technocratic. These comments—from a university rector, a women's rights advocate, and a radical teacher—point to the development of literacy and values as worthy of debate. The comments, and the conducts they seek to shape, show how the compulsion to seek better modes of education cuts across ideological divides.[5] Indeed, following Hunter's (1994) genealogy of schooling, opposing ideological perspectives, like the Marxian and liberal views espoused by the CNTE and UNAM, resemble one another. Focusing on the work of rural Oaxacan elementary educators, this chapter explores how quality, evident in the telenovelas commentaries, drives discussions of education and leaves openings for conducting quality differently.

Moving along the contours of quality, a tendency that is common to right- and left-wing perspectives, is quality framed within the mantle of scarcity or precarity. Education on the right often calls for technical education to solve real, lived problems, like the education of the millions of students in Lujambio's speech, which relates education to human capital development. Agencies on the left, such as the CNTE wing of the union and, more particularly, the Oaxacan teachers of the Sección 22, have a prevailing view that teachers should smuggle politics back into the teaching and learning, following perspectives like Giroux's (1988) critical pedagogy, as depoliticized education foments docility and keeps the poor, poor and the rich, rich.[6] The leftist view becomes apparent in the Paulo Freire (1994) critical pedagogy tradition that undergirds the CNTE dissidents' alternative education proposals across Mexico (CNTE, 2010) and in Oaxaca state (CEDES 22, 2009, 2010),[7] as we saw in Chapter One. The ways that different agents lean toward newer and better forms of education show that educational innovation is inescapably politics-riven, seen in the telenovela line of ideologically different responses. How has improved education become approachable enough for agents of differing beliefs and professions to call for it in their side of a public debate? Addressing this question, the subject of this second chapter, will help us recognize *quality* working as a friction and yield insight into how Oaxacan public intellectual teachers have come to spearhead political and pedagogical movements in street protests and in school-based teaching, which is elaborated in the ensuing chapters.

The Movement of Quality Education

By examining newspapers, policy documents, tourist booklets, teaching manuals, political speeches, high-brow magazines, development project user's guides, and elementary school textbooks from the 1880s to the present, the movements of diverse inquiries in this chapter form a *genealogy*[8] (McGushin, 2007), of quality education, an approach to reach outside the reduced, confined ways we perceive the problem today (p. xvii). As a reminder, the movement of diverse inquiries assembled in this book is ethnographic in its orientation and critical in its ethos. *Ethnographic friction* (Tsing, 2005), as I use it here, embraces points of contention that come to life through universal ideas carried out on the ground. Like the telenovela conversation on quality, ethnographic friction looks to "zones of awkward engagement, where words mean something different across a divide even as people agree to speak" (p. xi). *Frictions*, the "unequal, unstable and creative qualities of interconnection across difference" (p. 4), appear in the way Lujambio's telenovela and educational commentaries did, flashing local versions of the abstract concept of quality and rendering visible the confining aspects of the present use of quality education for critique. Movements of diverse inquiries, the way I approach the uneasy encounters of friction this book, begins where there is disagreement. In this chapter, the critical analysis starts through a contentious discussion on quality and leads to a genealogical exploration into how questions of quality education became discussion points to begin with.

For starters, genealogy is more ethos than concrete methodology. To call upon genealogy in social research is to reject easy causation and spurn notions of inevitability. One version of quality education comes into unequal engagement with another, and the friction this produces spells neither panacea nor panic for the possibility of alternative pedagogical projects. As a buzzword of good, progressive, and antipoverty education, quality may in fact dominate conversations among elite educational planners like Secretary Lujambio, the university rector, and the teachers' union operative, yet this conversation neither silences nor dominates other ones. Quality may play out in the everyday life of parents, teachers, and students, even if elite power brokers govern the media, police, research universities, and protesting teachers. To face diverse critical projects from non-elite actors, I take on quality (as well as patrimony and governability, as we will see later) through words, images, and thoughts that show it coming to differing forms. Assembling a genealogy is a critical approach for research (Dean, 2010, p. 54; Koopman, 2013, p. 16). It supplements my primary ethnographic approach in teaching and protest spaces in Oaxaca and Mexico City. As "incitement to study the form and consequences of universals in particular historical situations and practices grounded in problems raised in the course of particular social and political struggles" (Dean, 2010, p. 54), a genealogy traces out how the notions that drive quality education lead to a conversation carried out by trade unionists, educators, NGO leaders and politicians.

Genealogy in gathering and representing information from the field leads to as many questions as answers. Not seeking an underlying truth, genealogy less resembles a product of the Western scientific method than a platform to patch together the ways quality becomes a set of conflicting tangibles to act upon. A genealogy, sometimes considered a history of ideas, is focused on the present moment while drawing on what has passed (Koopman, 2013, p. 24). A researcher might start with quality as *sine qua non* of education, one that crosses political divides and methodological best practices and might argue that certain practices lead to excellence in teaching and learning more than others. In fact, I do make defining claims on the character of critical education at different points in this book. The manner of approach here, however, begins not with spelling out the necessary stages of how teachers have achieved higher quality, but rather how quality education has become a pedagogical concern worth asking about in the first place. Proceeding with questions about the notions and actions of quality—*problematizing* it rather than taking it as given, inevitable or naturally existing—characterizes the genealogical line of inquiry that follows and touches off the chapters of this book that follow. Genealogy, furthermore, works as a narrative device. In it, I turn to what is familiar to make it seem unfamiliar and to past texts, following Koopman, to familiarize the unfamiliar (p. 57). A social researcher builds a genealogy by stitching together narrative substance from divided and uneven sources, just as a compelling story tends to travel along simultaneous and disjointed pathways. In this book, across the movements of diverse inquiries into quality, patrimony, and governability, I see no reason to argue a unified, clear-cut account when outlying questions and reactions come up that merit attention, too. As a storytelling device, genealogy juxtaposes texts and other symbolic material that may seem ethnographically incoherent, turning what is apparent and taken for granted into what is intriguingly strange.

Instruction and Integration

The purposes for [the House of the People] are as follows:

I. *Social.* To construct schools for the community and the community for the schools …

II. *Economic.* … to cultivate habits of collaboration and cooperation and to promote the wellbeing of each associated person. …

III. *Moral.* To form free men. …

IV. *Intellectual.* To provide general knowledge according to different gradations of teaching without aiming to prepare the students for a brilliant exam where they might excel via incomprehensible encyclopedism (*enciclopedismo indigesto*) …

V. *Physical and aesthetic.* To develop habits of hygiene …. Softening [man's] personality via artistic manifestations related to the environment …

—From *Purposes for the House of the People, 1923* (Fuentes, 1986, pp. 32–33)

Quality education is not new. Oaxaca, as Mexico in general, has turned to educational quality for two centuries. The Spanish Constitution of 1812 mandated the literacy of all citizens by 1830 (Monarchy of Spain, 1820, p. 11). Prior to Mexico's early nineteenth-century independence from Spain, pedagogy, in an era of scientific positivism and liberalism, was spoken of as *instruction*.[9] The Colonial legal and administrative system before the 1810 independence movement had set up categories of racial classification (Wade, 1997, p. 29).[10] During the period after Independence, education through instruction would surface as a moral imperative to integrate and improve different groups that had been seen as peripheral.[11] The 1865 Mexican Law of Instruction stipulated that primary school instruction focus on religious principles, that the "local authorities shall take care that parents or tutors shall send their children or pupils, from the age of five, to public primary schools …" (Talavera, 1973, p. 137). By 1904, a state government document (Gobierno Constitucional del Estado Libre y Soberano de Oaxaca, 1904) includes in instruction an element of pastoral care for Indigenous Oaxacans.[12]

> In that the [Oaxacan] government truthfully wants to set up public instruction, [the government seeks] the most effective means for reaching solid progress for the pueblo, especially of the indigenous race, that solely via their intellectual perfection might abandon their current habits for ways that characterize the civilized races. This [instruction] shall show beneficial and direct influence and powerfully resolve important problems of a social, political and economic order, which have so worried and still worry us as public men (*hombres*). (p. 3).

The efforts to improve the thoughts and actions of an Indigenous other, according the public men concerned with the socioeconomic welfare of the Oaxacan pueblo, is not just about creating better polices. Instead, the document calls upon science for insight.

> We believe that the moment has arrived to begin a formal study to review the diverse laws of public instruction active in the state to find out how to follow through with imparting that which comes under the fomentation, care and orientation of the Government. (p. 3)

The Oaxacan official later suggests that the government would use scientific methods to measure compliance with the 1893 Law of Instruction and evaluate if the current "organization and teaching system" should undergo modification. The document also names the host of lawmakers, physicians, and teachers to serve as researcher-assessors in this process, dividing the scientific methods of a "civilized race" and a primordially backward, though teachable, Indigenous race.[13] Public men of Oaxaca created knowledge and policy around the educating of the uneducated as early as the nineteenth century.

With research-informed policy, instruction furthermore encompassed the conducts of moral rectitude. To enter a rural normal school and qualify for a teacher placement during this period required proof of good moral conduct. In 1883, a founding principle of one such teacher training facility mandated that successful teacher applicants "legally justify their civil and moral conduct, be that via persons of character or three witnesses ..." (Secretaría del Gobierno Constitucional del Estado Libre y Soberano de Oaxaca & Jiménez, 1883, p. 3). Once teacher candidates matriculated, the normal school director would ensure moral standards and "surveil the conduct of the practitioners and other subordinates, correcting their faults as necessary" and "[visit] district village schools once a month to correct the imperfections found there" (p. 9). Good moral standing of the teachers in the period of instruction differs from what we see today in terms of quality education, for morality resides inside the body and flourishes outside of teacher-student interactions. However, a proper teacher disposition—the quality embedded in their educator bones—remains infused with commitment and decency, and as we will see in this chapter and later, the modes of quality education that draw from and counteract official and elite versions of quality education gravitate toward social justice as the inheritance of the teachers.

Indeed, when different sociopolitical alliances became entangled in the 1910 Mexican Revolution, rural teachers with the "respect and trust" of the public became key actors in the nationwide upheaval (Cockcroft, 1967, p. 568).[14] Until the establishment of rural schools after the Revolution, school coverage remained limited farther away from cities. The great expansion came with philosopher-politician José Vasconcelos, who ran a volunteer-driven literacy campaign (Raby, 1974, p. 13). In 1921, he took directorship of the SEP and expanded rural education, particularly, as Carlos Monsiváis (2010) recalls, to institute secular and civic-focused literacy (pp. 114–115). But secularity did not spell the end of teaching as a moral act, as this period featured the creation of a corps of rural, primarily women, teachers to promote post-Revolutionary national integration (López, 2001; Vaughan, 1990, p. 143), which depended on conducting teachers toward socially committed civil service. Speaking in Washington DC, Vasconcelos (2009) shared his vision on how to "educate pure-blooded *[I]ndios*"[15] (p. 200) stating his "wish to educate the Indio in order to assimilate him (*asimilarlo*) into our nationality" (pp. 200–201) and, following the "great Spanish educators ...." adapt the [I]ndian to European civilization" and not "reduce them to isolation." (p. 201). Teaching in the post-Revolutionary period hinged on campaigning for the proper integration of racialized, rural, and needy others,[16] also evident in the Fuentes (1986) epigraph above on how education produced healthy, upstanding, and free citizens.

The post-Revolutionary period (1917–1940) progressed on the nation-building shoulders of teachers, particularly women. A unified nation carried out by pedagogical missionary work, Vasconcelos would hire Frida Kahlo's husband, muralist Diego Rivera, to paint iconic images in "dogmatic realism" (García Canclini, 2001, p. 53) where peasants and urban manufacturing workers in collective labor built a modern Mexico. In *La Maestra Rural*, a 1932 painting in Mexico City's SEP building, Diego Rivera portrays a teacher seated on her knees, on the iridescent yellow earth, in a circle of nine peasants, one in overalls and another with her long hair braided. The *maestra rural*, the rural teacher, in the earthen-hued dress of the peasants, keeping an open book in her left hand on her lap and extending the palm of her right, radiates like a saint in devotional iconography.[17] State-sponsored folkloric ballet would furthermore select from Indigenous textile patterns, village music, and dance numbers to shape a presumed Indigenous past into a deep-structure expression of what modern, post-Revolutionary Mexico might look like. The rural maestra, as village weaving and dancing, would publicize the products and practices of women in rural Oaxaca. Rural Oaxacan dance steps played a noteworthy role in cultivating national identity. A 1935 brochure that reports on La Guelaguetza, an annual Oaxaca City dance and music event, reads:

> As a moving tribute to the [1910] Mexican Revolution in its 25th anniversary, the pueblo of the State of Oaxaca presents, once again, the Guelaguetza festival that wondrously symbolizes the greatest example of the cooperation and solidarity that is cultivated in Oaxaca. … With this objective, racial values, better defined and consistent as they are, leave behind their farmlands and mountains and turn, enthusiastic and sincere, to the city to commemorate on this occasion the revitalizing (*revindicador*) [Mexican Revolution] movement that has moved the Nation in favor of a better life for all Mexicans. (Vargas, 1935, p. 3)

The Guelaguetza Festival today remains well attended by Oaxacans and visitors from across Mexico, as we will see in Chapter Five.[18] Nevertheless, official efforts to nationalize local differences in culture and in education would still provide openings for Oaxacans to steer the national integration project to their local advantage (Smith, 2008). Indeed, official efforts to make the mountainous and Indigenous state of Oaxaca resemble the rest of Mexico, since the nineteenth century, has taken on a particularly local zest (Caplan, 2010, p. 149). Even activists within the rural schooling systems designed specifically to integrate the communities to the nation could negotiate community-based education (González Apodaca, 2008, p. 240). The maestra rural, the rural teacher serving as a public functionary in a state system that organized teachers to integrate cultural difference, found openings for standing up for the local communities, their students, and themselves.

As much as the state addressed Indigenous communities in rural Mexico in hopeful and ameliorative terms, and carried out this work by women, it became essential to separate the knowledgeable from the needy. In the opening pages of a third-grade Mexican history textbook, Chávez Orozco (1937) directly lectures Mexican primary school students on the wretched condition of "[I]ndios" and the reasons why city dwellers need to lend devoted support to their rural, unassimilated cousins.

> When we go out to visit the countryside, we come across many men (*hombres*) that work the earth. These men go about poorly clad and generally live in straw (*zacate*) houses. We call the men that reside far from the great cities [I]ndios. Indios *earn little* money through their work, and thus they eat poorly. (Emphasis in original, p. 9)

The paucity of resources furthermore comes from a lack of schooling. "They do not always have the chance to go to school and they are ignorant. Generally, they can neither read nor write, but they know how to work. Indios work a lot" (p. 9). The fruits of that hard work from the rural hinterlands makes city life possible:

> The bread that we eat on our table is made with the wheat that the [I]ndios cultivate and harvest. The garments we put on our bodies are woven with wool from the sheep *shepherded* by the [I]ndios on their hillsides or come from the cotton that they sow and gather in their fields. We must love [I]ndios because without their effort we would not have many things that are *indispensable* for our lives. To demonstrate our love for [I]ndios, we must help them just as they help us. (Emphasis in original, p. 9)

This textbook excerpt renders quality education into the realm of teaching and learning on a few levels. First, directed to a national audience through the schools, it presents people of the pueblos originarios as a product of the primeval landscape, in mind and body; urban Mestizos and *Criollos* should "shepherd" and "sow and gather" this resource. Second, the textbook, from the period of socialist education in Mexico, posits Indigenous farmers as laborers who do not control the surplus value they create through their hard work. Third, because of this debt to the Indigenous worker, posited as "they," all other Mexicans becoming "we," owe a debt of gratitude. Overall, this schoolbook excerpt models *indigenismo*, a view of a unified Mexican nation forged out of Indigenous groups.[19] Indigenismo in this textbook uses the laborious, simple, and yet needed contribution of Indigenous people as requisite for modern, non-Indio, bread-on-our-table lifestyles. Pedagogically, the children and teachers engaging with the Chávez Orozco (1937) text reside in modernity,[20] a modernity with a responsibility for understanding the nation's origins and modes of production and for acting as curators of this cultural heritage and material abundance.[21]

This post-Revolutionary period cultivates teaching and learning as a morally committed and communalist social encounter. The rural Mexican school after 1921 became "the house of the pueblo" for promoting literacy, farming, public health, home economics, and other forms of social development (Loyo, 1985, p. 10). Official rural school pedagogy of this period favored experiential models under the leadership of Undersecretary of Education, Moisés Sáenz. A Columbia University student of educational philosopher John Dewey, Sáenz modeled the rural school on the "action school" of his northern mentor (p. 15). Speaking in 1925, Sáenz detailed his view of such schools:

> Observing, then, the activities in these rural mountain schools up front, the idea that the rural school is a social center for the community comes into full view. The rural school is the house of the pueblo, a meeting place for neighbors. It has connections and relations vital for the whole town. Mostly in these schools, we are constructing a little library, not just for the school but also for the whole town. (p. 21)

In the rural Oaxacan elementary school in Tecotitlán, eighty-five years later, I observed community-wide participation around sports competitions, school improvement efforts, reading festivals, and holiday celebrations. When I would ride along the access road back to Oaxaca with the assistant director of the school, adult men would stand up from working the fields to greet him and current and former students would stop him along the way to say hi and exchange news. Therefore, the rural Oaxacan school retains "social center for the community" status and teaching depends on engaging with villagers outside of school based on the rhythm of village life.

It would be inaccurate, however, to assume that Sáenz's official description of the newly established federal schools translated into uniform adherence to centralized mandates. Many schools ignored SEP mandates (Marentes, 2000), as the state's educational project never enjoyed the total adoption in the rural areas that the visionaries Vasconcelos and Sáenz had imagined. Rockwell (1996) noticed that in the state of Tlaxcala, the rural schools of the period resembled those of the instruction era, a generation before. More particularly, the regulation of education from the centralized state reduced municipal control over villages, which allowed teachers and families in the smaller communities a modicum of autonomy (pp. 316–317). What is more, Sáenz himself in 1932 would lament that the rural schools he visited in the state of Michoacán had failed to measure up:

> The schools do not deserve the … nickname of reading, writing and counting schools. The achievement of these fundamental arts, as we observe, is almost null…. So general and inexplicable is the deficiency that I have come to wonder if, while defining the rural school, we have not been ourselves victims of some mirage of idealism. The teaching program is a capricious creation of both circumstance and the teachers themselves. There are neither timetables nor order in what they do. Attendance is irregular…. (Raby, 1974, p. 32)

Therefore, from the very beginning, the centralizing impetus to foment Mexican subjects through literacy and social welfare met with localized impediments. From the period of instruction to the period of integration, the authorities tasked teachers with responsibilities to transform individuals and communities. As the state depended on building a moral *esprit de corps* among teachers to improve rural community conditions and help the underdeveloped rural peoples develop as individuals, the teachers and other community actors become empowered to interpret quality education in local terms. In 1932, Sáenz lamented that a mirage of idealism to develop rural education bamboozled him, but this cry is in vain because when a project depends on an embodied commitment to transform social conditions like poverty or low-quality education, actors respond to the local conditions with projects that may not resonate with the official projections. To comprehend quality education today, and to trace out how SEP director Lujambio's comments could meet with diverging verbal responses, we should also appreciate that schoolteachers and others address discourses at the policy level. This is a starting point for the first movement of this book, quality.

Nonmechanical Identities: Grasshopper Ladies

The actions of students played a part in how the Mexican state began to shift its policies away from a strong central state in the last quarter of the twentieth century. In 1968, weeks before the Mexico City Summer Olympics, and in the middle of a flowering of youth-centered social mobilization, President Gustavo Díaz Ordaz and his successor, Luis Echeverría, ordered the military to shoot at 10,000 protesting students at the Plaza of Three Cultures in Tlatelolco, Mexico City. Hundreds died, a massacre that affected Mexican policymaking (Torres, 1991), and shaped a generation of intellectuals, artists, and political actors nationwide

(Foweraker, 1993) and in Oaxaca (Albertani, 2009, p. 156). The repression of 1968 also prompted the state to soften its aggressive handling of social movement activity, among other compensatory measures to regain legitimacy. In the late 1970s, the CNTE teachers' movement within the mainstream SNTE gathered strength. Labeled "communists" and "snipers" (Yescas Martínez & Zafra, 1985, p. 133) and impeached for conspiring to destabilize Mexico (p. 145), the CNTE would eventually flourish, and Oaxaca's dissident local, the Sección 22, turned into the political and pedagogical force it is today. In addition to the rise in activism after the Tlatelolco state-sponsored repression, the state began to shift away from its universal commitment to public welfare. In southeastern Mexico, the decentralization of education had begun by 1974 (Hernández, 2009). When de la Madrid took office as president in 1982, he further pledged to decentralize some of the federal government's operations (Martínez Vásquez, 2004). His successor, Harvard-trained economist Carlos Salinas de Gortari, would turn Mexico further away from an interventionist and centralized state illustrated by the words of Vasconcelos and in the 1937 textbook example above. After President Salinas, public education remained important, but the ways teachers enjoyed benefits as civil servants, and how textbooks[22] trained students to think, shifted toward a pull-yourself-up-by-your-bootstraps independence. From here, quality teaching and learning begins to take its current form of shaping student and teacher thoughts and actions toward efficiency and individualism. This period coincided with the signing of the North American Free Trade Agreement (NAFTA), which would put Mexican education squarely within economic competitive models, and standardized curricula and assessment would retreat from collective responsibility in favor of quantitative testing, comparing the results from state to state.[23] The last two decades of Mexican neoliberal educational reform has promoted workforce development more than national integration and has looked to individuals to take care of their own needs instead of expecting the state to do it for them.[24]

This shift toward greater autonomy and accountability became palpable in terms of official views on race and ethnicity. President Vicente Fox's *2001–2006 Presidential Plan for National Development* (Fox Quesada, 2001) correlated education with the development category of rezago that Secretary Lujambio emphasized with his telenovelas comment above and thus located education in the domain of economic productivity. For example, President Fox's "strategy G" for social and human development attempts to "secure the direct participation of the Indigenous[25] in national development and combat the rezagos and structural causes of their marginalization…" (p. 86)[26]; and, "education must be linked to production, providing a basic cultural frame of arduous work to future workers and professionals so that they *see work as a medium of human becoming*" (emphasis added, p. 71). We see similar language of pastoral care, but with knowledge revolving around how to help individuals and groups to self-actualize rather than integrating them into the larger society. It is not all about economics, though, as ethnicity and identity politics remain important in this productivity turn for education. This *neoliberal multiculturalism* (Hale, 2005) validates how racial, language, and cultural differences exist in Mexico, and that these differences need to be validated and revitalized. President Fox's *Plan* further states:

> In the last thirty years, the conception Mexicans have toward the ethnic question has shifted in three fundamental aspects. First, today we recognize that the relationship between [I]ndigenous culture and identity is not mechanical. Therefore, cultural changes in a society do not necessarily imply a change in identity. Second, we have stopped thinking of the Mexican nation as something culturally homogenous, in fact, heterogeneousness has become manifest with greater vigor. Third, we recognize that [I]ndigenous people exist as political subjects. They represent their interests in terms of members of an ethnicity. In addition, today, [I]ndigenous organizations exist that powerfully influence the public sphere. (Fox Quesada, 2001, p. 36)

For Fox, who prided himself as serving as the first opposition party president in seventy years of Partido Revolucionario Institucional (PRI) hegemony, Mexico under his watch has progressed to the inclusion of all citizens.[27] As the 1937 textbook illustrated, Indigenous people have particular interests, rights, and knowledges that authorities must help revitalize.[28] However, in this neoliberal multicultural turn, the drive to improve the lives of Indigenous people targets their technological backwardness rather than their racial and cultural deficits. The president suggests an inclusive shift; though, this recognition of the "wealth of diverse cultural worlds" casts the risk and responsibility onto individuals and communities. Empowering the voices from the margins comes at a cost, for the state, the erstwhile pillar of social welfare, now *devolves* (Brown, 2015, p. 131) the responsibility of socioeconomic advancement onto the shoulders of the newly empowered.[29]

So far, we see that in the last two decades, along with signing NAFTA, the state officially recognizes language, culture, and identity. However, it is difficult to sustain fundamental policy shifts backed by productivity statistics alone. Here we see race and ethnicity featuring into the call for quality education across Mexico, as dark-skinned rural Oaxacans become representatively problematic. The May 2011 *Nexos* magazine issue, "The Scandal of Education: 2+2=5," published diverse angles on how Mexican education is in distress, presenting tedious statistics on rezago, and, written by a former SEP undersecretary, the magazine sketched out the ethnic and cultural visage of the predicament:

> Across the grass, a woman in Oaxaca drags a sack tied with woven palm reeds so it remains open. Grasshoppers fall in the trap. She empties them in a bag and separates out the garbage. She cooks the grasshoppers with water and lime. She sells them in the market. She is the grasshopper lady (*chapulinera*) with such a knowledge and practice for survival. She forms part of educational rezago [for] she studied until second grade. (Díaz de Cossío, 2011, p. 41)

Grasshoppers, *chapulines*, a Oaxacan delicacy, are commonly sold by women on the sidewalks by the 20 de Noviembre Market, in downtown Oaxaca City, a boisterous place that specializes in handicrafts, pirated CDs, and street vendor vocal appeals to prospective clients.[30] Ten blocks to the more affluent north, boutiques sell local wares, similar to those in the market, displaying them as art, not handicrafts.[31] The grasshopper lady, an informal market vendor, occupies the busy non-boutique market. Following the Díaz de Cossío narrative, she remains in the warren of a retrograde street, not because of her culture and ethnicity *per se*, but because quality education has remained beyond her reach. Díaz de Cossío's conclusion admonishes that "we can never be a developed and just society; we cannot aspire to be competitive in a globalized world with 70 percent of the population over fifteen in educational rezago" (p. 42). This compels the reader toward incorporating quality education, for without quality, young rural Oaxacan women will drag along as grasshopper ladies and not learn their way into developing Mexico. This imaginary implies that the unknowing and blameless grasshopper lady peddles her ancestral fare by default. An embodiment of rural Indigeneity, the "common patrimony of all Mexicans" (Bonfil Batalla, 1996, p. 128), she and Mexico both deserve better from teachers and administrators; education must help her surpass the 70 percent of Oaxacans in rezago and trade up her grasshopper-catching skills for more practiced ones.

Evolving beyond a Mexico of grasshopper ladies depends on bolstering educational quality that in recent years has meant reforming systems of assessment and evaluation.[32] The Instituto Nacional para la Evaluación de la Educación (INEE), a state organization founded in 2002 to oversee standardized testing, states that because education is an inalienable right, it must be quality-driven and target the "particular needs of the students" (INEE, 2010, p. 31). Attending to individual needs means favoring a "commitment to guarantee the right for a primary education provided for all children ... [that] does not distinguish between ethnic condition, place of residence, sex, socioeconomic condition and other characteristics"

(p. 39).[33] However inclusive and humanizing quality education may be, teachers and others are called to do their part. The INEE expressed concern that "rurality and poverty are phenomena that ... can construct impediments for reaching universal attendance and, therefore, the compliance of the right to an education" (p. 45). Missing school, one of the causes and outcomes of rezago, represents a problem, as "[n]on-attendance at school is a grave problem for populations at risk, which is something that brings up important deficits in resources of diverse types. This situation is ever more intense for those who live in isolated and Indigenous localities" (p. 130). The progression from grasshopper ladies to productive students is broken down here into calculable terms and categories. Rurality and Indigeneity become marginalizing categories not by racial typologies of inferiority but by poor academic output.

In addition to assessment, we see the state now solicits help from banks and nongovernmental organizations (NGOs) to oversee quality education. Antiquated teaching practices, according to World Bank assessors, is partly responsible for the problem. Traditional models of teaching need to give way to "cooperative, student-driven learning by investigation" where the teacher is not a "custodial controller" but instead a "critical thinking" and "time on-task" facilitator (Giugale, 2001, p. 13). Secretary of Education Josefina Vásquez Mota took up this challenge by gazing outside the fields conventionally associated with education. In the *Education Sector Program* (Secretaría de Educación Pública, 2007a) she suggested, at the beginning of the Calderón Presidency, "we shall incorporate civil society originations, professional training institutes, the private sector and the mass media into the task of education. The responsibility toward meeting ... student-based goals and grand objectives of national education is a collective" (p. 7). Education for national unity of the earlier era yields to education for student-based goals. This task is too variegated and onerous for the state alone, so she calls on NGOs, private schools, and profit-driven enterprises and venture philanthropic organizations like Fundación Alfredo Harp Helú (FAHH) and Mexicanos Primero.[34]

The *Education Sector Program* depends on the work of teachers, but places their work in instrumental rather than social terms. Using efficiency- and autonomy-focused verbs, the *Program* proposed ways to resolve educational rezago by shedding light on anti-rezago pedagogies. Focused on teaching, six objectives for education aim to "elevate" quality for achievement to contribute to national development; "expand" opportunities to reduce inequality; "stimulate" development and technology use; "offer" whole and values-based education; "offer" services to foment a sense of social responsibility for productivity; and "foment" school leadership (*gestión escolar*) for participation, decision making, and accountability (p. 14). Objective two becomes salient in that the *Program* suggests that Oaxaca is among the states with the most rezago in Mexico, so raising school participation becomes a goal for 2012 (p. 17). Objective three mentions the quantity of teachers receiving technological training (p. 19). Objective six lists among its indicators the percentage of federal school directors contracted by civil service exam (p. 22). In all, the secretary of education, through this sector plan, charts out pedagogy as an instrument and calls upon business and the development sector to lend a hand to save Mexico from backwardness.

Additionally, the neoliberal-era reforms beckon teacher-facilitators to implement their voluntary social welfare programs to keep families and children healthy for educational achievement. Oportunidades,[35] Mexico's "flagship welfare program" (Fox, 2007, p. 19), promotes public health, education, and nutrition. A brochure instructs teachers and school directors how to help students enroll in this "human development" program "to support families that live in dietary poverty [in order to] expand their alternatives to reach a better level of wellbeing…" (Gobierno Federal-SEDESOL, n.d., p. 1). Offering scholarships for families who submit successful applications, Oportunidades calls on teachers to shoulder the burden of paperwork, mandating that

> you as a teacher or director represent a large support system for families receiving program benefits in three fundamental aspects: [1] Certifying the enrollment of the children and correctly registering the statistics of each student … [2] Promoting student regular attendance in classes and improvement in their learning. [3] Registering the number of unjustified absences…. (p. 8)

In the above examples, the keen, efficient, and caring intervention of teachers into the lives of rural children and their families becomes vibrant in the shift from constant support to application-based support.

In addition to enrollee and teacher participation in Oportunidades, the Promajoven social welfare program incents school attendance for pregnant and sexually active female students to thwart transgenerational poverty via pedagogical assignation on sex and sexuality (Secretaría de Educación Pública, 2007b, p. 5). Promajoven takes school attendance as a human and constitutional right in that student pregnancy leads to discrimination by directors, teachers, and peers. I found the Promajoven teacher manual at one of the vinyl-tarped pavilions at the Oaxaca City education conference, seen in the initial pages of Chapter One. The manual detailed how teachers can help at-risk young women stay in school: "[i]t is necessary to recall that at school the teachers are the ones responsible for informing [students] on prevention[,] so that sexual practices in the early ages … if unavoidable, can be done responsibly" (p. 8). In addition, to achieve sexual abstinence and boost responsibility among students, teachers should liaise with families and the community on the topic of sexuality. "It is also the responsibility of the teacher to integrate with the community … relate with different members of the family and create communicative bridges that allow fathers and mothers to become sensitive to the different problems in which their children live" (p. 8). Discussing student sexual activity with parents and community members becomes pedagogical, according to the requirements of Promajoven; teen pregnancy and sexuality do not exclusively remain in the domain of the family or individual but rather become re-moralized into a learner's rights to quality schooling. The advocates for the potentially promiscuous youth and probable dropouts need to revere the self-actualizing potential of their charges by discussing responsibility and restraint.[36] Teachers need to guide their students toward a productive path, to step forward and ensure that students retain their rights to quality education and Mexico can optimize the potential of the grasshopper-lady rural citizen-subject.

Re-politicization

This chapter started with a series of political comments on what constitutes proper material for teaching and learning. These telenovela commentaries suggest politics and education are inseparable. The historical examples we have seen display that the state's relationship with rural, Indigenous, and lower-socioeconomic-status Mexicans has involved social dynamics of power. The reader might then appreciate education and politics as conjoined and view the Oaxacan teachers' attempt to re-politicize education as tautological. As my objective here is to show political struggles over quality education becoming frictions which flow differently across participants, my role is less to evaluate the (in)necessity of teacher claims and actions than to trace out how engaged universals like quality, patrimony, and governability flow. The dissidents in the teachers in the CNTE, including the Sección 22 in Oaxaca, call for quality education set along Marxian parameters.

Delving into politics for Oaxacan social movements and critical pedagogies calls for a bit of history. After the socialist education turn in the mid-1930s (Raby, 1974), by the late 1950s, radical elements of 1910 Mexican Revolution had become mainstream. Accordingly, the SNTE kept a "revolutionary" status quo while dissident teachers in 1958 rallied unsuccessfully to democratize their union (Loyo Brambila, 1979). A year later, the railroad workers' strike catalyzed Mexican social movements, drawing support from artists like David Siqueiros

(Dalton, 2007, p. 63). By the 1970s, the post-1968 Tlatelolco massacre social movements blossoming around Mexico would touch anti-oppression movements in Oaxaca (Campbell, 1989), with the teachers in Oaxaca and Chiapas organizing in 1979 to promote a livable wage and a democratic union (Yescas Martínez & Zafra, 1985). At the same time, a call for Indigenous-based liberation theologies based on an action-based reading of the Christian Bible would reach Oaxaca after a conference of bishops in Medellín, Colombia in 1968 (Norget, 2007). Liberation theology combined with social theories of education would inspire Paulo Freire, a major figure for dissident teachers, to theorize and exercise critical pedagogy. The liberation promised by Freire and Peter McLaren in his *La vida en las escuelas* (2005), mentioned in Chapter One, would drive teachers in the Sección 22 to publish alternative education training manuals for teachers to learn how to oppose the Mexican state's textbooks, timetables, and standardized testing (CEDES 22, 2009, p. 17). According to these guidebooks, "the neoliberal-impresario regime obliges us to rethink the public nature of the school, as conceived by Paulo Freire" (p. 4). Their in-service alternative education seminars attempt to put politics back into public schooling.

This re-politicization of education over the last decades has materialized in both grassroots and institutional spaces. On the grassroots side, Hernández (2009) reported how fourth-, fifth-, and sixth-grade teachers in the Mixe region had organized to analyze the content in the controversial Mexican history textbook (p. 334). In 2010, I would sit with a group of normal school students who, to counter the lack of cultural relevance of the 2009 edition of a sixth-grade textbook, introduced games already in practice and everyday tangible items into their teaching. These preservice candidates would respond to the textbooks via publishing an informal *gaceta* to validate and share the philosophy and outcomes of their work. At the same time, coordinated alternative education approaches have appeared, which may have started informally but now set the norms for what kind of critical pedagogy schoolchildren and their families deserve. In May 1991, the CNTE held a national conference on alternative education in which one mesa would suggest that "alternative" projects should "turn into a great National Pedagogical Movement[,] construct itself via a critical and democratic discussion … [and] maintain a critical and independent attitude toward the State educational proposal" (Hernández, 2009, p. 325). Seven years later, the pedagogical office of the Oaxacan dissident teachers, CEDES 22, published proceedings of the 1998 "Sixth Democratic Pre-conference," where one work table called for a "pedagogical movement" to help teachers exasperated with "sterile and indifferent" teaching and to recapture "human sensitivity" and "love toward our work" (pp. 329–330).

Two streams for a politicized pedagogy materialize, the development of independent teacher materials to counter the official textbooks and the organization of pedagogical conferences to plan radical teaching frameworks.

As discussed in Chapter One, *alternative* teaching tends toward a centralized and orthodox view of critical pedagogy. The mathematics teacher educator who mentored the students mentioned above came to tears when she related to me how the innovations she and her students developed met with scorn from CEDES 22 who called her strategies too connected with state-centered education. Being a radical teacher apparently depended on an outright embrace of the *official* alternative education and a total rejection of the state. When I asked teachers how they understood what alternative education would look like in the classroom, they called it "*puro planteamiento* (a mere proposal)" rather than a workable teaching model. An internal evaluation in 1990s found that dissident Oaxacan teachers responded ambivalently to implementing alternative education, while Sección 22 officials understood politics as coming through the trade union organizing rather than in the classroom (Hernández, 2009). These officials coordinated the annual Taller Estatal de Educación Alternativa (TEEA) trainings where teachers study the TEEA handbook, rich with political cartoons, informative tables, theoretical readings, and perspective on educational reform. The 2009–2010 handbook (CEDES 22, 2009) caricatures teacher education as a factory system, drawing individuals of different shapes and sizes on to a conveyor belt, plucking them up like slaughterhouse carnage, and injecting their heads with a liquid solution. Out of a side called "waste," diverse body types flush out of the factory through a culvert, and out of a conveyor belt called "uniformity" come a line of standardized body images, wearing the same glasses as the factory engineer on the top floor. Entitled "teacher training studies" and "the school machine" the visual bears an epigraph: "They plucked our fruits, busted our limbs, burned our trunks. ... But they cannot dry our roots" (p. 9).[37] Though humor and hyperbole permeate the visuals—flowers surrounding the factory, engineers sporting bushy mustaches, and the teacher candidates wiggling their rear ends when hooked and hung like meat—the school machine cartoon reveals a tragic, one-way process. The pedagogical challenge across this mechanized system seems to offer little recourse for actors save obstruction or revolt.

The same handbook provides the practitioner attending the TEEA workshop detail on how the struggle is grounded in social reality rather than abstract theory. "No educational proposal will be reached without putting it in practice. It is useless to establish principles of intervention from philosophical, juridical, psychological and sociocultural positing, if, in the end, it does not clearly address the human being" (p. 38). The human being is the locus of the teachers' "pedagogy of resistance" which is

> directed toward finding new ways of emancipatory human relations… to liberate ourselves from [official] conceptions and practices on testing and evaluation, which are assumed to be irreplaceable, truthful and effective.… Pedagogy focused on liberation and emancipation shall demystify oppressive education, making it possible for the agents involved to reorient their practices and be capable of creating the best life and development conditions for all. (p. 38)

While the conference proceedings cited earlier tend toward abstract views of alternative education, the TEEA booklet focuses on concrete educational praxis. Emancipation is an attitude toward people and deeds; alternative education thrives when lived, breathed, and related to others. The dissident teachers view the standardized system of the SEP as bereft of sympathy toward the participants in schools, and as such, emancipation touches on practices of government stretching out a vital and embodied alternative helping hand. Both the school factory cartoon and the block quote on pedagogies render pedagogical the practices of politically active and engaged teachers.

Quality Rendered Pedagogical

Just as the parents were able to use democracy as a friction in the conference, as discussed in the last chapter, on their way to talk back to the teachers' illegally charging fees, quality is a universal movement wielded in precise local contexts. Elite leaders can debate and gain media attention when they shrug their shoulders at Mexico's chief educator making fatuous comments on education, as quality education streams in the common currency of ideas, relating particularly to the vulnerability and promise of childhood. Quality plays out by grappling over what constitutes proper content and delivery of education. Through these competing discursive processes, quality is rendered into pedagogical parameters that teachers, administrators, and activists of different perspectives can address and add to.

Concentrated into thinkable and actionable terms, rival versions of quality become pedagogical. I appropriate the term rendering *pedagogical* from Tania Li's (2007) rendering *technical* (p. 7), which draws from Rose's (1999) work on practices of government. An ethnographer who focuses on NGOs in rural Indonesia, Li has examined how certain experts embody expertise while development beneficiaries embody deficiency. In her research, Li finds improvements take off when experts turn a problem like quality into improvable parameters, where experts articulate and approach the improvement scheme through non-ideological words and strategies. That is, rendering technical will start by addressing a crisis with consideration and expedience rather than by mission-driven principles or abstract observations on what a failure to improve might look like. Once a practitioner puts a socioeconomic problem into implementable steps, rendering technical involves the creation and dissemination of the key characteristics of the individuals endowed with technical expertise and that of the nonexpert individuals deserving a resolution.

In the case of quality education, read how the debaters spoke from executive seats in a research university, a teacher's union, and an NGO, and then appreciate how *La Jornada* carried the telenovelas debate for the public. This delivery confers technical credibility to quality experts, while parents, pupils, and classroom teachers remain on the other side, that of the telenovela watching beneficiaries. However, given SEP chief Vásquez Mota ascribing terms like *deliver, expand*, and *foment* to the labor of teachers, the Mexican state envisions the rural teachers on the giving end of quality education, too. Finally, rendering technical for Li depends on the experts calculating and representing the range of the problem at hand. We see this above with the construction of rezago, the embodiment of the grasshopper lady, and the flourishing of INEE standardized assessments. Li's observations on how rendering technical works, much like rendering pedagogical, emphasizes how problem-solving of this nature is expertly justified by social commitment, not politics. As Li points out, this impetus to improve the lives of the needy is not necessarily sinister, naïve, or cynical, but it works as a practice of power, even if unintentionally so.

Nevertheless, our quality education story here extends a step further. Systems of experts working with those in need have rendered quality pedagogical, sometimes as a strategy to make education more empowering. What is distinct about rendering it pedagogical in this chapter, and indeed the discursive groundings of the entire friction of quality education, is how teachers instill an acute left-wing will to empower. The CNTE caucus of the trade union, and particularly Oaxaca's Sección 22, struggles to keep teaching and learning radical and detached from state textbooks, assessments, and curricular maps. The CNTE response to Secretary Lujambio's telenovelas comment drew this out, calling the SEP boss's words capitalist subterfuge. The CEDES 22 in-service teacher training TEEA handbooks, as well as the comments and written proceedings from the alternative education conferences, inculcate unionized teachers to reject private and religious schooling and to refute the contemporary free-market-based public-school textbooks, standardized tests, and teacher training courses.

Notes

1. Former secretary of education Josefina Vásquez Mota eventually became the PAN candidate for the 2012 presidential elections, a disputed contest won by the former Governor of Mexico State, Enrique Peña Nieto of the ruling PRI.

2. This functionalist version of citizenship resonates with Banks (1990) and Gay (1997) calling for greater democratic and critical multicultural social participation. Such nation-state-centered citizenship, which accounts for majority of citizenship research (Sassen, 2002, p. 4), differs from *presence* (p. 22) and *postliberal* (Hernández Díaz, 2010) framings for participation among citizen-subjects.

3. No ally of bureaucrats like Lujambio, the CNTE dissident caucus organized in 1979–1980 to promote livable wages and to change the entrenched antidemocratic and official incorporation of the SNTE. For Oaxaca's leadership in the movement, consult Yescas Martínez and Zafra (1985).

4. The mega TV networks in Mexico limit the exposure of independent news but fail to monopolize the news. Vibrant alternatives to official media appear in street art (Nevaer & Sendyk, 2009), political cartoons (Schmidt, 1996), occupied radio stations (Stephen, 2007a), and word-of-mouth (Martínez Vásquez, 2009, pp. 344–345); overall, grassroots modes of communication helped stimulate autonomy and self-determination (Zires, 2009, p. 195).

5. Public debates on social welfare, such as this one on telenovelas, are often encouraged. See UNICEF-Mexico document (Mereles Gras, 2013), whose stated purpose is to serve as "an effective tool to measure the disparities that exist between carrying out the rights of childhood (*derechos de la infancia*) and to be a strategy to place this topic in the realm of public debate …" in "priority states" like Oaxaca (p. 4).

6. Many have explained how curriculum and instruction regimes commodify teaching and learning (Apple, 2004; Ball, 2003; Smyth, 1998). The topographies of the market and the social world that teachers and students operate in are not new to our understanding, for Marx, describing the working day in *Capital Volume One*, shows how capitalism is social and not just material (Harvey, 2010, pp. 135–162). Contemporary analyses take efficiency mechanisms as lived and embodied (Ong, 2006; Taylor, 2006) rather than deterministic. Indeed, deeming education as wholly dominated by economistic policies becomes difficult when political economists themselves take social class as a process rather than fixed and categorical (Resnik & Wolff, 1987) and theorize nonmarket relationships, like gift giving and theft, as economic (Gibson-Graham, 1996, 2006). So, as teaching and learning have become framed in economic terms, fluid social relationships of the political economy of teaching and learning seem more apt than assuming the business-sector techniques that hold teachers and students *accountable* for high-quality education delineate the parameters of how teachers and students can engage critically.

7. See Ellsworth (1992) and Lather (1998) for feminist poststructuralist and Comber (2001) and Luke (2000) for critical literacy interpretations on what counts as a politically engaged pedagogy.

8. For genealogy, see Dean (2010), Foucault (1980a), and Rose (1999) and see Hunter (1994) for an example of genealogy in education.

9. Like much of Hispanophone Latin America, Mexico's early nineteenth-century independence from Spain drew from the Enlightenment, a period when the concepts of individuality and reason countered the imperialist views of people as royal subjects and when logic began to supplant faith and superstition. The modern, liberal turn depended on an expansion of public education, a project that took more than a century to implement across Mexico.

10. Independence and mid-nineteenth-century liberal reforms brought new views on race and citizenship in Mexico. The history of African descendants in the Americas relates to the violent expansion of Christianity into Muslim territories in Spain and North Africa (Wade, 1997); however, the discursive construction of being "Indian" touched on vague religious and civil categories. Colonial authorities saw the Pueblos Originarios as both savage and innocent (p. 26). When the Independence from Spain began to move (1810–1821), the ideals of the Enlightenment guided a polity based on universal citizenship (p. 31; see also Knight, 1990, pp. 72–73).

11. Chassen de López (2004, p. 79) explains late nineteenth- to early twentieth-century social Darwinism in Oaxaca.

12. Pastoral care, like a shepherd leading a flock or a priest helping a sinner in the confessional, may appear a neutral effort to help others in need. Pastoral care for teachers and students cannot work without systems that index skills and knowledge as germane to the pastor and counterposing attributes of need proper to the flock. In my work in teacher education, I have found myself adding value to a system designed to shape how teachers think, act, stand, sit, and dress so that they can begin their careers as credible pastoral caregivers. As such, pastoral care, wielded to turn individuals into teachers, operates in the realm of the political. See Li (2007) for a corresponding description of aid workers in Indonesia conducted as *trustees*.

13. As touched on in Chapter One, shaping Indigeneity, as a practice of government, has a long history in Mexico. One of the ways such racialization is conducted is Indigeneity as a problem solved by modernity. In 1916, anthropologist Manuel Gamio (1960) integrated Indigeneity into the central narrative of the nation, constituted a problem that the expansion of rural education could fix.

14. Teachers factored into the Mexican Revolution by helping author the documents like the Plan de Ayala, serving as agitators, and, in the case of Oaxaca-born Flores Magón brothers, influencing the trajectory of Revolutionary politics (Cockcroft, 1967).

15. *Indio* for a person from a Pueblo Originario carries a negative connotation, especially when used by people outside the Pueblos Originarios. In social media, a racial epithet, "Indios of the CNTE" trivializes and compares Mexican teacher activism to

the mechanisms of power (Aristegui Noticias, 2017). Elsewhere in the Americas, the term has signified subjugation, visible in the 1952 National Revolutionary Movement reforms in Bolivia supplanting the term *indio* with *campesino* to mark incorporation in the larger society (Gustafson, 2009, p. 51).

16. Marentes (2000) analyzes how Vasconcelos' pan-Latin Americanist, Catholic, and Spain-oriented philosophy differed from the secular and Indigenismo-based views common in the post-Revolutionary period.

17. Garduño (1999) publishes a vivid array of images of the publicly funded art at the time of the expansion of public education. See also Museo Casa Estudio Diego Rivera y Frida Kahlo (1999) and López (2001).

18. A poet and member of the Mixtec Language Academy, an organization concerned with revitalizing culture and language in Oaxaca, discredited the Guelaguetza Festival as "*puro folklorismo* (pure tokenization of Oaxacan culture)." This suggests that the dance numbers and pageantry are invented and designed to entertain tourists. At the same time, protecting the integrity of the Guelaguetza as we see in Chapter Six should not be confused with a quest for dance authenticity, for the teachers know that the numbers have been invented and are divorced from specific village procession and fiesta practices. Still, dance has a powerful function in Oaxaca and beyond. Folkloric *baile* (lower-brow participative dance) or *danza* (choreographed pieces), which have come to their modern iteration through assimilationist policies of the 1930s (Hutchinson, 2009) across Mexico and in Mexican diasporic communities in the United States, have become re-appropriated. See Rodríguez (2009) for the interpretation of (in)authentic folkloric dance among Chicanos in the United States and Goertzen (2009) for the sociopolitical and gastronomic processes of Oaxacans occupying and sharing the free seats at the Guelaguetza performances.

19. Indigenismo drew from nineteenth-century social Darwinist discourses and Mexican policies on whitening the population (Knight, 1990, p. 79) and a Revolution period strategy to disempower regional non-Indigenous elites (p. 83).

20. García Canclini (2001) muses that Western versions of modernity are ill-suited to Latin America, where modernity has come unevenly and incompletely, a "modernism without modernization" (p. 41).

21. Indigenismo hinges on nostalgia, valorizing Indigenous traits as set in the glorious past rather than an active present for Mexico and Mexicans (Bonfil Batalla, 1996).

22. The free textbooks, prior to the 2009 editions, have also generated controversy. The 1992 versions retouched the image of historical figures, sparking an intense debate (Gilbert, 1997).

23. In Mexico during the run-up to the 1994 signing of NAFTA, a saying in Guadalajara was that there were three kinds of literacies du jour: Spanish, English, and computational. The individual needed to do their best help Mexico be on par with trade partners, Canada and the United States.

24. See Brenner and Theodore (2002) for how neoliberalism is more than a simple dismantling of the welfare state, for neoliberalization operates through creative processes, too. After 1968, the Mexican state relaxes the controls on organizations like the SNTE but then begins the process of decentralizing some of its core functions like education (Martínez Vásquez, 2004). Following Ong (2006), I use the term neoliberalism to refer to state, NGO, and for-profit agencies helping shape the lived lives of people. Those who once enjoyed equal rights under the law today are "not a citizen with claims on the state but a self-enterprising citizen-subject" (p. 14). Forces of neoliberalization are forces that conduct "self-propulsive individuals" (p. 16).

25. See Velez Bustillo (2001, p. 545) for World Bank reporting and comparing the standardized test results for rural and Indigenous schools versus the rest of Mexico.

26. As rural development projects for empowerment depend on local participation, it is important to emphasize that development, as a practice of government, is negotiated as much through the social world as the numeric and economic one (see Popkewitz, 2009, p. 229).

27. Work on *insurgent* (Atehortúa & Lalander, 2015; Gustafson 2009; Holston, 2009), *lived* (Rubin, Smilde & Junge, 2014), and *new* (Dagnino, 2007) citizenship expands the notions of citizenship as an individual's relationship with the nation-state across Latin America. President Fox here presents Indigeneity as a form of politics with all the rights and responsibilities of citizenship, a "permitted" (Hale, 2004), official form of being indigenous more than an autonomous or insurgent one. Cruikshank (1999) has explained how, through discursive impulses like the Fox comment practices, citizenship can guide individuals toward official rather than democratic ways of participating.

28. Identity formation and political process are now endorsed by the President. The year 2003 saw the passage of the General Law of the Rights of Indigenous Pueblos which was designed as an "instrument that helps to recognize and promote the use and respect of Indigenous languages in public and private domains" around Mexico (INALI, 2008, p. 5). One governmental response to this law was to create a linguistic catalog to help their planning and revitalization and "initiate the process of normalization" (p. 7), suggesting that speaking an Indigenous language is not about personal choice but of national heritage. A map of linguistic families in the guidebook shows intense coloration in the southeast, Oaxaca's region (p. 9). Finally, a fuller scope of the problem of Oaxacan languages at risk materializes with the posted 86 language groups and 364 variants.

29. An in-vogue neologism of quality education, *grit*, the inner resolve to overcome obstacles, helps illustrate devolution playing out on schooling. Grit, constructed as the ideal traits of effective teaching (Robertson-Kraft & Duckworth, 2014), accounts for student achievement solely on targeted care and commitment of individual teachers, not on measures that defund or shut down low-income-area schools.

30. Kristin Norget (2006) describes this market area in downtown Oaxaca City where villagers speaking indigenous Oaxacan languages sell *chapulines* (p. 28).

31. One incidence of turning the folk-based into luxury involved a shop in downtown Oaxaca City posting a sign in English: "single village mescal," a play on *single malt* scotch whiskey and *denomination of origin* wine. When I first sipped mescal in the late 1990s, a teacher had brought it from his village in a transparent plastic jug bearing no labels or markings; it was mescal from a village without any *single-village mescal* branding.

32. Neoliberal school reform in Mexico correlates with the ways that economic organizations like the OECD oversee educational achievement (see Hyslop-Margison & Sears, 2006, pp. 12–13). For the Mexico-specific World Bank poverty reduction through education, see Giugale, Lafourcade, and Nguyen (2001). Oaxacan teachers I met have avoided adding to the statistics that show Oaxaca as chronically underdeveloped which oftentimes corresponds to greater efforts from the state, NGOs and economists to change the social relationships of community life and put school-based learning into culturally irrelevant parameters, which, in the case of the grasshopper lady, sustain offensive racial stereotypes.

33. Achievement testing may be gender, color, class, and geography blind, as indicated by INEE (2010). Oaxacan teachers I spoke to have argued the opposite, that no standardized test can be fair given the socioeconomic inequalities and asymmetries of power from region to region and family to family.

34. Human capital development through public education becomes focal points for Mexicanos Primero (n.d.a, b) and FAHH (Holo, 2004).

35. Luccisano (2004) discusses how Oportunidades has attempted to use human capital investment as an entryway into conducting new kinds of "responsible," market-based and governable behaviors for the poor (p. 33). Sección 22 believes that Opportunidades "spoils (*se desvirtúa*)" public funding for education (CEDES 22, 2009, p. 33).

36. After a broad expansion of women in the teaching profession after 1921 (López, 2001, p. 235), the chastity of rural women teachers (*maestras rurales*) would preoccupy federal authorities. There were the "old" municipal teachers now joined by the "new" federal teachers, the latter with political consciousness formed in normal schools (pp. 219–223). Many documents from medical doctor reports to SEP regalements of the period evaluated the appropriateness of pregnant teachers, so that López concludes, the "maestras and their bodies were considered pedagogical and moral instruments" (p. 202).

37. The image furthermore depicts a barbed wire-encircled factory crowned by a SEP command gearbox and the SNTE hauling away buckets of money. The diverse human bodies of teacher candidates in the SEP/SNTE teacher education model move on a conveyor belt of "uniformity" (CEDES 22, 2009, p. 9). The epigraph of the cartoon reads, "They plucked our fruits, busted our limbs, burned our trunks

... But they cannot dry our roots" (p. 9). Finally, there is the "alternative education program" designed by the dissident teachers in CEDES 22 to halt this factory.

References

Albertani, C. (2009). *Espejo de México: (Crónicas de barbarie y resistencia).* San Pedro Cholula, Mexico: Altres Costa-Amic.

Apple, M. (2004). Schooling, markets, and an audit culture. *Educational Policy, 18*(4), 614–621.

Atehortúa, J. V., & Lalander, R. (2015). La ciudadanía insurgente de las mujeres de barrios populares en Venezuela: Reflexiones sobre los consejos comunales y las salas de batalla social. *Espacio Abierto: Cuaderno Venezolano De Sociología, 24*(3), 45–66.

Ball, S. J. (2003). The teacher's soul and the terrors of performativity. *Journal of Education Policy, 18*(1), 215–228.

Banks, J. A. (1990). Citizenship education for a pluralistic democratic society. *Social Studies, 81*(5), 210–214.

Bonfil Batalla, G. (1996). *México profundo: Reclaiming a civilization.* Austin, TX: University of Texas Press.

Brenner, N., & Theodore, N. (2002). Cities and the geographies of "actually existing neoliberalism." *Antipode, 34*(3), 349–379.

Brown, W. (2015). *Undoing the demos: Neoliberalism's stealth revolution.* New York, NY: Zone books.

Campbell, H. (1989). The COCEI: Culture, class, and politicized ethnicity in the Isthmus of Tehuantepec. *Ethnic Studies Report, 7*(2), 36–60.

Caplan, K. D. (2010). *Indigenous citizens: Local liberalism in early national Oaxaca and Yucatán.* Stanford, CA: Stanford University Press.

CEDES 22. (2009). *Taller estatal de educación alternativa: TEEA 2009–2010* (instructional material). Oaxaca, Mexico.

CEDES 22. (2010). *2010 Resolutivos del III congreso estatal de educación alternativa, 20–21 de mayo.* Oaxaca, Mexico: Sección 22, SNTE.

Chassen de López, F. R. (2004). *From liberal to Revolutionary Oaxaca: The view from the South, Mexico, 1867–1911.* University Park, PA: Pennsylvania State University Press.

Chávez Orozco, L. (1937). *Historia patria: Tercer año.* Mexico City: Editorial Patria.

CNTE. (2010, May). *Resolutivos, IV Congreso Nacional de Educación Alternativa, 28–30 de mayo* (Conference Proceedings). Mexico City.

Cockcroft, J. D. (1967). El maestro de primaria en la Revolución Mexicana. *Historia Mexicana, 16*(4), 565–587.

Comber, B. (2001). Classroom explorations in critical literacy. In H. Fehring & P. Green (Eds.), *Critical literacy: A collection of articles from the Australian Literacy Educators' Association* (pp. 90–102). Newark, DE: International Reading Association.

Cruikshank, B. (1999). *The will to empower: Democratic citizens and other subjects.* Ithaca, NY: Cornell University Press.

Dagnino, E. (2007). Dimensions of citizenship in contemporary Brazil. *Fordham Law Review*, *75*(5), 2469–2482.

Dalton, M. (2007). Los organismos civiles en Oaxaca y el movimiento ciudadano: Causas y consecuencias. *Cuadernos del Sur, 12* (24/25), 63–80.

Dean, M. (2010). *Governmentality: Power and rule in modern society*. Los Angeles, CA: SAGE.

Díaz de Cossío, R. (2011, May). La chapulinera. *Nexos, 401*, 41–42.

Ellsworth, E. (1992). Why doesn't this feel empowering? Working through the repressive myths of critical pedagogy. In C. Luke & J. Gore (Eds.), *Feminisms and critical pedagogy* (pp. 90–119). New York, NY: Routledge.

Foucault, M. (1980a). *The history of sexuality*, Vol. I. New York, NY: Vintage.

Foweraker, J. (1993). *Popular mobilization in Mexico: The teachers' movement 1977–87*. New York, NY: Cambridge University Press.

Fox, J. (2007). *Accountability politics: Power and voice in rural Mexico*. New York, NY: Oxford University Press.

Fox Quesada, V. (2001). *Plan nacional de desarrollo 2001–2006*. Gobierno de los Estados Unidos Mexicanos: Presidencia de la República. Retrieved from http://bibliotecadigital.conevyt.org.mx/colecciones/conevyt/plan_desarrollo.pdf

Freire, P. (1994). *Pedagogy of the oppressed* (new revised 20th anniversary edition). New York, NY: Continuum.

Fuentes, B. (Ed.). (1986). *Enrique Corona Morín y la educación rural*. Mexico City: SEP/Ediciones el Caballito.

Gamio, M. (1960). *Forjando patria*. Mexico City: Editorial Porrúa.

García Canclini, N. (2001). *Hybrid cultures: Strategies for entering and leaving modernity* (fourth printing). Minneapolis, MN: University of Minnesota Press.

Garduño, B. (1999). *Misiones culturales: Los años utópicos 1920–1938*. Mexico City: Consejo Nacional para la Cultura y las Artes.

Gay, G. (1997). The relationship between multicultural and democratic education. *Social Studies*, *88*(1), 5–11.

Gibson-Graham, J. K. (1996). *The end of capitalism (as we knew it): A feminist critique of political economy*. Oxford: Blackwell Publishers.

Gibson-Graham, J. K. (2006). *A postcapitalist politics*. Minneapolis, MN: University of Minnesota Press.

Gilbert, D. (1997). Rewriting history: Salinas, Zedillo and the 1992 textbook controversy. *Mexican Studies/Estudios Mexicanos, 13*(2), 271–297.

Giroux, H. A. (1988). *Teachers as intellectuals: Toward a critical pedagogy of learning*. Granby, MA: Bergin & Garvey.

Giugale, M. (2001). Synthesis. In M. Giugale, O. Lafourcade, & V. H. Nguyen (Eds.), *Mexico, a comprehensive development agenda for the new era* (pp. 1–47). Washington, DC: The World Bank.

Giugale, M., Lafourcade, O., & Nguyen, V. H. (Eds.). (2001). *Mexico, a comprehensive development agenda for the new era*. Washington, DC: The World Bank.

Gobierno Constitucional del Estado Libre y Soberano de Oaxaca. (1904, January 28). *Acuerdo*. State of Oaxaca Archive, Oaxaca, Mexico.

Gobierno Federal-SEDESOL. (n.d). *Información del programa oportunidades para directores y docentes de educación básica ciclo escolar 2010–2011.*

Goertzen, C. (2009). Dance, politics, and cultural tourism in Oaxaca's Guelaguetza. In O. Nájera-Ramírez., N. E. Cantú, & B. M. Romero (Eds.), *Dancing across borders: Danzas y bailes Mexicanos* (pp. 293–317). Urbana, IL: University of Illinois Press.

González Apodaca, E. (2008). *Los profesionistas indios en la educación intercultural: Etnicidad, intermediación y escuela en el territorio mixe.* Mexico City: *UAM-I*/Casa Juan Pablos.

Guichard, S. (2005). *The education challenge in Mexico: Delivering good quality education to all. OECD economics department working papers*, no. 447. Paris: OECD Publishing. http://dx.doi.org/10.1787/047122723082

Gustafson, B. (2009). *New languages of the estate: Indigenous resurgence and the politics of knowledge in Bolivia.* Durham, NC: Duke University Press.

Hale, C. R. (2004). Rethinking indigenous politics in the era of the 'indio permitido.' *NACLA Report on the Americas, 38*(2), 16–20.

Hale, C. R. (2005). Neoliberal multiculturalism: The remaking of cultural rights and racial dominance in Central America. *PoLAR: Political and Legal Anthropology Review, 28*(1), 10–28.

Harvey, D. (2010). *A companion to Marx's Capital.* New York, NY: Verso.

Hernández, F. G. (2009). La educación alternativa y el movimiento pedagógico en el discurso de los maestros democráticos de Oaxaca, como contexto de la educación bilingüe e intercultural. In M. J. Bailón Corres (Ed.), *Ensayos sobre historia, política, educación y literatura de Oaxaca* (pp. 288–340). Oaxaca, Mexico: IIHUABJO.

Hernández Díaz, J. (2010). La construcción de ciudadanías postliberales: Los reclamos de autonomía municipal y demandas indígenas en México. *Latin American Research Review, 45*(4), 138–165.

Holo, S. (2004). *Oaxaca at the crossroads: Managing memory, negotiating change.* Washington, DC: Smithsonian Books.

Holston, J. (2009). Insurgent citizenship in an era of global urban peripheries. *City & Society, 21*(2), 245–267.

Hunter, I. (1994). *Rethinking the school: Subjectivity, bureaucracy, criticism.* St. Leonards, NSW: Allen & Unwin.

Hutchinson, S. (2009). The Ballet Folklórico de México and the construction of the Mexican nation through dance. In O. Nájera-Ramírez, N. E. Cantú, & B. M. Romero (Eds.), *Dancing across borders: Danzas y bailes Mexicanos* (pp. 206–225). Urbana, IL: University of Illinois Press.

Hyslop-Margison, E. J., & Sears, A. M. (2006). *Neo-liberalism, globalization and human capital learning: Reclaiming education for democratic citizenship.* Dordrecht: Springer.

INALI. (2008). *Catálogo de las lenguas indígenas nacionales, cuaderno informativo.* Mexico City: Secretaría de Educación Pública.

INEE. (2010). *El derecho a la educación en México: Informe 2009* (report), Mexico City, Mexico.

Knight, A. (1990). Racism, revolution and indigenismo: Mexico, 1910–1940. In R. Graham (Ed.), *The idea of race in Latin America 1870–1940* (pp. 71–113). Austin, TX: The University of Texas Press.

Koopman, C. (2013). *Genealogy as critique: Foucault and the problems of modernity.* Bloomington, IN: Indiana University Press.

Lather, P. (1998). Critical pedagogy and its complicities: A praxis of stuck places. *Educational Theory, 48*(4), 511–519.

Li, T. (2007). *The will to improve: Governmentality, development, and the practice of politics.* Durham: Duke University Press.

López, O. (2001). *Alfabeto y enseñanzas domesticas: El arte de ser maestro rural en el Valle de Mezquital.* Mexico City: CIESAS.

Loyo, B. E. (1985). *La casa del pueblo y el maestro rural mexicano: Antología.* Mexico City: Secretaría de Educación Pública, Subsecretaría de Cultura, Dirección General de Publicaciones.

Loyo Brambila, A. (1979). *El movimiento magisterial de 1958 en México.* Mexico City: Ediciones Era.

Luccisano, L. (2004). Mexico's Progresa Program (1997–2000): An example of neo-liberal poverty alleviation programs concerned with gender, human capital development, responsibility and choice. *Journal of Poverty, 8*(4), 31–57.

Luke, A. (2000). Critical literacy in Australia: A matter of context and standpoint. *Journal of Adolescent & Adult Literacy, 43*, 448–461.

Maldonado, B. (2010). *Comunidad, comunalidad y colonialismo en Oaxaca, México: La nueva educación comunitaria y su contexto* (Doctoral dissertation, Department of Mesoamerican and Andean Cultures, Faculty of Archaeology, Leiden University).

Marentes, L. A. (2000). *Jose Vasconcelos and the writing of the Mexican revolution.* New York, NY: Twane Publishers.

Martínez Vásquez, V. R. (2004). *La educación en Oaxaca.* Oaxaca, Mexico: IISUABJO.

Martínez Vásquez, V. R. (2009). Antinomias y perspectivas del movimiento popular en Oaxaca. In V. R. Martínez Vásquez (Ed.), *La APPO: ¿Rebelión o movimiento social?: Nuevas formas de expresión ante la crisis* (pp. 329–347). Oaxaca, Mexico: IISUABJO.

McGushin, E. F. (2007). *Foucault's Askesis: An introduction to the philosophical life.* Evanston IL: Northwestern University Press.

McLaren, P. (2005). *La vida en las escuelas: una introducción a la pedagogía crítica en los fundamentos de la educación.* Mexico City: Siglo XXI.

Mereles Gras, L. (Ed.). (2013). *Los derechos de la infancia y la adolescencia en Oaxaca.* Mexico City: CIESAS Unidad Pacífico Sur/FLASCO/UNICEF México. Retrieved from http://www.unicef. org/mexico/spanish/SITAN2013_Oaxaca%281%29.pdf

Mexicanos Primero. (n.d.a). *¿En qué creemos?* (foundation website). Retrieved from http://www. mexicanosprimero.org/mexicanos-primero/ien-que-creemos.html

Mexicanos Primero. (n.d.b). *Lo que necesitas saber: ¡Conoce si tu derecho a la educación se está cumpliendo!* (foundation website). Retrieved from http://www.mexicanosprimero.org.mx/alum nos/lo-que-necesitas-saber.html

Monarchy of Spain. (1820). *Constitución Política de la Monarquía Española: Promulgada en Cádiz a 19 de marzo de 1812.* Madrid: La Imprenta Nacional de Madrid. Retrieved from http://www. famp.es/famp/intranet/documentos/const_facsimil.pdf

Monsiváis, C. (2010). *Historia mínima: La cultura mexicana en el siglo XX.* Mexico City: El Colegio de México AC.

Museo Casa Estudio Diego Rivera y Frida Kahlo. (1999). *Misiones culturales: Los años utópicos 1920–1938.* Mexico City: Consejo Nacional para la Cultura y las Artes.

Nevaer, L. E. V., & Sendyk, E. (2009). *Protest graffiti–Mexico: Oaxaca*. New York, NY: Mark Batty.

Norget, K. (2006). *Days of death, days of life: Ritual in the popular culture of Oaxaca*. New York, NY: Columbia University Press.

Norget, K. (2007). The drama of death: Popular religion and performing the good death in Oaxaca. In A. Gálvez (Ed.), *Performing religion in the Americas: Media, politics and devotional practices of the twenty-first century* (pp. 66–106). New York, NY: Seagull Books.

Olivares, E., & Morelos, R. (2011, February 19). Exhorta Narro a buscar estrategias más inteligentes contra analfabetismo. *La Jornada*. Retrieved from http://www.jornada.unam.mx/2011/03/19/politica/014n2pol

Ong, A. (2006). *Neoliberalism as exception: Mutations in citizenship and sovereignty*. Durham. NC: Duke University Press.

Popkewitz, T. (2009). Why the desire for university-school collaboration and the promise of pedagogical content knowledge may not matter as much as we think. In M. A. Peters, A. C. Besley, M. Olssen, S. Maurer, & S. Weber (Eds.), *Governmentality studies in education* (pp. 217–234). Rotterdam: Sense Publishers.

Poy, L. (2011, February 19). Exhorta Narro a buscar estrategias más inteligentes contra analfabetismo. *La Jornada*. Retrieved from http://www.jornada.unam.mx/2011/03/19/POLITICA/014N3POL

Raby, D. L. (1974). *Educación y revolución social en México*. Mexico City: Sep-Setentas.

Resnik, S., & Wolff, R. D. (1987). *Knowledge and class: A Marxist critique of political economy*. Chicago, IL: University of Chicago Press.

Robertson-Kraft, C., & Duckworth, A. L. (2014). True grit: Trait-level perseverance and passion for long-term goals predicts effectiveness and retention among novice teachers. *Teachers College Record, 116*(3), 1–27.

Rockwell, E. (1996). Keys to appropriation: Rural schooling in Mexico. In B. Levinson, D. E. Foley & D. C. Holland (Eds.), *Cultural production of the educated person: Critical ethnographies of schooling and local practice* (pp. 301–324). Albany, NY: State University of New York Press.

Rodríguez, R. (2009). Folklórico in the United States: Cultural preservation and disillusion. In O. Nájera-Ramírez, N. E. Cantú, & B. M. Romero (Eds.), *Dancing across borders: Danzas y bailes Mexicanos* (pp. 335–358). Urbana, IL: University of Illinois Press.

Román, J. A. (2011, March 18). Telenovelas, "instrumento importante" para abatir rezago educativo: Lujambio (p. 42). *La Jornada*. Retrieved from http://www.jornada.unam.mx/2011/03/18/sociedad/042n1soc

Rose, N. (1999). *Powers of freedom: Reframing political thought*. New York, NY: Cambridge University Press.

Rubin, J. W., Smilde, D., & Junge, B. (2014). Lived religion and lived citizenship in Latin America's zones of crisis: Introduction. *Latin American Research Review, 49*, 7–26.

Sassen, S. (2002). The repositioning of citizenship: Emergent subjects and spaces for politics. *Berkeley Journal of Sociology, 46*, 4–26.

Schmidt, S. (1996). *Humor en serio: Análisis del chiste político en México*. Mexico City: Aguilar.

Secretaría de Educación Pública. (2007a). *Programa Sectorial de Educación* (user's guide manual). Mexico City: Comisión Nacional de Libros de Texto Gratuitos.

Secretaría de Educación Pública. (2007b). *Estudiar es su derecho* (handbook). Mexico City: Dirección General del Desarrollo Curricular de la Subsecretaría de Educación Básica de la Secretaría de Educación Pública.

Secretaría del Gobierno Constitucional del Estado Libre y Soberano de Oaxaca & Jiménez, M. (1883). *Reglamento para la escuela normal*. Oaxaca State Archive, Oaxaca, Mexico.

Smith, B. (2008, April 1). Inventing tradition at gunpoint: Culture, caciquismo and state formation in the Region Mixe, Oaxaca (1930–1959). *Bulletin of Latin American Research, 27*(2), 215–234.

Smyth, J. (1998). Economic forces affecting supervision. In G. R. Firth, & E. F. Pajak (Eds.), *Handbook of research on school supervision* (pp. 1173–1183). New York, NY: Simon & Shuster Macmillan.

Stephen, L. (2007a). "We are brown, we are short, we are fat...we are the face of Oaxaca": Women leaders in the Oaxaca rebellion. *Socialism & Democracy, 21*(2), 97–112.

Talavera, A. (1973). *Liberalismo y educación*. Mexico City: SEP, Dirección General de Educación Audiovisual y Divulgación.

Taylor, M. (2006). *From Pinochet to the 'third way': Neoliberalism and social transformation in Chile*. Ann Arbor, MI: Pluto Press.

Torres, C. A. (1991). El corporativismo estatal, las políticas educativas y los movimientos estudiantiles y magisteriales en México. *Revista Mexicana de Sociología, 53*(2), 159–183.

Tsing, A. L. (2005). *Friction: An ethnography of global connection*. Princeton, NJ: Princeton University Press.

Vargas, A. (1935). *Guelaguetza: Costumbre racial oaxaqueña*. Oaxaca, Mexico: Imprenta del Gobierno del Estado.

Vasconcelos, J. (2009). *Antología de textos sobre educación*. Mexico City: Editorial Trillas.

Vaughan, M. K. (1990). Women school teachers in the Mexican Revolution: The story of Reyna's braids. *Journal of Women's History, 2*(1), 143–168.

Velez Bustillo, E. (2001). Education sector strategy. In M. Giugale, O. Lafourcade, & V. H. Nguyen (Eds.), *Mexico, a comprehensive development agenda for the new era* (pp. 446–478). Washington, DC: The World Bank.

Wade, P. (1997). *Race and ethnicity in Latin America*. London: Pluto Press.

Yescas Martínez, I., & Zafra, G. (1985). *La insurgencia magisterial en Oaxaca 1980*. Oaxaca, Mexico: IISUABJO.

Zires, M. (2009). Estrategias de comunicación y acción política: Movimiento social de la APPO 2006. In V. R. Martínez Vásquez (Ed.), *La APPO: ¿Rebelión o movimiento social?: Nuevas formas de expresión ante la crisis* (pp. 161–197). Oaxaca, Mexico: IISUABJO.

3

Quality Education through Self-managed Pedagogies

Que nos Den una Educación de Calidad

As the 2006 Movimiento on the streets in Oaxaca City waned by December, teachers resumed classes in their communities across the state. Among others, Marcos had participated in numerous protest encounters that involved open conversations on how to improve Oaxaca. There were dialog *mesas* held around town, such as the Citizens Dialog Initiative for Peace, Democracy and Justice. These were dubbed a "dialog space" (Martínez Vásquez, 2007, p. 133) for deliberations that sought common ground between the state, teachers, and the public in order "to achieve high-quality intercultural education" (p. 134). Marcos participated in the "Toward New Education in Oaxaca" conversations of the citizens' initiative and attended events with activist-performers like Lila Downs and Mujeres sin Miedo (Fearless Women).[1] These social spaces appealed to Marcos as a teacher, and during one of these encounters, he introduced himself to a man who called himself Don Luis Cuentacuentos (Don Luis Raconteur). When Don Luis found out that Marcos taught at a public school, he promised to come to Tecotitlán Elementary and narrate to Marcos's students.

Returning to the village school in December, Marcos and his Tecotitlán collaborators found it difficult to resume their classroom duties, for when they tried to enter the school grounds, they found the metal grating of the front door locked. The parents' committee and individual mothers and fathers had installed the lock, wanting the teachers to be replaced with others who would not abandon classes for protest activities. To break the impasse, one mother eventually said, "Let them pass, and let's hear what they have to say." With this, Marcos and his colleagues explained how the Movimiento waged in Oaxaca City also stood to promote better educational conditions in Tecotitlán. Now, to honor their community commitment, they would focus on the school-based part of their teaching. "Okay" responded the parents, still angry; "but for you to return, you must give our children *quality* education." Quality education, as we have seen in Chapter Two, is a discursively construed term most commonly wielded by neoliberal attempts to promote education for labor force development and by radical pedagogues intent on alternative education. In this instance, the parents showed they wanted instruction for their children as a daily commitment offered from teacher to student in an open and running school. In response to this, by operating under the "quality education" rubric, the Tecotitlán faculty came back to school in a way that was reasonable to parents and state officials alike. Promising quality education, the teachers convinced the parents to remove the chain. From the dialogs during the street protests to the agreement with village parents, the teachers operated through the movement of quality. This is where I caught up with Marcos and his colleagues, and how we came to a village school's effort to forment quality education.

Back in their post-Movimiento routine, Marcos and others in Tecotitlán debated how to implement the quality education the parents demanded. Marcos responded to this challenge in three ways. First, he undertook a research project on how people gather and organize in the village during the harvest, on feast days, and in quotidian family life that revealed the importance of classroom conversations where parents and students actively participate in every part of their learning. Second, he reread articles from a recent training seminar, pausing at Henry Giroux's (1988) call for making "the political more pedagogical and the pedagogical more political." Third, Marcos's version of politicizing his pedagogy related to the politics of the streets of Oaxaca during the most violent part of the Movement, when he attended the dialogs and performances. Specifically, he contacted Don Luis Cuentacuentos, and began inviting storytellers to school as part of a reading project he would initiate with his colleagues. When I asked him how he would describe this new pedagogy, he called it a *pedagogía autogestiva*, a self-managed and grassroots-funded approach to teaching and learning in and out of school, which resonates with the counter-pedagogies throughout this book.

This third chapter focuses on the autonomous pedagogies of quality, the ways teaching and learning flourished between the fissures of the state and the Sección 22 teachers' union apparatuses. Marcos and his coworkers taught this way to make their school an appealing social space for students and parents. Quality education ventured beyond supplanting teacher-centered school relations to include unlocking doors and encouraging students to paint the walls and ignore the bells of a preset class schedule.

Open Doors

After the upheavals of 2006, Tecotitlán Elementary teachers stopped locking the doors. I noticed this in my 2011 field visit when I shadowed Marcos for six weeks. One afternoon, before leaving for his home in Oaxaca City, Marcos, the assistant director of the school, stopped by the school library.[2] It is common to see him multitasking like this. Even when busy, he greets everyone from mule drivers passing with their alfalfa cargo to former students stopping by to say hi. He appears to take care in greeting parents and children, and as a result, people run to him to relate ordinary business like the results of a ball game. Seven or eight years before, a more formal division existed in Tecotitlán between teachers, students, and parents. Two parents I interviewed mentioned how the teachers since 2006 have become more present in the broader school community, while teachers reported a corresponding parental engagement. The school zone supervisor concurred with the spike in parental engagement, saying that she intervened in one school in the zone where parents demanded one teacher's removal, a parental move unheard of prior to 2006. The boost in school social commitment, even as it came to them through the locked school gate, has offered Tecotitlán pedagogues the platform to alter the school culture in favor of open doors whereby one of the open doors became the school library.

A decade prior, twelve class groups filled the twelve classrooms. In 2011, there were seven.[3] In the five vacated rooms, different projects have flourished. One classroom has become a library with newly acquired books and operated by a self-management checkout system; another two rooms are now repurposed as the *Enciclomedia*[4] computer-based research tool and the media room, respectively. Fewer groups mean fewer students in the three ball courts, the interior courtyard esplanade, and other corners on campus, including a mature ficus tree around which students often play. The parents, teachers, and administration worked with the students to cultivate a socially spaced, rather than an administratively ordered, school. The teachers worked particularly to ensure that student spaces expanded across the site. I observed this in Marcos's practice, when one day he and I went to lock up the library, hours after school had ended. When Marcos saw a student sitting inside, he stepped out to the hallway without urging the student to finish their business so we could lock up and go home. Outside the library waiting for the student to finish, Marcos and I stood facing a garden area between the library and the sixth-grade classroom block of buildings.

Marcos showed calm; he and I exchanged a glance when we saw a group of students playing in a ficus tree, which had knotted, sturdy limbs clawing to the left and right of a stump that must have been at one point trimmed. The level area above the stump and outward reaching branches had become a place students sat and socialized. Marcos had mentioned this tree earlier in the week when we traveled to Oaxaca City to meet with a venture philanthropy foundation that funded projects to foment reading for pleasure. At the city meeting, Marcos had mentioned the ficus tree as a site of unsupervised literacy practices among the students, and he intended to construct a tree house there to draw more students to read in an even more securely established student space, beyond the shadow of the teachers, parents, and administrators. With the aim of expanding storytelling and reading among his students, Marcos, three colleagues, and I sat under a Oaxaca City café parasol with the NGO program coordinator and had a soft drink (Sadlier & Morales Sánchez, 2012). The teachers had initially come to express thanks for a funded trip they had recently made to Monte Albán, the principal archeological site in the Central Valleys of Oaxaca.[5] "A tree house?" the NGO coordinator asked with surprise, "[w]hat if the kids fall" (p. 202). Marcos looked at me and then at the students playing in the area of the planned student shelter, and asked me if I thought those students sitting on the tree before us were in danger of falling and getting hurt. When the boy inside had walked out with his book, Marcos turned the metal key in the aluminum door handle to lock it shut, and we headed back to our homes in Oaxaca City.

During the drive home, Marcos and I discussed literacy practices that related to learner autonomy. For him, "unlocked doors" served as an ethos of openness and a practice of physical accessibility of official spaces of schooling. For too long, the students and their families had felt unwelcome on campus, while the doors to rooms where teachers and administrators held authority remained off-limits to student social life. An example of this ethos and practice of openness occurred when

> [O]ne day during recess, a sixth grader looking for a basketball scurried into the teachers' room [and] she found herself interrupting the teaching staff eating. She entered saying

'*con permiso, buen provecho*.' Con permiso, a respectful phrase said when crossing the personal space of another, neither asks for permission nor issues an apology. 'Buen provecho' as a courtesy phrase says 'I'm glad you've got a meal; it hope it agrees with you.' These phrases indicate the student knew she interrupted adults rather than peers, but she proceeded to enter the room until she found the ball. The teachers took no offense to this, responding politely: '*gracias, pásale*.' The student-teacher interaction does not suggest a student insurrection over teachers, for normative patterns of power remain. But the student enjoyed full access to the room, got the ball, and went about her tasks. So she was still at school, but the school had open doors for her. (p. 202)

The teachers often discussed tactics to manage school through more flexible[6] and activity-encouraging practices like unlocking doors, and as we get to below, painting the walls and scheduling classes at times outside regular hours.

Murals

The spatial rearrangement of the school also involved the informative and graphically symbolic act of painting the walls. In addition to the street art of protests, murals visually knit together different social circumstances, feelings, histories, and images; they form a social semiotics of Mexican public space. Many governmental buildings across the country display post-Revolutionary murals, didactic and socially realist representations of Mexican history, with heroes and villains in rural hinterlands and urban labor movements engaged in the sequential toil of producing modern Mexico. The muralists, who often painted themselves into their work, lived fabled lives themselves. For example, Diego Rivera, who reportedly defended his murals from censorship by pistol, socialized with Leon Trotsky and shared a life with Frida Kahlo. The muralists left behind wall art, which holds a special place in Mexico's public imaginary, a nostalgic residue, according to Octavio Paz, Mexico's noted postmodernist poet and cultural critic (Monsiváis, 2010, p. 102). Many schools contracted with one of the famous muralists to install wall art.[7] Just the same, murals can be unofficial. In Oaxaca during the 2006 protests, street artists engaged in the visual practice of *getting up* (De La Rosa & Schadl, 2014), painting and stenciling images in visible and well-trafficked areas (p. 7). Getting up is pedagogical, as one artist-activist related that their motivation was in "denouncing, though graphic art, what was happening in the city" and "translating a creative and comprehensible language into actions for a society living in conflict" (p. 7). Visual translation of issues through wall art, furthermore, depended on the historical significance of the *zócalo*. De La Rosa and Schadl believe that creating "images on the walls of a UNESCO World

Heritage site like Oaxaca's historic center" is "the epitome" of getting up (p. 10). The power of the street art gained the notice of the authorities to such a degree that when the federal police evicted protesters from the zócalo, they whitewashed the walls to remove all sign of the stencils, posters, *consigna* graffiti, and stickers (Lache Bolaños, 2009, p. 208). The teacher's choice to let students make murals follows a long tradition of scripted and graphic public communication on issues and feelings.

Murals on the streets met with murals created in schools. During my fieldwork, most of the walls in Tecotitlán Elementary featured student-painted murals. One of these covers a partition beside Marcos's classroom, which once bore the flaked image of soccer players with the heads of locally harvested produce painted as characters representing Marcos's book club drawings. The book club mural, dirty with spider webs and dusty cracks, seemed neglected. David, one of the young teachers, decided to clean the surface for his students to make a mural. Across the open-air esplanade on the school campus, three students in David's class began sketching on the wall, below two lingering posters on the anatomy of the nervous system. If not for the desks pulled from the classroom, the students might have been engaged in recess fun rather than a teacher-planned activity. Sometime later, David stood on one of the chairs sketching an image. Eventually, color would cover every corner of the white surface, the green frieze, and the cement posts that framed it (Sadlier & Morales Sánchez, 2012).

> For some students, this mural told of prior experiences, while for others it stood as an activity to do just for fun. I observed several boys at the mural one day and pointed to an image of a rabbit to ask about its origin. One boy informed me that the rabbit was *Tío Conejo*, a character introduced by Mexico City-based storyteller, María Antonia, through exaggerated body gestures and dissimilar voices to chronicle the adventures of one Tío Conejo or "uncle rabbit." The students had remembered the [Tío Conejo] story and chose to represent it in one of the mural frames. Asked about the mural, one day a group of boys responded by pointing to the images they had drawn and to other ones that remained unfinished. They said that the mural served to commemorate their time at the school. A year later when they would all graduate, they would have a ceremony by their collaborative wall art. In other conversations, the mural seemed more like play than reverie. When asked the topic of the mural, a girl said casually, 'we are just painting.' (p. 203)

The backside of the mural, the partition facing their classroom, bore all their names, and the students interacted with the wall as if it were their own. Over the weeks of the mural project, students often met, fingers pointing across the mural surface as they studied their collective work. Even when school-wide events took place on the ball courts, students often worked unsupervised on the mural.[8]

The murals became textual fruit of the reading project Marcos and his colleagues had established at school, though the social relationships established through writing on walls revealed a wider, inclusive shift in school culture to promote quality. The school director told me he welcomed the murals, provided they were done respectfully. Parents concurred, believing that school mural painting discouraged vandalism. David viewed the murals as pedagogically productive, forming what he called a "corner of diversity" to instill in the students a "sense of belonging (*sentido de pertenencia*)"[9]; in this migration-sending village, making murals in school would provide incentive for students to return to their fertile village (p. 203). This pedagogy of belonging corresponds to the politics of cultural and artistic elements of the 2006 Movimiento. Porras Ferreyra (2009) has observed that during the Movimiento, music, video making, and photography, among other written, performed, and textual arts, became sociopolitical, given how the visual and performative arts and the celebration of Oaxacan heritage had become embroiled in political corruption and kickback schemes in remodeling old buildings (pp. 228–239). The arts also directly related to the Tecotitlán reading projects through the fundraising efforts led by Marcos.[10]

Bells

After open doors and painted walls, a third way that teachers in Tecotitlán critically reframed the social life of their school after the 2006 Movimiento came about when teachers and students began disregarding the school bells. Alternative education proposals in Oaxaca (CEDES 22, 2010) have called out the factory-like regulation of the time and spaces of learning and teaching of the official curriculum as a breach in the sociocultural rhythm of village life, such as during the harvest when neighbors share resources and socialize over food and drink as part of the working day. Adherence to school timetables conducts efficient worker dispositions, ones vehemently opposed by CEDES 22, the wing of the Sección 22 in charge of framing the parameters of and training the classroom practitioners in the delivery of alternative education. In Tecotitlán, teachers and students apparently follow the formal time slots, for the bells still ring; nevertheless, they have chosen to start and stop classes at will.

The teachers and the administration have not rejected the bells outright, even as they select when and where to begin and end their class sessions. Even though others at Tecotitlán may ignore it, the teacher 'on-call' rings the school bell at 8:00 to start class, 10:20 for recess, 11:00 to end recess, and 12:30 to close out the day. Although this practice remains active, the bell ringers often miss the correct time and school community members maintain their prior activities when hearing the bell. More dynamic and personalized scheduling started as teachers in 2006 had promised parents that they would make up the time lost in the Movimiento. One parent noted that some teachers had been holding classes late in the afternoon and on weekends four years after missing months of class. (Sadlier & Morales Sánchez, 2012, p. 204)

The Book Fair events often take place during off-hours or conflict with programmed class hours.

The bells remain markers of time, though without signaling a change from one learning activity to the next, seen one day, when

at 8:00 a.m. while the bell rang, the students kept playing basketball and a teacher kept discussing the garlic harvest with a parent. The director exited his office where the bell is housed, and even as they saw him, the students and the teacher avoided rushing to class. By 10:33, Marcos's students remained in the library preparing a cultural performance on Benito Juárez's birthday, a school holiday. The bell never rang for recess, or if it had, nobody had paid attention. Eventually a student approached Marcos asking to break for recess. (p. 204)

A little while later, the male students begin to gather on the cement, not far from the ficus tree, to play the game of tops. I saw them from the jalousies in the classroom, where I saw most of them with female students, ready for the class to resume. Marcos had joined the circle of boys spinning their tops. "Come on, *Estif*," the girls gestured to me to come outside with them to join their classmates. Marcos seemed amused, laughing while spinning the plastic toy onto the Tecotitlán school courtyard sandy cement, which made his succeeding at getting a good spin more challenging. Soon enough, the whole class congregated under the tree. When others arrived, the game broke down, and the students, Marcos, and I returned to resume class. When the afternoon bell signaled the end of the school day, the students did not stir from their work, which on this particular day encompassed their performances for the Benito Juárez's birthday. With only a few days until their performance before peers, teachers, and community members, the students asked Marcos for more time to prepare during the coming weekend. Marcos lamented that he did not have time to come open up school that coming weekend, but the students needed to be ready for the performance just the same. Marcos released the class from their tasks forty minutes after the end-of-day bell.

In all, though the school bell rings, Marcos set the schedule with his students who had even asked him for class on a nonschool day.[11]

In support of educational quality, Tecotitlán Elementary school teachers opened doors, made wall murals, and disregarded schedules. The doors, bells, and walls of the school began to resemble the world outside the schoolyard, where conflict and contestation played out. Still, school remained a formal space of learning, too. The students occupy every corner of the school, often screaming and yelling, though bells and Monday morning homage to the flag rituals remain intact. Horizontal, community relationships filter into the school, while the institute retains its designation as a place of endorsed teaching and learning, rather than a wholly *powerful* literacy move (Gee, 2001) that students might take up at home or with peers outside of school. These counter-pedagogies followed the experiences of protest in 2006, where over 300 organizations lent structural support, public dialogs and cultural events occurred in Church atriums and unaffiliated individuals occupied public spaces in historic centers, the long-standing site of elite power. This is to say that the formal school institution, now inlaid with affinity spaces (Gee, 2004) where students feel at ease to interact as with friends over familiar tasks, has answered the parental demand for quality education.

Emergence

The Tecotitlán self-managed pedagogies of opening doors, ignoring bells, and painting walls represent a new turn. Schooling in Oaxaca involves a pedagogical conduct, where on the one hand, teachers should officially lead students and families toward greater intellectual output and more sober modes of managing the time and space, and on the other hand, teachers should radically delink their teaching from any mention of the state, as touched on in Chapter Two. As teachers let students negotiate learning outside the normal dimensions of time and space and yet still within the parentally approved notion of quality education, the state and the union-sanctioned pedagogies become counter-pedagogies that neither sanction nor subvert. That is, letting students play music from the director's office, suggesting that class begins and ends when the teachers and students say it does, and encouraging graffiti on campus offer the chance for an emergent and socially negotiated variety of quality education.

The socially negotiated multiplicity of activity that characterized the 2006 Movimiento, as well as the Tecotitlán Elementary book project explored in this chapter, are examples of emergent literacies, where different people collaborate over different projects (Botelho & Rudman, 2009, p. 58). While there is an appreciation of the politics of collectively dis-coordinated projects at protest events like anti-summit rallies (Maeckelbergh, 2009, p. 174), curriculum and instruction scholars are less likely to appreciate and plan for emergence in the classroom.[12] If we recall President Fox's linking education to production (Fox Quesada, 2001, p. 71), and a former Secretaría de Educación Pública executive describing the problem of Mexico as the problem of the Oaxacan grasshopper lady (Díaz de Cossío, 2011, p. 41), the social and embodied attending to the world outside the officialdom of the classroom becomes a counter-pedagogy of quality, as we see in the Book Fair below.

The Book Fair: *Animación a la Lectura*

Marcos

I met Marcos by chance in late June 2010 in Santa María el Tule, a village outside of Oaxaca City that is famous for country-style food. There, a signature of Oaxaca stands, *el árbol del Tule*, a *sabino*, a tri-millennial tree that fills a city block with its thirty-seven-foot trunk diameter venerated by arborists, tourists, and locals. The tree appeals to all ages, as a sixth-grade Tecotitlán boy, excited for the school field trip there, blurted out that they would see the "*nalgas de Thalia* (the buttocks of pop star, Thalia)" on a burl of the trunk. Much younger *sabinos* are common down that stretch of the valley where many noted archeological ruins dot the brown hills as well as artisan villages renowned for wool carpet weaving cooperatives described by Stephen (1991). Beside the sabinos, in some of the nearby villages, there are *mogotes*, little mounds of turf revered by people as historically significant, but which have avoided targeted archeological exploration. At a rustic eatery in El Tule I met Marcos, a veteran bilingual elementary educator, and learned about the annual Tecotitlán Book Fair.

The Book Fair has become part of a school project to stimulate reading. Over recent years, the school zone in that part of the valley has experienced a flowering of school-based projects like the one in Tecotitlán, though schools pick up different aspects of the elementary school curriculum. To illustrate, one school pulls from Mexican and international cinema, like the once-banned film *Rojo amanecer* on the 1968 Tlatelolco massacre, to historicize modern Mexico. For his part, Marcos's school centers on reading through popular practices of the harvest, fiestas, and family storytelling, the sites and scaffolding for understanding, sharing, and enjoying the written and spoken word. As a school-based project pioneer in the area, he presents his reading project at his associates' schools.

I accompanied Marcos to a day of training at the elementary school with the history project. Classes had shut down for this in-service training day, and Marcos stepped before the teachers, broke the group into teams, and sent them out into school grounds to capture landscape noises around the school and surrounding area. Sending the teachers out, he tasked us with gathering the sonic data for a performance on those noises and what they meant to our groups. Marcos turned toward me and sent me to join one group, and so we walked around the grounds, taking in the aesthetics. I stepped away from the teachers and noticed a groundskeeper burning brush that the school community had gathered during *tequio*,[13] a collective work project. Unlike the cemented ground in the Tecotitlán courtyard, the studentless greenery and playground game-filled land made this school seem like a rural summer camp in the offseason. Catching up with the teachers in my group, we shared sounds we had noticed on our jaunt.

As the group gathered on a ball court, one of the women chose to give the group a name, *los estevens*, drawing on my first name. The members of los estevens shared one main sound that captured their attention: the *perifoneo*, a loudspeaker attached to a car that drives through town, droning with announcements. This day, with the recording on a loop, we learned of shrimp prices at the market and put this reiterated sound into the official los estevens performance on the resonant scenario we had experienced. Upon performing the perifoneo to the other groups at the in-service, one teacher in another group expressed wonder at how she had never noticed the perifoneo in town, as the everyday-ness of it passed without her notice. Like the embodiment of opening doors, ignoring bells, and painting walls in Tecotitlán, developing an awareness of the sounds means developing a taste for the purposelessness of ambient noise. This squandering, antifunctional pedagogy counters the official policies to teach to assuage rezago in educational achievement and to engage in a radicalized praxis in critical pedagogy. Performing the sound of the price of shrimp on the perifoneo in town turns classroom awareness away from the unitary pedagogies of test score improvement and teachers' union radicalized alternative education, allowing the teachers to resuscitate a storyline out of the banality of everyday life, allowing perception, socialization, and performance to come out in the school. In addition to this participant-generated textual experience, later in the in-service calendar, Marcos coordinated a podium performance of printed story. However, stories that we come to read in books can be scaffolded by a teacher's ability to read and interpret the nonprint world of sound.

Texture and narration of sound is important to Marcos, a classroom practitioner intent on developing student interest in reading. This is a recent turn for him. With almost three decades in the classroom, when I asked how he came to his approach toward reading, Marcos emphasized that fomenting reading in experiential and ecological ways became urgent for him after the 2006 Movimiento on the streets of Oaxaca City. He mused on his time in protest:

> In 2006 we had a tough political conflict…. [This Book Fair], as a teacher-driven proposal, came to light precisely as this conflict passed…. This is to say, if we make, if we can make protests, we can also make pedagogical proposals. So then in the two years of research, we got anthropological references [from an ethnographic project on community practices]; we tasked ourselves to observe the lifestyle of the people.

From Marcos's perspective, project-based school learning resonates with the political protests on the streets.[14] It was no small thing to step away from the official curriculum and the Sección 22-sanctioned alternative education to establish a locally generated and alternatively funded reading project. Inspired and disturbed as he was by the events of the Movimiento and the repressive reaction of the state authorities, Marcos organized the Tecotitlán Book Fair, which met with immediate teacher resistance. Among teachers across the state, especially those active in the union, he observed, "critical and emancipatory discourses" rarely cemented into action. "What I have personally seen, the [emancipatory] projects are not grounded," he detailed. Standing apart from the radical bent of the Sección 22 that appears in Chapter Two, a teacher making independent pedagogical proposals runs a risk, for as Marcos said, "later the people in the union will peg (*tachan*) such a teacher, mark them with an X, [for doing] things that don't go with what they stand for. They start to put up obstacles, even try to ruin the project." Conceived at the street protests, in response to parental demands for quality education, and before the pedagogical uniformity of the teachers' union, Marcos coordinated the Tecotitlán Book Fair as *autogestivo*: a counter-pedagogy independent of direct union, Oaxaca state, and Mexico City oversight while, at the same time, drawing resources and materials from those same sites of officialdom when appropriate. The Book Fair asked for help from anyone who would offer it, yet the teachers would reject direct pedagogical mandates from the donors.[15]

The Puppet Show

The third day of the Tecotitlán Book Fair, the day after I met Marcos and the others at El Tule, I came to the events at the elementary school where the spoken word stood as one of the major subjects. Marcos observed that printed books are scarce in Tecotitlán, but parents and community leaders, according to his research and suggested in the trainings he gave to area teachers on the performance of sounds, show understanding of the written and lived word. The garlic and *chile de árbol* harvest are chief practices of multigenerational meeting; they occupy conversations and depend on transportation to market in Oaxaca City.[16] The transporting of goods to market in carts and taxis fuels networks within the community that extend out to the larger society in the Central Valleys region and Oaxaca City. Families, however, have often been kept apart from formal, learning-centered school practices, despite the ways that the rural elementary school communitarian legacy and teachers had once corporally punished students speaking Zapotec in school, as addressed earlier. According to the faculty, one purpose of the Book Fair was to incorporate communal ways of being together into literacy practices and to open the official learning in school to families in Tecotitlán and beyond. The embodied experience of sound, sonic literacy (Comstock & Hocks, 2006), became a vehicle for this.

This day of the Book Fair began with a "teaching concert." Clad in elegant white shirts, a group of troubadours sang and strummed songs from different regions of Oaxaca, and after each number explained the instrument choices to the audience. To the right of the ensemble, a puppet stage draped in black cloth was set tall enough so that a standing puppeteer could raise cloth dolls above her head and incite laughter and choral responses of the elementary students in the audience. Waxy green ficus trees appeared through the opening of the puppet stage and beside those trees, the brick-sided, detached buildings of the classrooms. About 200 people in all sat on folding chairs on red tiles on one of the ball courts of the elementary school, an area exposed to the burning sun on an ordinary school day when the parents' committee, who once clamored for quality education, had not tied up a theater roof of vinyl tarps to tree limbs and classroom buildings. Before the puppet stage, crayon-drawn book covers were taped and glued to the insides of straw baskets. One cover reads: "I'm enchanted by reading," another, with snail and scorpion drawings, "Invertebrate Animals" and one more: "The Little Black Sheep." Drawings of famous Disney and Simpsons characters as well as others stood out.

During the teaching concert, I examined the audience in this improvised auditorium beneath tarps: elementary school students remained seated, some in yellow school uniforms, others in red and white physical education tops and bottoms. Mixed in with students, parents held the hands of preschool children. Beside the stage, just outside of the student rows still under the tarp, I sat with other adults. María Antonia, the professional storyteller brought from Mexico City whom I had met with Marcos at El Tule the day before, sat beside me. Later, Theresa, the zone supervisor would sit with us in the line of chairs of adults.

As the concert progressed, puppets narrated the musical, gastronomic, and textile history of the ethnic regions of Oaxaca. To the left of the puppet stage, and in dialog with the puppets, taciturn-faced musicians played songs of yearning and love like *La canción de la Mixteca* which laments, "how far am I from the land that I love," then a courtship dance of *El palomo y la paloma*, the male and female dove. Between songs, the puppets introduced the audience to Indigenous words from diverse languages and traditional clothing. We heard music and learned about clothing from la Cuenca and la Cañada, far away from Tecotitlán. One puppet, the master of ceremonies, asked another puppet visiting from far away what it was like missing home and inquired about the agricultural products found in the visitor's distant region. We are in Tecotitlán, in Oaxaca's Central Valleys, a farming town that produces abundant produce, yet almost all families have or have had loved ones working in the United States. In Tecotitlán, people often come back to live after being away, oftentimes building larger, two-story houses that according to Marcos represent earnings from the States and oftentimes the continued absence of the ones working there. The puppet emcee, in greeting the visitor and asking about feelings of homeland, talked about longing and separation.

María Antonia and a Mother's Voice

Music, based on Marcos's research, mattered due to the sonorous capacity of the human voice. He taught the voice as a primary storytelling articulation device, and as such, it proved significant for increasing interest in reading, including the narration of fables and personal memories. Critical pedagogical approaches, underwritten by the transformative pedagogies attributed to Paulo Freire that the Sección 22's alternative education proposals depend on, have prized modern, progressive learning at the expense of oracy. To Freire, spoken language mattered less than learning print literacy (Bowers, 2005, p. 3). Yet, and in line with Marcos's self-managed and self-funded pedagogical interventions, across Oaxaca, a person's facility to speak well before others matters. Several mothers expressed satisfaction with the reading project at the school because they had witnessed their children's public speaking confidence grow. In public life, Oaxacans value accomplished orators. Speech making conducts leadership, especially in radical politics. The mystique surrounding the speeches of Polín, the legendary head of the rebel Coalición Obrera, Campesina, Estudiantil del Istmo (COCEI),[17] related to his double entendre-laced style (Campbell, 2001, p. 28); likewise, Mexico's great-est anarchist, Oaxaca-born Ricardo Flores Magón, charmed adversaries and allies alike through his lyrical eloquence (Hodges, 1995, p. 9). Oracy matters in local practice beyond its use as an intermediary from the voice to the printed word.

After the puppet show and musical performance, María Antonia got up from her seat beside me, and approached the stage. In her university-educated and upper middle-class Mexico City accent, she told a fable of an ant. She told the story with body posture shifts, gestures, and voices, turning through the kind of silliness that adults can get away with best when addressing children. The younger voices in the audience roared in unison and then paid silent attention to the details of the narrated adventures, appearing more focused on these stories than any other component of the day's events. Later, when she was sitting beside me, students approached her to ask for an autograph on the verso page of a paperback storybook. The same students would come back throughout the day, so that the storyteller progressively learned to address them by name.

By the afternoon, the group of students, parents, and teachers under the tarp broke into subsections to attend workshops throughout the school grounds. I stayed in the same shady spot while women came into a central ring of chairs, after the students had petered out into the classrooms for painting and dawning. Initially, I sat outside the circle until Marcos and María Antonia called people into an inner circle, which few ventured into. The two facilitators insisted, and grad-ually the mothers and grandmothers rounded the circle, the latter often stepping in as "parent" for children whose mother or father may have left Tecotitlán for work in the United States or northern Mexico. The circle of chairs became one of women, all of whom knew Marcos, as he had been teaching at the school for a decade. They seemed to offer deferential silence toward María Antonia who they had met only during the Book Fair. María Antonia, a fair-skinned, metropolitan, outsider like me, cofacilitated the Indigenous and *campesina* mother and grand-mother workshop on how to use the spoken word to generate interest in reading.

As a preamble, and to pace the spoken-word workshop, Marcos and María Antonia each related snapshots of a bygone meeting with an elder. First, Marcos narrated an instance when he rode on a bicycle crossbar with his father cycling to market, the grade-school Marcos protected by his father's strong limbs as they raced the darkening clouds of an approaching rainstorm. With a clear destination at the market, and in the race against a pluvial menace, Marcos related the youth-ful, sheltered exploration he undertook with his father as the rains overtook them. Pedagogically, Marcos's story led to his asking us at the workshop to clarify the bicycle's color in our mind's eye, as if the bike were just a bike until the recall of color delivered it into its experiential wholeness. His father's disused bike, stored at Marcos's house, triggered reverie, and stories like the rainstorm ride remained for him a living point of access with his father. When he saw the bicycle, he let a story come. After the bicycle-in-the-storm narrative, María Antonia gave us hers. While Marcos traced out a boy with his dad on a bike and a landscape of steel wool and charcoal clouds, María Antonia spoke through sensual impulses like the horizontal morning sun catching the dust of a barn and the warm sweet smell of milk drawn right from the cow. Her blurry and mysterious tableau came out faster as she concluded, almost as if she were dreaming and knew that very soon, she would awaken and the wholeness of the oblique rays of the morning sun would vanish. Like Marcos's story, her story felt exploratory and infantile, though without safety or companionship that, as a listener, I could identify. At our event, María Antonia had already established herself as a master storyteller before us, spinning fables on the stage now behind her, and now via the barn reverie she appeared indifferent to the listener as she soliloquized the memory's uninhabited, excessive details. At the point of milking, with light beaming through, if she had not already delivered the tale with the voice and corporeality established in her stage narrations, it all might have seemed too imaginary, too low-tech, and too bucolic to keep my interest. Her anachronistic and wistful delivery later helped her reveal how the barn milking came from her octogenarian mother's actual experience. Perhaps it was her mother's experience; though, since her mother told the story to the storyteller, María Antonia emphasized that she had inserted herself into it. Whoever possessed the authentic memory of the real event, no one could tell, she concluded. No one harnesses total or final rights to stories; the truthfulness of the prior events that are retold is no match for the truth that the performer gives them. Listeners can ingest stories that are not theirs to take in, for stories as collective endeavors need listeners to listen for the tellers retelling.

Once the bike and barn memories were completed, with the help of the mothers, Marcos emceed popular songs and then lullabies, which incorporated all of the mothers and grandmothers standing up and acting out gestures like the caressing of a baby, seen in figure 3.1. Lullaby, *arruyo* in Spanish, also means to caress or lull. On the microphone speaking to the circle of women, Marcos asked for a volunteer to lull an imaginary baby. At this point, the seemingly reserved and self-conscious mothers and grandmothers slowly became more expressive, surrendering to the imaginative body motions. Marcos then asked the women to adapt verses to the lullabies. Everyone knew some variation of the base stanzas, and different women led the others with their renditions. Chanting and slapping hands together to flatten an imaginary tortilla, a corn-based staple of Oaxacan cuisine,

Marcos and the women began to improvise a chain of verses which came out as a collectively expanding storyline through lullaby. Marcos offered the base verse: "*Tortillitas de maíz / Para la mamá que está feliz* (Tortillas[18] made of corn / For the mom who's happy.)" With the women standing, flattening imaginary tortillas and speaking in a nonschool voice to preschool children, the self-consciousness began to dissipate. Different women offered different extensions. The following one caused effusive laughter and chanting: "*Tortillitas de cebada / Para el papá que no hace nada,*" or "Tortillas made of barley / For the dad who does nothing."

This barley tortilla verse touched off such a ruckus that the pace of the workshop slowed down. Why such laughter? Maybe the mamá could get lost in lyrical appraisal of family life, passing this from mother to child. Weeks later when I questioned Marcos on why lullabies mattered to his work with the mothers and grandmothers, he reported that the workshop intended to connect fun, interaction, and melody in parent-to-child family histories. This would then show the women, many of whom visited school regularly, that they possessed the storyteller craft already. They spend hours uttering such stories to their children, stories that are rich in references to other stories, situations that allude to and depend on the understanding embedded in prior ones. However, these stories, like the lullabies, lack the formal endorsement of textbook learning. For Marcos, as the women sing these lullabies, their children feel the accounts, descriptions, and snippets of family lore. Making barley tortillas for the papá who does nothing at home, the mom who sings invents verses with her silent conversationalists, the small children and the unborn in the womb. As such, lullabies and their amended stanzas index a complex story, as textually varied as any *literature* found in a book, Marcos explained. Further still, storytelling like this at school becomes counter-pedagogical, for although "maternal language of domestic life" (Bonfil Batalla, 1996) stimulates rural area language development (p. 139), cradlesongs conduct a maternal narrative space rarely made pedagogical on school grounds.

Performing commonplace and home-based texts, like lullabies beneath the tarpaulin in the Book Fair, expands the range of what gets constituted as literacy and how the quality education that the same mothers demanded comes into school. Marcos's incursion into lullabies originates from his interest in the didactic pulse of the maternal voice. His teaching through lullabies came to him at a language and reading stimulation workshop delivered by Sierra Morales (2009), who stresses that storied embodiment involved a mother singing to her child, which then leads to children's reading habits.[19] For reading "is transmitting the emotions of the narrators with voice and gesticulation. It is learning that voices have rhythm and that the rhythm is carried in all my body" (para. 3). Translating the ideas of this workshop, Marcos introduced mother and grandmother expressions into his reading project, evident across the events of the Book Fair, including when Marcos remembered his father's protective embrace on the bicycle and María Antonia remembered her mother's memory. What is more, introducing lullabies into midweek daytime school learning draws from the nonschool family home. In Oaxaca, the kitchen, in particular, is praised as an important pedagogical space (Nahmad, 2004). Oaxaca reading and nutrition programs tie together food, learning, and Indigenous education, as family food preparation plays into the communitarian way of life. Therefore, teaching in this way is highly culturally relevant (p. 279). Work on *mujerista* or womanist pedagogies (Trinidad Galván, 2001), vibrant, interactive encounters where the body and emotion preside over learning, has also valued the kitchen spaces in rural Mexico. For Marcos and others, bringing such family and village *convivencia* (Trinidad Galván, 2015; Villenas, 2005) into formal schooling scaffolds pupil reading and shifts the school culture away from teacher-centered instruction toward a more embodied modality of quality education.

When the lullaby and personal story workshop with María Antonia and Marcos concluded, the mothers and grandmothers working on lullabies were joined by the students who posted artwork on a wall by the basketball court. The participants converged beneath the tarpaulin, Marcos on the microphone calling up representatives from each workshop to report back. A woman from the lullaby session, a blond-haired grandmother from the city of Guadalajara, a fifteen-hour drive to the northwest, approached the stage and reported in. She began by saying that she and her husband had been touring Oaxaca when they met someone from Tecotitlán who had invited them to the Book Fair, stressing how this little festival had become the highlight of their trip. Her attendance had meant a lot to her, for now she said she envisaged narrating to her grandchildren in the way she had experienced in the workshop. As much as the teaching concert and puppet show fomented cultural lessons on Indigenous traditions, artifacts, and fruits, the lullaby workshop drew from a more universal sonic literacy of (grand)mother to child. The voice, collective instrument of human interaction, carried implication and history to the born and the unborn alike. Mother or grandmother, the ones often cast off as unschooled, handle the literacy of the lullaby. Life's earliest voices, the storied melody of our pre- and postnatal caregivers, start modeling how to decipher stories; thus, the home-bound ephemeral feminism of lullabies meets the formal space of the public school where doors open, and families, pupils, and visitors gather under the tarpaulin, as they did during these days.

The Color of the Earth

The Book Fair was about to close when a student stepped on stage, grabbed the microphone, and called his peers to the basketball court beside the recently posted student artwork. A dozen or so students assembled in choreographed rows to perform, through gesture and recitation, a poem that one of their teachers had written years ago called *Los del color de la tierra* (People with earth-colored skin), a celebration of Oaxacan dark skin and of laboring close to the land in a land once conquered by Europeans, developed by big city technocrats, and now ushered into socioeconomic prosperity by US-based norms. Symbolically, *Los del color de la tierra* draws directly from a speech by Subcommander Marcos,[20] spokesperson for the Chiapas grassroots autonomy group, Ejercito Zapatista de Liberación Nacional (EZLN), Tecotitlán teachers informed me. Standing outside the shade of the tarpaulin, the students began to chant and dance to show their pride in having skin the color of the earth, as well as speaking languages, wearing clothing, and practicing traditions that predate the conquest of the Americas.[21]

The Zapatistas, and the subcommander in particular, have impacted education and social movements outside of Chiapas state. As policy makers and teachers since the 1920s and 1930s have used education to assimilate in the rural periphery of the Mexican state, autonomy-focused Indigenous education flourished after the 1994 EZLN uprising in Chiapas (Hernández Castillo, 2001, p. 212) and in Oaxaca (Maldonado, 2004, p. 36).[22] University-professor-turned-revolutionary Subcommander Marcos, for his part, led a 2001 rally on the Mexico City zócalo called "those who are the color of the earth," addressing Vicente Fox, "up there" in the lofty Palacio Federal:

> Up there they say that … we shall return to the land in which we are alone and empty. Up there they say that forgetting is defeat, and they want to wait for you to forget and to fail and to be defeated. They know up there, but they do not want to say it: *There will be no more forgetting, and defeat shall not be the crown for the color of the earth…* Now, and it is what they fear, there is no longer the "you" and the "we," because now we are all the color of the earth. (Marcos, Pena-Vargas, & Ruggiero, 2007, emphasis in original, p. 124)

The color of the earth here is a form of accompaniment, the footfalls where ancestors have lived and toiled. This integrated togetherness, voiced in a cultural and political ground zero of the nation, the Mexico City zócalo, includes others, not just Chiapan highlanders. When I asked the Tecotitlán school director why teachers and students chose this poem to close the Book Fair he said that it represented an expression of student "identity." This expression of identity differs from a separatist, primordial one consigned to essential traits. The color of the earth takes up more of a discursive position, one linked to Oaxaca and Tecotitlán, and also to Mexico City as well as the contemporary life of many other Mexicans. The color of the earth referrers *intertextually*[23] (Bloome & Bailey, 1992) to the EZLN leader's speech, and alludes to the prior contexts of the Zapatista's march to Mexico City, detailed in Chapter Two, where being color of the earth meant standing on the ground below the presidential balcony with everyone who has dealt with neoliberal reforms facing Mexico. As a performance, much like unlocking the doors, ignoring the bells, and painting the walls, the color of the earth is jocular, open air, and embodied, which counters the rational functionalism of officially sanctioned pedagogies.

Self-managed Pedagogies as Quality Education

Marcos calls the work carried out at Tecotitlán elementary a *self-managed pedagogy*. This is to say that the Book Fair, the open doors, painted walls, and ignored bells locally interpret official teaching and learning strategies endorsed by the state and the alternative education framed by the Sección 22. With representatives of the state, corporate sponsors, and radical union, a self-managed pedagogy becomes a different kind of quality education rather than a pedagogical rebellion.[24] In practice, self-government for Marcos denotes a way of knowing and joining together that is open to anyone willing to participate: parents, municipal leaders, and other visitors joining in the learning and fun under tarpaulins, inside of open rooms, and on ball courts. Self-managed pedagogies suggest self-government, akin to alternative education proposals described in Chapters One and Two; yet, for Marcos and his colleagues, such pedagogies mean asking for support from any individual or organization who will help them, echoing how organizations like churches and small businesses also participated in the Movimiento of 2006. Specifically, self-government has involved teachers bidding for three kinds of support: material,[25] professional,[26] and financial.[27] According to Marcos, to maintain the counter-pedagogical status has involved accepting support only if the teachers enjoyed freedom from intrusive monitoring and evaluation. Thus, the pedagogies are neither as ideologically nor institutionally self-governing as the Sección 22 wants nor as incorporated and standardized testing-based as the Instituto Estatal de Educación Pública de Oaxaca (IEEPO) wants. Rather, the counter-pedagogies above involve the vindication of the human body which in times of violence needs others around and in an age of standardized reforms casts the Oaxacan body, the grasshopper-lady-color-of-the-earth body, as *rezagado*. Self-government forms a critical resistance to the attempts to divide and disembody the streets and schools where Oaxacan teachers operate.

Notes

1. International and national solidarity with the protesters, including the work of Mujeres Sin Miedo, came through in manifestations, *encuentros*, conferences, and *plantones* (Martínez Vásquez, 2007, pp. 164–165).

2. Marcos has instituted a mobile library in Tecotitlán, a donkey-drawn cart made of plywood and recycled car tires, resembling what farmers use to transport alfalfa. From Marcos's ethnography of harvest practices, the cart passes through the town, serving as a lending library. Marcos mentioned he got the idea for the book cart from a mobile library in rural Colombia, called the *biblioburro*.

3. Across Oaxaca, fewer elementary students fill the classrooms. In 2010 one school principal, seated beside the Mexican flag encased in a glass box, told me that many working families stopped seasonal migration between the United States and Mexico out of fear that new anti-immigration measures in the United States would make it impossible to cross. As such, whole families, including the principal's own daughter, remained in the States, reducing Oaxacan elementary school enrollment. A principal at another elementary school, sitting below year-by-year school graduation photos with progressively fewer students, noticed that after 2000 her school began to lose enrollment. This trend has affected Tecotitlán, too.

4. One of the criticisms of *enciclomedia* is that the technology is delivered to schools without a maintenance plan. In Tecotitlán the data projector did not work, so students would gather around a single computer to read documents. In the alternative education conference in Mexico City (CNTE, 2010) the delegates at mesa once critiqued it for its private sector links that drain the coffers more than the public, and presumed costly, normal schools (p. 5).

5. Fomenting reading is a priority for the state and NGOs. When accompanying Lourdes on her site visits to a student teacher's practicum site in the interior of the Mixtec Region, we went to a library that occupied a large room. Lourdes indicated that such libraries popped up in remote regions under the conservative administration of Vicente Fox. When Lourdes and her colleague leafed through an art book, *Pintores mexicanos de la A la Z* (Olmos, 2012), they paused at a sensitive though immodest painting of a nude woman and laughingly wondered if those pushing the pro-Catholic agenda of the President's PAN would approve of children reading such "pornography." The library itself impressed them enough to take pictures of it. In the Central Valleys, hours to the west, an NGO had started a bookmobile to go to rural

communities. Marcos and his workmates often refer to reading project activities that depend on funding coming from special programs related to reading.

6. Flexibility, efficiency, and innovation are mechanisms of quality maximization that are extracted from the field of finance into the knowledge society (Sadlier & Arancibia, 2015), and "rites of exit" (García Canclini, 2001) compel modern artists to perpetual creative reinvention (p. 26). Flexibility enacted in this school's mural-making is more organic, for it allows a collective subjectivity, a *"nosotros,"* to Carlos Lenkersdorf (2003) in his Tojolabal-Maya village report, where a man goes confessing to the village priest that he had mistreated a saucepan and derided a dog. Though not Catholic sin, both acts offended the nosotros practiced in the Tojolabal-Maya village (pp. 28–29). Schools, like churches, historically tried to eradicate the nosotros. A schooled nosotros may be less malleable than a confessional one, given the high-stakes testing turn in the 2012 reforms have hyper-individualized assessment. Lenkersdorf (2002) reveals that individual evaluations go against the collective and collaborative problem-solving of village children.

7. A noteworthy academic institution mural of this period adorns the walls of Mexico City's Colegio de San Idelfonso. In the United States, Dartmouth College, New School for Social Research, and Pomona College have work by the Mexican muralists, too.

8. The students' painting the murals, for example, might qualify as vandalism, echoing the practices of graffiti on the streets of Oaxaca during 2006. If murals vandalize they carry out a different politics than if they are authorized. The graffiti in 2006 "transgresses because it appropriates space that many times issues warning to avoid 'posting' there" (Lache Bolaños, 2009, p. 200).

9. Near Tecotitlán elementary is the ENBIO, a bilingual and intercultural normal school. Though the two institutions address different populations, the sense of belonging becomes a credo for both, considering David's call for a sense of belonging through mural and the ENBIO's mission statement, to "train Indigenous teachers (*formar docentes indígenas*) from a bilingual and intercultural perspective … with a sense of belonging and identity" (García Ortega, Salvador, & Martínez, 2004, p. 488).

10. For our first interview, Marcos scheduled a meeting at the Instituto de Artes Gráficas in Oaxaca City. Entering the courtyard, he politely greeted the institute's founder, painter/activist Francisco Toledo, saying "Hello Maestro." As we discussed the reading project in his village school, artists sat at tables all around us in an old colonial courtyard working at their tables. Marcos informed me that Toledo funded the school reading project.

11. A Tecotitlán graduate reported that the bell ignoring is new. During her student days a decade earlier, students ran out after class. Ignoring the bells started when the teachers had come to the agreement that the normal hours were not enough to foment the level of quality education they had promised the parents. How the students stay in their classrooms, even an hour after school, and why Marcos's students express disappointment when he cannot come in on a Saturday, reveal the post-Movimiento

counter-pedagogical moves like ignoring bells has led to a variety of quality education of the students' and teachers' making.

12. For how formal spaces of classroom practices become sites of informal learning, see Botelho, Cohen, Leoni, Chow, and Sastri (2010).

13. Tequio is a noncommercial and nonmonetary public work project, which forms part of village governance in some Oaxacan communities. Because it involves neighborly support rather than contract-based relationships, tequio has inspired community-based popular education in Oaxaca such as the work of Acevedo et al. (2004).

14. Another master educator, who met Marcos during the dialogs in the 2006 Movimiento, accordingly took her experiences on the streets of Oaxaca City to make her secondary school more inclusive for students with handicaps, considering that solidarity with others that emerged in the conflict is something schools need to teach to all students, regardless of ability (Sadlier, 2014).

15. Self-managed pedagogies suggest self-government, something like the alternative education elaborated in Chapters One and Two, though not as partisan. See Appadurai (2002) for theoretical parameters on a similar political project in urban India.

16. Oaxaca is mountainous, and from valley to valley the village cultures vary; thus, traveling to the market becomes a cosmopolitan event. One teacher from a small highland city in the southwest of the state described the delivery of bread from a distant village. The bread was so distinct and its arrival so noteworthy that people in her city called it "*pan de burro*," named after the mode of transport, the burro, rather than its official name or ingredients. Marcos noted how for Tecotitlán farmers, selling in Oaxaca City's Mercado de Abastos represented a great journey into the outside world, even if the distance was rather short.

17. The ruling PRI has held power in regions of Oaxaca for over eighty years. In the Isthmus of Tehuantepec, radical local politics have a long history of contesting the PRI. People of the city of Juchitán, a four-hour drive southeast of Tecotitlán, elected the Coalición Obrera, Campesina, Estudiantil del Istmo (COCEI) into their city government in the early 1980s (Campbell, 1989, 1990, 1994; Rubin, 1994, 1997, 1998).

18. Aware that *ita* is a diminutive suffix for tortilla, I translate *tortillita* as tortilla, rather than *little tortilla*. For food, the "ita" may have nothing to do with reduced size but instead represents times of shared food. This is as if to say, *tortillitas, you know them, the ones I make for you,* instead of tortillas as a general food type. The diminutive shows storytelling relationships between the singer and the sung to; or, in the case here, the babies are only imaginary, so it is one mother to another.

19. For the narrativity of everyday life see Smith (2007).

20. *Zapatismo* has been translated into contexts beyond the highlands of eastern Chiapas. Works on the translocal, transnational, and translational political projects of the Zapatistas in Chiapas and beyond are numerous. For the use of memory work, see Jansen (2007) and for transnational activism, see Barmeyer (2009). For the ways

Zapatismo has influenced Oaxacan movements, see Stephen (2002) and for urban Mexican and U.S. interpretations of the movement, see Dellacioppa (2009).

21. As introduced in Chapter Two, inclusion requires clarification. Economic restructuring toward the free market has taken on a social and pedagogical function, the social policy of issuing "collective rights" to groups who lack them (Hale, 2005, p. 12) that draw the empowered into the free market vortex (p. 13). In Oaxaca and Chiapas, a tendency endures toward autonomy alongside inclusion. Oaxacan intercultural pedagogies (Meyer & Maldonado, 2004) that cultivate and revitalize the linguistic, festive, and work-based practices associated with the villages themselves thwart inclusion.

22. In addition to inspiring grassroots Indigenous education, the Zapatista uprising impacted state educational apparatuses, too (Figueroa Crespo, 2004, p. 239).

23. A "landscape of texts" (Bazerman, 2004, p. 64), intertextuality enables speakers and writers to draw from the verbiage of others to frame and understand new ones. Lullabies over the happy mother and the lazy father produce laughter not because the words themselves are funny but rather via recalling the lived worlds of mothers and fathers at home. The lullabies, then, are an intentional strategy to domesticate school, a self-managed pedagogical movement Marcos has described.

24. Work tables in an alternative education conference in 1998 had already conceptualized self-managed pedagogies, reporting that "self-management is indispensable (*imprescindible*) … No guidelines are drawn up for working in the schools. [Self-government in schools] must be rooted in the social encounter (*reencuentro*) and in the interrogation of the formats for linking children, parents and municipal authorities" (Hernández, 2009, p. 330).

25. The Catholic Church and a *chile* growers' association lent the chairs for the Book Fair.

26. IEEPO in-service trainers arrived to provide workshops for the students.

27. Grants came from individuals, corporate foundations, and NGOs in Oaxaca. A school district in the U.S. state of Georgia and an immigrant organization in southern California also contributed.

References

Acevedo, S., García, A., García, F., Gutiérrez, B., Bojórquez, F. S., Figueroa, E. M., … López, A. L. (2004). Tequio Pedagógico: Colaboración pedagógica en comunidad. In L. Meyer, B. Maldonado, R. Ortiz, & V. García (Eds.), *Entre la normatividad y la comunidad: Experiencias educativas innovadoras del Oaxaca indígena actual* (pp. 528–568). Oaxaca, Mexico: Fondo Editorial del Instituto Estatal de Educación Pública de Oaxaca (IEEPO).

Appadurai, A. (2002). Deep democracy: Urban governmentality and the horizon of politics. *Public Culture, 14*(1), 21–47.

Barmeyer, N. (2009). *Developing Zapatista autonomy: Conflict and NGO involvement in rebel Chiapas*. Albuquerque, NM: University of New Mexico Press.

Bazerman, C. (2004). Intertextualities: Volosinov, Bakhtin, literary theory, and literary studies. In A. F. Ball & S. Warshauer Freedman (Eds.), *Bakhtinian perspectives on language, literacy and learning* (pp. 53–64). Cambridge: Cambridge University Press.

Bloome, D., & Bailey, F. (1992). Studying language and literacy through events, particularity, and intertextuality. In R. Beach, J. Green, M. Kamil, & T. Shanahan (Eds.), *Multiple disciplinary approaches to researching language and literacy* (pp. 181–210). Urbana, IL: NCTE & NCRE.

Bonfil Batalla, G. (1996). *México profundo: Reclaiming a civilization.* Austin, TX: University of Texas Press.

Botelho, M. J., Cohen, S. L., Leoni, L., Chow, P., & Sastri, P. (2010). Respecting children's cultural and linguistic knowledge: The pedagogical possibilities and challenges of multiliteracies in schools. In M. L. Dantas & P. C. Manyak (Eds.), *Home-school connections in a multicultural society: Learning from and with culturally and linguistically diverse families* (pp. 237–256). New York, NY: Routledge.

Botelho, M. J., & Rudman, M. K. (2009). *Critical multicultural analysis of children's literature: Mirrors, windows, and doors.* New York, NY: Routledge.

Bowers, C. A. (2005). Introduction. In C. A. Bowers & F. Apffel Marglin (Eds.), *Rethinking Freire: Globalization and the environmental crisis* (pp. 1–12). Mahwah, NJ: Lawrence Erlbaum.

Campbell, H. (1989). The COCEI: Culture, class, and politicized ethnicity in the Isthmus of Tehuantepec. *Ethnic Studies Report, 7*(2), 36–60.

Campbell, H. (1994). *Zapotec renaissance: Ethnic politics and cultural revivalism in southern Mexico.* Albuquerque, NM: University of New Mexico.

Campbell, H. (2001). *Mexican Memoir: A personal account of anthropology and radical politics in Oaxaca.* Westport, CT: Bergin & Garvey.

Campbell, H. B. (1990). *Zapotec ethnic politics and the politics of culture in Juchitán, Oaxaca (1350–1990)* (dissertation). University of Wisconsin-Madison.

CEDES 22. (2010). *2010 Resolutivos del III congreso estatal de educación alternativa, 20–21 de mayo.* Oaxaca, Mexico: Sección 22, SNTE.

CNTE. (2010, May). *Resolutivos, IV Congreso Nacional de Educación Alternativa,* 28–30 de mayo (Conference Proceedings). Mexico City.

Comstock, M., & Hocks, E. M. (2006). Voice in the cultural soundscape: Sonic literacy in composition studies. *Computers and Composition Online, 23*(3), 444–455.

De La Rosa, M. G., & Schadl, S. M. (2014). *Getting up for the people: The visual revolution of ASAR-Oaxaca.* Oakland, CA: PM Press.

Dellacioppa, K. Z. (2009). *This bridge called Zapatismo: Building alternative political cultures in Mexico City, Los Angeles, and beyond.* Lanham, MD: Lexington Books.

Díaz de Cossío, R. (2011, May). La chapulinera. *Nexos, 401,* 41–42.

Figueroa Crespo, G. (2004). Programa Aula Abierta. In L. M. Meyer & B. Maldonado (Eds.), *Entre la normatividad y la comunalidad: Experiencias innovadoras del Oaxaca indígena actual* (pp. 234–276). Oaxaca, Mexico: IEEPO/Colección Voces del Fondo; Serie Molinos de viento.

Fox Quesada, V. (2001). *Plan nacional de desarrollo 2001-2006.* Gobierno de los Estados Unidos Mexicanos: Presidencia de la República. Retrieved from http://bibliotecadigital.conevyt.org.mx/colecciones/conevyt/plan_desarrollo.pdf

García Canclini, N. (2001). *Hybrid cultures: Strategies for entering and leaving modernity* (fourth printing). Minneapolis, MN: University of Minnesota Press.

García Ortega, E., Llaguno Salvador, I., & Méndez Martínez, C. (2004). La Escuela Normal Bilingüe Intercultural de Oaxaca. In L. M. Meyer & B. Maldonado (Eds.), *Entre la normatividad y la comunalidad: Experiencias innovadoras del Oaxaca indígena actual* (pp. 476–510). Oaxaca, Mexico: IEEPO/Colección Voces del Fondo; Serie Molinos de viento.

Gee, J. P. (2001). What is literacy? In P. Shannon (Ed.), *Becoming political, too: New readings and writings on the politics of literacy education* (pp. 1–9). Portsmouth, NH: Heinemann.

Gee, J. P. (2004). *Situated language and learning: A critique of traditional schooling.* London: Routledge.

Giroux, H. A. (1988). *Teachers as intellectuals: Toward a critical pedagogy of learning.* Granby, MA: Bergin & Garvey.

Hale, C. (2005). Neoliberal multiculturalism: The remaking of cultural rights and racial dominance in Central America. *PoLAR: Political and Legal Anthropology Review, 28*(1), 10–28.

Hernández, F. G. (2009). La educación alternativa y el movimiento pedagógico en el discurso de los maestros democráticos de Oaxaca, como contexto de la educación bilingüe e intercultural. In M. J. Bailón Corres (Ed.), *Ensayos sobre historia, política, educación y literatura de Oaxaca* (pp. 288–340). Oaxaca, Mexico: IIHUABJO.

Hernández Castillo, R. A. (2001). *Histories and stories from Chiapas: Border identities in southern Mexico.* Austin, TX: University of Texas Press.

Hodges, D. C. (1995). *Mexican anarchism after the revolution.* Austin, TX: University of Texas Press.

Jansen, R. S. (2007). Resurrection and appropriation: Reputational trajectories, memory work, and the political use of historical figures. *American Journal of Sociology, 112*(4), 953–1007.

Lache Bolaños, N. P. (2009). La calle es nuestra: Intervenciones plásticas en el entorno de la Asemblea Popular de los Pueblos de Oaxaca. In V. R. Martínez Vásquez (Ed.), *La APPO: ¿Rebelión o movimiento social?: Nuevas formas de expresión ante la crisis* (pp. 199–217). Oaxaca, Mexico: IISUABJO.

Lenkersdorf, C. (2002). Aspectos de educación desde la perspectiva maya-tojolabal. *Reencuentro, 33,* 66–74.

Lenkersdorf, C. (2003). Otra lengua, otra cultura, otro derecho: Un ejemplo de los maya-tojolabales. In J. E. Ordóñez Cifuentes (Ed.), *El derecho a la lengua de los pueblos indígenas:* Jornadas Lascasianas 11, No. 59 (pp. 17–29). Mexico City: Instituto de Investigaciones Jurídicas, Universidad Nacional Autónoma de México.

Maeckelbergh, M. (2009). *The will of the many: How the alterglobalization movement is changing the face of democracy.* London: Pluto Press.

Maldonado, B. (2004). Comunalidad y educación en Oaxaca indígenas. In L. M. Meyer & B. Maldonado (Eds.), *Entre la normatividad y la comunalidad: Experiencias innovadoras del Oaxaca indígena actual* (pp. 24–42). Oaxaca, Mexico: IEEPO/Colección Voces del Fondo; Serie Molinos de viento.

Marcos, S., Pena-Vargas, C., & Ruggiero, G. (2007). *The speed of dreams: Selected writings, 2001–2007.* San Francisco, CA: City Lights.

Martínez Vásquez, V. R. (2007). *Autoritarismo, movimiento popular y crisis política: Oaxaca 2006.* Oaxaca, Mexico: UABJO.

Meyer, L. M., & Maldonado, B. (Eds.). (2004). *Entre la normatividad y la comunalidad: Experiencias innovadoras del Oaxaca indígena actual.* Oaxaca, Mexico: IEEPO/Colección Voces del Fondo; Serie Molinos de viento.

Monsiváis, C. (2010). *Historia mínima: La cultura mexicana en el siglo XX.* Mexico City: El Colegio de México AC.

Nahmad, S. S. (2004). Aula Abierta. In L. M. Meyer & B. Maldonado (Eds.), *Entre la normatividad y la comunalidad: Experiencias innovadoras del Oaxaca indígena actual* (pp. 277–281). Oaxaca: IEEPO/Colección Voces del Fondo; Serie Molinos de viento.

Olmos, G. (2012). *Pintores mexicanos de la A a la Z* (2nd ed.). Mexico City: Artes De Mexico/Libros del Alba.

Porras Ferreyra, J. (2009). Las expresiones artísticas y la participación política: El conflicto oaxaqueño de 2006. In V. R. Martínez Vásquez (Ed.), *La APPO: ¿Rebelión o movimiento social?: Nuevas formas de expresión ante la crisis* (pp. 219–245). Oaxaca, Mexico: IISUABJO.

Rubin, J. (1998). Ambiguity and contradiction in a radical popular movement. In S. E. Álvarez, E. Dagnino, & A. Escobar (Eds.), *Cultures of politics/politics of cultures: Re-visioning Latin American social movements* (pp. 141–164). Boulder, CO: Westview Press.

Rubin, J. W. (1994). COCEI in Juchitán: Grassroots radicalism and regional history. *Journal of Latin American Studies, 26*(01), 109–136.

Rubin, J. W. (1997). *Decentering the regime: Ethnicity, radicalism, and democracy in Juchitán, Mexico.* Durham, NC: Duke University Press.

Sadlier, S. T. (2014). The tarpaulin and the tablecloth: Cover and non-traditional education in traditional spaces of schooling. In P. R. Carr & B. J. Porfilio (Eds.), *Informal education, childhood and youth: Geographies, histories and practices* (pp. 97–111). New York, NY: Palgrave Macmillan.

Sadlier, S. T., & Arancibia, M. C. (2015). Toward a society where everyone is always studying: Access at an elite Chilean research university. *International Journal of Qualitative Studies in Education, 28*(9), 1049–1064.

Sadlier, S. T., & Morales Sánchez, I. R. (2012). Open the doors, paint the walls and ignore the bells: Refashioning the post-movimiento classroom to foment "civic space" ties. In S. Mills & P. Kraftl (Eds.), *Educating for peace in a time of permanent war: Are schools part of the solution or the problem?* (pp. 197–208). New York, NY: Routledge.

Sierra Morales, M. L. (2009). Taller de estimulación del lenguaje y la lectura…Una experiencia singular. *Consejo Estatal para la Cultura y las Artes: Revista digital de la Biblioteca Central del Estado de Hidalgo.* Retrieved from https://bcehricardogaribay.wordpress.com/2009/02/10/%E2%80%9C taller-de-estimulacion-del-lenguaje-y-la-lectura%E2%80%9D%E2%80%A6una-experien cia-singular/

Smith, B. (2007). The state of the art in narrative inquiry: Some reflections. *Narrative Inquiry, 17*(2), 391–398.

Stephen, L. (1991). *Zapotec women.* Austin, TX: University of Texas Press.

Stephen, L. (2002). *¡Zapata Lives!: Histories and cultural politics in Southern Mexico.* Berkeley, CA: University of California Press.

Trinidad Galván, R. (2001). Portraits of mujeres desjuiciadas: Womanist pedagogies of the everyday, the mundane and the ordinary. *International Journal of Qualitative Studies in Education (QSE)*, *14*(5), 603–621.

Trinidad Galván, R. (2015). *Women who stay behind: Pedagogies of survival in rural transmigrant Mexico*. Tucson, AZ: University of Arizona Press.

Villenas, S. A. (2005). Commentary: Latina literacies in "convivencia": Communal spaces of teaching and learning. *Anthropology & Education Quarterly, 36*(3), 273–277.

Movement II: Patrimony

4

Marching for Patrimony

The name of the southeastern Mexican state of Oaxaca comes from the *guaje* tree (Norget, 2006, p. 31). People in cities and towns across the state love their guajes and other trees, in part because some are ancient and monumental, and others are endangered. Trees engender political and pedagogical movement in part because in Oaxaca they are patrimonial: they form part of the historical commons, the inheritance of all. Oaxaca is a place of trees. How heritage plays out across space and time is the focus of this fourth chapter.

This initial chapter on the movement of patrimony begins with a fallen tree. In spring of 2005, a hullaballoo occurred over a fallen tree in the center of Oaxaca City. A landscaping project, the Plan Paisajístico del Zócalo y la Alameda, stalled when an ancient shade-casting *laurel de la India* tree toppled over and fell into the façade of Palacio de Gobierno, stirring protests (Ruiz Arrazola, 2005).[1] According to one protester's testimony (Verástegui, 2010), the fallen tree motivated a protest against the impulsive remodeling, which had moved without public input and ended up demolishing the *zócalo* (p. 291), the city center's primary green space and a registered United Nations Educational, Scientific and Cultural Organization (UNESCO) World Heritage (*Patrimonio de la Humanidad*) site. Such negligence toward the trees and the park rallied Oaxacans of diverse social classes, such as bar employees, street venders, shoe shiners, store owners, and pedestrians, to take to the streets, where they served on rotational shifts to guard the toppled tree in the heart of the old colonial city (p. 291). Then, according to the account, the chief of the Oaxacan office of Public Security showed up with laborers and riot police (*granaderos*) who were geared up for battle in helmets, shields, night sticks, and gasmasks to haul away the fallen tree (p. 292). Though ready for conflict, the protesters sought dialog, as the *comandante* seemed amenable. Then a protester produced a picture of the zócalo in 1874 with the laureles de la India and called the trees "living historical monuments of Mexico" that deserved respect (p. 292), to appeal to the comandante's sense of Oaxacan heritage.

The destruction of the laurel tree stimulates public and pedagogical responses, which are interventions designed to facilitate change and create a visibly meaningful act in schools and in street protests.[2] Public outcry developed when citizens took duty shifts on the zócalo and physically obstructed the trees to prevent further damage and then approached the comandante, the top cop overseeing the progress of the governor's construction project. Then, one person safeguarded the trees at another level, by using historical photographic documentation. By showing the officer proof of the tree's primordial stature on the public square, important enough in the nineteenth century to come out in a magazine, he indexed the intrinsic historical value in the tree-lined central square of the state's capital. Here, patrimony becomes a movement observable to us: no individual, least of all an elected state leader, can willfully damage a tree without public scrutiny and pedagogical responses. As a public pedagogy (Biesta, 2012; Christen, 2009; Sandlin & Milam, 2008; Sandlin, Schultz, & Burdick, 2009) the defense of the tree's legacy in the public square exposes the contention between neighbors attesting to the antiquity of downtown, a governor's renovation project to beautify a city park, and police protecting construction workers. Featuring a series of protest marches, this chapter gazes into the social, political, and economic construct of patrimony, as it moves across events like the tree dispute above. The chapter closes with the practice of patrimonial counter-conducts, public pedagogies that call upon the words, thoughts, and bodies of renowned heritage, in ways unanticipated by official versions of patrimony.

Patrimonial Impressions

Competing versions of what has come before, clashing with pedagogies of current-day public education, may seem an unlikely friction. Schools, where most teachers work, is an enterprise of progress. Liberal, progressive beliefs and epistemologies that predominate in schooling demand growth from students, parents, teachers, and policy. In Chapter Two, we saw the cult of progress develop from the age of instruction (Talavera, 1973) after the nineteenth century formation of a new state in the breakup of the Spanish Viceroyalty and during the Post-Revolutionary socialist education turn in the 1930s (Raby, 1974). Additive notions of education continue to dominate a contemporary workforce development turn, as we observed with Oaxacan women cast as culturally deficit "grasshopper ladies" (Díaz de Cossío, 2011, p. 41) in need of school completion to take up better jobs. Similarly, the critical-dialectical approaches coming from the current-day radical pedagogies of the Coordinadora Nacional de Trabajadores de la Educación (CNTE) and Sección 22 also adopt future-focused education, as evident in alternative education conferences taking on new educational approaches as remedy for the nation's ills (CNTE, 2010, 2013). Outside Mexico, multicultural approaches to teaching and learning valorize socioeconomic status factoring in student learning; however, at present writing, it seems unfathomable to engender critical multicultural conversations without recognizing that learning involves a constant process of becoming more knowledgeable (Nieto & Bode, 2008, p. 52), especially when asymmetries in economic resources and learning expectations create undue burden on students (p. 11). This is to say that liberal, functionalist, and critical teaching look more toward the present and future than toward the past. In addition, considering Oaxaca ranks at the bottom among Mexican states in the globally comparable, business-model indices on subjects like the Programme for International Student Assessment (PISA) test results, Spanish-language proficiency, human development, and food security, a reader might reasonably wonder how a past-focused universal like patrimony matters in the movement of diverse inquiries in a book about rural Oaxacan public educators. An answer, which becomes clearer in the movement of diverse inquiries below, resides in how patrimony becomes a site of present-focused pedagogies and situates the contention for moral high ground on whose heritage matters more, and whose heritage, like the tree activism, is at risk of collapse.

Authenticity and Conflict

Patrimony drives a movement. Patrimony is an inheritance that refers more to the present than to the past. Working out a vocabulary around the meanings of patrimony, the focus of Chapters Four and Five, becomes imperative. Conflict over authenticity is the starting point in the movement of patrimony, as the activism around the trees of Oaxaca makes clear. The above-described zócalo construction project to beautify the historic downtown to promote tourism, and the engagement with the comandante over the fallen laureles de la India, index competing and uneven struggles over primordiality and vulnerability. The zócalo trees example is a patrimonially telling one; upon their felling, the trees are converted into "founding objects" (García Canclini, 2001, p. 133) for Oaxacans who came to the streets to confront police. A founding object has value not just because it's old but because it mile-marks a process that still has social currency. Such an object is also important because it cannot speak for itself without the active participation of its offspring. The zócalo trees witness the city's history; uprooted and dilapidated, they add authenticity to Oaxaca that they may not have had to give when standing. The laureles were not just any trees, but the sun cover of a main square in town, one that faces the stone facades of the power elite in the Catholic Church and the Oaxaca state and city governments. A founding object,[3] decipherable to passersby, residents, and visitors alike, enhances the patrimonial value of a site. Then the tree-filled zócalo

> becomes ceremonial by virtue of containing the symbols of identity, objects and souvenirs of the best heroes and battles, something that no longer exists but is preserved because it alludes to origins and essence. It is there that the model of identity—the authentic version—is conserved. (p. 133)

If the historical purchase of the zócalo does not naturally dwell within the tempered trees and emblematic lime green façades, patrimony is substantiated when the trees and buildings witness the topographies of conflict with the governor, the impunity of the political elite, and the sidewalk pushback of actors like the teachers.[4]

This monumentalizing of the trees and the public inheritance of the zócalo in general meet the national and international agencies that consecrate the sites' value by *listing* them. By listing world heritage sites, UNESCO locates historic places like the shady zócalo, replete with founding objects, as a bequest that our forbearers have made for all of humanity. The UNESCO World Heritage Committee (2013) praised the zócalo for its "iconic architecture and the buildings [which are] representative of a cultural tradition of more than four centuries of art and history,"[5] and the "19th-century buildings in [the] city that was the birthplace of Benito Juárez"[6] (p. 185). UNESCO's acknowledgement of the zócalo matches that of Mexican state agencies[7] who during my fieldwork celebrated the zócalo's twenty-fourth anniversary as a UNESCO World Heritage site.[8] Oaxacan activists rallying around centenarian trees damaged by the governor, and as we will see, the teachers that the governor repressed with police, turn to national and transnational organizations to suggest that the activists more authentically represent Oaxaca and Oaxacans.

Patrimony-as-authenticity accompanies another struggle for heritage, patrimony-in-conflict.[9] Flashing an old photograph to the police (Verástegui, 2010, p. 292) reveals the defaced trees in youth, a living culture of trees that coagulates when trees are felled and chopped up under police supervision.[10] A threat of violence against someone's identifiable cultural group can shape self- or other-designations of originality.

It is difficult to pinpoint what counts as someone's true origins without understanding conflict. Though a government-issued cultural atlas demarcates one cultural group in Mexico from another (Consejo Nacional para la Cultura y las Artes, 2010), Oaxacans living in the Zapotec-speaking Central Valleys may identify with their individual village rather than a pan-ethnicity like Zapotec. According to Stephen (1996), who has completed fieldwork in the Central Valleys for decades, ethnic definitions shift when politics shift (p. 99). A legacy of village-to-village conflicts in the Mixtec region, four hours to the west, makes *Mixtec* self-identification less frequent while living in the region (Nagengast & Kearney, 1990, p. 72) than across the U.S. border in California, where *Mixtecos* appeal to *Mixtec* origins when that becomes useful in the wider frame of transborder issues of race, class, and ethnicity (p. 77). This suggests that claiming an identity for Oaxacans depends on where a person is and how the cultural politics plays out.

Even as some Oaxacans claim different origins when traversing village, state, and national boundaries, others have claimed they have unique and aboriginal rights to be and act in their localities. Today, teachers marching against the federal government and facing police batons and tear gas have turned to singing the national anthem (Loyo Brambila, 1979; Santiago Cruz, 2010). At the same protests, the teachers shout out subversive *consignas*, rally chants like "*lucha, lucha, lucha, no dejes de luchar, por un gobierno obrero, campesino y popular* (fight, fight, fight, and don't stop fighting, for a government of workers, peasants and the people)," suggesting if they claim original rights to being Mexican, the teachers avoid acquiescing to mainstream politics. Claiming rights to be and act in a primordially Oaxacan or Mexican way has become politically and economically strategic. Politicians elected in the Zapotec-Spanish bilingual city of Juchitán, Oaxaca have addressed the public in Zapotec to position Spanish-only speakers as outsiders (Campbell, 1990, pp. 363–365). In the 1930s, Oaxacan carpet weavers petitioned the president to intervene when Japanese carpets began to show up with Oaxacan cultural motifs (Stephen, 2005, pp. 136–137), and in 2015, French designer Isabel Marant styled a blouse with Tlahuitoltepec embroidery (Larsson, 2015), which was denounced on Twitter as plagiarism (see #miblusadetlahui). In conflicting ways, appealing to privileged access to Mexican or Oaxacan roots opens ground for political economic action.[11]

In addition to demarcating trees, people, and designs as culturally and historically significant, the political movement of patrimony extends to immaterial expressions of culture. Defending patrimony in recent decades has encompassed *intangible* culture. UNESCO (n.d.) reports:

> The term 'cultural heritage' has changed content considerably in recent decades, partially owing to the instruments developed by UNESCO. Cultural heritage does not end at monuments and collections of objects. It also includes traditions or living expressions inherited from our ancestors and passed on to our descendants, such as oral traditions, performing arts, social practices, rituals, festive events, knowledge and practices concerning nature and the universe or the knowledge and skills to produce traditional crafts. (p. 3)

Through the action of intellectuals, like John Ruskin who was distressed over a Victorian building boom vandalizing medieval England or post-World War II rebuilders, who saw the Cologne Cathedral amid rubble, intangible culture under threat becomes patrimonial when experts are concerned that a craft will pass into oblivion. Pedagogically, preserving intangible culture is supporting the time, space, and action where masters preside (Kirshenblatt-Gimblett, 2004, p. 53). Distinct from the call to protect a tree or a blouse, this immaterial turn incorporates learning and carrying out the trade, how the "life space and social world" operates in schools, institutes, or galleries (p. 54). Recognizing intangible culture means recognizing a craftsperson as a "living archive," as a fountainhead of knowledge worthy of transferal down the generations (Kirshenblatt-Gimblett, 2006, pp. 179–180). Classroom teachers, as we will see, recalling their forbearers descending upon the hinterlands, supplanting religious faith with science, and turning peasant servitude with democratic participation, operate in friction with the ways educational reform and privatization threaten the Oaxacan teachers.

In preserving the lifeways of the masters, we begin to trace patrimony moving on the streets and in schools. Oaxacan teachers, for their part, often recount the bygone days of teaching in remote schools and militating for funding for free, secular, and universal public education. Such claims harken back to the 1920s and 1930s, for example, the summoning of committed young people to fix the social problems of Mexico through rural schooling when teachers became *cultural missionaries* (Santiago Sierra, 1973) who were visible through iconic block prints and murals (Museo Casa Estudio Diego Rivera y Frida Kahlo, 1999).[12] Teacher commitment to relieving the suffering of the rural poor endured long after this phase. By the late 1970s, a teachers' movement to democratize the trade union gathered force in Oaxaca and Chiapas (Yescas Martínez & Zafra, 1985). A 1980 teacher *manifiesto* written to Oaxacans, including the teaching force itself, lauded the immaterial heritage of the Oaxacan teacher in service of the public:

> Many have praised the Mexican teacher, locating them at highest levels of in terms of the truth and spirit of service … Today, Oaxacan teachers have taken up the glorious Mexican teacher (*mentores*) tradition of the struggle (*lucha*); [furthermore, as teachers] we demand the right to a life of dignity, which enhances the performance of what we do (nuestras funciones) and makes the development of the state and country possible. (Martínez Vásquez, 2005, p. 159)

Organizing for better working conditions, the teachers link their social service to the legacy of Mexican teachers of days gone by. The call for professional dignity is not just one of financial motivations, as the endangered teacher way of life is worthy of support because the teaching helps Oaxaca and Mexico prosper.

Three decades after the 1980 spirit of teacher service manifesto, the integrity of this civic commitment faces further challenges. During my research, a new policy to promote private education allowed parents to deduct school tuition fees from their taxes. This de facto voucher system inhibits the free, obligatory, and secular nature of teaching and learning. What is more, to deflect the centrality of the preservice teacher candidate pathways through the state-funded normal schools that have produced civic-minded rural educators, a civil service exam (Concurso de Oposición) has enabled private institute graduates access to public school teaching positions. The demise of state-financed, public-service teaching troubled many Oaxacan teachers during my 2010–2011 research, demonstrated in an in-service teaching manual (Cuadernillo del Taller Estatal de Educación Alternativa), that asserted that schooling in Mexico is less identifiable with Mexico today (CEDES 22, 2009, p. 7) for the activist teachers in the union

> feel and see that the people are moving in the wrong direction, manipulated by consumerism, alienation (*enajenación*) and the fallacies of the modern world. We see how outside ideas are regulating (*modulando*) a *malinchista* (favoring what's foreign over what is Mexican)[13] spirit and an immense loss of identity; to this end, governmental programs that generate spiritual and economic poverty unite. (p. 9)

Still, the Oaxacan public educator, by looking at heritage, can resolve this problem:

> We must attempt new educational politics which promote collectively learning our roots, so we can regenerate what is ours, listen to one another, to interact with nature and people…. [and to] develop culturally-derived knowledge which is directly connected the spiritual and the useful…. (p. 9)

Education, then, homogenizes our true nature and fulfills false needs. We need more of what we really are, and we need teachers, the living treasures of community involvement, to override the cultural forfeiture of our modern educational system in favor of our cultural heritage.

As a friction, patrimony moves when social actors struggle over what kind of growth and progress is to come. The Oaxacan governor can renovate a historic center with greater license if he claims that the renovation is to improve tourism, but the people push back when a tree falls, presenting the commandant with a historic photo with the tall trees forming part of the beauty. Protecting and promoting what is germane to a given place or group of people also relates to cultural products like an embroidered motif and practices like using Zapotec in public speeches. The lifeworld and performances of an expert in a craft have also motivated restoration efforts when that craft is in danger of extinction. Below, patrimony moves on the streets and in schools: public schoolteachers demonstrating against the inauguration of a private Catholic university and mobilizing in response to police violence; members of the public supporting the Oaxaca tourism industry and in opposition of the teachers' defacing of historical buildings; and teachers meeting in support of a sick colleague. To approach the patrimonial sway of critical pedagogy in practice, I close the chapter by presenting an example of how the movement of patrimony might look like as a counter-pedagogy.

Teachers and Police

Eating and Texting

One day in mid-February, I went to meet the teachers for a late lunch after spending the morning with Marcos and the sixth graders in Tecotitlán. Because of the delays on the road from the disturbances, I arrived at the restaurant after all had finished, but they insisted that I eat unrushed. All of the teachers had come from other cities and towns to Oaxaca City either to submit paperwork at the Instituto Estatal de Educación Pública de Oaxaca (IEEPO) or to accompany someone who did. Now a group of five sat at ease at about 4:00 p.m. and exchanged bits of news. The day that had started quietly ended up tense because of the teacher stand-off with the police;

this meant that my tablemates, keener to get updates on the disturbances, talked very little. With their plates cleared, Wendy and Lourdes checked their email and text messages for news, finding the violence still raging in the Oaxaca City zócalo. Wendy got a text and uttered as a reminder that President Calderón had come from Mexico City to meet newly elected Governor Gabino Cué and banking magnate Alfredo Harp Helú to inaugurate the Oaxaca City campus of Universidad LaSalle, a private Catholic university Harp Helú bankrolled.[14] Oaxacan teachers, fierce defenders of Article Three of the 1917 Constitution which guarantees secular, free, obligatory and universal education, maintained guarded optimism over Governor Cué, who had not yet completed 80 days of his term as the first opposition governor in eighty years. If the teachers felt sympathy with Governor Cué, they reviled President Calderón because of his 2006 electoral fraud, his ardent Catholicism and, most of all, his role in the 2006 violence. Calderón had just made headlines on the subject of private education when days before he provided a tax exemption against the payment of private school tuition. Here he got to Oaxaca on Governor Cue's invitation to inaugurate LaSalle, a private Catholic university that might draw students away from public ones. As we sat at lunch, the teachers caught reports that protesting teachers in the zócalo were beaten by the granaderos and that this event would provoke the Sección 22 to respond.

Private Education Affront

The indignation at the private university has context. Amid the morass of the bloody, multi-faction Mexican Revolution, officials drafted the 1917 Constitution, steeped in nineteenth-century anti-Church liberalism and science, which hit on two issues still germane for teachers today: free, universal, and secular education and the right to unionize and strike.[15] CNTE and Sección 22 justify the public struggle for education on these grounds. In all, public teachers for generations have formed a key part of the Post-Revolutionary nation-building project through the expansion of public education,[16] the patrimony of Mexican public schoolteacher. In 1911, in the throes of the Revolution, President Madero presaged the task ahead for the public educator by lauding the Reform laws of the prior century for setting out free thought and curtailing the power of the clergy (Monsiváis, 2010, p. 114). Schoolteachers descending upon rural areas would craft scientific awareness out of superstition and conduct a modern Mexico via sports, hygiene, and patriotic symbols (Raby, 1974; Vaughan, 1982). The Secretaría de Educación Pública (SEP), formed to deliver this to the peripheries of the nation (Vaughan, 1997), by the 1930s aimed for a science-based and communalist school for all (Montes, 1998, p. 23). Secretary of Education García Téllez in 1935 mandated each school have a "social action committee" involved in the defense of the *ejido* public land system (Raby, 1974, p. 59).[17] In this way, the rural school spearheaded teaching and learning through a curriculum interconnected with peasant life welfare (p. 48).[18] With this public, secular, and collectivist lineage, science and social action are ingrained in the Oaxacan teacher. With the visit of the Catholic Calderón and the billionaire Harp Helú to inaugurate the private, tuition-charging university in the territory of the Oaxacan public elementary educator, the teachers clasp on to the public and secular anchorages for education.

This chapter progresses through a series of events that surround the February 2011 teacher manifestation and stand-off with police over the inauguration of LaSalle University in Oaxaca and how various patrimonial claims underscored rival public pedagogical projects. Specifically, I examine the ways that teachers, threatened by the changes in their craft, take care of one another, including sitting around a table, eating, and checking text messages on the clash with police. I also describe a protest procession led by 70,000 teachers against police violence and showcase a smaller march in favor of law, order, and tourism. Finally, I close with how a sick friend and former mentor and colleague motivates a social gathering in Oaxaca City.

The Cross-party Meetings

Sitting at the restaurant with the teachers on this February afternoon, reports of police violence against the teachers kept coming to Wendy's cell phone. With headphones attached to his telephone, Luis had heard that the violence had led the Sección 22 to mobilize in the coming days against Governor Cué for sending the police to batter the protesting teachers on the zócalo. In addition to the inauguration, Governor Cué had also met President Calderón in the Palacio de Gobierno. Facing the protests in 2006, Governor Ruiz Ortiz had then abandoned the Palacio, carrying out his functions as governor in a hangar by the airport (LASA, 2007, p. 166), turning the "symbolic" Palacio into a museum (Martínez Vásquez, 2007, p. 45). By summer 2010, the palace balcony still faced the teachers' annual *plantón* where music, speeches, and consigna chants belted satire and scorn via loudspeaker.

The arrival of the president in Oaxaca on this day represented a conciliatory attempt to bridge party lines, which the teachers considered proof of elite leaders colluding against them. Calderón and Cué came from rival factions: Calderón, from the neoconservative[19] and neoliberal Partido Acción Nacional (PAN) and Cué, widely considered to have been fraudulently denied of the governorship in 2004

(Dalton, 2007, p. 78), from the Oaxacan conglomerate of left-wing parties unified against the Partido Revolucionario Institucional (PRI). The two may seem like
uneasy allies, but party lines at this elite level are blurry. Cué, for instance, was a loyal
Oaxacan PRI assessor, and assembled at this inauguration was Diódoro Carrasco,
former PRI governor of Oaxaca and cabinet member during the PRI Presidency of
Ernesto Zedillo (1994–2000). In his days before joining the opposition, Cué had
once served as aide to Governor Carrasco; the nationally distributed, left-leaning
Mexico City daily paper, *La Jornada,* reported Cué as making amends with his
former mentor (Herrera Beltrán, 2011, p. 5). Cué's obsequiousness, according to
Rodríguez Cortés (2011), extended to his treatment of Calderón, which inspired
the "rancor" of the teachers and others on the streets who in turn shouted a humorous consigna: "*Calderón borracho, la estás regando gacho* (Calderón, drunkard, you
are screwing it all up)" (p. 4). Finally, Alfredo Harp Helú attended the inauguration,
lamenting the "precarious state under which many Oaxacan schools operate" (Herrera Beltrán, 2011, p. 5). This exclusive congregation of private education advocates
compelled a small contingent of the Oaxacan public teachers to protest in the zócalo
where the granaderos attacked.

Figure 4.1: Mexico City zócalo and Felipe Calderón mockery. A sign featuring Felipe
Calderón wearing the presidential sash with alcoholic bubbles, saying: "Felipe Calderón in
illicit collusion with the mafia: 1. He stole the presidency. 2. He robbed the (now defunct)

State Light and Power Corporation and the work of 44,000 workers from the Electricians Union" during the electricians' strike, 2011. Source: Author.

Infiltrados *and* Trancazos

During my lunch with Lourdes, Wendy, and their colleagues, news kept arriving of teachers wounded by the granaderos. Wendy and Lourdes seemed dismayed at the violence, which benefited neither Governor Cué nor the Sección 22. Wendy suggested PRI agents provocateurs (*infiltrados*) had incited the blood-stained event, as the PRI had lost the governorship after 2010, and the failure of the new opposition administration served their interests. After 80 years of PRI governors, Cué's arrival to the Oaxaca state executive chambers in 2010 promised little real change. An article in *La Jornada* mockingly placed quotation marks around the term '"New Era"' of Gabino Cué (Herrera Beltrán, 2011, p. 5), suggesting that his politics were business as usual. Still, attacking protesting teachers would damage Cué, so it seemed unlikely to Wendy that his people ordered it. For his part, Cué's defeated PRI opponent for the 2010 gubernatorial race, Eviel Pérez Magaña, claimed that the violence against the protesters in hardly three months delegitimized Cué's democratic credibility (Méndez & Martínez, 2011, p. 7). Recited consignas and sprayed graffiti began to call Cué a "repressor" of the same ilk as Ruiz Ortiz and Calderón. Cué may have sensed the political danger of the police action against the teachers, for he issued an apology over the violent events of February 15. This information would come later. For now, upon hearing Lourdes's and Wendy's updates on the fighting between the teachers and the police, I made my way toward the zócalo to see the skirmish for myself. Leaving the restaurant, Luis, a teacher whom I have known for over a decade, was getting his own updates. In a cautious voice he addressed me, saying "they are still exchanging blows, trancazos, downtown," so "don't go down there, okay?" Out on the street with the teachers, though I saw military troop transporters filled with men in fatigues, no trancazos became apparent. Pointing at the men in military dress, Wendy noticed they were "special forces" to accompany the president. Despite the emails and text messages on violence in the zócalo, the soldiers remained off to the side in their vehicle, blocks away from the action.

To the Zócalo

Parting with Wendy, Lourdes, and Luis, I walked toward the zócalo. Along the way, the agreeable, professional, and efficient nature of the uniformed officers stood out. I have noticed members of the *gendarmería,* which includes soldiers and state and municipal police, becoming more present around Mexico. More uniformed men and women have filled the streets and in militarized roadblocks after the 1994 Ejército Zapatista de Liberación Nacional (EZLN) insurrection in Chiapas, one state to the east of Oaxaca. Unlike many other regimes in Latin America, no pervasive repressive system has taken command of modern-era Mexico. Instead, the state has maintained power via inclusion and corporatism more than overt repression (Haber, 2007). The teacher, as a tlacuache at the science institute introduced in Chapter One, as a cultural missionary in the rural village, or through their incorporation in the Sindicato Nacional de Trabajadores de la Educación (SNTE), formed part of this soft-handed and social form of control. Here on the streets and restaurants, I observed the teachers texting about the violence juxtaposed with the well-equipped presidential guards in waiting. The teacher and solider are comparable state functionaries: both take special training in public institutes and serve in ministerial agencies; both are subject to professionalization with reformed techniques and technologies. The state-run normal schools for teachers are, however, on the decline. The privatization measures of the recent reforms to education enable nonpublicly trained teachers to serve in public schools.[20] Likewise, the government, supported by venture philanthropy foundations, has expanded scholarships, as seen in Chapter Two, and incorporated private school options, such as tax breaks for tuition, into domains of public education. The military and police training faculties, in contrast, remain vibrant, and their graduates take on active roles in struggles around the country. In all, I saw the teachers were bitter over their lot, while the military and state police I found were polite and gentle. As I found myself civilly ignored or addressed with respect by the security forces on a day they engaged in a violent clash, I turned to ruminating on state functionaries in Mexico. If the police in neoliberal and neoconservative times occupy the streets during teacher protests, which remain constitutionally protected, could security forces be taking on a more pedagogical role?[21] As a green-eyed visitor and teacher in Mexico over the decades, I have found the military and police never as amiable as I saw here in Oaxaca.

As I approached the zócalo I noticed greater militarization. I stopped and asked two police officers, who wore camouflage helmets and were carrying rifles, if the walkway toward the zócalo remained closed. No, they said with responsive eye contact, "it's fine." Then I came to Alcalá Street, by Santo Domingo Church, a major stop on the tourist corridor. Before me dozens of officers swiftly detached the interlocking, metallic riot fences and hoisted these portable bulwarks on trailer trucks. Pedestrians beside me had been waiting for the way to clear. In a matter of minutes, the defensive barriers are stacked in the trailer trucks, the fortressization of the city, breaks down, and passages open up, just as the police had assured. I was standing for a few minutes at Santo Domingo, which had been a combative place in 2006. While I watched the dismantling of riot fencing, I turned to ask a young woman dressed in a restaurant uniform how long the street had been closed by the defensive barriers. She did not answer me, but an older woman beside her, who presented herself as a tour guide waiting to return to her museum inside a nearby church, indicated that the police and military presence was all "normal." She emphasized that I should not worry about all this, as it is for our protection, "so that there is respect for law and order." I asked the tour guide if the "disturbance" on the zócalo, five blocks to the south, was more organized, or if it occurred spontaneously. She stressed that it was just a little thing, one that's settled in a minute, that the disturbances in Europe are even worse,[22] and there was nothing for me to worry about. I had asked out of curiosity instead of concern, so I felt that she addressed me as a tourist who was preoccupied with safe access to the city. I sensed in her the same push to appease me that I felt with the militarized police.

The Spectacle of a Burning Trailer

When the security forces finished removing the barriers, I proceeded down the pedestrian-only tourist walkway of Alcalá Street, toward the zócalo. A group of helmeted male and female granaderos walked toward me, toting their night sticks and lugging their shields. One of them had the plexiglass shattered at the top of their shield. The column of granaderos strode uphill, bantering among themselves as they passed, paying no attention to me. I detected in them the routine weariness of the end of the workday, and that if I had walked into them, they would have parted ranks around me, broken shields and all. After they had passed, I continued toward the still, bodiless street corner by the Law Faculty of the state university where a pile of bonfire ashes remained in a smolder. Littering the road and sidewalk, I saw broken off debris of green cantera stone,[23] the color of the Law Faculty.

Along the way, it became clear from the façades that some of the stones had been cracked off of the window casings and thresholds of centuries-old colonial buildings. Ahead of me, as I turned the corner toward the cathedral on the north side of the zócalo, people stood as if cordoned off in a half-moon line, snapping pictures and shooting cell phone movies as thirty-foot flames billowed out of a trailer truck, the twin of the vehicle I had observed where police had hoisted riot fence partitions by Santo Domingo. The agitation had ended and only a raging fire cracked and sparked a few feet from the laureles de la India trees. Among the crowd, I saw a reporter on camera speaking into a microphone, saying, "you can feel the burning from here." The next day, the image of the burning trailer made the cover of *La Jornada*, above the fold, and I would pass by the same site, underneath the zócalo tree canopies, to observe that the charred wreck had been cleared away. Vendors had returned, and a *danzón*-playing band chimed the marimba at a *bajo el laurel*, below the laurel tree, event. Just like the swift removal of metallic anti-riot fences, the city had returned from battle zone to cultural and social space.

Figure 4.2: Oaxaca City zócalo, February 2011. Trailer truck in flames after clash between teachers and police. Note the laurel de la India, whose limbs are above and right of the vehicle hood and whose canopy extends to the left of the ashen cloud. Source: Author.

The Response of the Sección 22: Marching from the IEEPO

If the zócalo would return to the comforts and pleasures of urban leisure by the following evening, another teacher protest was yet to come. In response to the violence against the teachers and the affront of the private Catholic university's inauguration in the heartland of public, secular teacher dissent, the Sección 22 had suspended classes statewide and 70,000 teachers hit the streets. On the morning of this march, Marcos forwarded me an email that had been circulated among his teacher colleagues. Akin to the texts and emails Wendy and Lourdes had shared over lunch the day before, the message, forwarded to scores of others, included the copy from three news articles of the aggression and how it prompted the Sección 22 to sever relationships with Governor Cué. Tens of thousands of teachers, few of whom had attended the protest or faced violence on the zócalo the day before, had assembled in a matter of hours. Marcos canceled our scheduled meeting, so the school-based pedagogies I had anticipated observing in his village would have to wait, as the pedagogies of the march would occupy us this day.

Creating Rezago

To historicize the march, Mexico has a twentieth-century tradition of centralized education with a federated SEP in Mexico City. By 1992, two years prior to signing North American Free Trade Agreement (NAFTA), Mexico had formally deconcentrated some SEP functions to the individual states, the IEEPO becoming Oaxaca's SEP chapter, which to this day monitors and evaluates teaching and learning outcomes (Martínez Vásquez, 2004).[24] As I mentioned in Chapter Two, the Sección 22 has, in response, maintained strident critiques of the IEEPO; nevertheless, the teacher-dissidents in Sección 22 and the teacher-functionaries in the IEEPO will work in partnership, even as they clash ideologically. The antipathy toward private education at the Catholic university inauguration, and the ensuing violence against dissenting teachers, complicates the Oaxacan public educators' collaborating with the IEEPO, even under the new governor they helped elect.

As we have seen, the Sección 22 in my research has also opposed recent educational reforms. Specifically, the Sección 22 rejects the 2009 SEP textbook reforms, saying these new editions have transformed the free-of-charge and available textbooks into a series of technical manuals, alien to Oaxacan actualities.[25] According to a teacher trainer at a normal school, a math problem in the new textbooks uses Mexico City subway stations as contextual cues, while children in many Oaxacan communities have never seen as much as an automobile.[26] In addition, by officially rejecting the reformed textbooks, the Sección 22 also rebuffs standardized testing measures, which have both calculated and created the dimensions for educational rezago. The federal government in 2002 started the Instituto Nacional para la Evaluación de la Educación (INEE), which implements the PISA test, whose results funnel into educational achievement ranking (INEE, 2010). These data, driven by economic development mandates, locate education as both urgent and calculable, so the standardized assessments become seen as imperative, too. The results of such testing sound daunting, as Muñoz Izquierdo and Ulloa (2011) reported that Mexico had placed last in the PISA among the thirty-four countries affiliated in the Organisation for Economic Co-operation and Development (OCDE) (p. 39). Such statistics that present Mexico as in rezago often point to the southeastern states of Oaxaca, Chiapas, and Guerrero, consummate contenders for last place nationwide in standardized test rankings.[27] This makes Oaxaca the site of further educational reforms along economistic parameters and ushers forward venture philanthropic organizations like the Alfredo Harp Helú Foundation (FAHH) to promote alternatives like private universities in Oaxaca.

All this groundswell of educational reform depends on the creation and publishing of the dimensions of rezago. Elevated levels of educational rezago are presented as an offense to the human rights of Mexicans. Rezago surfaces in presidential documents (Calderón Hinojoso, 2007; Fox Quesada, 2001) and in the words of venture philanthropists (Mexicanos Primero, n.d.), where it menaces the hard-working people of Mexico. For this, the burden falls on the shoulders of public educators, students, and their families, ignoring the gaps in economic resources and teacher expectations that already overburden the children of the poor. Stopping educational rezago has been constructed as so urgent that former Undersecretary of Education Roger Díaz de Cossío (2011) used war metaphors in suggesting education is a "battle that never ends" (p. 41). The problem facing a state like Oaxaca involves other factors such as cultural deprivation of rural agricultural life, which often forces students to miss school (p. 42).[28] This undersecretary's placement of the problem is echoed by David Calderón, founder of Mexicanos Primero, who called for "authentic professionalizing" of teachers (Calderón, 2011, p. 44). The teachers, for their part, are well equipped with devices to contest this deficiency hypothesis and, as we will see, constructing the rural public schoolteacher as patrimonial to Mexico.

The Protest March, 10:20 a.m., Westward from the IEEPO toward the Zócalo

The march the day after the infiltrados and trancazos on the zócalo started in the mid-morning. Men and women took turns speaking via *perifoneo* angled toward the 70,000 teachers and members of other civil groups like the Asemblea Popular de los Pueblos de Oaxaca (APPO) who answered the call to march. Teachers passed along the crown of the road, many toting cell phones, texting, or speaking among themselves. In the front line of walkers, the Sección 22 General Secretary Azael Santiago Chepi strode shoulder-to-shoulder with several others, in entourage style, while other teachers in the multitude walked in smaller groups or alone. Cameras, from the long lenses of the press to the low-pixel cell phone of the amateur, snapped shots of the horizon of bodies beneath umbrellas and hats. As the front of the march passed under a pedestrian overpass, dozens of photographers and videographers peered down through viewfinders at the marchers.

On the two-hour path toward the zócalo via the broad avenue, the march pushed on. Transit police at successive intersections whistled and indexed oncoming traffic to turn away from the marchers. Outside of few transit police, I saw no other uniforms, in stark contrast to the prior day's drama of fatigues, shields, nightsticks, and trailer trucks of anti-riot fencing. Leading the teachers, the perifoneo pace car rolled slowly forward. Beside the car, speakers alternated with the microphone and denounced yesterday's repression against the teachers and condemned the ongoing neoliberal reforms and push for privatization. The rhetorical style of the speeches took on a persuasive polemic on the grim certainty facing teachers and dissident leaders, though the consignas seemed more diverse and playful than the gloomy speeches.

The speakers, through consignas and speeches, singled out several individuals as guilty of betraying the public. First, they denounced Alfredo Harp Helú and his bankrolling the newly inaugurated LaSalle University, shouting "we owe him nothing, he is not our benefactor." Second, they blasted the recent President Calderón decree to allow parents to deduct private school tuition from federal taxes. To the speakers, this measure meant privatization and a weakening of the Third Article of the 1917 Constitution. Similarly, they slammed yesterday's violence against teachers who were exercising their Constitutional right to stage public manifestations. They also critiqued Calderón's push for "educational quality" which further diminished the public character of education. Most of all, Gabino Cué and his cabinet became the targets of the consignas and speeches, as these local functionaries had received a public mandate for change after eighty years of PRI rule in Oaxaca. "We voted for you Gabino" one said, and "we want change not just in name but in the way things are done," said another. Other speeches demanded the immediate resignation of Secretary of the Interior, Irma Piñeyro, called a mere puppet of reviled SNTE president, Elba Esther Gordillo, the arch enemy of the Sección 22. Though speeches called for Piñeyro's resignation and insisted on Cué's apology to the teachers, the bulk of the rhetoric of the march had been prepared prior to the events of the day before. Yet the salient motive for keeping up the mobilizations was Cué's treachery, as his administration was in the pocket of enemies of the people of Oaxaca.

Recalling the Constitution, Dreaming of Sovereignty

> Today we, the teachers of Oaxaca, have returned to the glorious tradition of the militant
> Mexican teacher. We demand the dignity of life that allows us to carry out our tasks with
> greater effect and makes the development of our state possible.
>
> —From a 1980 Oaxacan teachers' movement call to action
> (Martínez Vásquez, 2005, p. 159)

The orators asked for a return to better days for Oaxaca, calling out unreasonable student testing practices. Chanting to support the vindication of Article Three of the 1917 Constitution that ensured "secular, free and obligatory" education, the perifoneo carried denouncements of the 2008 educational reforms and standardized tests which privatized education.[29] The Alianza por la Calidad de la Educación (ACE) reforms trouble the teachers for allowing private institute graduates who pass the *Oposición* exam to become public school pedagogues. The Evaluación Nacional de Logro Académico en Centros Escolares (ENLACE),[30] applied to the last three years of primary school and the first two of secondary, provides a single, nationwide measuring stick for the subjects of Spanish, mathematics, science, civics, ethics, and history. Alongside the PISA test indicated above, the ENLACE compiles data that compares educational achievement and rezago from region to region. One of the speakers at the march addressed this exact point, saying that tests that are standardized for an unfortunate student from the Mixe region, several hours to the northeast of Oaxaca City, cannot fairly compare to another student in Monterrey, a wealthy city in the north of Mexico.

This march followed the ways standardized reforms have met forceful opposition by dissident teachers. Oaxacan teachers have keenly promoted counter-pedagogies, including the self-managed and independently funded pedagogies discussed in Chapter Three and the national alternative education conference discussed in Chapter Two. Prior to the Mexico City conference conveyed in Chapter Two, in May 2010, the Sección 22 in Oaxaca held a regional conference to contest educational reforms and articulate a pedagogical response that would feed into the national conference on alternative education. Azael Santiago Chepi, General Secretary of the Sección 22, stated in the conference proceedings from the Oaxacan conference that "[t]he heroic Sección 22 cannot and should not act with passivity before the most lethal offensive that today is taken up against public education via the ACE. Faced with this challenge, the response must be immediate and definitive" (CEDES 22, 2010, p. 4). The conference also reported: "Mexican education is suffering a ferocious attack from the educational reforms

…[involving] modifying the articles of the Political Constitution of the United States of Mexico and the General Law of Education" (p. 5). The conference participants then went on to conjoin education to issues of national sovereignty as they suggested defending the "essence and spirit" of the 1917 Constitution to repudiate both the educational and state worker reforms (p. 6).[31] Then they asked for a "return to the essences of UNESCO" which proposes education budgets equate to 12 percent of the gross domestic product (p. 6).[32] Referring to the 1917 Constitution and UNESCO allows the teachers to take moral high ground and stand on juridical and organizational authority that trumps the current reforms fads. The reference to the 1917 Constitution and UNESCO locates alternative education as organically pro-Mexico and raises the Sección 22 to the level of a veritable political party with interests outside of teaching and learning. The march, and the education project of the dissident teachers in general, presents the public function of teaching as more ingrained in what's an Oaxacan than the staid textbooks in their reissued form and the ribbon-cutting power elites gathered at the Catholic university's inauguration.

Dissonance and Filthy Dogs

Still, if marching forms a core part of a teacher's way of being, how do others in Oaxaca see it? The choral harmony, the striking audacity of graffiti writers working in plain daylight, and the 70,000 mobilized teachers on twelve-hours' notice indicate that teachers speak in multiple voices. Oaxacans present diverse, often negative, opinions about the teachers. During the February 2011 Oaxaca march outlined above, one roadside vender toting a straw basket full of gum and candy told me that most people are with the teachers, as I asked her opinion on the marching teachers. Similarly, an older woman inside a shop on a side road by the march indicated that the teachers were angry about the day before but that people in general felt that the teachers were holding up the dialog with Governor Cué. In my research, it became common to hear individuals, even teachers themselves, complaining about the teachers' marches. When one veteran teacher told me that classes were canceled for March 8th, International Women's Day, she proposed that if teachers wanted to celebrate women, "they should give us a dance" rather than a boring march.

Since the 1980s, the democratic teachers' movement has tried to democratize the SNTE, a movement in which we have seen the Oaxacan Sección 22 among the most active nationwide. Through this, the public has had an up-and-down relationship with the teachers. One teacher, who worked at a politically radical rural normal school, painted Oaxaca as persistently besieged, not always in open conflict like the 2006 Movimiento, but in a "low-intensity war (*Guerra de baja intensidad*)." When we sat and talked over coffee, he related how in this conflict, the Oaxacan public tolerates the teachers the way they would a neighborhood "filthy dog (*perro roñoso*)." He illustrated this to me via a parable of the teachers as this filthy dog living among the public: you do not like the dog to be around so much, but it is around, and you tolerate it, even feeding it, but you wish it would wander off and bother someone else. However, when an intruder enters the neighborhood, as in the police raids of 2006, and kicks the *perro roñoso*, the people defend it as if it were their own house pet. The filth of the dog becomes relative to the aggression it faces at the hands of the more commanding and nefarious; over violence, annoyance turns to endearment. Another teacher would tell me how in the days of the tensest period of 2006, an elderly woman selling candies out of a basket on a street corner approached her to offer her prayer cards to protect the teachers against encroaching police (Sadlier, 2014). The teachers submit that the public holds the teachers in esteem, albeit with weary frustration. In the end, the teachers enjoy the people's support especially when they face repressive violence (Martínez Vásquez, 2009, p. 338),[33] observable in 2006 as hundreds of thousands marched alongside the teachers, only days after the beginning of the police raids.[34] Furthermore, it seems that the state, the public, and the teachers are aware of the limits and consequences of state-sponsored violence against the teachers. I asked Luis, the teacher whom I had eaten lunch with the day before and whom I ran across at the February 2011 march, if there would be trouble today with the police. Attacking the teachers today "does not suit them," he responded, as public sympathy with the filthy dogs can rekindle in outbreaks of authoritarianism.

When the march turned toward the city center, the bodies bottlenecked down the colonial streets, protected as a UNESCO World Heritage site. Along this path with high walls at our sides, graffiti writers scribed consignas linking Gabino Cué to Ulises Ruiz Ortiz while denouncing Felipe Calderón. I also viewed more sophisticated stencils of ski-masked faces, ones resembling Chiapan EZLN leader Subcomandante Marcos as well as a series of multicolored political cartoon-like mockeries of President Calderón standing on a tank, in an absurd military uniform that fit him too loosely, a recurrent graffiti image on walls all the way to the zócalo. To appreciate the work of street art better, I let the rear of the line pass me by. In the wake of the march, office workers and neighbors came out of their newly unlocked iron bar doors and inspected the street.[35] At the Universidad Tecnológica de la Mixteca tourism department hotel, a woman in a uniform vest and a teenage boy came out to examine the spray can tagging. Four hours later, walking past the same hotel façade, I noticed that they had covered the graffiti with paint that perfectly matched the red building façade. At another moment, a police officer curiously touched the silvery paint of one of the Marcos mask stencils. Marking walls in the historic district of downtown Oaxaca is forbidden and generates public attention, according to members of the artist assembly, Asamblea de Artistas Revolucionarios de Oaxaca (ASARO) (De La Rosa & Schadl, 2014), who post street art "to reverse the social order" (p. 10). Marchers left behind a spray painted and stenciled footprint that garnered public attention as they progressed to the zócalo.

By the zócalo and cathedral atrium, the teachers clustered in bands in their delegation nuclei, each with a numbered and lettered sign that marchers had toted along the way.[36] Delegation meetings of this sort often feed into Sección 22 assemblies whereby the delegates gather the opinions of the rank and file teachers then amass in the Teachers' Hotel to the west of the zócalo and come to a decision on the next steps of action. One teacher noted that the delegation gatherings in the zócalo for events like the march end up serving the banal functions of attendance record-keeping, the meetings functioning more for regulation than for solidarizing. Instead, teachers get to see and hear what others are thinking and feeling at the marches. The delegation meetings link the teachers with Sección 22 business items. To illustrate, in the last week of June 2010, I had observed the teachers in the plantón before and after a Sección 22 state assembly. When the delegates had gotten out of the assembly, the rank and file learned that the Sección 22 would end the weeks-old plantón on the zócalo and return to their communities across the state in order to observe the polling stations of gubernatorial elections and support the electoral democratic process in which Gabino Cué would triumph. Teachers in the march described above would take Cué to task for this electoral victory and the police under his command who attached the same teachers.

Arrival at the zócalo and the forming of delegation-based clusters marked the end of the February 2011 march, but events continued on. At the *quiosco* (bandstand) at the center of the zócalo, at the *mitin* (political gathering), a group orated and took pictures of others holding signs. They were not all teachers. I tried to get up on the platform around the gazebo, but men were standing should to shoulder, letting some pass while keeping others out. An hour later, by 1:00 p.m., the zócalo was cleared of marchers altogether, and business as usual returned. As the teacher Luis had predicted, the police presence had been hidden. The teachers had their day of marching, and now by the early afternoon, with the exception of the graffiti, the marchers' path to the zócalo returned to its routine.

I Raise My Voice in Defense of Cultural Patrimony

As suggested above, the teachers as filthy dogs enjoy a complicated relationship with the public. Many sectors of Oaxaca stand vehemently against the teachers as an organized group, opposing their marches and the absenteeism in schools. Individual teachers, even as they may earn community respect for their arduous work, also contend with the suite of political activities that the Sección 22 undertakes as a collective. The business sector at times has supported the teachers, and at other times it organizes against them when protests obstruct tourism, as seen below.

On February 20, four days after the Sección 22 march, an anti-teacher countermarch took place from Santo Domingo Church, where I had seen police removing the riot fencing on the first day of the hostilities. Led by a young bearded man with a bullhorn, a white shirt-wearing group lingered around by Santo Domingo in anticipation of the late morning march. The bearded man addressed 200 or so marchers saying that they did not want "complaints or denouncements but need proposals from the citizens." The marchers appeared to be composed of mostly men over fifty and women of all ages who wore comfortable clothes of natural fibers rather than the polyester and patched up garb worn by the educational marchers days before. A lawyer in her early thirties, whom I had met the day before, approached me as she joined in with the march. When I asked why they opposed the shouting of consignas, the woman next to her related that the group was from "civil society," neither against the teachers nor the state. This suggests that she believed consignas are a radical counter-position and that civil society groups are devoid of political positions. The two women joined the others dressed in white, and slowly as a convoy made their way to the zócalo in less than five minutes. At the zócalo, below the laureles de la India they circumambulated the square twice, avoiding the central *quiosco* where the teachers and the other militants often make speeches. On one of the zócalo turns, I heard the people in white chanting consignas: "No more violence; we want peace" and "Oaxaca deserves to live in peace," both led by the bearded bullhorn organizer. At other times, the marchers continued at a normal walking pace and then froze in a voiceless posed position when one person chimed a bell.

Business owners might seem unlikely to opt for social mobilization, but in Oaxaca and Mexico as a whole, there is an impresario activist. By the 1970s, in the wake of the 1968 Mexico City student movement, rural and urban working class, student, and guerrilla groups confronted the political leadership (Zafra, Hernández Díaz, & Garza Zepeda, 2002, p. 13), as Oaxaca and the adjacent state of Guerrero experienced significant militancy (p. 14) and business leaders stood up for their interests, too (Zafra, 2002, p. 83). In Mexico, the PRI, whose mid-twentieth-century political base had been peasant organizations and urban trade unions, began to cater to business interests for help undertaking his economic policies (p. 92). Then, López Portillo nationalized the banks in 1982, the business class turned adversarial (p. 101), while the pro-business PAN challenged the PRI over issues of corruption and waste (Meyer, 1992, cited in Zafra, 2002, p. 102). Throughout much of rural Oaxaca, the PRI has enjoyed a hold, even with supporters of grassroots mobilizations that one might consider at odds with an entrenched capital city political party (Stephen, 1997). The elite of the more urban Central Valleys region of Oaxaca remains a powerful force in the state, and when antigovernment uprisings surfaced in 1977, business elites would help oust Oaxaca Governor, Manuel Zárate Aquino.[37] There is no natural hostility between the teachers and the business sector. The teachers, struggling for salary and democracy, got paid by the state, though with greater mobilization, the business sector saw their needs clashing with the teachers' needs (Zafra, 2002, p. 95). By 2005, with the restoration of the zócalo and the uprooted tree, many Oaxacan business leaders clashed with Ruiz Ortiz. These elites today are more politically fragmented than they were during the mobilizations of the 1970s, with different Oaxaca-based business families supporting different opposition parties (Gloria Zafra, personal communication). By the time of this march in 2011, the Oaxacan business sector drew on decades of social movement experience. In addition, though some business leaders had supported the protesters in the 2006 Movimiento against Ruiz Ortiz, the teachers breaking off green cantera from the façades of the old buildings to throw at police disrupted the flow of the city, impeded tourism, and exasperated the business sector. The march sprouts out from this frustration.

At the zócalo, the marchers doing their rounds articulated their positions through Oaxacan patrimonial images. They carried placards with handwritten quotations of the fabled Oaxaca-born Mexican President Benito Juárez: "The respect of others' rights is peace" and "nothing by force, everything by reason." They toted a printed vinyl banner that read, "teachers, we want you to let us work," sponsored by a construction consortium and a placard that read, "there is no way to peace, peace is the way," all texts and sign systems common in peace movements. They also deployed the image of Juárez, a practice common in teacher marches and, as I show in Chapter Four, school reading events. Stephen (2002) noted that no one ideological stance holds dominion over famous Mexican leaders, and in the case of the most venerated leaders, like liberal reformer Juárez and radical revolutionary Emiliano Zapata, Stephen has observed the radical left and the neoliberal right honoring and deploying the same images for their own ends

(Stephen, 2002). Depicting Juárez has specific significance here, for the former president hails from two hours north of Oaxaca City.

After two turns around the zócalo, the lead marcher marshaled everyone together on the side of the atrium of the cathedral, the spot where I stood a few days prior to witness the torched trailer truck. The leader asked the marchers to introduce themselves to the people standing beside them so that each person could voice their views on the challenges facing Oaxaca. In this he talked about the entity of Oaxaca as if it were alive, an anthropomorphic presence rather than a site or a political domain. After the greeting, the organizers distributed paper upon which each marcher was encouraged to write down a proposal for Oaxaca. Several women circulated among the multitude and spoke to groups of five or six people, gathering the proposals. One man appearing to be in his forties penned: "Legislate in favor of jail for people who damage the patrimony of all, like historical [sites]." Around the people standing in the assembly, remnants from the teacher stone projectiles from the colonial buildings like the Law School at the Universidad Autónoma Benito Juárez de Oaxaca (UABJO) still remained, though the piles of rubble had been cleaned up. The architectural damage and the positioning of Oaxaca as a living individual situated the public demonstration within the dimensions of patrimony.

This version of patrimony involved progressive rather than nostalgic politics. The leader continued to shout through the bullhorn at the bajo el laurel site, saying that these proposals would be uploaded on the Levanto la Voz Facebook page. I reviewed the page the day of the march, which under "*información*" indicated that "we must make it so that Oaxaca itself lives better. If you complain, leave a proposal. If you can, carry it out. The ... group has neither political nor economic pretentions." Along with the verbal ban on consignas, a fear of a "political" project comes up here, as if to say that politics is what the state and the teachers do, but the group is striving for a forward-thinking solution to the problems faced by all. One Facebook comment echoed the call for the defense of patrimony by specifically railing against the teachers. In text-messaging shorthand, it read: "... *de que sirve k digan k son 'maestros' si no cuidan el patrimonio, k es eso de estar destruyendo la c.d, igual y no son todos pero justos pagamos por pekadores!!!!!*" (Levanto la Voz, Facebook Page, February, 16, 2011). This might translate as: "... what's the use if according to them they are 'teachers' if they don't take care of our patrimony, what's this about destroying the city, though not all of them, but all of us end up paying for the sinners!!!!!" The teachers, then, lack civil servant credibility because they destroy the patrimony of Oaxaca City. Instead, a peaceful and inclusive politics is needed, according to this.

The organized meeting of white shirt marchers led by the bearded man was about to break up. He said that next week they were meeting at the Fountain of the Eight Regions, but they should come respectfully and bring "balloons and placards, but nothing offensive," for "as Oaxacans we are brothers and sisters and want peace." To close, about a hundred marchers collectively chanted Spanish lyrics to Beethoven's Ninth Symphony. Instead of leaving, however, smaller groupings of people loitered, chatting between the zócalo and the cathedral atrium. I overheard a curly haired young woman speaking with strangers, whom she took leave with a friendly, "nice to meet you to," expressing disfavor with the teachers and the Asamblea Popular de los Pueblos de Oaxaca (APPO).[38] Ten or so similar horizontal chats occurred between the newly acquainted marchers. Another woman, a gatherer of the pro-Oaxaca proposals, instructed a group of women on the group's procedures, saying "we help by channeling the proposals" made by the individuals. The social aspect of this meeting ended up straying from concrete proposals on how to improve Oaxaca, and sound like a group of friends meeting bajo el laurel on a Sunday.

Still lingering at the assembly site below the trees, members of the press interviewed the bearded man, who said on camera: "We are a city that lives by tourism; we are an image that projects a good image for coming here" reported Ricárdez (2011, min. 50) who detailed that the business owners, students, and residents of the historic center of Oaxaca City made up the majority of the protest group. The same news report also gave a response from Oaxaca Archbishop José Luis Chaves Botello, who had addressed the zócalo violence of days prior: "Yet again, the violent acts of this week shout out to us that some do not want what is good for society. They do not want to step up and promote a better phase for Oaxaca" (min. 1:18). The Archbishop's comments, among others at the protest citing Benito Juárez's views on peace, designated a sovereign and rights-endowed Oaxaca imperiled by protests.

The kernel component of mobilization in the protests described above is the defense of patrimony. Patrimony here comes out at first glance as an abstract concept that is unworthy of a public manifestation. To start, the green-stoned historic center of Oaxaca, protected as a UNESCO World Heritage site, differentiates Oaxaca from its rivals and brings in tourism revenue. Discursive markers of patrimony make Oaxaca, like Benito Juárez himself, iconic but at the same time alive and unfinished. Patrimony may seem retrograde, a nationalist call for authentic origins, and marchers here did refer to Oaxaca as a rights-endowed individual, yet the marchers were struggling in the present. The teachers recalled the intangible heritage of rural education that they have enjoyed since the free, secular, and universal educational mandate of the 1917 Constitution. The marchers in white shirts recalled Benito Juárez and railed against the teachers who destroyed colonial façades as others had done before the fallen laurel de la India in 2005. The teachers feel that violence, the incursion of private education, and decades of one-party rule threaten their world as much as do the white shirt-wearing marchers. They are fearful that more disturbances might lead to a shutdown of 2006 proportions and reckon their world is at risk from the teachers and the state government. Both go marching, taking their solutions to the streets; both defend their dimensions of patrimony-at-risk. Thus, rifts over patrimony present an active fault line in which the organized teachers feel they represent the linchpin of popular power, while the white shirt-wearing activists from the private sector position themselves as protectors of a peaceful and tourist-friendly Oaxaca.

Wendy and *La Maestra* and Everyone Else: Teachers as Living Archives

The day before the white shirt march and several days after the Sección 22 march to protest the Catholic university inauguration and violence against the teachers, I got a text from Raquel who indicated that her former teacher, Wendy, was in the hospital. The health scare had mobilized a group of Wendy's people, all teachers, to travel to Oaxaca City to support their friend. When I got in touch with Raquel, hours after the peace march, she said Wendy remained in good spirits, and was now discharged and surrounded by "*los amigos*" eating a late lunch at a small eatery by Santo Domingo Church. Raquel invited me to stop by to wish Wendy well. When I got there, I hugged Raquel at the door and then proceeded to the teacher table to sit down. A group much larger than I imagined had gathered in Oaxaca City from across the state, from places as far as the homes of the teachers at the march a few days ago. At the table, Wendy was sitting in front of her mother. Beside Wendy, going counterclockwise, sat Antonio and then Clitlálic, who lived three hours away. At the head of the table sat Marco Antonio, Wendy's former teacher, colleague, and subordinate. I sat down between Marco Antonio and a veteran teacher whom the others referred to as "*la maestra.*"[39] Wendy knew that I knew most everyone but reminded me by saying: "you've met la maestra, Stephen, when you spoke last summer on critical pedagogy at the normal school."

All those present except Raquel and me had traveled hours to see Wendy and now found her recovered and engaged in divergent conversation from the casual to cultural critique. Raquel, who often uses the restaurant for her meetings with other teachers, ended up serving tables around us as the owner found herself understaffed. Because she was in and out of the back room, Raquel served us food and mescal. In all, this gathering involved a tight-knit teacher network composed of plural and complex modes of contact which united us on this day over food, drink, and Wendy's continued good health.

As I sat down, Marco Antonio filled a shot glass with mescal, and I was urged to drink my fill. When Wendy asked about my recent activities, I said I had marched with the white shirt-wearing group earlier in the day. I realized I made the faux pas of saying I "marched" instead of "saw," for immediately Wendy retorted: "The enemy?!" in a serious and inquisitive way. I was just there to learn, I responded. The rest of the teachers looked at me in silence, as they knew I had attended teacher protest marches and blockades with them. Wendy has a way of feigning scandal, especially with me when I make linguistic or cultural lapses, so it resembled a common conversation between us, and my offending her dissipated in a matter of seconds. The restaurant bustled. For several hours the teachers at the table energized the room in part because of the dialog between the owner, the special bottle of mescal that appeared without being ordered, and Raquel circulating the floor as impromptu server. Raquel had apparently spent the entire day at the restaurant, having met with María Antonia, the storyteller, and Elena, the novelist, two visitors from Mexico City who had participated in a weekend-long storytelling workshop with Raquel. Raquel took over the restaurant and maintained the prominence of teachers among the smaller groups who came and went.

The table conversation is an expression of the intangible cultural heritage of teachers. They are such large, obstinate, and loyal agents who bring multiple performances and roles into their daily lives as teachers. Being a teacher resembles serving as a community member in a village that practices *guelaguetza*, that is, the practice of mutual aid. Guelaguetza can involve practices of helping others during a harvest or for a party. In guelaguetza, individuals help one person, and that person responds by providing food and drink. It is important, according to Maldonado (2004), in village practices of mutual aid that the work is undertaken with pleasure, with mescal, and with different generations present (p. 29). The social, festive, and familial intermingle with a teacher's working obligation. Maldonado further signals that such village practices of work and togetherness are "equalizing symbols" even when social positioning varies (p. 29). This is to say that coming together over Wendy's illness involves a communal outpouring of support, shared gladly with spirits and food. In such a teacher's lifeworld, Raquel can easily go about multitasking in the kitchen without neglecting Wendy, in that the encounter in practice already involved work, play, and support. Through these kinds of social gatherings, the patrimony of the teachers becomes more outwardly distinguishable as a critical practice. The solidarity Wendy enjoyed in this chapter also emerges in Oaxaca through conflict like the 2006 Movimiento where activists "constructed a collective being ... [and] a political community" among protesters where people across the range of protest events saw each other, regardless of age, gender, sexuality, or political difference, as part of the same struggle (Martínez Vásquez, 2009, p. 338). The solidarity shown to Wendy has roots in the Oaxacan village life and in conflict on the city streets after the 2006 Movimiento, both sites where teachers have vindicated their collective social roles.

In this chapter I started and ended with the gatherings of teachers to talk about crises, one based on police violence and another based on a sick friend. These meetings assert performing as teacher: being together, eating, sitting, and seemingly wasting time in an educational system that gravitates toward greater efficiency. The eating sessions also mark people's comings and goings; when someone arrives to town you go eat. Food relationships situate the "civic space"[40] (Martínez Vásquez, 2009) that links teachers and creates opportunities for neighbors to gossip, ask for help, and find out what is going on. Such a space for teachers and other members of the Movimiento "does not have a formally defined or definite structure [or] personalized leadership" but "functions under the principles of solidarity, respect of autonomy [and] via its heterogeneous attributes, it promotes horizontality" (p. 345). With such diversity among the teachers, a set agenda is undesirable, and even unachievable. The marches presented in this chapter hinge on being together, knowing one another, and possessing a particular presence in the face of another. Being together as a social practice becomes a vital tool of reclaiming roles and knowing who is doing what, which includes issues of teaching, learning, marching, and camping out in plantones. This being together is well established in the teachers through the institutional affiliations, the Sección 22, and the enduring bonds that bring people together over specific issues close to them.

Patrimonial Counter-conducts

Unlike quality, examined in Chapters Two and Three, patrimony might seem a less workable teaching strategy. Patrimony, as we see here, speaks through the vetted, established, delinquent, and conflicted; it may be measured, identified, debated, and defended by experts, agencies, and pedestrians. Claiming a practice, product, or person bears patrimonial power is claiming the right to take up the good fight.

How does patrimony help render a text, practice, or idea pedagogical? First, patrimony is what we enact. On a classroom wall at the normal school where

Dalia and Lourdes taught, a poster entitled "*La Patria eres tú* (The Fatherland is you)" stands, one of 829,000 of its type distributed to Mexican schools during the Fox administration (Herrera Beltrán, 2004, p. 43). The poster shows the Mexican flag waving in the center foreground with the words "Our flag symbolizes independence, honor, institutions and the nation's territorial integrity. [The flag] is venerated by daily effort of all Mexicans—Vicente Fox Quesada." The flag that represents the fatherland is not just cloth draped on a wall or carried in a ceremony. As *you are the fatherland,* you may disagree with the government or feel unjustly treated by a policy, but the patria transcends the issues and squabbles and merits your daily veneration. Second, patrimony is not only what we do, but who we are. To illustrate, as described in Chapter One, in late May 2010, teachers carried a painted image of the Madre Patria in a protest march through downtown Mexico City. Officially the Madre Patria, the "Mother of the Fatherland" is an imaginary image of an Indigenous-featured woman in a Greco-Roman tunic standing as the matron of Mexico. The image of the Madre Patria adorns student textbooks and posters bearing the national anthem in schools.[41] We have seen how universal schooling has been a major vehicle for constructing Mexico out of hundreds of desperate communities and fashioning the Mexican citizen out of millions of bodies with ancestral ties to lands between Mesoamerica and the Great Plains of North America. Through this history, the Mexicanization of common Indigenous traits has been seen as a form of white supremacy, akin to the melting pot view of ethnicity in the United States and Racial Democracy construction of postracial politics in Brazil.[42] This is to say that, a generation after glorifying the heroes of Mexico's aboriginal past through classical European visages (Alonso, 2004, p. 462), the state *officialized* select Indigenous features to *patrimonialize* their hold on to power; they officialized this Madre rather than let Indigenous maternity remain unofficial and community-based. She became a visual standard to draw individuals and groups into the larger state. This is the Madre Patria—or one version of her—which, alongside the *you are the fatherland* poster, puts heritage into pedagogical terms and opens up the possibility of counter-pedagogies.[43]

A counter-pedagogical madre appears beside the classical, official one, in the visage of a radical madre carried by the teachers. Scores of dissident teachers passing through Mexico City, some of whom arrived at an alternative education conference discussed in Chapter One, would chant consignas against the state and in favor of the workers; they would attend work *mesas* and *talleres* on how to supplant the federal textbooks with more locally viable materials; they also carried a madre patria, an instrument of consensus when writ large, but now bearing features and clothes of non-assimilation, a radical madre materializes. The official Madre Patria in civics textbooks posits an "imaginary Mexico," instead of a lived one (Bonfil Batalla, 1996, p. 126). The Madre Patria, the countenance of Indigeneity integrity, self-constraint, and chisel-feature beauty, teaches active civic participation in Mexico. A child can kind of see herself in the Madre, or she can see her mother in the Madre. As far as this official icon taps into patrimony, an unofficial madre, a counter-conduct madre, becomes possible. The dissident teachers are aware of how authorities have imagined liberal democratic Mexico with figures like the Madre Patria, one forged of a uniform base stock of a nation and crafted into its ideal form by devices like the Madre Patria, the *bondadosa feminidad*, the lady bountiful *a la mexicana*. In her life-sized likeness, she marches, communicates in the multiple conversations and witnesses the participants' struggles on the streets

Figure 4.3: The Madre Patria, above image in white carrying a green flag, left, beside "down with [SNTE president] Elba Ester [Gordillo] and FECAL [President of Mexico, Felipe Calderón]." To the Madre Patria's right stands a muscular woman carrying a red and black radical flag and wearing an Indigenous shawl (*rebozo*), instead of the Hellenic white robe of the Madre Patria from school textbooks and nationalist symbolism. The title before the Indigenous women reads: "We defend." Source: Author.

and in schools. Her use here turns *their* Madre to *our* madre (see Figure 4.3). This is a public pedagogical rather than a classroom instructional use of patrimony. As we see in the following chapter, teachers turn to a national hero to open the doors of a school during a national holiday to a community-wide event.

Notes

1. The remodeling project in 2005 became a "watershed of great public discontent" against the Oaxaca state government (Meixueiro, 2007 p. 143).

2. In a lecture at the Universidad de la Tierra, Gustavo Esteva described a park in Oaxaca City, north of downtown, in the lap of the Sierra Juárez to the north. The park had been the water source for the old colonial city; the park's old trees in the green space had been overtaken by urbanization. A supermarket chain had appropriated the public park and had commissioned, illegally, the construction. Shrouded by darkness, Gustavo related that one night workers came with chainsaws and cut down the trees. Neighbors awoke to a park stripped of its foliage, and Gustavo would join a group who organized to halt the construction, by any legal means. It turned out that groundwater studies were needed to start a construction project; this forced a hiatus in more destruction to this public space. Even as he expressed enthusiasm over the victory, Gustavo lamented that the trees would never grow back. Hearing the activism around the natural spaces of Oaxaca tuned me on to how trees mattered in Oaxaca, by providing shelter and a link to the past.

3. As medieval buildings during Victorian England faced defacement, the Society for the Protection of Ancient Buildings began in 1877 to impede builders defacing English patrimony. The society's founder, William Morris, has inspired current-day professional historic preservationists to safeguard constructed patrimony (Chapman & Texas Historical Foundation, 1990, p. 6). The concept and legislation of patrimony of founding objects would solidify into its current iteration after World War II, as Europe lay in ruins. The newly formed UNESCO preserved books, artwork, and monuments as elements of "world's inheritance" (Musitelli, 2002, p. 323).

4. Living in Oaxaca, meeting at the shady cafes at *los Portales* (the arches) became customary; in my research, participants would suggest we meet *bajo el laurel* (below the laurel trees that cover the Portales) either because paths often crisscross the shady, protected zócalo or because the trees themselves are protected public spaces to meet up, free of sun glare.

5. The International Council on Monuments and Sites (ICOMOS) (1986), a heritage management NGO, further locates the patrimony of the space around the fallen tree within the realm of authenticity by recommending it for UNESCO, based on "criteria I, II, III and IV" (p. 1), counting the number of city blocks "classified" in "Zone A" and "Zone B" (p. 2) and by affirming that King of Spain and Holy Roman Emperor, Charles the Fifth, authorized the city's founding in 1526 (p. 2).

6. President Benito Juárez, a mid-nineteenth-century liberal reformer, came to Oaxaca City from a Zapotec-speaking village in the mountains in the north. His arrival to the state capital has been celebrated and critiqued, as addressed in greater detail in Chapter Five.

7. Mexico's Instituto Nacional de Antropología e Historia (INAH) was founded in 1939 to protect tangible and intangible heritage in Mexico (Yáñez Reyes, 2006, p. 48).

8. The National Museum of Anthropology and History through "monumentalization and nationalist ritualization of culture" (García Canclini, 2001, p. 120) crafts a founding story for Mexico in an accessible and a dogma-free way (p. 126).

9. To illustrate world heritage in conflict, Gillman (2010) recalls the Buddha statues in Bamiyan, Afghanistan, that were dynamited in 2001 by the Taliban (pp. 9–13). That the people in Bamiyan once endeavored to hew the statues from the rockface would not safeguard the Buddhas from pulverization. Listing the cultural legacy of a given community as a good for everyone becomes useful when products, practices, or notions lose favor with those overseeing them (p. 15), as was the case with the Bamiyan Buddhas.

10. Verástegui emailed me a video that appreciates ancient trees in Oaxaca, starting with the name *Oaxaca* coined by the Aztecs for the prevalence of *guaje* trees in the area (Oaxaca Fértil, n.d.). It also notes the mystical and curative magnificence of the *árbol del Tule*, which requires two score people with latched hands to surround the trunk. The video concludes with the report of a citizen's action committee to save an *ahue-huete* tree beside the Museo del Ferrocarril Mexicano del Sur, the railroad museum. Since the damage on the zócalo in 2005, trees have remained part of a strategy to protect the green spaces in the state.

11. Thousands of architectural sites in Oaxaca remain unexcavated, and are still part of someone's plowed fields, in the liminal space between the world of artifacts and the labors of daily subsistence. A week after noticing a pyramid shape on the north side of the highway just west of the turnoff to the city of *Tlaxiaco*, my colleague and I returned to see if what I had seen was a hill or a pyramid. At a collective taxi stop, a woman in casual, professional clothing advanced and interrogated us on who we were, why we were there, and if we were collecting artifacts in our backpacks. In areas where tourists are expected, an international-looking visitor is welcome, but to this person, we were not welcome. When our *colectivo* came, I felt like an intruder. My colleague and I had understood we needed to ask permission from *las authoridades* to go exploring in the fields, but it never occurred to me that a stranger in an open, public colectivo stop would surveil us. Around thirty minutes later, we were meeting with the village author-ity who, in clear, soft-spoken Spanish revealed it was perfectly fine for us to walk across the fields, his fields, to confirm that the hill was an old pyramid. Before we left on our wander he asked us to wait. Ten minutes later he called us over to the side of an adobe building, where on the coarse sandy ground a series of clay statuettes stood out which resembled the pre-Columbian artifacts I had seen in community museums in Oaxacan villages and in archeology museums in Mexico City and fine art museums in New York and Boston...."How much?" he asked.... I clarified that we had come as explorers rather than artifact collectors. ..."How much to take them away?"

12. Drawing on a cultural missionary legacy for teachers today does not mean uniform consent to state policy. For a contemporary example, NGOs promote empowerment among women educators in Pakistan, though the teachers rally around a family-centered traditionalism at cross purposes with the progressive NGOs (Khurshid, 2012).

13. *Malinchista*, a term for a person who thinks products from the United States and physical traits of whiteness stand for virtue (Norget, 2006, p. 57), derides a person for being not Mexican enough. It is drawn from La Malinche, an early sixteenth-century resident of the Gulf of Mexico who guided Spanish conquistador, Hernán Cortés, in defeating and subjugating the Aztecs, the preconquest residents of what is now metropolitan Mexico City.

14. For a sympathetic view of Harp's Oaxacan philanthropy efforts, derived from his surviving a kidnapping, see Holo (2004, p. 111). Harp Helú became a committed enterprise philanthropist after being kidnapped in 1994, promising that if he was released, he would "serve the neediest, enjoy every minute of life and dedicate himself to baseball" (Holo, 2004, p. 111). The FAHH insignia is common on event posters and in museum exhibits, cultural magazines, and projects to promote reading.

15. Liberalism in Mexico became a political friction of enlightenment and reason in the period after independence from Spain when the conservatives in the Spain-oriented Catholic Church and landed oligarchy struggled to keep their hegemony in the newly independent state.

16. Education and modern secular nationhood date farther back than 1917, to Article 18 of the 1857 Constitution, which was designed to challenge the stronghold of the Catholic Church over education (Vaughan, 1982, p. 17). By 1888–1890, a law and a national conference on instruction inspired innovations in public schooling. Rural educators would become an important part of the Mexican anarchist and Revolutionary movements that undid the Díaz dictatorship in 1910 (Cockcroft, 1967).

17. Seventy-seven percent of Oaxaca is public land, 47 percent of which is *ejido* (Eisenstadt, 2011, p. 29).

18. Scholars have identified the formation of the rural school and nation building as less radicalized and comprehensive than policymakers expected. Rockwell (1996) saw the academic and social side of schooling as Post-Revolutionary hegemony that borrowed from the more radical land reforms of martyred revolutionaries like Zapata but changed little from the nineteenth-century liberal project. Rural schooling ended up bringing peasant groups closer toward state policy (p. 304). To Raby (1974), teachers ended up serving on the front lines of federal programs, like the support of the ejido system.

19. Neoconservatism sets new public norms and rules for moral rectitude, law, and order. Prior to the 1857 Reforms, the Catholic Church, not the state, issued birth, death, and marriage certificates (Flota Ocampo, 1993). The state enacted policies of liberal secularism, particularly in education, until President Carlos Salinas's 1991 constitutional reforms lifted the prohibition on religious involvement in public

schools (p. 66). Anti-crime and drug efforts since 2007 have led to a more militarized Mexico (Main, 2014).

20. Elba Ester Gordillo, former president of the SNTE, suggested that normal schools should become tourism colleges to serve Mexico's need for skilled agents to serve international visitors, according to Avilés (2009) in an article that Lourdes handed me to describe the current devaluation of normal schools.

21. Living in Guadalajara from 1991–1995, high-profile figures such as the archbishop and the attorney general got gunned down, yet I rarely observed armed police. In contrast, my time in Oaxaca (1997–1999, 2010–2011) I noticed a visibly militarized police presence. Widely discussed reports of a counterinsurgent police force trained by crack Guatemalan Kaibiles (Sotelo Marbán, 2008, p. 81) and of plainclothes para-militaries (el Alebrije, 2007; CCIODH, 2007, p. 34) have put the police on the pedagogical landscape of Oaxacan streets.

22. The movement later dubbed the Arab Spring, well publicized in Mexico, materialized during these weeks.

23. Green cantera stone, emblematic of the colonial architecture of Oaxaca City, is some-times called "*la verde Antequera*," in reference to the city's colonial name, Antequera, and the green stone used in the colonial architecture. The public protested when the governor restored the fabled dance venue, La Plaza de la Danza, by replacing the cantera with cement (Martínez Vásquez, 2006, p. 141).

24. In 1992 Oaxaca Governor, Heladio Ramírez López, signed the Acuerdo Nacional para la Modernización de la Educación Básica y Normal, which, along with agree-ments made with the Sección 22, ushered in the IEPPO and the deconcentrating of administrative functions from Mexico City (Yescas Martínez, 2006, p. 25).

25. At the start of the 2014 academic year, education critics, César Navarro Gallegos and Tatiana Coll Lebedef, observed how that year's revised sixth-grade history textbooks had lost their critical content; the term *conquest* replaced the more administrative *viceroyalty* (Poy Solano, 2014), and the textbooks became "history light" (p. 36).

26. This same normal schoolteacher trainer with her student teachers in the elementary teaching degree program would publish an informal newsletter on teaching math, a *gaceta*, which paid special attention to playfulness and games. In all, the gaceta served as a compendium to facilitate student- and community-centered techniques for teaching mathematics. When the teacher trainer, however, shared these ideas with the Sección 22, she faced a combination of apathy and scorn. The union saw these teaching practices as not alternative enough for them.

27. The United Nations Development Programme (2007), referring to water security, explains to the reader how Oaxaca and neighboring Chiapas and Guerrero fall within the country's "poverty belt," as compared to the "more prosperous northern states" (p. 54).

28. As I accompanied Wendy and Lourdes on their supervisory site visits to rural ele-mentary schools, I observed that students would often arrive at school after complet-ing farm chores. In villages with an unstable year-round water supply, able-bodied

children are needed to fetch water and feed animals. In some of those same villages, the mothers would show up to bring food during school recess. In one village, during the middle of the school day, the mothers and fathers on the parents' committees were preparing for a concert and measuring classroom windows for curtains. If the village daily labor schedule did not match those of the urban middle class, this failed to signal a lack of village educational values.

29. The vindicating efforts around the Third Article of the Constitution in general, and the defense of secular education in specific, might give the impression that activists and educators scorn the Catholic Church. In fact, the Church in rural Oaxaca has long been radicalized (Norget, 1997). Such political praxis draws from the Liberation theology movements of the late 1960s, which had called upon the Vatican II view of spreading the gospel through intervening in local socioeconomic conditions. Rural Catholicism often dovetails with the communalist strategies of teachers and Indigenous rights advocates (p. 110). It has been the Evangelical Protestant churches, with their individualized resistance to village mutual aid projects, which rural activists have critiqued more than the Catholic Church (Maldonado, 2002).

30. The ENLACE standardized test in reading and mathematics, critiqued by teachers in Chapter Two, is taken by private and public school pupils, the results of which are compared and disseminated. The objective of the test, according to the SEP is: "to be able to know to what measure young people are capable to put basic disciplinary competencies in practice in the face of real-world situations" (Secretaría de Educación Pública, 2014, para. 3).

31. In 1992, drawn from structural adjustments from the International Monetary Fund and the World Bank, the administration of President Salinas turned education away from the Third Article of the Constitution. From this turn came the standardized tests PISA and ENLACE, which through their auditing calculations, found the Mexican fifteen-year-old to be deficient vis-à-vis those in the "developed world" (CNTE, 2010, p. 3, see also Navaro Gallegos, 2013). This has justified widespread reforms toward productivity, standardized tests, and "flexible" teaching as a practice of the civil service (p. 4). All of this leads the dissident teachers of the CNTE to seek "vindication" of education which has lost its "social and transformational character" (p. 8). Faced with such reform, marches and conferences form a part of the pedagogical heritage of the dissident teacher.

32. The proceedings from the national CNTE conference on alternative education three years later reiterated this demand for 12 percent of the GDP to go to education (CNTE, 2013, p. 15), having asked for 8 percent at the first of such conferences in 1991 (Hernández, 2009, p. 304).

33. Rockwell (1996) explains that community-teacher solidarity occurred in the postrevolutionary period when villagers adopted the federal mandates that suited them and supported teachers' labor struggles against the federal government (p. 317).

34. Osorno and Meyer (2007), in one of the most cited chronicles of the 2006 Movimiento, observed how the many repressive and aloof actions of the Ulises Ruiz Ortiz

administration caused widespread anger against the governor. In joining them, some in the Movimiento may have had no sympathy with the teachers at all but instead used the occasion to express other grievances.

35. Despite the support the public may have for the teachers and the legality of union manifestations, the march led residents and vendors to secure doors and windows with metal curtains and iron bars.

36. As colonial officials in Oaxaca incorporated Indigenous peoples (Bautista Martínez, 2010), church atria served as pedagogical spaces for becoming loyal Catholic subjects. One teacher educator described when he advised a student teacher's research into the mass rituals before rural colonial churches, like the one pictured in Teposcolula, with atria so large that thousands of Oaxacans could be baptized at once (see figure 4.4).

Figure 4.4: Church atrium of a Teposcolulan colonial church.
Source: Author.

37. Public pressure has ousted three Oaxaca governors: Edmundo Sánchez Cano in 1947, Manuel Mayoral Heredia in 1952, and Zárate Aquino in 1977 (Sotelo Marbán, 2008, p. 110).

38. The APPO, a "convergence of movements" (Esteva, 2007, p. 20), formed from long-standing Oaxacan forms of resistance, though it is "strictly contemporary in its nature, perspectives and openness toward the world" (p. 21). Proposed by the Sección 22 teachers, the APPO became a "space of movement deliberation and management," and assembled first on June 17, 2006, to deal with the diverse interests infused into *megamarchas* (Ortega, 2009, p. 20).

39. *Maestra* or *maestro* offers "mastery" status. Students in school often use it to address their teachers, as used here by the group. Marcos used "Maestro Toledo" when he addressed Oaxacan activist-artist Francisco Toledo. The term does, however, connote a practitioner rather than a coordinator or thinker. In other fields of knowledge, the preferred term of respect is commonly *licenciada* or *licenciado*, meaning, bachelor's degree holder in the study of law. The term maestro, particularly in the diminutive "*ma'e*" can become a classist insult, as it refers to master laborer, or *maestro albañil*. The term maestra given here bestows status but also with social class limits.

40. The civic space is neither a space or an organization itself but a "conjunction" or a "network" of sundry organizations and individuals that visibly gelled after the June 14, 2006, attack on the teachers (Martínez Vásquez, 2009, pp. 344–345).

41. See Carrie Chorba's (2007) analysis of the controversial NAFTA-era 1992 textbooks and their use of the Madre Patria. She relates the European sartorial presentation of the Madre alongside the textbooks' revitalizing of pro-international Porfirio Díaz (1830–1915) and submerges defenders of Mexican sovereignty, like the Niños Heroes, military school cadets who died defending Chapultepec Castle against the United States in 1847.

42. For the construction of race in Mexico vis-à-vis elsewhere in Latin America, see Wade (1997, pp. 40–47).

43. A figure of the hegemonic consensus building taken up by the federal government, and more specifically, the education authorities in the SEP, the Madre Patria might seem an unlikely point of departure for critical counter-conducts. Though Oaxaca, as across much of *deep Mexico* (Bonfil Batalla, 1996), respect for authority (*respeto*), and relationships of solidarity (*confianza*) coexist (Norget, 2006, pp. 46–47), while "selective use of tradition and projection of the past into the present" facilitates the appropriation of state-generated national heroes into struggles for autonomy (Stephen, 1997, p. 43).

References

Alonso, A. M. (2004). Conforming disconformity: "Mestizaje," hybridity, and the aesthetics of Mexican nationalism. *Cultural Anthropology, 19*(4), 459–490.

Arellanes Meixueiro, A. (2007). Un zócalo destruido, pueblo enfurecido. *Cuadernos del Sur, 11*(24–25), 139–148.

Avilés, K. (2009, July 30). Insiste Gordillo en cambiar de vocación a las normales; niega la venta de plazas. *La Jornada* (p. 15). Retrieved from http://www.jornada.unam.mx/2009/07/30/politica/015n1pol

Bautista Martínez, E. (2010). *Los nudos del régimen autoritario: Ajustes y continuidades de la dominación en dos ciudades de Oaxaca.* Oaxaca, Mexico: IISUABJO.

Biesta, G. (2012). Becoming public: Public pedagogy, citizenship and the public sphere. *Social & Cultural Geography, 13*(7), 683–697.

Bonfil Batalla, G. (1996). *México profundo: Reclaiming a civilization.* Austin, TX: University of Texas Press.

Calderón, D. (2011, May). Brechas y puentes. *Nexos, 401,* 42–44.

Calderón Hinojoso, F. (2007). *Plan nacional de desarrollo 2001–2006.* Gobierno de los Estados Unidos Mexicanos: Presidencia de la República. Retrieved from http://www.snieg.mx/conteni dos/espanol/normatividad/marcojuridico/PND_2007–2012.pdf

Campbell, H. B. (1990). *Zapotec ethnic politics and the politics of culture in Juchitán, Oaxaca (1350– 1990)* (Dissertation). University of Wisconsin–Madison.

CCIODH. (2007). *Informe sobre los hechos de Oaxaca. Quinta visita del 16 de diciembre de 2006 al 20 de enero de 2007* (Report). Barcelona: CCIODH. Retrieved from http://cciodh.pangea.org/

CEDES 22. (2009). *Taller estatal de educación alternativa: TEEA 2009–2010* (instructional material). Oaxaca, Mexico.

CEDES 22. (2010). *2010 Resolutivos del III congreso estatal de educación alternativa, 20–21 de mayo.* Oaxaca, Mexico: Sección 22, SNTE.

Chapman, W., & Texas Historical Foundation. (1990). William Morris and the Anti-Scrape Society: Reflections on the Origin of an Ethos. *Heritage, 8*(3), 6–13. Retrieved from http://texash istory.unt.edu/ark:/67531/metapth45427/m1/6/

Chorba, C. C. (2007). *Mexico, from mestizo to multicultural: National identity and recent representations of the conquest.* Nashville, TN: Vanderbilt University Press.

Christen, R. S. (2009). Graffiti as public educator of urban teenagers. In J. A. Sandlin, B. D. Schultz, & J. Burdick (Eds.), *Handbook of public pedagogy: Education and learning beyond schooling* (pp. 233–243). New York, NY: Routledge.

CNTE. (2010, May). *Resolutivos, IV Congreso Nacional de Educación Alternativa,* 28–30 de mayo (Conference Proceedings). Mexico City.

CNTE. (2013). *Resolutivos, V Congreso Nacional de Educación Alternativa, 25–27 de abril de 2013* (Conference Proceedings), Mexico City.

Cockcroft, J. D. (1967). El maestro de primaria en la Revolución Mexicana. *Historia Mexicana, 16*(4), 565–587.

Consejo Nacional para la Cultura y las Artes. (2010). *Atlas de infraestructura y patrimonio cultural de México.* Mexico City: Gobierno Federal de Mexico (Government document). Retrieved from http://sic.gob.mx/atlas2010/fo/ATLAS-1a-parte.pdf

Dalton, M. (2007). Los organismos civiles en Oaxaca y el movimiento ciudadano: Causas y consecuencias. *Cuadernos del Sur, 12*(24/25), 63–80.

De La Rosa, M. G., & Schadl, S. M. (2014). *Getting up for the people: The visual revolution of ASAR-Oaxaca.* Oakland, CA: PM Press.

Díaz de Cossío, R. (2011, May). La chapulinera. *Nexos, 401,* 41–42.

Eisenstadt, T. A. (2011). *Politics, identity, and Mexico's Indigenous rights movements.* New York, NY: Cambridge University Press.

el Alebrije. (2007). Las noches en la Ciudad de la Resistencia: Entrevista a "El Alebrije." In C. Beas Torres (Ed.), *La batalla por Oaxaca* (pp. 197–202). Oaxaca, Mexico: Ediciones Yope Power.

Esteva, G. (2007, November). La otra campaña, la APPO y la izquierda: Revindicar una alternativa. *Cuadernos del Sur, 12*(24/25), 5–37.

Flota Ocampo, E. (1993). Relaciones Iglesia – Estado en México. *Xipe Totek, 2*(1), 62–77.

Fox Quesada, V. (2001). *Plan nacional de desarrollo 2001–2006.* Gobierno de los Estados Unidos Mexicanos: Presidencia de la República. Retrieved from http://bibliotecadigital.conevyt.org. mx/colecciones/conevyt/plan_desarrollo.pdf

García Canclini, N. (2001). *Hybrid cultures: Strategies for entering and leaving modernity* (fourth printing). Minneapolis, MN: University of Minnesota Press.

Gillman, D. (2010). *The idea of cultural heritage.* New York, NY: Cambridge University Press.

Haber, P. L. (2007). *Power from experience: Urban popular movements in late twentieth-century Mexico.* University Park, PA: Pennsylvania State University Press.

Hernández, F. G. (2009). La educación alternativa y el movimiento pedagógico en el discurso de los maestros democráticos de Oaxaca, como contexto de la educación bilingüe e intercultural. In M. J. Bailón Corres (Ed.), *Ensayos sobre historia, política, educación y literatura de Oaxaca* (pp. 288–340). Oaxaca, Mexico: IIHUABJO.

Herrera Beltrán, C. (2004, February 12). Con frases de Fox, la SEP viste salones de clase. *La jornada* (Newspaper). Retrieved from http://www.jornada.unam.mx/2004/02/12/04021202.pdf

Herrera Beltrán, C. (2011, February 16). Al iniciar la "nueva era", Oaxaca recibió entre protestas a Calderón. *La jornada* (Newspaper). Retrieved from http://www.jornada.unam. mx/2011/02/16/politica/005n1pol

Holo, S. (2004). *Oaxaca at the crossroads: Managing memory, negotiating change.* Washington, DC: Smithsonian Books.

ICOMOS. (1986). *The city of Oaxaca, the archaeological site of Monte Alban and the site of Cuilapan.* World Heritage List, 415. Retrieved from file:///C:/Users/ssadlier/Down loads/415-ICOMOS-478-en.pdf

INEE. (2010). *El derecho a la educación en México: Informe 2009.* Mexico City, Mexico.

Khurshid, A. (2012). A transnational community of Pakistani Muslim women: Narratives of rights, honor, and wisdom in a women's education project. *Anthropology & Education Quarterly, 43*(3), 235–252.

Kirshenblatt-Gimblett, B. (2004). Intangible heritage as metacultural production. *Museum International, 56*(1–2), 52–65.

Kirshenblatt-Gimblett, B. (2006). World heritage and cultural economics. In I. Karp & Rockefeller Foundation (Eds.), *Museum frictions: Public cultures/global transformations* (pp. 161–202). Durham, NC: Duke University Press.

Larsson, N. (2015, June 17). Inspiration or plagiarism? Mexicans seek reparations for French designer's look-alike blouse. *The Guardian.* Retrieved from http://www.theguardian. com/global-development-professionals-network/2015/jun/17/mexican-mixe-blouse-isa bel-marant

LASA. (2007). Violaciones contra la libertad académica y de expresión en Oaxaca de Juárez: Informe presentado por la delegación de la Asociación de Estudios Latinoamericanos (LASA) encargada de investigar los hechos relacionados con el impacto del conflicto social del año 2006. *Cuadernos del Sur, 11*(24–25), 155–171.

Levanto la Voz. (n.d.). Facebook page. Retrieved from http://es-la.facebook.com/pages/Levanto-la-voz/100447570010778

Loyo Brambila, A. (1979). *El movimiento magisterial de 1958 en México*. Mexico City: Ediciones Era.

Main, A. (2014). The U.S. re-militarization of Central America and Mexico. *NACLA Report on the Americas*, *47*(2), 65–70.

Maldonado, B. (2002). *Los indios en las aulas: Dinámica de dominación y resistencia en Oaxaca*. Mexico City: Instituto Nacional de Antropología e Historia.

Maldonado, B. (2004). Comunalidad y educación en Oaxaca indígenas. In L. M. Meyer & B. Maldonado (Eds.), *Entre la normatividad y la comunalidad: Experiencias innovadoras del Oaxaca indígena actual* (pp. 24–42). Oaxaca, Mexico: IEEPO/Colección Voces del Fondo; Serie Molinos de viento.

Martínez Vásquez, V. R. (2004). *La educación en Oaxaca*. Oaxaca, Mexico: IISUABJO.

Martínez Vásquez, V. R. (2005). ¡No que no, sí que sí!: Testimonios y crónicas del movimiento magisterial oaxaqueño. Oaxaca, Mexico: SNTE.

Martínez Vásquez, V. R. (2006). Movimiento magisterial y crisis política en Oaxaca. In J. V. Cortés (Ed.), *Educación sindicalismo y gobernabilidad en Oaxaca* (pp. 125–149). Oaxaca, Mexico: SNTE.

Martínez Vásquez, V. R. (2007). Crisis política en Oaxaca. *Cuadernos del Sur*, *11*(24–25), 39–62.

Martínez Vásquez, V. R. (2009). Antinomias y perspectivas del movimiento popular en Oaxaca. In V. R. Martínez Vásquez (Ed.), *La APPO: ¿Rebelión o movimiento social?: Nuevas formas de expresión ante la crisis* (pp. 329–347). Oaxaca, Mexico: IISUABJO.

Méndez, E., & Martínez, F. (2011, February 16). Exigen PRI, PRD y PT investigar la "agresión". *La Jornada*, year 27, number 9523.

Mexicanos Primero. (n.d.). ¿En qué creemos? Retrieved from http://www.mexicanosprimero.org/mexicanos-primero/ien-que-creemos.html

Monsiváis, C. (2010). *Historia mínima: La cultura mexicana en el siglo XX*. Mexico City: El Colegio de México AC.

Montes, O. N. E. (1998). *La educación socialista en el Estado de México, 1934–1940: Una historia olvidada*. Zinacantepec, Mexico: Colegio Mexiquense.

Muñoz Izquierdo, C., & Ulloa M. I. (2011, May). Últimos en la Prueba PISA. *Nexos*, *401*, 39–40.

Museo Casa Estudio Diego Rivera y Frida Kahlo. (1999). *Misiones culturales: Los años utópicos 1920–1938*. Mexico City: Consejo Nacional para la Cultura y las Artes.

Musitelli, J. (2002). World heritage, between universalism and globalization. *International Journal of Cultural Property*, *11*(02), 323–336.

Nagengast, C., & Kearney, M. (1990, January 1). Mixtec ethnicity: Social identity, political consciousness, and political activism. *Latin American Research Review*, *25*(2), 61–91.

Navaro Gallegos, C. (2013). La reforma educativa: Despojo y castigo constitucional al magisterio. *El Cotidiano*, *179*, 77–98.

Nieto, S., & Bode, P. (2008). *Affirming diversity: The sociopolitical context of multicultural education* (Custom ed.). Boston, MA: Pearson.

Norget, K. (1997). The politics of liberation: The popular church, Indigenous theology, and grassroots mobilization in Oaxaca, Mexico. *Latin American Perspectives*, *24*(5), 96–127.

Norget, K. (2006). *Days of death, days of life: Ritual in the popular culture of Oaxaca*. New York, NY: Columbia University Press.

Oaxaca Fértil. (n.d.). *El árbol patrimonio vivo de la humanidad parte 1* (video). Accessed from https://www.youtube.com/watch?v=5t_Q8IiGnME

Ortega, J. (2009). La crisis de la hegemonía en Oaxaca: El conflicto político de 2006. In V. R. Martínez Vásquez (Ed.), *La APPO: ¿Rebelión o movimiento social?: Nuevas formas de expresión ante la crisis* (pp. 11–44). Oaxaca, Mexico: IISUABJO.

Osorno, D. E., & Meyer, L. (2007). *Oaxaca sitiada: La primera Insurrección del siglo XXI*. Mexico City: Random House Mondadori.

Poy Solano, L. (2014, August 11). Convirtieron los libros de texto en "informes gubernamentales". Retrieved from http://www.jornada.unam.mx/2014/08/11/sociedad/036n1soc

Raby, D. L. (1974). *Educación y revolución social en México*. Mexico City: Sep-Setentas.

Ricárdez, A. (2011, February 21). Marchan en Oaxaca por la paz. *El Universal*. Retrieved from http://www.youtube.com/watch?v=sjfLPq-yvUQ

Rockwell, E. (1996). Keys to appropriation: Rural schooling in Mexico. In B. Levinson, D. E. Foley, & D. C. Holland (Eds.), *Cultural production of the educated person: Critical ethnographies of schooling and local practice* (pp. 301–324). Albany, NY: State University of New York Press.

Rodríguez Cortés, R. (2011, February 21). Gran angular: De la farsa a la crisis. *El Correo de Oaxaca*, 4(199), 4.

Ruiz Arrazola, V. (2005, June 29). Retiran artistas proyecto para el zócalo de Oaxaca: Aducen insultos y falta de respeto del comité de vigilancia. *La Jornada*. Retrieved from http://www.jornada.unam.mx/2005/06/29/index.php?section=estados&article=041n1est

Sadlier, S. T. (2014). The tarpaulin and the tablecloth: Cover and non-traditional education in traditional spaces of schooling. In P. R. Carr & B. J. Porfilio (Eds.), *Informal education, childhood and youth: Geographies, histories and practices* (pp. 97–111). New York, NY: Palgrave Macmillan.

Sandlin, J. A., & Milam, J. L. (2008). 'Mixing pop (culture) and politics': Cultural resistance, cultural jamming, and anti-consumption activism as critical public pedagogy. *Curriculum Inquiry*, 38(3), 323–350.

Sandlin, J. A., Schultz, B. D., & Burdick J. (Eds.). (2009). *Handbook of public pedagogy: Education and learning beyond schooling*. New York, NY: Routledge.

Santiago Cruz, R. M. (2010). 14 de Junio: La unidad popular. In M. A. Damián (Ed.), *Educación popular: Apuntes de una experiencia liberadora* (pp. 62–67). Oaxaca, Mexico: La Mano.

Santiago Sierra, A. (1973). *Las Misiones Culturales*. (SEP/Setentas Number 113). Mexico City: Secretaría de Educación Pública.

Secretaría de Educación Pública. (2014). *Educacion Media Superior. Preguntas frequentes*. (Government website). Mexico City: SEP. Retrieved from http://www.enlace.sep.gob.mx/ms/preguntas_frecuentes/

Sotelo Marbán, J. (2008). *Oaxaca: Insurgencia civil y terrorismo de estado*. Mexico City: Era.

Stephen, L. (1996). The creation and recreation of ethnicity: Lessons from the Zapotec and Mixtec of Oaxaca. In H. Campbell (Ed.), *The politics of ethnicity in southern Mexico* (pp. 99–132). Nashville, TN: Vanderbilt University.

Stephen, L. (1997). Pro-Zapatista and pro-PRI: Resolving the contradictions of Zapatismo in rural Oaxaca. *Latin American Research Review, 32*(2), 41–70.

Stephen, L. (2002). *¡Zapata Lives!: Histories and cultural politics in Southern Mexico.* Berkeley, CA: University of California Press.

Stephen, L. (2005). *Zapotec women: Gender, class, and ethnicity in globalized Oaxaca.* Durham, NC: Duke University Press.

Talavera, A. (1973). *Liberalismo y educación.* Mexico City: SEP, Dirección General de Educación Audiovisual y Divulgación.

The United Nations Development Programme. (2007). *Human development report 2006 published for the United Nations Development Programme (UNDP) beyond scarcity: Power, poverty and the global water crisis* (Report). New York, NY: Palgrave Macmillan. Retrieved from file:///C:/Users/ssadlier/Downloads/HDR-2006-Beyond%20scarcity-Power-poverty-and-the-global-water-crisis.pdf

UNESCO World Heritage Committee. (2013, May 17). *Convention concerning the production of the world cultural and natural heritage. Thirty-seventh session 16 – 27 June 2013.* (Government Document). Retrieved from: https://whc.unesco.org/archive/2013/whc13-37com-8E-en.pdf

UNESCO. (n.d.). *What is intangible cultural heritage?* (Web page). Retrieved from https://ich.unesco.org/doc/src/01851-EN.pdf

Vaughan, M. K. (1982). *The state, education and social class in Mexico 1880–1928.* DeKalb, IL: Northern Illinois University Press.

Vaughan, M. K. (1997). *Cultural politics in revolution: Teachers, peasants, and schools in Mexico, 1930–1940.* Tucson, AZ: University of Arizona Press.

Verástegui, F. (2010). Oaxaca: Arboles y resistencia civil. In I. Yescas Martínez & C. Sánchez Islas (Eds.), *Oaxaca 2010: Voces de la transición* (pp. 290–297). Oaxaca, Mexico: Carteles Editores.

Wade, P. (1997). *Race and ethnicity in Latin America.* London: Pluto Press.

Yáñez Reyes, S. (2006). El Instituto Nacional de Antropología e Historia: Antecedentes, trayectoria y cambios a partir de la creación del CONACULTA. *Cuicuilco, 13*(38), 47–72.

Yescas Martínez, I. (2006). *Al cielo por asalto: (Notas sobre el movimiento magisterial de Oaxaca).* In J. V. Cortés (Ed.), *Educación, sindicalismo y gobernabilidad en Oaxaca* (pp. 19–31). Oaxaca, Mexico: SNTE/Editorial del Magisterio Benito Juárez.

Yescas Martínez, I., & Zafra, G. (1985). *La insurgencia magisterial en Oaxaca 1980.* Oaxaca, Mexico: IISUABJO.

Zafra, G. (2002). Los empresarios en y contra los movimientos sociales. In G. Zafra, J. Hernández Díaz, & M. Garza Zepeda (Eds.), *Organización popular y oposición empresarial: Manifestaciones de la acción colectiva en Oaxaca* (pp. 79–110). México: Plaza y Valdés Editores.

Zafra, G., Hernández Díaz, J., & Garza Zepeda, M. (2002). *Organización Popular y oposición empresarial: Manifestaciones de la acción colectiva en Oaxaca.* Mexico City: Plaza y Valdés Editores.

5

Benito Juárez as Pedagogical Package

"*¡Si Juárez viviera, a Gabino le escupiera!*"
(If Juárez were alive, he would spit on [Oaxacan Governor] Gabino [Cué]!)

      —Oaxacan teachers' rally chant, February 2011, Oaxaca City

"*Nada con la fuerza todo con la razón—Benito Juárez*"
(Nothing by force, everything with reasoning—Benito Juárez)

    —Pro-business sector and anti-teacher rally placard, February 2011, Oaxaca City

During the marches discussed in Chapter Four, I noticed the two epigraphs above whereby the two opposing factions, the teachers and the small business owners, summoned up the same Benito Juárez for their cause. Recalling how celebrating heroes and holidays has been viewed as a noncritical variety of multicultural education, I paused at the protest uses of Juárez and took greater notice as sixth-grade teachers taught through the historical figure. This chapter recognizes a call for a politically engaged epistemology and praxis that is articulated by multicultural educators (Amosa & Gorski, 2008; Banks, 2008; McGee Banks & Banks, 1995; Nieto, 2010) but signals how summoning up Oaxacan patrimony through Juárez has become a galvanizing device in a critical multicultural intervention in Tecotitlán Elementary School.

Free Us of the Weight of Juárez

Benito Juárez (1806–1872) holds a revered place in Mexican political history, and his origins in Oaxaca enable the state to claim him as an illustrious personage. The International Council on Monuments and Sites (ICOMOS, 1986) deemed downtown Oaxaca City worthy of a United Nations Educational, Scientific and Cultural Organization (UNESCO) World Heritage site designation, in part because of its association with Benito Juárez, whose visage beyond Oaxaca is emblematic. "He's the Mexican Abraham Lincoln" one person once told me. This presidential comparison does not resonate exclusively based on the two presidents' humble origins but instead is based on their roles in keeping their nations together in the face of war, or more particularly, in signifying national unity in the political projects that followed them. The political weight of liberal reformist President Juárez is best understood in the ways others have used him, Charles Weeks (1987) suggesting, "Juárez dead was worth more than Juárez alive" (p. 80).[1] In the decades after his death, conservative and liberal political factions began to draw on the Juárez legacy to legitimize their regimes. When in 1903 conservative historian Francisco Bulnes derided Juárez's leadership during the French invasion of the 1860s, popular support for Juárez turned the former president into a liberal hero (p. 70). As disparate intellectuals and politicians over the ensuing century, from the anarchist Flores Magón brothers to status quo leaders in the Partido Revolucionario Institucional (PRI), would laud Juárez, his figure validates the authenticity of political projects. For example, as many credit Juárez for setting Mexico on an anticlerical path that lasted a century, official celebrations across Mexico in 2006 commemorated the bicentenary of his birth, though Mexico's key leaders at the time came from a pro-Catholic Partido Acción Nacional (PAN).[2] Marshalling the service of Benito Juárez, then, casts a project into greater legitimacy.

The year 2006 marked the bicentenary of Juárez's birth, though not everyone across Mexico was celebrating. In that year, the Movimiento erupted against the Oaxaca governor.[3] In that grassroots struggle, Oaxaca-born Juárez made an appearance among the protesters, with his name, adages, and visage appearing in rally chants and on graffiti and posters around town to support the resistance against the state officials. During my yearlong ethnographic research five years after the Movimiento, I noticed the two epigraphs above whereby two opposing factions in Oaxaca City summoned the same Benito Juárez for their cause. I paused at the protest uses of Juárez, thirty kilometers away in Tecotitlán, particularly on how sixth-grade teachers taught through the example of Oaxaca's most famous denizen. This fifth chapter describes the town coming to the elementary school on March 21, 2011, a nonschool holiday, to commemorate Juárez's birthday, and accordingly established a different framework for socialization, play, and relations of power.

Before exploring his power to call people together in an elementary school project, I should recognize how Juárez's legacy is contentious across Mexico. One afternoon when I was perusing books in a protest-free downtown Oaxaca City, I opened the book *Señor Juárez* to a chapter by public intellectual Gustavo Esteva (2007a) whose title whispered like a prayer: "*Líbranos del peso juarista* (free us from the weight of Juárez)." Unlike the representations at street demonstrations and in elementary schools where I had been researching, Esteva critiqued Juárez for becoming the clarion call for economic and social development initiatives in areas like public health and education, as we saw in Chapter Two. Esteva heard comments like "in any one of these villages there could be a Juárez" as an indicator that finding new Juárezes will save Mexico from underdevelopment (p. 20). The hopeful naiveté implies that Juárez did something noble and patriotic by leaving his native village, moving to the city, and assuming a modern lifestyle. While social movement practices may deploy Juárez in their placards and chants, for many intellectuals like Esteva, the hero's bequest to modern Mexico also embodies a puzzling tradition of progress and development as an inevitable deliverance for Mexico.

Benito Juárez of Oaxaca deserves a bit of background. Raised in the Northern Sierra of Oaxaca, Juárez served five terms as president of Mexico. As Esteva noted, he stands as an exemplar of Indigenous[4] educational achievement: hailing from a village, he learned Spanish, became a lawyer, a judge, and then president. He would thwart French imperial initiatives against the *patria mexicana* and turn into an emblematic national hero, celebrated by Mexico City politicians who sought to unify the multiple ethnicities and languages in Mexico under a one-nation-one-people banner (Gutiérrez, 1999, p. 57).

Institutionally, as the Secretaría de Educación Pública (SEP) was established in 1921 to expand and equip rural schools with carrying out such national integration, schooling coverage would expand in Juárez's rural, mountainous state of Oaxaca, which boasts a quarter of the total number of municipalities nationwide on only 5 percent of the nation's land mass. Key SEP officials of the day, like Moisés Sáenz, would establish schooling on the shoulders of Indigenous heroes like Juárez, who indicated at a Dallas, Texas, conference that Benito Juárez, who unified Mexico, was a "pure-blooded Indio," and so, in the post-Revolution rebuilding, "we have decided to bring Indios to the bosom of our Mexican family.

Through the rural school we ensure their incorporation to this type of civilization that at present constructs our nationality" (p. 26). Taking the example of Benito Juárez, Sáenz suggests that Indios do not wish to remain on the fringes of the nation and that schooling can bring the nation to them. As I will show Juárez used for critical purposes, I begin by conceding his use in governmental programs aptly critiqued by public intellectuals like Gustavo Esteva.

In this chapter, I focus on how a group of elementary teachers venerated Benito Juárez as a patrimonial pedagogical project after a period of conflict and violence. Just as Juárez stirs up controversy, celebrating what is conceptualized as *heroes and holidays* is deemed problematic within critical multicultural education, an approach which strives toward identifying and transforming practices, policies, and texts that marginalize historically nondominant groups (Amosa & Gorski, 2008; Nieto, 2010; Sensoy et al., 2010). Honoring Juárez with an interdisciplinary curricular unit and community-wide gathering, following Banks (2008), resembles outdated models of national identity and citizenship (p. 132), while Nieto studies how heroes and holidays perpetuate rather than question racialized stereotypes (pp. 68–69). Given how Amosa and Gorski (2008) have applauded the diminishing numbers of heroes and holiday sessions at a recent National Association for Multicultural Education (NAME) conference, the future of the field, shaped at conferences like NAME, has progressed beyond the kind of work on Juárez undertaken by the teachers I observed in Oaxaca. Still, despite these critiques, as I will show, critical ethnographic examination in Oaxaca expresses Juárez as a "pedagogical package," an allegoric device deployed by activist teachers adept at dissident union-based politics to make schooling less based on the state-sanctioned timetables and curricular maps and more of the alternative education that Oaxacan teachers have sought for decades.

Activist and Pedagogical Packaging

A critical literacies (Botelho & Rudman, 2009; Kamler, 2001) and public pedagogical (Sandlin & Milam, 2008) usage of a nationalist icon in classroom instruction and teacher activism needs further clarification. When I taught in Oaxaca in the 1990s, organized schoolteacher activism was so menacing that an academic dean in the nonunionized science institute forbade groups of five or more of us instructors from sitting together at the campus café. Here I turn to teacher affinity spaces (Gee, 2004) that materialized after the 2006 Movimiento, when teachers spent May to November out of the classroom facing police and paramilitary violence on the streets of Oaxaca City. As noted, independent of the smaller protest events such as those described in Chapter Four, my fieldwork came four years after the intensified protests. Teachers had returned to teaching in their communities, so I depended on the Movimiento testimonials and analyses of others (Bautista Martínez, 2010; Dalton, 2007; Esteva, 2007b; Martínez Vásquez 2007; Nevaer & Sendyk, 2009; Osorno & Meyer, 2007; Sotelo Marbán, 2008) to situate activism and observe the use of heroes and from there, find linkages with classroom practices.[5] Though my fieldwork came at a much quieter period of protest, classroom teachers regularly told stories about the marches, *plantones*, roadblocks, conferences, and assemblies that militants in the Oaxacan Sección 22[6] of the Sindicato Nacional de Trabajadores de la Educación (SNTE) teachers' union had undertaken. For this reason, classroom pedagogies never strayed too far from public pedagogies, and so I began to appreciate Benito Juárez's symbolic use as an activist package in street protests and as pedagogical package in the classroom.

This fifth chapter takes root in Tecotitlán Elementary in the Central Valleys of Oaxaca state, just outside Oaxaca City where I spent part of summer 2010 and winter and spring 2011. There, I observed and participated in an interdisciplinary reading project, part of the teacher Marcos's modes of teaching which were teaching practices apart from, but not totally independent of, the official SEP curriculum and the Sección 22-sponsored alternatives. The reading project depended on funding from many sources, including the private sector, community-based nongovernmental organizations, the Catholic Church, and a group of interested teachers from the United States. As a self-managed project, the teachers rejected any external monitoring and evaluation; only by controlling the approaches and outcomes would they accept financial or in-kind support. As part of this independently coordinated effort to promote reading through oral storytelling, performance, and playfulness, the teachers had chosen to open the school gates on March 21, 2011, a national holiday to celebrate the birth of Benito Juárez.

Signaling the heroic stature of Benito Juárez, protesters in Oaxaca have used him as an *activist package*, a term I borrow from Tsing (2005). Activist packages are

> allegorical modules that speak to the possibilities of making a cause heard. These packages feature images, songs, morals, organizational plans or stories. They introduce us to heroes and villains; they show us how an unrepresented group can become a political force. Like all socially effective allegories, activist packages are formed in a political and cultural location that gives their stories meaning and makes them work as social interventions. This location need not be a single place; it may be a widespread political culture, or the meeting point between two or more political cultures.... The effect of a new allegory is most

striking when it inspires unexpected social collaborations, which realign the social field…
in coming together, they make a difference in what counts as politics. (pp. 227–228)

Tsing exemplifies an activist package[7] as Brazilian Chico Mendes, represented in an English language HBO Channel biopic, who became a galvanizing symbol for environmental activists in Indonesia (p. 234). In Mexico, other examples abound. Lynn Stephen (2002) has shown how elite Mexico City politicians celebrated the martyred revolutionary Emiliano Zapata, while Zapatista (EZLN) autonomy activists in conflict with the elite politicians have also gathered under the example of Zapata, as have, following De La Rosa and Schadl (2014), Oaxacan street artists.[8] When establishment politicians, hilltop insurgents, and urban stencilists find currency in the singular figure of Zapata, interpreting his usage defies clear-cut ideological explanation. Indeed, the Zapata activist package shows "contradictory models of solidarity" (Tsing, 2005, pp. 233–234) playing into the dissemination of political messaging.[9]

Akin to the activist package, a *pedagogical package*, thickly described below, encompasses the celebration of a widely respected hero that provides a surface for teachers, pupils, and a community to convene. The politics of schooling in Oaxaca state and across Mexico are shifting, from a welfare state system for universal public education to one with greater pressure placed on teachers and pupils to produce knowledge through standardized tests and official textbooks. Additionally, potential teachers are now able to find work via passing the Oposición test, putting the traditional public normal schools, affordable options for low-income teacher candidates, at risk of closure. The private sector has more vigorously sponsored public school projects with foundations like Mexicanos Primero helping write school textbooks and the Fundación Alfredo Harp Helú (FAHH) promoting schoolchildren's reading habits. Such pro-business activists are perturbed by how Mexico has hit the bottom of international educational achievement tables (OECD & Ramos, 2016), with Oaxaca ranked in last place in Mexico (Dirección de Información y Comunicación Social, 2011, p. 2), which has put the nation on the brink of further educational backwardness (Díaz de Cossío, 2011). Standardized and individualized notions of quality education have become a concern for businesses and public agencies.

As we have seen thus far, Oaxacan elementary teachers, faced with reformed textbooks and standardized tests, organize against and seek curricular content to elide state reforms. Through radical approaches underwritten with action research, local epistemologies (Maldonado, 2010), and the radical teaching approaches of Paulo Freire (CEDES 22, 2009, 2010) teachers offer alternatives to the cognitive individualism in the SEP curriculum in Oaxaca, a state with vibrant communalo-cratic modes of knowing and living (Martínez Luna, 2007, p. 96). This chap-ter shows how teachers at Tecotitlán Elementary used the patrimonial stature of national hero Benito Juárez, used elsewhere as the visage of assimilation, to gather the school and village community to implement an alternative curricular unit.

The Guelaguetza and Cultural Battlefields

Just as in the close of the previous chapter where marching teachers toted the image of the official Madre Patria alongside the unofficial, the teachers discussed in this chapter draw upon the cultural legacy of Benito Juárez, albeit a slightly dif-ferent version of the hero. For sure, Oaxacan cultural repression has been used for state hegemony,[10] though competing articulations of culture, like activist packages noted above, show how heroes become importable and for other political pur-poses. This is because cultural representation is part of globally interconnected frictions of understanding and meaning.

To contextualize cultural battlefields of representations of Oaxaca inside Mexico, one day, Tecotitlán Elementary teacher, Marcos, described his reading project. Since part of his school's project involved relating the human voice to printed word, he once hired a professional Argentine storyteller to narrate to the schoolchildren. The narrator, on a Mexico tour, would end up in the northern part of the country, seen internally in Mexico as more urbane and modern than Oaxaca. The Argentine reported to Marcos that *norteños* (northern people) asked him why an Argentine storyteller would bother going down to backward Oaxaca. Marcos explained to the storyteller that outside Oaxaca, people think that "*Oaxaca aun vive en la prehistoria* (Oaxaca still lives in prehistory)." Additionally, Marcos described how living in prehistory is a "label" that Oaxacans themselves can come to believe in.

Guelaguetza, the well-known festival introduced in Chapter Two, was orga-nized in Oaxaca in 1932 and plays a role in sustaining and contesting the view of Oaxacans as folkloric. Guelaguetza is a communalocratic practice whereby a neighbor answers the call to support another during the harvest or the organi-zation of a party (Stephen, 1991). Guelaguetza stands as a concrete economic practice in many Oaxacan communities;[11] though it is drawn into urban cele-brations, Guelaguetza symbolizes the "prehistory" label.[12] Just after Moisés Sáenz used schooling to "bring Indios to the bosom of our Mexican family," officials used folkloric ballet numbers in the Guelaguetza Festival as a tool of national integration (Nagengast & Kearney, 1990). This is palpable in how a guidebook (Vargas, 1935) from the fourth year of the Guelaguetza Festival refers to it as a "racial tradition of Oaxaca [which is the] proof of unbreakable solidarity that is observed in Oaxacan pueblos and villages" (p. 3). This indissoluble harmony ascribed to the festival in the vintage guidebook further benefits state governors presiding in places of distinction in the Guelaguetza Auditorium, as we will see in Chapter Six. Because of how the guelaguetza communalocratic mutual aid practices became officially appropriated by the state-sponsored dance event, the Guelaguetza Festival, like the legacy of Juárez, provokes controversy.[13]

To be sure, neither the governors nor residents of the urban and industrialized north of Mexico have won the battle of representation at the expense of Oaxacan teachers like Marcos, as the Guelaguetza Festival and the image of Benito Juárez have become a terrain of struggle. In recent years, the festival has grown in popularity, which has set the event in further conflict. To start, Oaxacans have adopted the festival, one teacher informed me, as we stood with 300 others on avenue below the Guelaguetza Auditorium, just north of downtown. As the festival has gotten more touristic, many locals cannot afford to go.[14] Correspondingly, the relationship between the Oaxacan public and the governors began to deteriorate as the selection process for dance ensembles had become fraught with nepotism. Then, without public discussion, contractors began to restore historic parks and buildings around town at great markup prices (Sotelo Marbán, 2008, p. 44). The remodeling of the iconic green-stoned Guelaguetza Auditorium and the overall mismanagement of the construction across the city, as we saw with the public rallying around the damaged zócalo trees, spurred movement against the governor, including at the Auditorium itself. In this we see the appearance of Benito Juárez when a visible hillside sculpture near the Auditorium of a Juárez quote, reading: "*El respeto al derecho ajeno es la paz* (The respect of the rights of others is peace)" got damaged by the rebuilding; the final word "paz (peace)" turned to rubble down the slope. In response, jokes circulated about the governor's inability to maintain the peace (Colectivo Producciones Vanguardia Proletária, 2006, min. 11:31), and so the governor's mishandling of the construction projects is met with Juárez deployed on the side of protesters.

By summer 2006, facing the full-throttle Movimiento against his leadership, the governor scrapped that year's Guelaguetza Festival. In reaction, teachers organized an alternative festival, the *Guelaguetza Popular*, which by 2009 boasted 40,000 attendees (Davies, 2007). By my 2010 field visit, I stood with the 300 teachers mentioned above in the middle of a major thoroughfare to obstruct construction vehicles going up to the Guelaguetza Auditorium, so that by the upcoming overpriced performances, the half-finished amphitheater would shame the governor. Even as the folklorism of the Festival represents Oaxaca as blissfully backward, Oaxacans have come to love the event enough to defend its "iconic" stature and to use it as a point of disputation against a repressive and corrupt political machine.[15] The official and popular standing of the festival becomes less a contest over purity and truth than a cultural trench within which the teachers and others have hunkered down as partisans. As the life of the Guelaguetza Festival has simmered with the broth of the hegemonic depiction and sprouted out in grassroots activism, Oaxaca-born hero, Benito Juárez, whose statue stands by the Guelaguetza Auditorium, and whose monumental "peace" slid down a hillside, has also become an activist and pedagogical package that is useful for political advantages, as we will see below.

Juárez as Pedagogical Package

In this section, I describe the events of March 21, 2011 the national holiday for Benito Juárez.

Pausing at the Periódico Mural

I rode to Tecotitlán with Marcos, as was our custom each morning during the winter and spring months, though as the national holiday in memory of President Juárez today seemed less formal. Our commute chat centered on the Sección 22 *bloqueos* (roadblocks)[16] planned in two days and, more importantly, the disappearance of a noted Oaxacan teacher that occurred the week before. Marcos knew of the teacher's work visiting different villages to monitor alternative education projects in the face of the Alianza por la Calidad de la Educación (ACE) standardized educational reforms. Posters and graffiti that were visible around town demanded the teacher's safe return, exclaiming "because he was taken alive we want him returned alive." This suggested that the teacher had been taken against his will rather than merely wandering off. As there had been little information and no ransom demands, I asked Marcos for clarification. Marcos responded with perturbation about the lack of news on the teacher. I asked why someone might take this teacher, a known critical pedagogue and not a key figure in the Sección 22 political side, like the secretary general. He said that the political operatives who engage in disappearing people are too smart; they know who is who. This suggested to me that teachers centering on classroom approaches stand amidst political fault lines.

As we arrived at the town, we passed along a well-maintained access road that was raised a little above the surface of the cultivated, moist fields to either side. In an arid region, this farming town has water, and this year, farmers had reported that the aquifer was particularly high. Marcos parked his car and we entered the school grounds through the metal grate doorway that the parents had locked to prevent teachers from entering after the 2006 protests. When we entered, ahead of us in the school's interior courtyard, parents had made a makeshift theater of foldable chairs below a vinyl tarp roof. We walked to the left of the *periódico mural*, a plywood sheet affixed to the iron bars on a building window. Two weeks ago, after the Monday morning *homage to the flag* ceremony that begins each school week, Marcos had remained outside with his sixth-grade students standing before the periódico mural before heading to their classroom. In many schools like Tecotitlán Elementary, the periódico mural as a literacy space functions as a student-organized bulletin board for current events during the month. On Valentine's Day, the previous month, student inscriptions on love and friendship filled the board; often, students throughout the day would pause there and read the writing of their peers. For the month of March, an outstanding mural headline recalled the life of liberal reformer Benito Juárez.

At this spot two weeks prior, Marcos began class facing the mural.[17] Marcos had been coordinating his sixth-grade group's "performance" on Juárez's life for the celebration day. Like the teacher whose group had posted their work on the periódico mural, he would base the presentations on research. In the classroom stood a "Performance on Benito Juárez García" poster: "Performance, an English word which we'll understand as representation with various artistic activities (theater, music, dance, poetry, song …). How can we make our performance the way we need to? Creativity. Know the history of Juárez. Sources to check: books, the internet, Encarta [Microsoft digital encyclopedia]." Finally, the page featured a flowchart of arrows: "research it ⇒ result ⇒ learning." In practice, research on the former president meant visits to the Enciclomedia, the classroom computer program installed in the early 2000s, to read Juárez's letters to his children and to Emperor Maximiliano and to listen to a ballad about Juárez's life. Marcos had also read aloud from books from his personal collection. The class furthermore visited the school library and the computer room (*aula de medios*) to watch the 1954 film, *El jóven Juárez*, when, before his students Marcos explained, "we are going to watch a film … sure, it is a movie, but it is based on research the director made…." In this way, Marcos scaffolded student research skills for the project.

As the sixth-grade group paused at the periódico mural a week later, the students had yet to plan their performance, and Marcos was not happy. Facing the mural, Marcos asked the class to take out the photo albums on Benito Juárez they had assembled for homework. One student showed me his construction paper collection covered with glued glossy *lámina* cards, which are available at any stationary store. I asked him where he had gotten the words that he had written below the cards; he remarked that he had copied them off the backs of the lámina cards and affixed them to the construction paper. Wanting to challenge his mechanical effort, I gave a brief appraisal, choosing to step back from being a teacher myself to await Marcos's response. Marcos, before the mural, appeared in full classroom mode. Irritated with the students' cut-and-paste job, he pronounced that the cards were a last resort, not the main source. Reminding them of the visits to the Enciclomedia and the aula de medios, he challenged them: "What is the good of taking notes if you don't use them?" His irritation segued into a new task, having the students read the periódico mural to verify how well the information there resonated with their homework. Marcos and the students proceeded with the comparison line-by-line. Two weeks later, however, Marcos and I walked past the mural without pausing, as the atmosphere was informal and before us stood staging for the day's celebration.

Performances and Basketball

When Marcos and I had walked beyond the periódico mural and stepped out into the cement, sand, and brick surface of the central square, he would step away to coordinate the Juárez celebration event. I stood to the side to perceive the panorama of the event. Soon, Marcos spoke via loudspeaker before the students, teachers, the parents' committee, and the municipal officials who had shown up on this nonwork day. He began to discuss the importance of self-government, how infringements on sovereignty like the ongoing U.S. military strikes in Libya are among the many violations of our contemporary world. Juárez in his time stood up to the infringements to sovereignty. What's more, Juárez emerged from a nearby town and went on to greatness. He was a man of his time, and he was full of flaws. That is not the point. He stood up to the conservatives who, according to a student speech later, had invited a Maximilian, a European emperor, to run out of fear that the United States of America would take more of their land.[18] However, Juárez confronted these conservatives and their fears, executed Emperor Maximiliano, and honored Mexico's sovereignty. The flawed but memorable

Juárez, Marcos reiterated, stood up to such affronts after coming from a Oaxacan village to the president's palace.

After Marcos's speech, before the whole Tecotitlán community, the students under the vinyl tarp engaged in performances on the life of Juárez, the heart of the day's celebrations, where a parent brought a live sheep and the children dressed in period costumes and posted drawings of landscapes and biographic timelines. Marcos's sixth graders sang a ballad on the life of Juárez as different students acted out the thematic content of the song. As noted by Marcos's earlier exasperation, the students had not assembled or performed a substantial text compared to the other groups. Later in the day, two of the girls in the group approached me distraught because Marcos had given them a grade of five out of ten for the performance. Though the volume of the taped music drowned them out, "we were singing" they insisted and did not deserve a low mark.

After the performances, the all-female honor guard, filled with several of Marcos's students, executed the homage to the flag ceremony which signaled the shift from commemorative performance to sport, as the basketball league finals were about to start. When the matches began, Marcos grabbed the same microphone he had used in his speech, sat under the tarp, and called the play-by-play for two simultaneous matches. He referred to students by their nicknames and with warm wittiness announced the details of what he saw, commenting once, "In an extraordinary manner, Pepe has made a shot but missed the mark." When the students in the lower grades finally scored a point, the whole court erupted in cheers. Marcos turned his attention to them and said, "and it seems the first point has been scored; yes, the first basket in one and a half games!" The entire school, and indeed, the whole Tecotitlán community, had congregated at these games.

While calling the games, Marcos had suddenly noticed me perched behind a lime tree running my video camera. In English, he beckoned to me, "Steve, come on, please." I walked beneath the shady space in the tarpaulin toward the main court to see what he wanted and noticed the sixth-grade girls' match on the main court. Marcos revealed that they lacked a coach, so "go and coach them," he ordered. I ran to the court, and saying nothing, huddled the team up for a moment, until the referee whistled for them to play on. At the end of the game, which my sixth graders won 2-0, I called them in for final pointers, saying "next game, when you get the ball, keep calm, settle down, nobody is going to steal it from you if you are holding it!" Monday-to-Friday school days, bustling with student and teacher movement from one activity to another, are not conducive for pep talks and strategic huddles, but on this day off the pattern had shifted, and I took the time to bond with them after their victory. Later in the day, the parents' committee awarded basketballs and school supplies to each winning team. One of the victorious sixth graders came into the quiet classroom and interrupted me, her coach for ten minutes, from my field note scribing. She revealed the prize and shouted, "Look, Estif, we won a ball!" The competition gave diverse members of the community interactive space in school that broke from the attributed roles. Any one of the adults, even me as international researcher, became teacher or coach while the students would at times wander from the pack and paint on or read one of the several student-designed wall artworks around the courtyard.

After awarding prizes to the winning teams, the male teachers took to the court in a grudge match against the fathers.[19] Marcos had asked me to play for the teachers; however, one of the fathers rejected the teachers calling for *refuerzos*, or backup, especially for foreigners who were "too tall." Marcos found this amusing and taunted them on the loud speaker: "Why you all worked up about with the backup?" Despite Marcos's lightheartedness, it was clear that the game meant a lot to the men's pride. Then, just before the jump ball, as a compromise the director handed me the official whistle and asked me to referee instead of play. Eventually, the game was close with the teachers securing victory, even as they donned leather-soled shoes and collared shirts while the fathers wore more flexible tee shirts and jeans. Yet calling the teacher victory was premature, as one of the fathers requested a ten-minute overtime. Just before the whistle, a father looked at me and said, "and don't be calling it for teachers this time!" I countered, "score more points, then, and your problem goes away" in the mock irritation of sports trash-talk. This extra time proved more intense with the director changing his collared shirt for a tank top, reducing the residual veneer of formality and freeing up the joints for this extra round. The teachers ended up winning, though the fathers had narrowed the margin.

Drinking Beer Under the Tarp

When the basketball game ended, the players sat below the tarp on in a circle. One of the fathers placed a case of Corona beer on the brick surface. At this time, almost everyone had left the school grounds save the fifteen or so male teachers, the fathers, and me. One of the fathers had his son and daughter present for a time, sitting on his lap and side. When I looked at him, I saw his fingernails were covered with blue paint worn off on all but the corners and edges of the nails. These were working hands. Drinking beer and sitting in the shade after sports enabled a brand of conversation with flexibility and ease unlike the conversations I experienced during many meals and informal chats with teachers and parents.

The beer under the tarp involved cautious solidarity and a quiet social eyes-to-the ground introversion, though the men below the tarp do not enjoy a carefree relationship given teacher absence during protests. During months of observing the teachers, I had encountered many parents, including some of these fathers. On my right sat a father who had lived in California and, hearing me mention New England, in English asked me if I lived near Yale University. In the beer-drinking circle, he was talking about business, the legal patents for Atlanta-based Coca Cola. The school director then brought up that the Chinese were beginning to patent a type of *nopal*, a cactus that in Mexico figures as both a national symbol and a delicacy. Despite the Mexicanity of the nopal, Chinese manufacturers began to take part of the market away from Mexican producers. Then, the conversation shifted to the recent devastating tsunami in the northeast coast of Japan.[20] The men discussed disasters and school preparedness; the director interjected, assuring that protocol was in order with the pupils exiting the individual buildings to the ball courts, the site of our present conversation. The director talked about how Japan had responded so differently than Haiti had in the quake a year before. After this, the discussion turned to the U.S. bombing campaign in Libya. Someone also brought up the disappeared teacher that Marcos and I had discussed on our ride to town and how this unresolved event would lead to an intensification of teachers' union political action. The conversations remained primarily among the whole group, and focused largely on current affairs.

The conversations, accompanied by the huffing and puffing of competitive, out of shape men, had departed from the roles I had perceived over the last six weeks. Marcos, the school assistant director, hardly spoke. The director was loquacious; having, however, dismounted from a leadership position, he physically changed from collared shirt to tank top and he never took charge; though he spoke as the principal when the topic of student safety arose. It happened that some of the most verbal participants in the conversation had less sway in the school and community, such as a recently hired young teacher who mockingly dragged the case of beer away from the reach of anyone who uttered something absurd, gesturing, "you are cut off from the booze!" The open exchanges, Marcos reported later, enabled the teachers to level the parent relations that had remained tense since the 2006 class cancelation due to street mobilizations, when the parents locked the gate on the absentee teachers. Now the doors were open on Benito Juárez Day, and a group of teachers remained seated with a group of parents well into the late afternoon. The basketball, conversation, and beer converted the meeting into one of competition and solidarity. On our drive home to Oaxaca City, Marcos, who often calls on community support for his reading project activities, suggested things might go a little smoother with parents now after today's events.

A Patrimonial Convocation

To wrap up the pedagogical packaging of Benito Juárez in Tecotitlán Elementary, I return to examples of protest in Oaxaca state that are well known to teachers. A book, *La batalla por Oaxaca,* compiled by Beas Torres (2007a), contains song lyrics, policy documents, political analyses, and testimonials on Oaxacan gubernatorial authoritarianism. The book, published in Oaxaca City without a listed editor or principal author, presents an array of voices and stories from the internationally renowned Immanuel Wallerstein to the roadblock activist, El Alebrije. A focal piece is a fifty-eight-page analysis by Carlos Beas Torres (2007b), coordinator and advisor to varied groups of pueblos across Mexico, that explores militarism, linkages between Oaxaca 2006 and others in Mexico, radical artist contributions, and the "Oaxacan Fascism" connection with that of Guatemala, Argentina, and Chile (p. 45). Its local specificity aside, the Oaxaca uprising intersected with events and individuals far beyond the state. The cover of the *La batalla* book reprints a protest poster from the street art: the visage of Benito Juárez in a beret with a commandant's star, subtitled, "If by asking for justice one's labeled a 'guerrilla,' then I'm a guerrilla, too, compatriot." The book cover, drawn from the sidewalks of the 2006 Oaxaca Movimiento, positions Juárez as a Che figure, an activist package that connected people and ideas across time and space, even as inside, the content came as plurivocal and disjointed as the Movimiento itself.

Just as activists can package Juárez as Che, the teachers who serve in the same popular struggles also use him in their classroom practice. The pedagogical package of the Oaxaca-born president helped teachers organize a curricular unit and community-wide celebration on a nonwork day. This celebration incorporated schoolchildren, community leaders, and parents who had disapproved of the protest-focused teacher absence in 2006. Juárez, who was celebrated by student performances, served as a worthy and answerable beckoning into the official space of the school's interior courtyard and occasioned a special effort on a holiday to lay a tarp over one of the ball fields and open the doors to all who wished to attend. This respite from routine marked a rupture in the class schedule and reached beyond the curricular SEP flowcharts and the radical idealism of the Sección 22-sponsored alternative education. As a pedagogical package, Juárez services the teacher work in implementing an ongoing reading project in the classroom.

As we see in the above narratives, the celebration also featured an unofficial social reconnection among children, parents, community members, and teachers—all in the official space of the school. There is not time during the ordinary working week to pause for a day, play, dance, and interact on sundry topics in the rural school, which as we have seen, has exerted pressure on communities to centralize, modernize, and flexiblize. As the Juárez pedagogical package unfolds in the heart of the school, it embraces the homage to the flag ceremonialism; it taps into the research-based studies of the prior weeks. All of this lends the event legitimacy that draws in a community. Additionally, the teachers and other adults took the opportunity to converse on natural disasters, recent technology, and state politics in ways that cannot occur while burdened with the timetables and curricular maps of their working day. Like the vinyl tarp lapping above them, celebrating Juárez informally in the formal setting of the elementary school on a national holiday locates the teachers' work in local, regional, national, and international scope and allows them to negotiate how they will situate their work in the community.

By showing celebration becoming a critical pedagogical choice, I am not railing against Gustavo Esteva's critique of the use of the president or arguing against multicultural educators who seek teaching that goes beyond heroes and holidays. Indeed, in a period of *neoliberal multiculturalism* (Hale, 2005) a figure like Juárez has current purchase for imbuing in rural schools a more efficient, inclusive, and flexible set of habits in the interest of the state and corporate affiliates. By the pedagogical package, however, I suggest looking at how curricular thematic content, like celebrating the life of a fabled president, opens conversations, gives activists cover from the pressures to produce, and creates openings for students, parents, and community members who historically clash with the teachers to reconnect.

Notes

1. Juárez has enjoyed political currency long after his death, but the dead in Oaxacan everyday life interact with the living (Norget, 2006), as "living is such that even the dead must pull their weight, and death is such that even the living must contribute to the welfare of the dead" (p. 114).

2. In the nineteenth century, liberals in Mexico sought rational and positivistic futures for a modern and developed Mexico. Their rivals, the conservatives, enjoyed a tighter relationship with the Catholic Church and the Spanish Bourbon dynasty. In this, the secularism of Juárez and his successors became a nationalist and power-consolidation strategy, while Catholicism through this period persisted, to Norget (2006), as an "interiorized" practice within individual believers rather than as a collective political

identity (p. 100). Until the presidency of Carlos Salinas (1988–1994), Mexican politics under the PRI remained officially opposed to the Catholic Church, while Salinas would restore diplomatic links with the Vatican, and in 2000, the conservative PAN won the presidency. See Sheppard (2011, p. 510) for the PRI's use of Juárez to defend secularism in the early 1980s.

3. See Gibler (2009) for a brief sketch of the eviction of street vendors and police violence in San Salvador Atenco, 20 miles outside of Mexico City, and how other activists rallied to their support (pp. 72–80). From conversations with Oaxacan teachers, I learned about the musical connection between Oaxaca and Atenco in the ballads of José de Molina who in 2006 attended both protest movements and whose songs appeared in the Oaxaca plantón.

4. I use *Indigenous* here as an invented identity group. As introduced in Chapter One, the term started as a state-fabricated catch-all descriptor for the products, practices, and phenotypes of hundreds of different racial, ethnic, political, and linguistic groups in Mexico claiming pre-conquest origins. See Kearney (1995, 1996), Martínez Novo (2006), Nagengast and Kearney (1990), and Stephen (2007) for how outside of Oaxaca in Mexico and across the border and in the United States differing Indigenous identifications become possible while in Oaxaca self-identification is less flexible.

5. In the fall of 2013, a groundswell of teacher activism across Mexico made the front pages of national dailies, showing the movement's ongoing struggle against educational reform and the vindication of teacher public intellectual work.

6. Democracy and salary battles had surfaced within the nationwide SNTE teacher union prior to the late 1970s when a sustained dissident caucus, the CNTE, would concretize. The Sección 22 in Oaxaca has spearheaded this nationwide movement (Cook, 1996; Yescas Martínez & Zafra, 1985).

7. An activist package further resembles *détournement*, the ways protest images are reused elsewhere (Gun Cuninghame, 2007), and how texts theoretically always draw from texts that have come before (Bakhtin & Holquist, 1981).

8. Stencils of a gasmask-wearing Mother Mary, a "Virgin of the Barrikadas" (sic) (Nevaer & Sendyk, 2009), shrouded in a cloak of burning tires (p. 63) appeared in the 2006 Movimiento. Consult Norget (2009) for more on the Virgin of the Barricades and the role of liberation theologians in the 2006 Movimiento.

9. Brunk (1998) shows the recollection of Zapata in Oaxaca by state governors and grassroots activists (pp. 481–484).

10. I use the term *hegemony* here as many Oaxacan teachers do, as the ways elites maintain their class position via presenting their needs, like a unified and monocultural Mexico, as universal.

11. One Tecotitlán farmer in the peak of the garlic harvest reported to me that he preferred to undertake work projects by paying his neighbors rather than the mutual exchange of guelaguetza.

12. See Goertzen (2009) for the sociopolitical and gastronomic processes of Oaxacans occupying and sharing the free seats at the Guelaguetza performances.

13. Albro (1998) discussed how provincial authorities in Bolivia strategically deployed the defense patrimony around a local festival to thwart privatization.

14. For the Guelaguetza dance festival, "[t]here is no point in arguing that the Guelaguetza is no longer 'authentic,'" argues Norget (2006), "perhaps it has never been 'authentic'… More interesting, in my view, would be an examination of the way the state government has used its 'production' of the Guelaguetza as an indigenous festival as a catalyst for tourism …" (p. 235).

15. Oaxacan icons are source material for artistic production. Consider street artist Ita (De La Rosa & Schadl, 2014), the "remixing" of iconic images, saying that the "icons are a way for young people to express their power. To say, 'well, okay, let's use these image that the State has appropriated but they can also be ours with sombilism that come from the youth'" (p. 17).

16. When the radical teachers organized a *bloqueo* as a scheduled event it operated differently than when neighborhood residents set up Movimiento barricades. The bloqueos obstructed traffic the way a plantón does, for a specific political objective, while the *barricadas* served as ongoing defenses (CCIODH, 2007, 196, p. 62; Sotelo Marbán, 2008, pp. 118–119) at the height of the Movimiento. For more on Oaxacan barricadas, see the testimony of el Alebrije (2007), the film by Mal de Ojo TV and Comité de Liberación 25 de Noviembre (2007), and the Albertani (2009, p. 180) description of barricada music.

17. Consider Marco's indexing of the *periódico* mural through Geneva Gay's (2002) discussion of the ways "culturally responsive" teachers analyze and construct the use of the "symbolic curriculum" carried by graphic spaces like the mural (pp. 108–109).

18. By 1844, the United States had appropriated half of Mexico's territory.

19. The mothers are more visible at school, especially at the start of the day and during recess. A group of preservice teacher candidates from a women's rural normal school undertook their practice there, and one day during my fieldwork, they faced the mothers in a basketball game.

20. During recess at a nearby village school, I sat with teachers who were checking their text messages when two of them blurted out the news that a tsunami had just hit Japan.

References

Albertani, C. (2009). *Espejo de México: (Crónicas de barbarie y resistencia)*. San Pedro Cholula, Mexico: Altres Costa-Amic.

Albro, R. (1998). Neoliberal ritualists of Urkupina: Bedeviling patrimonial identity in a Bolivian patronal fiesta. *Ethnology, 37*(2), 133–164.

Amosa, W., & Gorski, P. C. (2008). Directions and mis-directions in multicultural education: An analysis of session offerings at the annual conference of the National Association for Multicultural Education. *Multicultural Perspectives, 10*(3), 167–174.

Bakhtin, M. M., & Holquist, M. (1981). *The dialogic imagination: Four essays.* Austin, TX: University of Texas Press.

Banks, J. A. (2008). Diversity, group identity, and citizenship education in a global age. *Educacional Researcher, 37*(3), 129–139.

Bautista Martínez, E. (2010). *Los nudos del régimen autoritario: Ajustes y continuidades de la dominación en dos ciudades de Oaxaca.* Oaxaca, Mexico: IISUABJO.

Beas Torres, C. (Ed.). (2007a). *La batalla por Oaxaca.* Oaxaca, Mexico: Ediciones Yope Power.

Beas Torres, C. (2007b). La batalla por Oaxaca. In C. Beas Torres (Ed.), *La batalla por Oaxaca* (pp. 21–79). Oaxaca, Mexico: Ediciones Yope Power.

Botelho, M. J., & Rudman, M. K. (2009). *Critical multicultural analysis of children's literature: Mirrors, windows, and doors.* New York, NY: Routledge.

Brunk, S. (1998, August 1). Remembering Emiliano Zapata: Three moments in the posthumous career of the martyr of Chinameca. *Hispanic American Historical Review, 78*(3), 457–490.

CCIODH. (2007). *Informe sobre los hechos de Oaxaca. Quinta visita del 16 de diciembre de 2006 al 20 de enero de 2007* (Report). Barcelona: CCIODH. Retrieved from http://cciodh.pangea.org/

CEDES 22. (2009). *Taller estatal de educación alternativa: TEEA 2009–2010* (Instruccional material). Oaxaca, Mexico.

CEDES 22. (2010). *2010 Resolutivos del III congreso estatal de educación alternativa, 20–21 de mayo.* Oaxaca, Mexico: Sección 22, SNTE.

Colectivo Producciones Vanguardia Proletária. (2006). ¡Venceremos!: La otra historia de Oaxaca. Retrieved from http://www.oaxacaenpiedelucha.info/2007/02/venceremos-la-historia-de-la-appo.html

Cook, M. L. (1996). *Organizing dissent: Unions, the state and the democratic teachers' movement in Mexico.* University Park, PA: The Pennsylvania State University Press.

Dalton, M. (2007). Los organismos civiles en Oaxaca y el movimiento ciudadano: Causas y consecuencias. *Cuadernos del Sur, 12*(24/25), 63–80.

Davies, N. (2007, July 17). Oaxaca government armed forces use violence to prevent the people's use of the Guelaguetza Auditorium. *The Narco News Bulletin.* Retrieved from http://www.narconews.com/Issue46/article2735.html

De La Rosa, M. G., & Schadl, S. M. (2014). *Getting up for the people: The visual revolution of ASAR-Oaxaca.* Oakland, CA: PM Press.

Díaz de Cossío, R. (2011, May). La chapulinera. *Nexos, 401*, 41–42.

Dirección de Información y Comunicación Social. (2011). *Presenta CONEVAL Estimaciones del índice de rezago social 2010: A nivel municipal y por localidad* (Press release no. 012). Mexico City: Consejo Nacional de Evaluación de la Política de Desarrollo Social. Retrieved from http://www.coneval.gob.mx/Informes/COMUNICADOS_DE_PRENSA/COMUNICADO_012_indice_de_rezago_social_2010.pdf

el Alebrije. (2007). Las noches en la Ciudad de la Resistencia: Entrevista a "El Alebrije." In C. Beas Torres (Ed.), *La batalla por Oaxaca* (pp. 197–202). Oaxaca, Mexico: Ediciones Yope Power.

Esteva, G. (2007a). Líbranos del peso juarista. In G. Esteva, F. Gargallo, J. Martínez Luna, & J. Pech Casanova (Eds.), *Señor Juárez* (pp. 17–49). Oaxaca, Mexico: Archipiélago.

Esteva, G. (2007b, November). La otra campaña, la APPO y la izquierda: Revindicar una alternativa. *Cuadernos del Sur, 12*(24/25), 5–37.

Gay, G. (2002). Preparing for culturally responsive teaching. *Journal Teacher Education, 53*(2), 106–116.

Gee, J. P. (2004). *Situated language and learning: A critique of traditional schooling.* London: Routledge.

Gibler, J. (2009). *Mexico unconquered: Chronicles of power and revolt.* San Francisco, CA: City Lights.

Goertzen, C. (2009). Dance, politics, and cultural tourism in Oaxaca's Guelaguetza. In O. Nájera-Ramírez, N. E. Cantú, & B. M. Romero (Eds.), *Dancing across borders: Danzas y bailes Mexicanos* (pp. 293–317). Urbana, IL: University of Illinois Press.

Gun Cuninghame, P. (2007). "A laughter that will bury you all": Irony as protest and language as struggle in the Italian 1977 movement. *International Review of Social History, 52*(15), 153–168.

Gutiérrez, N. (1999). *Nationalist myths and ethnic identities: Indigenous intellectuals and the Mexican state.* Lincoln, NE: University of Nebraska Press.

Hale, C. (2005). Neoliberal multiculturalism: The remaking of cultural rights and racial dominance in Central America. *PoLAR: Political and Legal Anthropology Review, 28*(1), 10–28.

ICOMOS. (1986). *The city of Oaxaca, the archaeological site of Monte Alban and the site of Cuilapan.* World Heritage List, 415. Retrieved from file:///C:/Users/ssadlier/Downloads/415-ICOMOS-478-en.pdf

Kamler, B. (2001). *Relocating the personal: A critical writing pedagogy.* Albany, NY: State University of New York Press.

Kearney, M. M. (1995). The local and the global: The anthropology of globalization and transnationalism. *Annual Review of Anthropology, 24*(1), 547–565.

Kearney, M. M. (1996). *Reconceptualizing the peasantry.* Boulder, CO: Westview Press.

Mal de Ojo TV, & Comité de Liberación 25 de Noviembre. (2007). (DVD). *Compromiso cumplido.* Oaxaca, Mexico: Mal de Ojo TV.

Maldonado, B. (2010). *Comunidad, comunalidad y colonialismo en Oaxaca, México: La nueva educación comunitaria y su contexto* (Doctoral dissertation, Department of Mesoamerican and Andean Cultures, Faculty of Archaeology, Leiden University).

Martínez Luna, J. (2007). De Juárez a García. In G. Esteva, F. Gargallo, J. Martínez Luna, & J. Pech Casanova (Eds.), *Señor Juárez* (pp. 73–99). Oaxaca, Mexico: Archipiélago.

Martínez Novo, C. (2006). *Who defines Indigenous? Identities, development, intellectuals, and the state in northern Mexico.* New Brunswick, NJ: Rutgers University Press.

Martínez Vásquez, V. R. (2007). *Autoritarismo, movimiento popular y crisis política: Oaxaca 2006.* Oaxaca, Mexico: UABJO.

McGee Banks, C. A., & Banks, J. A. (1995). Equity pedagogy: An essential component of multicultural education. *Theory into Practice, 34*(3), 152–158.

Nagengast, C., & Kearney, M. (1990, January 1). Mixtec ethnicity: Social identity, political consciousness, and political activism. *Latin American Research Review, 25*(2), 61–91.

Nevaer, L. E. V., & Sendyk, E. (2009). *Protest graffiti–Mexico: Oaxaca.* New York, NY: Mark Batty.

Nieto, S. (2010). *Language, culture and teaching: Critical perspectives* (2nd ed.). New York, NY: Routledge.

Norget, K. (2006). *Days of death, days of life: Ritual in the popular culture of Oaxaca.* New York. NY: Columbia University Press.

Norget, K. (2009). La Virgen de las barricadas: La Iglesia Católica, religiosidad popular y el movimiento de la Asamblea Popular de los Pueblos de Oaxaca. In V. R. Martínez Vásquez (Ed.), *La APPO: ¿Rebelión o movimiento social?: Nuevas formas de expresión ante la crisis* (pp. 301–328). Oaxaca, Mexico: IISUABJO.

OECD, & Ramos, G. (2016). *Country Note: Results from PISA 2015 Mexico.* Retrieved from https://www.oecd.org/pisa/PISA-2015-Mexico.pdf

Osorno, D. E., & Meyer, L. (2007). *Oaxaca sitiada: La primera Insurrección del siglo XXI.* Mexico City: Random House Mondadori.

Sandlin, J. A., & Milam, J. L. (2008). 'Mixing pop (culture) and politics': Cultural resistance, cultural jamming, and anti-consumption activism as critical public pedagogy. *Curriculum Inquiry, 38*(3), 323–350.

Sensoy, O., Sanghera, R., Parmar, G., Parhar, N., Nosyk, L., & Anderson, M. (2010). Moving beyond "Dance, dress, and dining" in multicultural Canada. *International Journal of Multicultural Education, 12*(1), 1–15.

Sheppard, R. (2011, July 1). Nationalism, economic crisis and 'realistic revolution' in 1980s Mexico. *Nations and Nationalism, 17*(3), 500–519.

Sotelo Marbán, J. (2008). *Oaxaca: Insurgencia civil y terrorismo de estado.* Mexico City: Era.

Stephen, L. (1991). *Zapotec women.* Austin, TX: University of Texas Press.

Stephen, L. (2002). ¡Zapata Lives!: Histories and cultural politics in Southern Mexico. Berkeley, CA: University of California Press.

Stephen, L. (2007). *Transborder Lives: Indigenous Oaxacans in Mexico, California, and Oregon.* Durham, NC: Duke University Press.

Tsing, A. L. (2005). *Friction: An ethnography of global connection.* Princeton, NJ: Princeton University Press.

Vargas, A. (1935). *Guelaguetza: Costumbre racial oaxaqueña.* Oaxaca, Mexico: Imprenta del Gobierno del Estado.

Weeks, C. A. (1987). *The Juárez Myth in Mexico.* Tuscaloosa, AL: University of Alabama Press.

Yescas Martínez, I., & Zafra, G. (1985). *La insurgencia magisterial en Oaxaca 1980.* Oaxaca, Mexico: IISUABJO.

Movement III: Governability

6

Blocking the Road

Governability

The state's effectiveness in its intervention and development strategies is further debilitated by the fact that its very structure includes contradictory societal relations and structures. In order to dominate, opposing groups must be either repressed or co-opted into the state; if co-opted, their demands must be at least partially met. As a consequence, the success of the state's development strategies is determined not only by its own policies and actions, but also by the dynamics of social movements and by the political confrontations that permanently modify the configuration of society.

—Noel McGinn and Susan Street (1984, p. 324)

One day, a civil servant in the cultural affairs section of the Oaxaca state government met me for coffee under the stone-pillared archways at a café, beneath the leafy *laurel de la India* canopies of the *zócalo*. I had met her at the reading festival in Llano Park, described in Chapter One and at the Tecotitlán Book Fair discussed in Chapter Three, and wanted to learn more about how the state promoted reading. She started by describing the first book launch she had organized, which she publicized with a few days' notice and mainly in the central areas of Oaxaca City. In anticipating a smaller crowd, she queried attendees on how they had heard about the literary event. Many reported that a neighbor had told them about the event. Information spreads quickly, she related, through urban neighborhoods or rural dirt streets via *perifoneo*, a megaphone mounted on a car. These transmissions, noted earlier, serve in marches for call-and-response *consigna* chants as well as in the villages, where they act as town crier, radio transmitter, and product advertiser. Circulating the streets with its tinny droning announcements, this mode of information sharing sets off strings of neighborly conversations, emails, and text messages. Publicity for her event, she realized, would work best by tapping into informal information-sharing networks. Self-consciously, she confessed that Oaxacans like to gossip, a trait that increases attendance at the cultural events she plans. Gossiping taps into governability.

Staring out of the blinds and sharing an egg with a neighbor are practices of government, pedagogies of daily life that turn into wider solidarity networks when trouble starts. In Oaxaca, this has been termed the "civic space," the peer-to-peer social dynamic that helped inflate public participation once the 2006 Movimiento took shape (Martínez Vásquez, 2009, pp. 344–345). However radical the Movimiento became, the word-of-mouth civic space networks that drew a crowd for the book launch also turned a teachers' union-driven protest in May into a statewide social movement in June. On a day-to-day basis, the civic space unites people through play, competition, and shared projects; it is a purpose-fulness that materializes in action (Sadlier & Morales Sánchez, 2012). The civic space may not become apparent until an event like the teachers' protest *plantón* encounters police violence, when the mundane, everyday interactions of the civic turn into solidarity and compassion among strangers. When the police attacked on June 14, residents opened doors to shelter teachers and hand them sticks and stones for pushing back the police, who had expelled 30,000 comrades from the encampments by the laureles de la India in the city center. Though they may complain about the teachers as the filthy dogs of the neighborhood, the *perros roñosos* described in Chapter Four, enjoy public protection.[1]

In addition to teachers eventually pushing back the police and reoccupying the city center, the violence against them led to a spillover for pent-up public indignation over Governor Ruiz Ortiz. A chronicler of Oaxaca in 2006, Davies (2007a) reported public opposition to Ruiz Ortiz's Mexico City campaigning for his party's 2006 presidential candidate (p. 13), his use of repressive force, and his "unwillingness to consult the citizenry about the public works that are destroying Oaxaca's cultural heritage" (p. 17). The public also stood against Ruiz Ortiz for social and affective rather than resistance reasons, when neighbors constructed defensive roadblocks without direction from the larger movement or a stated ideological stance (el Alebrije, 2007). As the Federal Preventative Police (PFP)[2] militarized Oaxaca City, neighborly solidarity strengthened. The teacher Andrea, for example, received a gift of prayer cards from a street vendor, worried about the teachers' safety with news of the advancing federal officers. When police detained protesters, strangers gave financial support to their family members.[3] Informal social networks that ordinarily go unnoticed or discredited as trivial when sharing a cup of sugar with a neighbor cement into action when the state and federal police move against the citizenry, and the civic space goes from gossip to camaraderie. The civic space might appear politically insubstantial under normal circumstances until bad governance of the authorities makes neighborly cohesion essential.[4] The intensification of the civic space from nosy neighbor to social solidarity is a starting point for approaching movement of governability as a critical practice.

To be precise, moving against illegitimate governance of a repressive state is neither the only nor primary movement of governability in this region. The movement of good governance, for many, is about autonomy, a group's "reclaiming their rights to exist according to their own values and forms of social organization" (Hernández Díaz, 2007, p. 35). The right to exist is particularly poignant for *pueblos* choosing to maintain ancestral systems of mutual aid, language practices, and collective decision making outside the norms of modern, nation-state-centered, pro-development strategies. Even projects to defend "human rights," which are hardly controversial or ideological to many, become systems of colonial domination for autonomy advocates like Gustavo Esteva (2007, p. 8). Most communities in Oaxaca are governed by community-based decision making and mutual aid (Martínez Luna, 2007), social and economic relations that reject decision making by political parties and demand civic participation by collective, nonmonetary contributions.

Most of the school actors in this study work inside the wider system rather than autonomous of it. Despite its credo of "opposition to the official established model" (Cortés, 2006, p. 59), the Oaxacan teachers' movement strives to promote better salary and trade-union democracy as state-paid civil servants. The teachers, furthermore, celebrate protest marches that have led to an increase in public funding. Many of the marches start or end at the principal offices of state power. The music they play, too, resonates below the gubernatorial balcony in the central square, as I heard transmitted June 14, 2010 (by me in original, translated by me) via loudspeaker from the Oaxaca City teachers' protest plantón, recalling the June 14, 2006, *desalojo*:

> *Y el pueblo en general también llegó a apoyar*
> *Exigiendo cumplimiento a diferentes demandas*
> *Libertad para los presos, contra el fraude electoral*
> *Presupuesto educativo, productivo y de salud*
> *Que se largue de Oaxaca el ratero Ulises Ruiz*
> *Y también Radio Plantón difundió la información*

Enfrentando eficazmente tanta manipulación
Y Radio Universidad también dio buena ayudada
Aunque los pinches priistas le dieron su balaceada
Y también la Guelaguetza del gobierno-cancelaron
Para que el gobierno y patrones no lucren con tradiciones
De ancestrales poblaciones se hizo un festival gratuito,
Guelaguetza popular
The pueblo[5] in general came out to lend a hand
Calling for adherence to different demands
Freedom for prisoners, no electoral fraud
Funding for education, productivity and healthcare
And for the *ratero*[6] Ulises Ruiz Ortiz to leave Oaxaca
And Radio Plantón[7] circulated information
Effectively opposing so much manipulation
Radio Universidad did their part too
Even if the *pinches*[8] *priistas*[9] shot up the station
And the official Guelaguetza[10] got called off
To stop government and the bosses
Getting rich off ancestral traditions
They made a festival free to all
The Guelaguetza Popular[11]

The ballad narrates the achievements made by the teachers and other activists four years earlier to increase public funding and access to information and to stop ruling party elites from profiteering off the Guelaguetza Festival and committing electoral fraud. The attention paid to the urban public sphere reveals a movement of governability from within the state system, and so Chapters Six and Seven focus on governability not as autonomy practices from outside the state system but rather from within civic life and civil service. Governability, among the teachers described here, as a movement on the streets and in schools, interacts with the politics of the nation-state, especially when the officials in charge, like governors or union presidents, become vulnerable and resort to authoritarianism, as Oaxacans have witnessed with greater intensity since 2000.[12]

For his part, Governor Ruiz Ortiz, completely aware of the movement of governability, justified his use of force against the teachers and other activists in 2006 on good-governance grounds, citing the "*estado de derecho* (rule of law)" as essential to uphold, even by force (Martínez Vásquez, 2007a, p. 44). The Movimiento would get labeled as an armed insurgency by Oaxacan Attorney General, Lizbeth Caña (Martínez, 2006). This justified battle-readiness in the name of Oaxaca, at the risk of falling into chaos under the work of dangerous vandals, not civil servants engaged in a legal protest. Because Caña moved through governability, force became discursively defensible, even obligatory for a responsible public figure. In the teachers' social movement response, they and others condemned the same executives in the state government as incompetent leaders. Just as quality education was a movement apparent in the debates that union, educational and political leaders took up and patrimony a movement seen in rival notions of heritage and history, governability is a movement where rival demands for good governance clash. If the civic space is where governability lingers until called upon, the friction between rivals is what shapes the movement of governability on the streets and in schools.

With police and paramilitary violence, barricades, and traffic-stopping marches, governability is embodied. To practice governability is to name people, stare them down, and deride them. In the struggles over what counts as legitimate governance, a principal point of contention became the figure of Governor Ruiz Ortiz himself. Ruiz Ortiz was a longtime political operative turned lawmaker and then governor. Social movement actors called him out as an election-rigging operative (*mapache*) (p. 41) who hired student thugs (*porros*)[13] (p. 43) and hack journalists (*chayotes*) (p. 44) to hold power by force and chicanery rather than public administration. Social movement actors turned to satire to address the absurdity of a leader who kills members of the public and justifies his actions as reasonable. One veteran teacher activist, López Aguilar (2010), expressed mock gratitude for the misrule stirred up by Ruiz Ortiz. He called the chief, "*Ulises Ruin Botín*, (Ulises Ruin Plunder—a consonant pun of the Governor's name)," a "despotic and repressive" state agent that "motivated the pueblo to unite once again and to remind the teachers of Oaxaca of their origins among the pueblo" (p. 115). Ruiz Ortiz, for his (mis)rule of law, faced mockery and derision, though the Oaxacan teachers spoke solemnly through the acts of ridicule. One activist's play on words labeled Ruiz Ortiz a "*des-gobernador*" (non-governor/misrule-er) (CCIODH, 2007b, p. 176). For Martínez Vásquez (2006), a key participant and theorist of the movement, the struggle at hand is one of "governability," the pathways taken through institutions, agencies, and individual performances on the streets where versions of honesty, lawfulness, and accountability vie for territory. He deployed *granadero* police to negotiate with teachers, an action that proved Ruiz Ortiz's illegitimacy as governor to many in Oaxaca (p. 145). Still, the teachers, in abandoning their students and obstructing tourism with protest activities, face pointed critique on their legitimacy as public servants in charge of developing the youth of Oaxaca.

To approach the creative tensions of governability that helped shape the counter-conducts on the streets and in schools, I describe an afternoon spent with normal school teachers Wendy and Lourdes at a June 2010 teachers' *bloqueo*, a body blocking of traffic on a major thoroughfare. I link the bloqueo with earlier practices of embodied obstruction in teacher activism from Oaxaca and across Mexico. I then relate the bloqueo to the 2006 Movement, the uprising in Oaxaca City, namely, roadblocks and *barricadas* (defensive barricades), where teachers and others amassed on streets in sufficient numbers to obstruct vehicle passage and safeguard the social movement from uniformed police and paramilitaries wandering the streets at will.

El Bloqueo, June 21, 2010, 1 p.m., Oaxaca City

One Monday, *La maestra* Lourdes and I made our way to the plantón in the central streets and squares of Oaxaca City. Lourdes, a mid-career educator, is a faculty member at a normal school who prepares elementary teachers for service in rural communities. A former elementary school teacher, she has worked in remote *escuelas multigrado*, schools where class grades are mixed in a single classroom. Students often come to class after completing chores and without eating breakfast and teachers promote social and economic welfare—all mainstays of the teaching profession.[14] On our way toward Oaxaca City via curvy mountain passes, I could mark when we left Lourdes's drier region, for the soil turned darker, moister and the recently furrowed fields attested to the more intensive agrarian attention the farther east we got. Today would have been a school day, had the Sección 22 not suspended classes so Lourdes and her colleagues could take their turn at a Oaxaca City plantón event.

I knew Lourdes well. Thirteen years before, I had taught a small group of her teacher colleagues, and she and I became friends. Discussing critical pedagogy, a view that schooling reinforces domination without teaching to raise consciousness and intervene in systems of oppression, she and I had kept in touch over the years. Lourdes eventually encouraged me to carry out my research in Oaxaca. Lourdes herself remained unconvinced that official protest actions of the union was the critical pedagogical intervention her students needed most, even as the leaders of the trade union insist that political change by protest is necessary. Her personal commitment to classroom teaching sometimes clashed with the attention she devoted to the plantones and *megamarchas*, given how the school-based, open-air, resistance-oriented teaching pressured those in village schools outside of Oaxaca City and the surrounding Central Valleys. In the car on the way to

Oaxaca City, I asked her to explain the challenges in balancing protesting and classroom teaching:

> I have considered this, and I tell it to my students. Being teacher (*maestra o maestro*)[15] in Oaxaca involves a dual effort, because you have to follow through in the labor union struggle, which in some ways represents, um, being against the oppressor, or whatever term the others want to call it. This is to say, against all the policies the state puts forward. So I tell [my preservice teachers] that it represents a dual effort, as you have to deliver on that side and also in the rural communities. In the communities, the kids have to be well-served academically. They need to be diligent students. As a teacher, you've got to train yourself. Apart from politically, you have to do it intellectually.

Lourdes's classroom pedagogies end up clashing with her protesting. This *dual effort*[16] burdens the rural teacher with answering classroom needs and the teachers' union demands for participation in events like the bloqueo.[17] Just as state officials struggle to maintain legitimacy to preserve power, the rural teacher struggles to maintain an academically rigorous and socially committed presence in the villages.

Dual Efforts

To be a legitimate maestra or maestro is to balance the professional commitments of classroom teaching and the dissidence obligations of the Sección 22. Lourdes using gender-inclusive speech submits that being maestra deserves specific mention on account of women taking on the greater responsibility of classroom instruction, household management, and trade union activism. Lourdes and Wendy would often mention the way men are the most ardent, vocal militants in the Sección 22, while the women do most of the actual teaching and, as we see below, cooking at protest events like the plantones.[18] English (2005) notices that women educators in the global south negotiate their work between formal or informal spaces, while across rural Mexico, such emergent and interstitial spatiality of doing and knowing becomes a feminist pedagogical space (Trinidad Galván, 2001, 2005). Women spearhead Mexico's teachers (Howell, 1997; Street, 1996, 2001), from a 1916 feminist conference (Cortina, 1990) to the "sustaining force" of women in the Oaxacan teachers' movement to this day (Zafra, 2006, p. 228). Still, women regularly handle more than their share of the dual effort of classes and union activities, as they face male superiors who sexually harass them (Cortina, 1990; Street, 1996) and valorize the women's contributions as more social than issue based (Cortina, 1990, p. 256). Even if their romantic partners are teachers, women balance the union and classroom-based teaching with stay-at-home-mom-level household commitments (Zafra, 2006, p. 247). For women teachers, the dual effort becomes a multiple one.

The multiple effort required of women educators allows little leeway. Teachers who are absent from school, according to Lourdes, easily evoke the indignation of parents who label them "lazy" and "uncommitted." Likewise, teachers who are absent from plantones and megamarchas incur union penalties.

> [Before working as a normal school professor] I was a teacher in an escuela multigrado. I remember that they were always calling us for union related activities, to meetings, to union representation in the plantón …. It turned out that I ended up having just two classes a week. No way! I was ashamed about it all. "You know what" I told the supervisor, "it doesn't seem fair that they always call us in as if we taught in the city, you know? In the union [I said the same thing] too. We cannot get involved the same way an urban school does, because here [by my going to union activities] the school shuts down. I *am* the staff, you know.

Teaching in an *escuela multigrado* encumbers the multiple efforts required of Lourdes. As the rural multigrado teachers need to address a broader range of student needs than their urban single-grade teacher counterparts, union activities in the city amasses more work upon returning. One career teacher, who was currently serving as a regional supervisor, pulled me aside after I introduced my research project on critical teaching, and said that the heart of the struggle for transformation for her cannot be at the marches and union assemblies, but rather, in the rural classrooms where learners depend on teachers who matter most in socially just education.

With classes officially canceled that day, Lourdes and I had just arrived in the city to participate in the bloqueo, an obstruction at a busy intersection inside the city limits. When Lourdes and I parked just outside of the Oaxaca City zócalo, the midday June sunlight blazed at a ninety-degree angle and showed no signs of rain, though the rainy season had started, and the brown hills of winter and spring grew verdant. Lourdes began to walk, and as she took a cell phone call, I stepped toward the broken curb sidewalk of the narrow colonial street and gazed east. Six blocks away stood the venerable laureles de la India that cast shade over the core of the city's pedestrian-filled historic district, the site that united the public to protest the destruction of Oaxacan patrimony. The canopies, as I saw, stretched above the stone buildings and inclined into the street, disobeying the rules of order that cars have first right to a streetscape. Historic Mexican cities often redirect foot and wheel traffic away from an old tree, just as subsistence farmers will plow around the tuft of land that an aged tree stands on. Despite the monumental treescape, this was an urban corridor. Below the trees, blue and green vinyl tarpaulins extended below the leafy awning that the trees made, and there a multitude of teachers, tourists and vendors passed at street level. In this part of the plantón, where the zócalo spilled into Alameda Park in front of the cathedral, near the café where I met the civil servant for coffee, protesters sat-in and passersby passed by, as if the plantones belonged not to the teachers but to the city itself. When Lourdes hung up, she shouted over to me as I was gawking treeward, signaling that we should leave the zócalo area and return an intersection in the direction from which we had come, where teachers in her delegation had begun assembling to obstruct traffic.

Against Terrorism of the State

After eating eggs and corn tortillas and drinking instant coffee, Lourdes and I took a city bus to the bloqueo, where she and I joined Wendy and others from Lourdes's union delegation in Santa Clara.[19] All around, teachers wore hats and loose-fitting clothes, an unambiguous departure from the tidy, comfortable attire at the two normal schools where I had been observing Lourdes and Wendy in the weeks prior. Upon our arrival, someone handed Lourdes a clipboard with a sheet of paper with Sección 22 letterhead, the attendance control mechanism for the bloqueo event. Lourdes and the others dutifully signed the sheet. Below the document's letterhead, it read: "the state plantón staffed by teachers from different regions on a rotating system" and below that, a mission statement: "for education, justice and against state terrorism."[20] State terrorism referred both to the state-sponsored violence and the anti-teacher smear campaigns of current Governor Ruiz Ortiz (Sotelo Marbán, 2008). Curiously, teachers signing in at the plantón to avoid penalties link the Sección 22 with Ruiz Ortiz, who threatened to sue teachers for abandoning their classes (Martínez Vásquez, 2007b, p. 47). The trade union calculates teacher rates in flesh-and-blood presence at the protest rallies to conduct radical-enough participation at the delegation level, and the state conducts responsible-enough teaching by physical presence in the classrooms. The project of governability for teachers is the project of vital politics.

The weather got hot and remained dry, now into the afternoon, and the hills to the north remained lush with sustained rain. Lourdes, Wendy, another colleague, and I stood beneath a bright red flapping campaign banner reading, "Eviel," the first name of the Partido Revolucionario Institucional (PRI) gubernatorial candidate, who would eventually lose the 2010 elections to Gabino Cué and pass the Oaxaca state government to the opposition for the first time in eight decades.[21] Looking toward the hill, people were lining under any slip of shade, including the swiveled cement rise of a pedestrian overpass. The road toward the hill lay in solitude as the traffic rushing by us passed unnervingly close, for I felt discomfort at having my body, among hundreds of others, serve as an obstacle that diverted traffic. As I observed Wendy greeting her colleagues as if at a café, the obstruction our bodies made seemed routine; around us, vendors stood next to load-carrying tricycles with carriages in the front full of water for sale. At one instance, an ambulance nudged its bumper into the line of bodies by the traffic side of the bloqueo. Without a word, the teachers standing there broke their line, ran to the curbsides, grabbed the lapping twine that held up the tarpaulins, and produced an ambulance-sized opening for the vehicle to pass. Despite the traffic disruption as an act of protest, an ambulance could pass with full teacher cooperation. After that, Wendy and I sat off to the side under an umbrella that she had brought. We got talking.

Guelaguetza

I asked Wendy why this intersection in Oaxaca City mattered so much for teachers who live and work across a mountain range, hours away, given that none of the teachers at the bloqueo had come from Oaxaca City or nearby Central Valley union delegations. She said that it was the time of year that Governor Ulises Ruiz Ortiz prepared to celebrate the Guelaguetza Festival in Oaxaca City, which would take place above us on the Cerro del Fortín, a hill in the city. Billed as the Bicentenary Guelaguezta this year, Governor Ruiz Ortiz, at the end of his six-year term, had erected a roof to cover the Guelaguetza Auditorium, an incomplete project that depended on the flow of traffic of construction vehicles up the hill. The bloqueo, by amassing teachers' bodies to prevent construction, protected the integrity of the Guelaguetza Festival, which had until recently been inexpensive enough for locals to enjoy while being exposed to seasonal rain.

Defending the public and accessible pedigree of the festival, the teachers entered into friction with deep historical and symbolic intonations and implications. A communal practice proper to Oaxaca City and the neighboring valleys, guelaguetza serves as a form of mutual aid among families and remains an example of alternative economic practices (Cohen, 1999; Maldonado, 2004; Stephen, 1991). The Zapotec term *guelaguetza*, following Stephen's (1991) work on rural women weavers, becomes a labor exchange resource between households for festivals and parties (pp. 32–33). It plays a political economic role in community life, as a person may reciprocate for the money, labor, and in-kind exchanges decades later, even through the borrower's decedents. As such, guelaguetza allows people who are harvesting and celebrating to distribute the responsibility communally and avoid undue debts of a given family (p. 104); additionally, guelaguetza stands against the market-based relationships implemented in recent decades through the North American Free Trade Agreement (NAFTA) and World Bank adjustments to labor and agriculture[22] which favor specialization and individualization. Most of Oaxaca runs on community-based decision making, a nonparty-based communal governance called *usos y costumbres*, which has been legally protected since 1995 and in practice in 418 of the 570 Oaxacan municipalities. Though many people in villages that practice guelaguetza may opt for market-based or salaried work contracts[23] during the harvest seasons, guelaguetza persists. Many Oaxacans, like the teachers, stand against economic efficiency, agricultural commodification, and labor flexibility, the hallmarks of neoliberal modifications to turn Oaxaca into a more prosperous and governable state. In a site the Spanish had never fully conquered,[24] where Catholic ceremonies syncretized with native religious practices,[25] and where the Mexican efforts to modernize often adapt to what's Oaxacan,[26] the ancestral practice of guelaguetza is the inspiration for the Guelaguetza Festival. Today, the Sección 22 summoned Wendy and Lourdes's delegation to Oaxaca City to obstruct traffic so that a governor would sit beneath an unfinished roof as he inaugurates the festival.

"What's the importance of the Guelaguetza Auditorium?" I asked

"It's an icon," she replied and narrated the recent history of the Guelaguetza Festival and explained why the event and the auditorium are so significant.

The festival has patrimonial importance that overlaps with the teachers' importance, for during the days of the Guelaguetza Festival, Wendy explained, "the eyes of the world" look upon Oaxaca. We see the "harmony of the masses," and for Oaxacans it is "a space for diversity." In recent years, the selection process for representatives from each of the state's regions has become mired in nepotism and cronyism. From the state to municipal levels of government, administrators in the dominant political party in Oaxaca for eighty years, the PRI, have co-opted the process of dance troupe selection, so that the Guelaguetza Festival now, to Wendy, "is another extension of political power." Indeed, the annual festival, such as this year's, promoted alongside Mexico's 1810–2010 bicentennial celebrations, turned into a political display at the expense of its communal Oaxacan roots. "The high feast of the people of Oaxaca" to Martínez Vásquez (2007a) has converted into "political catwalk (*pasarela política*)" where the dance ensembles pay homage to the governor, seated among his guests (p. 90).[27]

In response to the manipulation of the festival's selection process and the symbolic capital garnered by the presiding governor in his seat of honor, Sección 22 members created the Guelaguetza Popular, a free cultural event occurring on the same days as the official one (pp. 89–92). The Guelaguetza Popular has featured instrumental dance-march *calendas*, circumventing the touristic and ritzy thoroughfares in favor of the streets of the lower socioeconomic status neighborhoods across Oaxaca City, inviting the public out onto the streets for the party. This people's fete countered the governor's, and according to Wendy, it lent "voice to groups that had never participated" in the official Guelaguetza. Organizing and carrying out the Guelaguetza Popular has come at a cost. In 2007, the police prevented the teachers from using the Guelaguetza Auditorium, which set off violence that injured over forty people, including twenty police (Davies, 2007b).[28] Such clashes with the police at as historically important a space as the Guelaguetza Auditorium consecrated the Guelaguetza Popular event as part of the pueblo's struggle against the illegitimate authority of the state.

In addition to its corrupt selection process and the clashes with police, the Guelaguetza Auditorium became a point of contention when in 2006 Governor Ruiz Ortiz contracted with his brother to restore historic points of Oaxaca, including the Auditorium. The Sección 22, in their plantón activities, deliberately situated the bloqueo I presently described to channel traffic away from the roof project in order to delay construction. Five years prior, activists impeded construction projects on the Auditorium's "symbolic" hill (Martínez Vásquez, 2006, p. 141). By the time of the current bloqueo, Governor Ruiz Ortiz's construction projects had become part of a kickback scheme, involving invoicing as much as 100 times above the going rate (Sotelo Marbán, 2008, p. 44). Most significantly, the governor's restoration of the Auditorium on the Cerro del Fortín replaced the traditional green *cantera* stone with cement. Thus, hampering the flows of materials and workers up and down the hill is as much a patrimonial intervention as it is a teacher offensive against gubernatorial corruption, arrogance, and misrule. The teacher bloqueo of the Guelaguetza Auditorium in 2010, which interconnects with the teachers' Guelaguetza Popular festival of the prior years, thus vindicated two emblems of Oaxaca: the Auditorium and the teachers as visible agents of community resistance. Traffic would bottleneck; pedestrians and motorists would take notice of teachers teaching during their protest day. Thus, the bloqueo isolates the governor from his project as it embodies the greater public mission that the teachers' movement professes.

Historical Antecedents of Embodied Obstruction

Until now, we have seen the bloqueo as a modern tactic to defy the governor and portray the Oaxacan teachers on the defense in a battlefield of cultural politics and good governance. Below, I present provisional embodied obstructions in prior struggles across Mexico to show how congested contestation has moved against bad governance.

Plantones and Campamentos, 1958

Teacher-embodied obstructions go back at least a half century. In 1958, Mexico City elementary teachers petitioned for salary increases and created what they called a *campamento*, or encampment in the SEP building, a major office of state power (Loyo Brambila, 1979). Contrasting reports of the encampment appeared. Some witnesses called it a "democratic zone," with an atmosphere of "combativeness, authentic collegiality, a real exception to the general run of politics" (p. 55). This democratic space involved the teachers singing the national anthem when questions came up about the their patriotism. Other reports of the campamento were less flattering, such as the *Excélsior* newspaper calling the campamento a "dirty camp of Gypsies" full of drunkards, beggars, and agitators (p. 55). The Mexican president in turn commented in a Teachers' Day speech that the camped-out teachers lacked the discipline needed for teaching (p. 61). This act of obstruction in 1958 physically blocked the ancient SEP building and impeded the politics-as-usual flows in and out of the primary edifice of public school teaching in Mexico which elicited direct commentary from the press and a president in his speech that traditionally pays tribute to teachers as a countrywide force for good.

1980

The 1958 movement centered on capital city teachers; by 1980, we see a broader national democratic teachers' movement with roots in the southeastern states of Chiapas and Oaxaca (Yescas Martínez & Zafra, 1985). This period saw the rise of plantones positioned in front of the executive offices of state power. Mexican social movements had emerged through the 1968 massacre of student activists at Tlatelolco, in Mexico City. As noted in Chapter Two, that sad night in Tlatelolco inspired generations of intellectuals, artists, and political actors (Foweraker, 1993) and teachers.[29] Still, the democratic teachers' movement of 1980 began not as an urban social movement in the nation's center but as a movement in the rural southeast where Oaxacan teachers were protagonists (Foweraker, 1993). Labeled "communists" and "snipers," teachers in 1980, just as in 1958, faced character defamation (Yescas Martínez & Zafra, 1985, p. 133). Fidel Velázquez, a fabled union boss who was affiliated with corporatism-centralized state power, categorized the events as a conspiracy to destabilize Mexico (p. 145). In response to their critics, the teachers formed a June plantón in Mexico City, a "dignity encampment" replete with "committees of struggle," "mobile support-teams (*brigadas*)," and a defense force (p. 143). An observer reported, "in the plantón, there was an interesting life, real communality like … it was a total place of the people, *era todo un pueblo*" (p. 147). Mexican teachers' union democratization efforts take their current form in 1980.

2006–2010, Complications at the Plantón

Looking back to 1958, the Mexican president chided teachers on his May 15 Teachers Day speech. Teachers Day, by 1980, would signal the beginning of the Oaxacan teachers' cycle of resistance, plantón season. On Teachers Day 2006, the teachers set up the annual plantón and detailed their proposals for democracy and higher salaries, and the plantón became a living place for families, teachers, vendors, and shoe shiners and an organizational space for protests alongside other social actors like Indigenous groups. In the car on the way to the Auditorium bloqueo described above, I asked Lourdes to describe her view of the cultural life of the plantones, if she felt these represented in-service training or meaning making for teachers:

> There was none of that. Before there was something, each union delegation had to present a dance number or poetry. But nothing more than that, but now there isn't even that. Before they did things but in the permanent plantones, now they don't, I don't know what they do now.

Lourdes describes how these provisional embodied obstructions echo the uneven social relationships in the workplace and at home. However, the plantones to her are less pedagogically varied in that they resemble the same forms of traditional relations of power of home and the schools. Coming to the plantones, teachers tote televisions and kitchens, and there, Lourdes reported, male teachers ask the women to cook for them as if they were stay-at-home wives. Male teachers expect women who work in Indigenous education, even after marching all day, to cook and clean, Lourdes added. Plantón friends and comrades, for Lourdes, would end up letting her down, while others turn out "on your side (*solidaria*) when you need them." The men teachers who voice the most radical politics can turn out in the plantón to do the least amount of work. "So you go about making friends and similarly dropping others, you know. Why do you want to have these people around during these moments when you need help and they don't give it?" Just the same, communal support flourishes at the plantones. Teachers there, to Lourdes, "have their own ways of self-organizing." As I had seen cell phones charging and lights shining in the evenings, I asked Lourdes how the plantones on public property got electricity. "Somebody goes over and steals the energy … they make metallic *diablitos* (coat-hanger devices to pirate electricity)." Teachers know how to do all these things via their work in rural areas and bring this knowledge to the plantones. In 2010, I would notice teachers climbing up the façades of colonial buildings to fasten a tarpaulin from one side of the street to the next and others cheering the feat from below. Then, the next day, after a union assembly had concluded, teachers on that same street corner were texting in simultaneous silence.

A book describing the 2006 Movimiento, *Teaching Rebellion: Stories from the Grassroots Mobilization in Oaxaca*, becomes more nostalgic than Lourdes on the life of the plantones as a teacher named Eleuterio described the vitality and patience at the provisional space. He noted that "walking through the jungle of plastic tarps, you caught glimpses of all kinds of conversations, but mostly what you heard were teachers discussing the conflict, analyzing social problems, thinking about how to organize" (Denham & C.A.S.A. Collective, 2008, p. 48). Eleuterio detailed a lifeworld of squatters and teachers "sitting on the asphalt, on pieces of cardboard, on plastic chairs … backpacks strewn about over straw mats." There they passed the time "reading newspapers or cheap magazines, planning lessons for when they returned to classes, playing chess or dominos, sewing and embroidering" (p. 47). This description presents the plantones as less combative than the barricadas occurring around the city at the same time.

Lourdes and Eleuterio present a living pulse to the plantón; for tourism industry people, these obstructions disturb their livelihood. For example, a week after the 2010 bloqueo, over a hundred signatures from the Oaxacan business community questioned the 2010 bloqueo and the motives of the dissident teachers in a whole-page ad in *La Jornada*, a left-leaning Mexico City newspaper (Cervantes Navarro, 2010, p. 11). The title read "WOMEN AND MEN OF OAXACA SAY: ENOUGH ALREADY!" and that "society" is now sick of having their businesses fail because of "having no more Guelaguetza and thus no tourism" based on teacher disturbances (p. 11, emphasis in original); Oaxaca, meanwhile, remains in last place in "educational achievement (*aprovechamiento escolar*)." Most emphatically, the ad said that nobody is above the law, a common human rights response to impunity in Mexico, and concluded:

Women and men of Oaxaca will not permit another 2006. WE DEMAND:

- That the teachers (*magisterio*) return to their classrooms and not get involved in political matters.
- That the state government enforce the law and respect of the democratic rule of law (*estado de derecho*).
- That we hold the Federal government responsible for any act of violence or confrontation between Oaxacans. (p. 11)

The appeal for law-and-order and democratic governance by business leaders in a national newspaper reveals a responsiveness toward different social texts and contexts around governability. The ad speaks through the rights of the indignant, using consigna phraseology in declaring that "women and men of Oaxaca say enough already," though not rhythmic or wry in the way the call-and-response consignas often are. The teachers lose legitimacy right from the start: Oaxaca has poor educational performance, the responsibility and livelihood of the *magisterio*, and the teachers interfere with the tourism industry, the responsibility and livelihood of the business sector. Professional specialization matters, for teachers need to leave politics to the politicians and get back to raising skills in reading, writing, and arithmetic. Nevertheless, the state government must carry out the rule of law with respect for democracy and peace. Expressions of discontent with the magisterio are often less reasonable. Business leaders, state authorities, and teachers maintain movement over legitimacy; the business sector calls for better governance on the part of the teachers and the state. The charges against the teachers show less restraint, such as "Love Oaxaca, Kill a teacher," penned on poster pasted on the façade of colonial building in downtown Oaxaca in June 2010.

The campamentos and plantones described above have presaged the conflictive and complex spaces I observed at the bloqueo in 2010. Horizontal relationships intermingle with male nonindigenous dominance of women and indigenous teachers, where radical teachers reproduce the traditional power relations found in schools and in domestic life. It might be tempting to deem the teachers' spaces discussed here as exemplary zones of rebellion and teachers as harbingers of a radical utopian "Oaxaca commune" (Román & Velasco Arregui, 2008) for their blocking construction, redirecting traffic, stealing electricity, defending popular culture, and troubling the business community. Such a celebration of the teachers-as-radicals, as alluring as it may be, would obscure other aspects of the

Movement. The teacher encampments and plantones are acts that speak directly to the summit of executive and business elite power; they are in friction with mass media and political discourses, and for this they use their positions as Mexican state functionaries and Oaxacan citizens as much as village teachers in Indigenous communities. For example, to contest charges of communism, teachers exercised their Mexicanity by singing the national anthem. Teachers would labor peacefully within the public eye while presidential and gubernatorial addresses cast them as negligent or insidiously violent. Even with their roots in the grassroots civic space, the campamentos and plantones come to public visibility in front of the façades of law and instruction, not in the confines of classrooms, peripheral neighborhoods, or village squares. Acts of embodied obstruction draw from an attempt to shape the parameters of governability with their interlocutors in the state regime and the business community. These obstructions often emerge self-managed over centrally coordinated ways, a trait recently noticed in alter-globalization movements across the world (Maeckelbergh, 2009).

Violent Overtures and the Desalojo

The embodied acts of obstruction—the June 21, 2010, bloqueo and its linkages with plantones and campamentos—have elicited critique and scorn from diverse sectors of society, including teachers like Lourdes. The spaces of resistance in public view perform a pedagogy woven into other templates of power, the obstructions interventions of primarily symbolic import. With violence becoming more recurrent in Latin American public protests (Auyero, 2007), the public and performative also become defensive. In Oaxaca, resistance turned belligerent as the teachers' plantón in the early hours of June 14, 2006, filled with 2,000–2,500 officers evicting the teachers from the central areas of the city. Conflict escalated over the months after June 14, with rampart barricadas blocking traffic and protecting neighborhoods across Oaxaca City (El Alebrije, 2007). This is the *desalojo*, the starting point of the 2006 Movimiento.

Wendy, who at the time was a school director, narrated her experience at the 2006 desalojo. On June 13th, she had attended the events at the zócalo plantón. That day, the plantón ran with rumors of police action against the striking and camped-out teachers. A contact of Wendy's in the *Procuraduría*, the State Attorney General's office, informed her of a buildup of police outside the city. Nobody in the plantón, according to Wendy, believed these rumors; the police would never dare attack. Without fear of violence, many slept that night on cardboard mattresses beneath the zigzagging maze of vinyl tarpaulins secure in the knowledge that their greater numbers and the fortitude of the Sección 22 protected them. In Wendy's words, "there are three things that move the state economy: drugs, tourism, and the teachers." With her colleagues, Wendy never fathomed that the governor would use the public employees in the police force to attack their equals in the schools.

On the night of June 13th, after serving her time at the plantón, Wendy took leave to spend the night in a soft bed at her house outside the city center. When she arrived at the door, the taxi driver asked if she planned to return to the plantón, and warned her to stay home that night, for something was brewing. Later, in the wee hours of the next day, Wendy's uncle Francisco, an active member of the Sección 22 and veteran of the 1980 movements, ended up phoning her to tell her that she should stay at home because the police were attacking with a full-on strike. Instead of staying at home, she returned to the city center crossing the names off a sheet for each of the teachers in her school that she found safe. She spent the next hours on the phone, pacing through tear gas-filled streets, searching for the final unaccounted-for teachers. Through the streets of Oaxaca, she would pass houses where she would hear residents shout, "teacher, come in the house," as it was not safe for her there. Wendy balked, responding, "No, I can't. I'm looking for my colleagues." Wendy was not afraid of dying, but rather felt "incensed" at witnessing events such as a friend with a cut cheek from a tear gas canister that a sniper had shot down from a helicopter.

Throughout the heart of the city, principally at the Sección 22 building by the zócalo and the Teachers' Hotel where union assemblies took place several blocks away, the teachers confronted police violence and threats. Then they began to regroup. At Radio Plantón, the teacher radio station within the Sección 22 building, reports surfaced of the police throwing acid in teachers' faces and shouting: "son of a bitch, you're gonna die" (Martínez Vásquez, 2007a, p. 64). In the same building, Osorno and Meyer (2007) noted how women were gathered in the bathrooms, reminded of the recent police violence against civilians in San Salvador Atenco, and threatened with rape (p. 37). Out on the streets, in the plantón itself, the teachers faced encroaching police. Even in their retreat, teachers began to turn the tide. Rosa María Santiago Cruz (2010) narrated how she fled north to Santo Domingo Church. Like the teachers in 1958, she heard her colleagues singing the Mexican national anthem. When she got to the church, she encountered a teacher calling out on a megaphone to his union delegation, the group of teachers who clustered together in plantón sectors. When nobody answered him, Rosa María asserted, "hey man, it's now past the time for delegations" (p. 65). Now in a melee, the smaller divisions of the teachers' union no longer shielded the teachers in safety or led them with democratic governance. Something else was needed to converge in response to the desalojo.

After initially fleeing the plantón, the teachers gathered their wits, and their response came before the tear gas had settled: let's turn against the police and take back the plantón. Unarmed and facing a militarized force, the teachers turned around and marched back to the zócalo, meeting residents from along the streets stepping out of their houses to give the regrouping teachers weapons to take back the plantón. Cuevas Martínez (2010) recalls that the teachers at this point were filled less with the indignation Wendy had mentioned than with a sense of "warranted violence" against the police and the repressive governor who sent them.

> Stones and sticks in the hands of a people tired of lies, tired of poverty, tired of promises, tired of repression and killing, tired of total abandonment—all became a weapon that defended the dignity of the pueblo which is our human dignity. Everything against the powers that be, against the oppressor. (p. 59)

Likewise, Rosa María Santiago Cruz (2010) witnessed the teachers reengaging the unsuspecting police, breaking their line:

> We arrived at the corner of Matamoros and García Vigil [streets], two blocks from the Alameda [park]; there, our colleagues were resisting. The helicopter flew above and shot down tear gas canisters. I saw my colleagues pick up those canisters and toss them back over by the police. In the end, we broke the police perimeter at that street corner and we entered the zócalo! (p. 66)

These testimonials suggest that the desalojo and the teachers' efforts to thwart it released the strain of multiple grievances. The initial violence led to the organized retaking of the plantón, an achievement that became an allegory of democratic teacher resistance, while at the same time the perro roñoso teachers drew bystanders and neighbors onto the streets.

During the desalojo and the retaking of the plantón, Wendy, for her part, never battled with stones or sticks, but rather labored on to locate her evicted teacher subordinates from her school. Her friends and colleagues, she once told me, were more important to her identity as a teacher than the fighting and the union organizing. Then something snapped with the police attack. Wendy faced the corporeality of the desalojo every time she found a protester back from the front lines. With sweat, dust, and glistening coloration, their faces told a striking story, "This is the way wars are," she recalled thinking. The week before our participation at the bloqueo of the Auditorium in 2010, at the four-year anniversary of the desalojo and retaking of the plantón, Wendy found herself in Oaxaca City, listening to a radio program memorializing the 2006 events. Four years on and the teachers were back at the plantón, but relations with the authorities were quiet this year. The year 2006 was not over in Wendy's heart. Hearing these stories on the radio caused tears to stream down her face. The events of June 2006, though the physical wounds may have healed, became steeped in recollection that far outlasted the specific circumstances of the events.

In the end, Governor Ruiz Ortiz's police assault to dismantle the teachers' plantón had failed to break up the teachers. Furthermore, the terrain of that day had become part of a teacher narrative of resistance; the indignity of the teachers facing snipers and nightsticks while exercising their constitutional right to protest publicly had become pedagogical. On June 14 at the 2010 plantón, blaring via loudspeaker before the windows of the Palacio de Gobierno, I heard a recorded ballad that lauded the events of the desalojo: "The troops were pulling back, running in fear / The teachers advanced, the repression was confronted / And they cursed him, that ass (*culero*) Ulises Ruiz Ortiz." Just as street art in Oaxaca 2006 satirized elite leaders and retook the streets for protesters (Lache Bolaños, 2009, p. 209), songs became part of the semiotic imaginary of resistance (Albertani, 2009). For this, according to the teacher Santiago Cruz (2010), Oaxaca became "city of resistance," where "well water got stained blood red; there was sorrow, pain, rage and destruction. Above all, that destruction started to ask for justice! The unity of the people was at hand!" (pp. 66–67). These events confirm that violent repression catalyzed resistance of diverse sectors of society, that bad governance of the state united people (Sotelo Marbán, 2008, p. 63). The violence would intensify, though. Two months after the desalojo and the teachers' retaking of the zócalo, defensive barricadas popped up all around the city to protect the city from police and plainclothes para-police.

The Barricadas

> Education is a territory in which struggles and disputes unfold.
>
> —María de la Luz Arriaga Lemus (2016, p. 107)

On August 21, 2006, more than two months after the desalojo, roving bands of para-police and paramilitaries against the protesters began to shoot the antennas of the independent press, a key source of news in the Movimiento. The now bustling movement grew beyond the trade union concerns of teachers, the plantón no longer formed a single nerve center of the resistance. The shot-out antennas marked the moment when thousands of barricadas went up to protect the media (Sotelo Marbán, 2008, pp. 118–119). In contrast to the plantones as obstructions, the barricadas emerged in 2006 as bulwarks. While the plantón corresponded to the teachers' petitioning for better working conditions and pay, the barricadas emblematized the 2006 Movimiento, as *Son de la barricada* became an anthem of the Movimiento (Albertani, 2009, p. 180).[30]

If the plantones coincide with the triumph of the desalojo, the barricadas coincide with low-intensity warfare. By July 2006, pro-government civilian paramilitary and para-police squads had begun encircling Oaxaca City killing people and restricting the independent press (CCIODH, 2007a, p. 34). These agents also set up anti-Movimiento barricades as checkpoints to restrict the press in town. According to a human rights report:

> On July 18, in the middle of the Guelaguetza, the most important local festival, masked men entered shooting, taking advantage of the fireworks. They took over a building after making a barricada with the objective of impeding the arrival of the press. They destroyed the computers and expelled 31 journalists with gratuitous violence. They hurt one of Ismael Sanmartín's eyes and kidneys. The police never intervened at any moment. (p. 47)

In response to this open aggression and the lack of police protection, locals organized their own protection, the barricadas. At first, this safeguarded the free press outlets and journalists themselves; then, as more violence occurred throughout the summer, defensive barricades protected everyone else. Another Comisión Civil Internacional de Observación de los Derechos Humanos (CCIODH) human rights report testimonial describes these self-defensive mechanisms:

> So you are at a barricada, you don't know at what moment someone could arrive. I was there, for example, the day they killed the architect. It's precisely for that reason that this was at the barricadas. Before the death of the architect, there were barricadas only to protect the places that people had taken, that's it. They were only barricadas for protecting the radio or the office. (CCIODH, 2007a, p. 62)

With killings, the barricadas proliferated, not just to impede traffic but also to protect people.

Additionally, meeting at barricadas, which obstructed the passage of armed groups, the neighbors collaborated and communicated with the rest of the city in resistance, though not always peacefully. Though many at the barricadas came out without any stated political purpose (El Alebrije, 2007), some felt forced to pick sides, for the barricadas "forced the Oaxacan society to be either with or against" the Movimiento (p. 34). While the barricadas forced for-or-against responses, these spaces may have in fact intensified the violence against people in the Movement. Another CCIODH (2007a) testimonial reported that "when there started being barricadas precisely to protect the movement, that's when the hardest repression started. That's when the telephone calls begin coming in, saying that they are going to kill us, that they are going to rape us …" (CCIODH, 2007a, p. 69). Alongside the threat of violence, the barricadas furthermore became points of discursive attacks that were generated in the mainstream pro-Ruiz Ortiz media, which had been vocal since the desalojo on June 14. Reports targeted teachers for not supporting the rights of children (Martínez Vásquez, 2007b, p. 46). Radio and TV messages from a nonexistent parents' association presented children shouting, "teachers back to class not to plantones" (Martínez Vásquez, 2006, p. 142). The expansion of the provisional enactments of obstruction met with discursive attempts against the responsibility of the activists.[31]

As the barricadas were places of violence, the media pressure against the barricadists took a hard-line tenor. The period of the barricadas coincided with Attorney General calling the Movimiento a guerrilla uprising (Martínez, 2006). Other press outlets, following this wave, attempted to discredit the barricadists and call for their removal:

> By October 26[32] it stands out that a radio station appears, Citizen Radio … that transmitted hate messages against the teachers that were supporting URO [Ulises Ruiz Ortiz] [and] called for the ending of the movement of the barricadas, "ending once and for all these dirty pigs at the barricadas." (CCIODH, 2007a, p. 38)

Calling the teachers at the barricades dirty pigs recalls the "dirty camp of Gypsies" comment in the 1958 newspaper report on the Mexico City encampment.

Clear-cut heroes and villains, however, were hard to identify at the barricadas. Frustration and dissonance within the barricadas became visible as teachers considered the barricadists opportunists who took hold of the site, cut down trees, and burned tires. One teacher reported, "I had students who couldn't go to school because they were sick from the burning of tires. That's no good; it's an aggressive attack …" (CCIODH, 2007a, p. 129). Another testimony portrays the teachers at the barricadas as even more violent and anti-communitarian:

> At the teachers' barricadas they impeded the free flow of traffic. They asked people for money in order to go by. There have been cases of assaults with high-powered weapons and people in masks. Those are people who have been paid by teachers to take care of the barricadas. When power is exercised from below, anarchy is above, and it's what happened those days. (CCIODH, 2007a, p. 130)

The teachers at the barricadas, according to this report, took advantage of the chaos, adding to the misrule the advertisement expressed (Cervantes Navarro, 2010, p. 11).

The teachers may well have abused their power at the barricades, though the misrule of the state authorities endorsed the good governance of the teachers, clearing space for them and their allies to intensify their movement of governability. A teacher named Jiménez Felipe (2010) described this in a prose poem: "Accused of being violent, I'm a teacher, disappeared, hurt, dead. I've come back to life.... I'm a new man. I'm expectation, song, struggle, APPO. I'm barricada.... Creator of a thousand battles.... I am ever the people" (p. 131).

Bloqueo Closure

For Wendy, Lourdes, and me, the closure to the bloqueo of June 21, 2010, went more gently than the violence of the desalojo and barricadas depicted above. The afternoon of the bloqueo, I spent two hours with Wendy, Lourdes, and the teachers from their region. Then we left the site and went to a village where we ran across a group of teachers. One teacher, Raquel, came over to greet us. Wendy had been her teacher a decade prior at a rural normal school and Raquel was now on staff at a teachers' center that focused on in-service training. Raquel came by to greet Wendy and describe her recent reading and storytelling activities at Tecotitlán, the rural elementary school outside of Oaxaca City described earlier. Later in the week, Raquel and her colleagues reported they would take their turn at the regional rotational plantón, as the Santa Clara teachers with Wendy and Lourdes had done at the bloqueo earlier that day. For now, Raquel focused her energies on providing trainings at the school. Wendy, in turn, told her about our day, how we had been at the bloqueo. She told Raquel that she and Lourdes needed to report later at the main plantón under the laurel trees on the zócalo, but they would make a quick appearance and return, so we could all visit that evening. I spent the rest of the afternoon with Raquel and the storyteller María Antonia at a textile museum, while Lourdes and Wendy went to check in at the plantón. On our way to the museum, Raquel, María Antonia, and I passed the crossing where Lourdes, Wendy, and I were standing in the bloqueo, which had now reverted to its normal volume of traffic flow.

Governability

Good governance moves on the streets in two ways, plurality and centrality. First, the practices of embodied obstruction on the streets and in parks establish safety in numbers. Barricades, plantones, and megamarchas include nonactivist participation; they express civic space networks that exist latently in neighborhoods and villages and come to public visibility when repressive force becomes visible. This became apparent when women who had never participated in acts of public resistance occupied a radio station (Stephen, 2007) and when the teacher Andrea accepted prayer cards for her teacher colleagues, a gift a lone street vendor provided to the secular, even atheist, corps of public school teachers. The civic space reserve of community support may lack identifiable political forethought, though governability moves in this way as much as a trade union assembly deciding on a collective course of action. As el Alebrije (2007) observed, the roadblocks popped up without anticipation with neighbors sharing food rather than discussing critical social theories. Their spontaneity and plurality, rather than their ideological coherence and formal planning, noted Maeckelbergh (2009), may make multiple, self-managed social movement practices more successful than coordinated, issue-specific ones.

The movement of governability has a second side seen here: a targeted strategy to take down the governor. This occurs in two ways: demonstrating his absence and exposing his inability to maintain a functioning government. The national Senate in Mexico City can determine if a state like Oaxaca has fallen into misrule, "the inability to respond to the demands made by groups in a society" (Martínez Vásquez, 2007a, p. 79), in legal terms, the "disappearance of the powers" (Cámara de Diputados del H. Congreso de la Unión, 1978, p. 1). If lawmakers, judges, or the governor in a state appears to "abandon the exercise of their duties" or are "physically incapacitated" from carrying out their tasks, the federal Senate can nominate a provisional governor (p. 1). Protest marches serve to obstruct the branches of state government from these two conditions that are necessary for constitutional legitimacy. During 2006, the Oaxaca Senate postponed making a decision on ungovernability, in part, Davies (2007a) believed, because lawmakers feared a domino effect of social movements hitting other states (p. 111). Common interests among supposed rival political parties[33] during an election year may have also contributed to political rivals supporting the Ulises Ruiz Ortiz hold on the Oaxaca state government, despite the overwhelming entreaties for his resignation. Ruiz Ortiz for his part revealed his uneasiness about a provisional governor taking his place under a declaration of ungovernability at an October 19, 2006, vote, when he provided documents to prove "state functions are continuing" (p. 138). The senate voted against removing Ruiz Ortiz (p. 142).

The plurality and centrality in the movements of governability are not, however, restricted to activists drawing upon the civic space and legal frameworks, for friction can cut both ways. The teachers' movement, in demanding Lourdes and her colleagues carry out a dual effort of teaching in rural schools and marching in urban protests, becomes the subject of critique. Parents call teachers lazy for absenteeism; even if the union mobilizes the teaching masses in favor of higher-quality education, parents expect teachers' physical presence in the community. Governor Ruiz Ortiz and his team understood this well enough during 2006 to create a phantom parents' organization and broadcast video clips of children changing for the return of classes. Martínez Vásquez (2007a), a sociologist who was active in the 2006 Movimiento, sums up people's frustration with Oaxacan teacher politics:

> It seems to me that the teachers' movement has not been sufficiently self-critical but rather self-complacent. The political discourse has become more dogmatic, sectarian, simplistic [and] black-and-white (*maniqueo*). It has stayed exclusively in the terrain of contestation. (p. 57)

Martínez Vásquez continues with the lack of achievement among Oaxacan schoolchildren, underserved by the dogmatism of the teacher's movement, which "has not gotten past the discourse of 'alternative education' and its call for a 'pedagogical movement'" (p. 58). With low student rates of reading and writing, access to preschool, and high dropout rates in elementary and middle school, "the [state of Oaxaca's negative] results have become clear" (p. 58). Just as repression and educational reforms have provided the points of departure for counter-pedagogies, the teachers expose themselves to critique when their work as activists and practitioners appears unsatisfactory for a public servant in the schools. Thus, on the streets, in the media, and in public intuitions, the state and the private sector keep in dynamic tension with the teachers, per the movement of governability.

Notes

1. The solidarity for the Oaxacan teachers when police on June 19, 2016, killed nine protesters extended internationally. Canadian Prime Minister Justin Trudeau, for instance, discussed human rights and the plight of teachers with Mexican President Enrique Peña Nieto in Ottawa (Maloney, 2016). New York Collective of Radical

Educators (NYCoRE) forwarded a link from Alliance for Global Justice (2016) calling for solidarity with Oaxaca. Moreover, the U.S. embassy, Athens (2016), reported on its Citizen Service page that "Anarchists" (para. 5) planned a July 2 demonstration at the Mexican Embassy.

2. The PFP is a militarized police force, with ex-soldiers dressed in black who form part of the "neoliberal neofascism of our times," according to Esteban.

3. The November altercations with the PFP included protesters with different agendas, not just members of the formal organizations like the APPO and Sección 22 (Martínez Vásquez, 2007a). There were the *chavos banda,* the kids in gangs, who refused to follow any leader in their fight against the police (p. 169). The one unifying demand was the call for Governor Ruiz Ortiz's departure (Martínez Vásquez, 2007b, p. 50).

4. On solidarity, see Gibler (2009) for police violence against street vendors in San Salvador Atenco, 20 miles outside of Mexico City, and the Zapatistas rallying in support (pp. 72–80).

5. The *pueblo*, when referred to in grassroots terms, means the *trusted populous* or *our* people.

6. Minor crook.

7. Radio stations in the Movimiento played a significant role in the Movimiento (El Alebrije, 2007, p. 199). Radio also became the site of participation of many, especially women (Stephen, 2007, 2013).

8. Adjective to describe a negative characteristic, considered vulgar.

9. Supporters and beneficiaries of Governor Ruiz Ortiz's political party, the PRI.

10. The "official" Guelaguetza Festival, as it is called here, refers to a summer folkloric dance performance popular with tourists and locals.

11. Boycotting the official Guelaguetza Festival, the teachers planned their own, the Guelaguetza Popular. *Popular* here is "of the pueblo."

12. The year 2000 became important when the PAN opposition won the presidency in Mexico City, while the ruling PRI still held control of Oaxaca. Without a president in their party, Oaxacan governors became quasi-sovereign and carried out "subnational authoritarianism" (Martínez Vásquez, 2007a) in their handing of intrastate politics (p. 17). Without a president in Mexico City to answer to, they were able to make decisions with fewer out-of-state repercussions. "Authoritarian gubernatorialism" (p. 16) has involved intensified political violence, including the 2010 paramilitary murder of Triqui activist Bety Cariño and international aid worker Jyri Jaakkola.

13. For almost a century, paid student porros have infiltrated and attacked groups that go against school, university, or political party interests (Hodges, 1995, p. 123).

14. Normal school teachers have labeled multigrade school pedagogies as alternative, as the teacher and the community attempt to address the unique needs and conditions of a remote rural area in this way. Still, the work of such teachers has not gone

unnoticed by the Mexican state and the World Bank, as achievement in such schools has been calculated and reported and compared (Velez Bustillo, 2001, p. 454).

15. Gender-inclusive practices to mention collective female nouns and adjectives, rather than defaulting to the masculine, have grown.

16. The Sección 22, according to one commentator (Martínez, 2007), has turned into the repressive and nondemocratic agency that it once opposed (p. 88). A dual effort means the community side of teaching often suffers when protesting becomes mandatory.

17. In interviewing Oaxacan women teachers, Howell (1997) found their participation in union activities led to family accusations of impropriety (pp. 268–269), and partners still expected protesting women teachers to complete domestic tasks (Zafra, 2006, pp. 246–247).

18. Lourdes and Wendy disagreed that radical structuralist framings for critical teaching and activism mattered more than social and community-based ones. The two teachers often expressed exasperation with the rigidity among male teachers in the union, recalling the critical poststructural feminist (Ellsworth, 1992; Lather, 1998) critique of male theorists (Freire, 1994; Giroux, 1988; McLaren, 1999) for being too structuralist.

19. The bloqueo formed part of the rotational regional plantón where teachers from various parts of Oaxaca completed their duty as Sección 22 militants at one or another designated protest spots. This was one of many tactics to engage in simultaneous protests and/or avoid depopulating the local schools of teachers. A delegation is a subunit of the union with forty or more members.

20. Oaxacan teachers have long spearheaded the democratization of their national trade union, the SNTE (Hernández Ruiz, 2006, p. 89). In one of my interviews, a teacher pridefully called the Sección 22 the "spinal column" of the democratic teachers' movement across Mexico. Bautista Martínez (2010) noted that the teachers have been fighting for decades for revitalization of the union and their public acts have become more perceptible, yet their activism has been "institutionalized" whereby union leaders have profited from it all (p. 231).

21. Eviel Pérez Magaña stood as PRI candidate for the 2010 governorship that was eventually won by Gabino Cué, a triumph of the opposition over the PRI, according to many Oaxacan teachers I spoke with, carried on the shoulders of the Sección 22. This debt proved costly to Cué when in February 2011 state police beat up teachers who were protesting the arrival of the president in Oaxaca (see Chapter Two).

22. Structural adjustments have been pressures to devalue the Mexican Peso, cut back on government spending, and reduce tariffs and other barriers to international flows of capital, though, instead of stimulating trade, this led to an economic crisis in Mexico in 1994 (Havard, 1995).

23. In the village of Tecotitlán, a farmer identified how he used the guelaguetza mutual support system for harvesting beans but not garlic. Guelaguetza in the bean harvest

would involve calling his friends to pull the produce, which became less efficient because it included a social pact with workers, serving them food and drink. A system of paid contracts rather than mutual exchanges becomes easier for garlic as the farmer could focus on work and get the goods to market faster. In this way, at least for the agricultural practice of guelaguetza, we see the traditional practice in active combination with wage contracts. In all, the farmers engaging in harvest guelaguetza comes as a conscious choice between multiple options. In the end, even if teachers rally to preserve the Guelaguetza Festival via the bloqueo, the communal act of guelaguetza cannot be revived because it already exists as one among many options.

24. Rubin (1994) and Campbell (1994) address Zapotec cultural politics of resistance in the Istmo region.

25. Norget (2006) explains how Catholicism combined with pre-Hispanic procession and veneration practices.

26. Caplan (2010) discusses local liberalism in Oaxacan history.

27. See Osorno and Meyer (2007, pp. 55–56) on the politician and local tourist industry influence on the festival.

28. The festival's roots stem from communal agricultural and religious practices (Albertani, 2009, pp. 118–119).

29. Castellanos and Jiménez (2007) cover mid-twentieth-century urban and rural armed movements on the Mexican left and right, depicting teacher militancy as produced in normal schools (p. 71) and in opposition to *caciquismo* (p. 65). They show how teachers interpreted urban and rural struggles at home and abroad and drew from manuals like Che Guevara's *Guerra de Guerrillas* (p. 78). Teacher activism even in the most remote corners of Mexico has maintained ties with other struggles blurring a teachers' "Movement" with the pain and triumphs of others.

30. For visual and testimonial accounts of the formation of the barricadas and political impunity, see the short film *Compromiso cumplido* (Mal de Ojo TV & Comité de Liberación 25 de Noviembre, 2007). The title means "fulfilling our public commitment," mockingly drawn from Ruiz Ortiz's public account of how the government has worked alongside the teachers following the nonviolent example set by Benito Juárez.

31. Attacks against the teachers intensified a decade on from the 2006 Movimiento. According to activist teacher Arriaga Lemus (2016), protesting the privatization of education has become criminalized (p. 107), and as "[t]eachers as social leaders endanger the neoliberal system" (p. 111), "[s]mbolic lynching takes place in a media that calls for the repression of 'violent' teachers" (p. 112).

32. One week prior, the Mexican Senate recognized "ungovernability" in Oaxaca, but did not vote for the removal of Ruiz Ortiz from the governorship, a decision that intensified the violence against the teachers (Martínez Vásquez, 2007b, p. 52). Ruiz Ortiz avoided political demise, a *desaparición de poderes*, in part because the PAN colluded

with the PRI in supporting the beleaguered Oaxaca governor (Saldierna & Muñoz, 2006).

33. Newspapers, flyers, and placards have long quipped that the two main parties, the PRI and the PAN are one: the PRIAN.

References

Albertani, C. (2009). *Espejo de México: (Crónicas de barbarie y resistencia)*. San Pedro Cholula, Mexico: Altres Costa-Amic.

Alliance for Global Justice. (2016, June 21). *Urgent call for solidarity with Oaxaca's teachers Union* (Organization website). Retrieved from https://afgj.org/urgent-call-for-solidarity-with-oaxacas-teachers-union

Arriaga Lemus, M. L. (2016). The Mexican teachers' movement: Thirty years of struggle for union democracy and the defense of public education. *Social Justice*, *42*(3), 104–117. Retrieved from https://ezproxy.spscc.edu/login?url=http://search.proquest.com /docview/1802183693?accountid=1172

Auyero, J. (2007). *Routine politics and violence in Argentina: The gray zone of state power*. New York, NY: Cambridge University Press.

Bautista Martínez, E. (2010). *Los nudos del régimen autoritario: Ajustes y continuidades de la dominación en dos ciudades de Oaxaca*. Oaxaca, Mexico: IISUABJO.

Cámara de Diputados del H. Congreso de la Unión. (1978, December 29). *Ley Reglamentaria de la Fracción V del Artículo 76 de la Constitución General de la República* (Federal Law). Retrieved from http://www.diputados.gob.mx/LeyesBiblio/pdf/202.pdf

Campbell, H. (1994). *Zapotec renaissance: Ethnic politics and cultural revivalism in southern Mexico*. Albuquerque, NM: University of New Mexico.

Caplan, K. D. (2010). *Indigenous citizens: Local liberalism in early national Oaxaca and Yucatán*. Stanford, CA: Stanford University Press.

Castellanos, L., & Jiménez, M. C. A. (2007). *México armado 1943–1981*. Mexico City: Ediciones Era.

CCIODH. (2007a). *Informe sobre los hechos de Oaxaca. Quinta visita del 16 de diciembre de 2006 al 20 de enero de 2007* (Report). Barcelona: CCIODH. Retrieved from http://cciodh.pangea.org/

CCIODH. (2007b). Entrevista a la Doctora Berta Elena Muñoz. In C. Beas Torres (Ed.), *La batalla por Oaxaca* (pp. 171–182). Oaxaca, Mexico: Ediciones Yope Power.

Cervantes Navarro, R. (2010, June 29). Las oaxaqueñas y los oaxaqueños decimos: Ya basta. (Advertisement). *La Jornada*.

Cohen, J. H. (1999). *Cooperation and community: Economy and society in Oaxaca*. Austin, TX: University of Texas Press.

Cortés, J. V. (2006). El movimiento magisterial Oaxaqueño: Una aproximación a sus orígenes, periodización, funcionamiento y grupos político–sindicales. In J. V. Cortés (Ed.), *Educación, sindicalismo y gobernabilidad en Oaxaca* (pp. 33–86). Oaxaca, Mexico: Editorial del Magisterio Benito Juárez/SNTE.

Cortina, R. (1990). Gender and power in the teacher's union of Mexico. *Mexican Studies/Estudios Mexicanos, 6*(2), 241–262.

Cuevas Martínez, N. (2010). "La barricada más grande lo llevo en el corazón." In M. A. Damián (Ed.), *Educación popular: Apuntes de una experiencia liberadora* (pp. 57–61). Oaxaca, Mexico: La Mano.

Davies, N. (2007a). *The people decide: Oaxaca's popular assembly.* Natick, MA: Narco News Books.

Davies, N. (2007b, July 17). Oaxaca government armed forces use violence to prevent the people's use of the Guelaguetza Auditorium. *The Narco News Bulletin.* Retrieved from http://www.narconews.com/Issue46/article2735.html

Denham, D., & C.A.S.A. Collective. (2008). *Teaching rebellion: Stories from the grassroots mobilization in Oaxaca.* Oakland, CA: PM Press.

el Alebrije. (2007). Las noches en la Ciudad de la Resistencia: Entrevista a "El Alebrije." In. C. Beas Torres (Ed.), *La batalla por Oaxaca* (pp. 197–202). Oaxaca, Mexico: Ediciones Yope Power.

Ellsworth, E. (1992). Why doesn't this feel empowering? Working through the repressive myths of critical pedagogy. In C. Luke & J. Gore (Eds.), *Feminisms and critical pedagogy* (pp. 90–119). New York, NY: Routledge.

English, L. M. (2005). Third-space practitioners: Women educating for justice in the global south. *Adult Education Quarterly, 55*(2), 85–100.

Esteva, G. (2007, November). La otra campaña, la APPO y la izquierda: Revindicar una alternativa. *Cuadernos del Sur, 12*(24/25), 5–37.

Foweraker, J. (1993). *Popular mobilization in Mexico: The teachers' movement 1977–87.* New York, NY: Cambridge University Press.

Freire, P. (1994). *Pedagogy of the oppressed* (New revised 20th anniversary ed.). New York, NY: Continuum.

Gibler, J. (2009). *Mexico unconquered: Chronicles of power and revolt.* San Francisco, CA: City Lights.

Giroux, H. A. (1988). *Teachers as intellectuals: Toward a critical pedagogy of learning.* Granby, MA: Bergin & Garvey.

Havard, J. (1995, February 11). World summit on social development. *Lancet, 345*(8946), 335–336.

Hernández Díaz, J. (2007). Los dilemas en la construcción de ciudadanías diferenciadas en un espacio multicultural: El caso de Oaxaca. In J. Hernández Díaz (Ed.), *Ciudadanías diferenciadas en un estado multicultural: Los usos y costumbres en Oaxaca* (pp. 35–86). Mexico City: Siglo XXI Editores/Universidad Autónoma Benito Juárez de Oaxaca.

Hernández Ruiz, S. (2006). Insurgencia magisterial y violencia gubernamental en Oaxaca. In J. V. Cortés (Ed.), *Educación, sindicalismo y gobernabilidad en Oaxaca* (pp. 87–123). Oaxaca, Mexico: SNTE.

Hodges, D. C. (1995). Mexican anarchism after the Revolution. Austin, TX: University of Texas Press.

Howell, J. (1997). 'This job is harder than it looks': Rural Oaxacan women explain why they became teachers. *Anthropology & Education Quarterly, 28*(2), 251. Retrieved from Bibliography of Native North Americans database.

Jiménez Felipe, L. (2010). Pueblo Soy. In M. A. Damián (Ed.), *Educación popular: Apuntes de una experiencia liberadora* (pp. 131–132). Oaxaca, Mexico: La Mano.

Lache Bolaños, N. P. (2009). La calle es nuestra: Intervenciones plásticas en el entorno de la Asamblea Popular de los Pueblos de Oaxaca. In V. R. Martínez Vásquez (Ed.), *La APPO: ¿Rebelión o movimiento social?: Nuevas formas de expresión ante la crisis* (pp. 199–217). Oaxaca, Mexico: IISUABJO.

Lather, P. (1998). Critical pedagogy and its complicities: A praxis of stuck places. *Educational Theory, 48*(4), 511–519.

López Aguilar, S. J. (2010). Origen de un maestro. In M. Areva Damián (Ed.), *Educación popular: Apuntes de una experiencia liberadora* (pp. 89–90). Oaxaca, Mexico: La Mano.

Loyo Brambila, A. (1979). *El movimiento magisterial de 1958 en México.* Mexico City: Ediciones Era.

Maeckelbergh, M. (2009). *The will of the many: How the alterglobalization movement is changing the face of democracy.* London: Pluto Press.

Mal de Ojo TV, & Comité de Liberación 25 de Noviembre. (2007). (DVD). *Compromiso cumplido.* Oaxaca, Mexico: Mal de Ojo TV.

Maldonado, B. (2004). Comunalidad y educación en Oaxaca indígenas. In L. M. Meyer & B. Maldonado (Eds.), *Entre la normatividad y la comunalidad: Experiencias innovadoras del Oaxaca indígena actual* (pp. 24–42). Oaxaca, Mexico: IEEPO/Colección Voces del Fondo; Serie Molinos de viento.

Maloney, R. (2016, June 28). Trudeau discusses deaths of protesting Mexican teachers at presser with Enrique Pena Nieto. *The Huffington Post Canada.* Retrieved from http://www.huffington post.ca/ 2016/06/28/trudeau-mexican-teachers-enrique-pena-nieto_n_10718790.html

Martínez, N. (2006, August 22). Califica Procuraduría a APPO de guerrilla urbana. *El Universal.* Retrieved from http://www.eluniversal.com.mx/notas/370333.html

Martínez, V. L. J. (2007). ¡Ya cayó! ¡Ya Cayó!: Colapso del Sistema político en Oaxaca. *Cuadernos del Sur, 11*(24–25), 81–106.

Martínez Luna, J. (2007). De Juárez a García. In G. Esteva, F. Gargallo, J. Martínez Luna, & J. Pech Casanova (Eds.), *Señor Juárez* (pp. 73–99). Oaxaca, Mexico: Archipiélago.

Martínez Vásquez, V. R. (2006). Movimiento magisterial y crisis política en Oaxaca. In J. V. Cortés (Ed.), *Educación sindicalismo y gobernabilidad en Oaxaca* (pp. 125–149). Oaxaca, Mexico: SNTE.

Martínez Vásquez, V. R. (2007a). *Autoritarismo, movimiento popular y crisis política: Oaxaca 2006.* Oaxaca, Mexico: UABJO.

Martínez Vásquez, V. R. (2007b). Crisis política en Oaxaca. *Cuadernos del Sur, 11*(24–25), 39–62.

Martínez Vásquez, V. R. (2009). Antinomias y perspectivas del movimiento popular en Oaxaca. In V. R. Martínez Vásquez (Ed.), *La APPO: ¿Rebelión o movimiento social?: Nuevas formas de expresión ante la crisis* (pp. 329–347). Oaxaca, Mexico: IISUABJO.

McGinn, N., & Street, S. (1984). Has Mexican education generated human or political capital? *Comparative Education, 20*(3), 323–338.

McLaren, P. (1999). *Schooling as a ritual performance: Toward a political economy of educational symbols and gestures.* Lanham, MD: Rowman & Littlefield.

Norget, K. (2006). *Days of death, days of life: Ritual in the popular culture of Oaxaca.* New York. NY: Columbia University Press.

Osorno, D. E., & Meyer, L. (2007). *Oaxaca sitiada: La primera Insurrección del siglo XXI*. Mexico City: Random House Mondadori.

Román, R., & Velasco Arregui, E. (2008). Mexico's Oaxaca commune. *Socialist register, 44*, 248-264

Rubin, J. W. (1994). COCEI in Juchitán: Grassroots radicalism and regional history. *Journal of Latin American Studies, 26*(01), 109–136.

Sadlier, S. T., & Morales Sánchez, I. R. (2012). Open the doors, paint the walls and ignore the bells: Refashioning the post-movimiento classroom to foment "civic space" ties. In S. Mills & P. Kraftl (Eds.), *Educating for peace in a time of permanent war: Are schools part of the solution or the problem?* (pp. 197–208). New York, NY: Routledge.

Saldierna, G., & Muñoz, A. E. (2006, October 19). Hay ingobernabilidad, pero no procede la desaparición de poderes. *La Jornada*. Retrieved from http://www.jornada.unam.mx/2006/10/19/index.php?section=politica&article=007n1pol

Santiago Cruz, R. M. (2010). 14 de Junio: La unidad popular. In M. A. Damián (Ed.), *Educación popular: Apuntes de una experiencia liberadora* (pp. 62–67). Oaxaca, Mexico: La Mano.

Sotelo Marbán, J. (2008). *Oaxaca: Insurgencia civil y terrorismo de estado*. Mexico City: Era.

Stephen, L. (1991). *Zapotec women*. Austin, TX: University of Texas Press.

Stephen, L. (2007). "We are brown, we are short, we are fat...we are the face of Oaxaca": Women leaders in the Oaxaca rebellion. *Socialism & Democracy, 21*(2), 97–112.

Stephen, L. (2013). *We are the face of Oaxaca: Testimony and social movements*. Durham, NC: Duke University Press.

Street, S. (1996, January 1). Democratization "from below" and popular culture: Teachers from Chiapas, Mexico. *Studies in Latin American Popular Culture, 15*, 261–278.

Street, S. (2001). When politics becomes pedagogy: Oppositional discourse as policy in Mexican teachers' struggles for union democracy. In M. Sutton & B. A. Levinson (Eds.), *Policy as practice: Toward a comparative sociocultural analysis of educational policy* (pp. 145–166). Stamford, CT: Ablex Publisher.

Trinidad Galván, R. (2001). Portraits of mujeres desjuiciadas: Womanist pedagogies of the everyday, the mundane and the ordinary. *International Journal of Qualitative Studies in Education (QSE), 14*(5), 603–621.

Trinidad Galván, R. (2005). Transnational communities en la lucha: Campesinas and grassroots organizations "Globalizing from below." *Journal of Latinos & Education, 4*(1), 3–20. Retrieved from ERIC database.

U.S. Embassy Athens. (2016, July 1). *Security message for U.S. citizens: Demonstrations and strike*. US Department of State: US Citizens service (website). Retrieved from http://athens.usembassy.gov/demonstrations3.html

Velez Bustillo, E. (2001). Education sector strategy. In M. Giugale, O. Lafourcade, & V. H. Nguyen (Eds.), *Mexico, a comprehensive development agenda for the new era* (pp. 446–478). Washington, DC: The World Bank.

Yescas Martínez, I., & Zafra, G. (1985). *La insurgencia magisterial en Oaxaca 1980*. Oaxaca, Mexico: IISUABJO.

Zafra, G. (2006). Género y educación: Las mujeres del movimiento magisterial Oaxaqueño. In J. V. Cortés (Ed.), *Educación, sindicalismo y gobernabilidad en Oaxaca* (pp. 223–248). Oaxaca, Mexico: SNTE/Editorial del Magisterio Benito Juárez.

7

Laughing in Protest

Laughter Lends a Movement Meaning

Soundscapes of Protest

In April 2011, I had not seen Yolanda, an elementary teacher at a school outside of Oaxaca City, for three weeks when she called to say that she would be at the *plantón* in the *zócalo*, and that I could come by in the morning to catch up on her efforts to foment reading. Yolanda and I met during my time shadowing rural sixth-grade teacher, Marcos, in his self-managed pedagogies described at length in Chapter Three. I met Yolanda at a reading workshop in a Oaxaca City elementary school gymnasium, as we performed lectern-based dramatic readings of popular children's texts. With text performativity established among the teacher participants, Marcos assigned us to groups to interpret and represent a key feature of a lower-grade student book from our workshop. Yolanda and I drew the same text about a fruit tree and a fountain. I performed tree to Yolanda's fountain, and our interpretation of the leafy and watery scenario before the workshop participants led us to talking about elementary school practices for reading for pleasure. "Come to the protest on Saturday," Yolanda suggested.

That Saturday of a teacher protest, few patrons sat in the terrace of the restaurant as I waited for Yolanda. I turned to the server to ask if the teachers' plantones led to more customers.

"No, there is less business," she said, tapping her elbow with the palm of her opposite hand, gesturing, "*son codos los maestros* (the teachers are cheapskates)."

I finished breakfast at the restaurant area off to the east side of the zócalo, when I discerned, with curiosity more than with concern, helicopters thumping overhead. Helicopters are iconic, linked to the 2006 repression, as graffiti and placards over the years have used the helicopter as a metaphor of misrule. However, in my years as teacher and researcher in Oaxaca, I almost never saw or heard actual air traffic. Although circling airplanes form a constant part of the Mexico City landscape, descending south over the western suburbs, to Periférico Sur, to the runways on the eastern side of the dried-out lakebed that is Mexico City, Oaxacan skies are different. I would sometimes retreat to a cool nighttime roof and observe the glittery sky. I learned to discern far-off voices and identify the course of a satellite, like a ball bearing passing beneath the nighttime vault. Not seeing air traffic in Oaxacan skies reveals my sheltered view of the conflicts that have gone on around me. Nancy Davies (2007) observed that police helicopters shattered car window glass with sniper-launched tear gas canisters (pp. 10–11), which offered optimism to one neighbor who exclaimed, "we are hostages in our own city! [The helicopters] can clean out these [protesters]" (p. 131). Five years on, waiting for Yolanda at the 2011 teacher protest, the helicopter thundered so abruptly that I felt air press against my chest and sensed the roar of the choppers pulling above the treetops.

The aircraft sounds grew distant as a distinct persistent noise grew more prominent. Emanating from 30 yards away, I heard a *corrido*, a ballad, transmitted over a loudspeaker at the central table of the plantón, the information booth at the façade of the Palacio, where speeches and music bellowed out, like the song presented in Chapter Six. It was a song I had heard before, "*El corrido del magisterio*" (the ballad[1] of the teachers), which went, "*Ulises Ortiz hermano / del perro y del marrano / mapache de nacimiento / no quieres entender / ¡Aplaudan! ¡Aplaudan! / No dejen de aplaudir / El pinche de Ulises se tiene que salir.*" This lyrical storytelling, directed at the former Governor, Ulises Ortiz, in English would read as, "Ulises Ortiz brother / Of the dog and swine / *Mapache* by nature / You won't ever get a clue / Applaud, won't you applaud! / Don't stop your applause / The *pinche* Ulises has got to be gone!"

"The ballad of the teachers" played from the central table some days before, and its use of adolescent vulgarity and mockery through animal-reference assaults, all within the ballad genre of Mexican folkloric music, captivated me.[2] Ballading with playful crudeness on the "dog and swine" seems juvenile and light, but it works as an aural analysis of the misrule governing state politics. The term *mapache*, the Maya word for raccoon, in political discourse describes a person who goes about rigging elections on the sly. The political mapache, or party hack, has become synonymous with the impunity of the electoral system that had kept the Partido Revolucionario Institucional (PRI) in power in Oaxaca for eighty-one years. To call a politician *mapache* suggests their cleverness and treachery, not their skillful leadership. Furthermore, mapache garners offensive attention by assigning zoomorphic traits to humans, an insult to demean a public servant.

During the ballad, I scanned the crowd for Yolanda, hoping to begin our discussion on reading in village schools. Another track came on the teacher plantón loudspeaker, a mock-advertisement for an upcoming circus, a hyperbolic boasting of the death-defying feats of the state government in their handling of the protesting teachers in 2006. If the ballad had sounded out state repression against teachers in vocally addressed historical terms, like Woody Guthrie chronicling the Sacco and Vanzetti murder trial, the mock circus ad does something different: it laughs at tyranny.

The zócalo around me had been the scene of teacher protest and repression over the decades in Oaxaca City. On this day, Yolanda's protest involved only a few dozen *primaria* teachers who, instead of shouting out radical *consignas*, played songs and jokes over a loudspeaker before the *Palacio de Gobierno*, just below the governor's balcony. After a few tracks, they played the mock advertisement for a circus that introduced the listener to Oaxaca Governor, Ulises Ruiz Ortiz, calling him "Uli URO" a mapache party hack who sent the police to raid a peaceful protest encampment, the *desalojo*, which touched off the 2006 Movimiento.[3] The mock circus ad begins:

> Ladies and gentlemen, boys and girls, welcome to the *Totopo*, Shrimp, and Cheese Circus where we have the most useless jugglers, acrobats, and clowns (trumpet circus music). At the head of the circus, we welcome the mapache that speaks, Ulises Ruiz Ortiz (applause) followed by the evil little doll, "El Chucky," Jorge Franco (screams of terror).[4] Now, it would be a mistake to leave out our feminine beauty, dressed in a mini thong and riding a pony: here is our beloved Lizbeth Caña, who shall hang from her own tongue. A round of applause, if you will (applause)…. Coming next, we have our first number, with our star juggler, in one of his most far-out acts that he has never, never, never been able to achieve: here is Uli URO with his act, the desalojo … (build up noise) … (helicopter and gunshot noises)…. URO, not at the children!

The announcement, transmitted by the teachers at the plantón, portrays Governor Ruiz Ortiz, his Secretary of the Interior, Jorge Franco, and Attorney General,

Lizbeth Caña, as hapless and violent circus performers. If they cannot get through a circus performance, they cannot perform their functions as civil servants, the satirical tone suggests. More seriously, if lawmakers designate Oaxaca as in a state of misrule (*ingobernabilidad*), leaders run the risk of removal from office (*desaparición de poderes*).[5] Using humor, the circus announcement delivered snippets of recent history to passersby, onlookers, and the teachers themselves.

As I heard this absurd circus ad on a serious theme from the central table of the teachers' protest encampment, not ten meters from the gubernatorial balcony, I realized that the humorous protest practices carried a sonic history, a history that was altogether distinct from testimonials (Stephen, 2013), journalism (Osorno & Meyer, 2007), human rights' reports (Comisión Civil Internacional de Observación por los Derechos Humanos, 2007), political analyses (Martínez Vásquez, 2006), and the teachers' ballad. I met Yolanda and asked her how the overstated and irrational humor at a conflictive site became meaningful to the teachers who survived the repression. She downplayed the importance of humor, commenting that the Totopo, Shrimp, and Cheese circus advertisement counted as the funny side of sending a political message.[6] Reading the sonic literacy of humor—the penetration of melody, meter, metaphor, mockery, and memorialization—seemed to be a provocative angle to the critical project Oaxacan teachers and their affiliates across Mexico carry out. This seventh chapter makes space for how humor condenses and carries messages on the current state of good and bad governance, and it explores how humor influences the public record of state repression and educational reform in ways that direct, sober speech cannot.

Absurdity and the Formal

Instead of conversing with Yolanda at the plantón about reading and writing practices as I had intended, the Totopo, Shrimp, and Cheese Circus announcement made me pause at humor juxtaposed with misrule. Upon meeting Yolanda, I had come to a crossroads in my ethnographic fieldwork on the pedagogies of the Oaxacan teachers' movement, the three-decade-old democratic campaign among educators in the Sección 22, the state's local of the Sindicato Nacional de Trabajadores de la Educación (SNTE) (Yescas Martínez & Zafra, 1985). Teachers across Mexico have long taken up village-centered "intellectuals of the poor" positions (Foweraker, 1993, p. 19), which have featured union-centered projects, ones involving salary, democratic decision making, and social movement work concerning a broader roster of civil society struggles.[7] This is to suggest that being political implies different things to different teachers. In my own teaching and research, I have noticed how Oaxacan teachers locate themselves as defenders of public education and opponents of standardized and decontextualized education. For teachers, this commitment links theory, practice, policy, and pedagogy, all of which intertwine teachers' lives with many forms of politics and pedagogies. For instance, speaking with the teacher trainer and her preservice teacher candidates who were developing an ethnomathematical project using popular games and pasta piece manipulables, as reported in Chapters One and Two, the pedagogies worked with practices and items that are culturally relevant to village life. The trainer and her charges suggested that the 2009 reformed sixth-grade textbooks, just off the press, furnished mathematical examples that are inaccessible to elementary pupils in rural Oaxacan schools. Pulling the textbook off the shelf, they showed me an image of a Mexico City subway station in a word problem that compared ticket prices (Balbuena Corro, 2009, p. 117). The group called this official textbook example bizarre and disturbing as children at their teaching sites would get no scaffolding by teaching through subways. They told me how introducing games and pasta pieces strung together like a bracelet to teach "seriation, classification, and addition" helped them work with "concrete, abstract, and symbolic" values and stave off the damage of the abstruse textbook exercises. The question of how to provide quality education among Oaxacan elementary educators, then, has drawn on popular practices, which turned my attention to the everyday popularity of humor.

A year after the math teachers had shown me how popular games worked better than subway cars, I had gathered most of my data and turned to the description of how teachers and their pupils engaged in critical literacies (Comber, 2001). In researching teacher literacies through communities of practice (Lave & Wenger, 1991) and affinity spaces (Gee, 2004), the use of the voice kept surfacing as important regarding reading, writing, and socializing. For instance, in one village school with a cross-disciplinary reading project, parents recalled a boom in their children's verbal self-confidence as a sign that the reading project was working for them. Oral persuasiveness mattered to Oaxaca-born anarchist, Ricardo Flores Magón, who persuaded ideological opponents by using his lyrical oratory (Hodges, 1995, p. 9), and politicians from the Isthmus of Tehuantepec used Zapotec rather than Spanish in official spaces like Juchitán City Hall to address local listeners and exclude outsiders (Stephen, 1996, p. 109). The day I heard the humor in the circus ad, I had already been following teachers around to different social spaces and cities as if I were a traveling circus performer myself. It seemed right to travel beyond the classrooms in pursuit of the teachers, for methodologically, I took power not as lingering within single schoolrooms or communities but instead as relational, "rooted in the whole network of the social" (Foucault, 1998, p. 141). For this reason, this chapter draws on fieldwork and document analysis from public squares, rural homes, mealtime conversations, and weekend storytelling seminars to examine oracy and literacy practices.

For decades, Oaxacan teachers have explored education and power in their alternative education responses to state-centered (subway car-riddled) curricula (Hernández, 2009). Teachers often lack the skills that are needed to implement such proposals. So the question of how to implement such pedagogies in the classroom has driven national (CNTE, 2010, 2013) and Oaxacan (CEDES 22, 2009) teacher conferences and annual in-service critical pedagogy and action research workshops that teachers attend prior to the start of each school year (CEDES 22, 2010). Conversations I have heard around these training events often get gridlocked in theoretical debates or avoid theory altogether and only center on practice.[8] In practice, however, just like pasta piece manipulables, teachers have embraced the human voice as an alternative educational device, something I observed in two schools I visited in the Central Valleys region of the state. Then, upon listening to the humorous circus ad in the central square of Oaxaca City, I considered the vocal grounding for alternative education and drew on Gustavo Esteva's (2010) critique of formal schooling and Meyer and Maldonado (2004) who helped instigate Indigenous education proposals that were rooted in communalist epistemologies and governance apropos to rural Oaxacan community life. Below, I show how spoken and written humor has become a critical pedagogical practice of teachers engaged in union- and school-based political projects, which offer insight into how alternative educational incursions are emerging in teacher practice.

Just as a sociocultural turn has enabled literacy projects that hit at a more human and personal level than decoding texts, in recent decades, a cultural turn has enveloped the study of social movement politics. Social movement practices call upon the arts to broaden participation (Reed, 2005). Across the globe and in Latin America, where textual practices like the circus ad at the plantón become public pedagogies, humor and wordplay take political messages down to the level of everyday life on the streets. While artists in Oaxaca have long deployed their craft to effect change in socioeconomic life (Albertani, 2009), humor forms a serious part of struggles, too. In philosophy, psychology, and folklore studies, humor has enjoyed a long-standing status as worthy of study. In social movement studies, less has come to us on the power of the jocular. Humor has called out the humorlessness of the German state in the 1960s (Teune, 2007), while in Poland, the Orange absurdists reminded people that the Solidarity Movement, which had become mainstream by the 1980s, originated among the people (Romanienko, 2007, p. 144). In urban Peru and Mexico, Vich, Edwards, and Nicolini (2004) and Haviland (2011) portray how humorous street performers occupy public spaces that would normally be off-limits to people of the performers' provincial backgrounds and working-class status. Olesen (2007) has explored the humor used by the Zapatistas in Chiapas, Mexico, to promote their movement's humanity and accessibility. Social movement research on humor has shown the door that humor opens toward public participation. However, Goldstein (2003), whose work on laughter in Brazilian shantytowns cautions against considering it a resistance tactic (p. 9), implies that social change calls for more direct political action than laughter provides.[9] Most social movement analysts who discuss humor read it as a culturally specific or interactively appropriate mode of communication, but the immediate and humanizing pull of humor that I observed among teachers facing repressive policies and precarious working conditions touches a deeper chord of critical literacy than an exchange of textual information.

Goldstein rightly measures her expectations on laughter's ability to change the material conditions of repression. The problems of bad governance—elected leaders who attack public-service-oriented teachers in the Oaxacan parks—set up a problem which humor on its own cannot fix. The circus advertisement may offer no change, though the playful mockery represents a deliberate practice of politics and signals a potential pathway into critical teaching that more abstemious and direct actions do not. Examples of this abound: civil rights leaders Miles Horton and Paulo Freire made use of humor in their long careers in folk and popular education (Horton & Freire, 1990), and McLaren (1999) observed laughter helping students decenter the teacher. Additionally, Mayo (2010) drew out humorous "provisional fields" linking students via "enjoyment" to change thought and social patterns (p. 511). These are apt overtures to appreciating humor as a critical literacies practice, though the critical purchase of humor remains underdeveloped.

How does humor work politically? Delving into two points of theory, the *anti-rite* and *presence*, helps us appreciate how humor works when the stakes are high and direct transformation of social and economic conditions is not yet possible. Rites in the world around us, for starters, are inflexible reinforcers of the status quo (García Canclini, 2001, p. 134). A council member in my home city once explained to me how members of the public might have an ongoing grievance written up in editorials, discussed in neighborhood meetings, and brought to the city hall foyer with activist fervor. Coming up to the podium to address the council, their tone softens and the militancy of their argument dissolves. It is not as if they are addressing the United Nations or standing on the spot of a famous speech, for this is just city council. The discursive experience of entering chambers, facing a circle of elected officials, speaking into a microphone, taking up an allotted spot, and forming part of the meeting's public record makes such a presentation of a public grievance a *rite*. Sometimes the power of rites and rituals overwhelms an individual who approaches the podium unarmed and disrobed. Humor can become a delivery mechanism for public responses in circumstances where rites and rituals disempower individuals. The practice of humor establishes *anti-rite* capacity.

> The anti-rite of the joke shows the sheer contingency or arbitrariness of the social rites in which we engage. By producing a consciousness of contingency, humor can change a situation in which we find ourselves, and can even have a critical function with respect to society. (Critchley, 2002, p. 10)

Humor as an anti-rite suggests that many of the products, practices, and events that surround us are often propped up as truthful, ritualistic, or merely *there*. The anti-rite involves a communicative play on social convention to shake up the staid formality, foment a consciousness of contingency, a presence (Sassen, 2002) across spaces where a social actor has no permission to be (p. 11). We have seen the anti-rite and presence described by Mikhail Bakhtin (1984) in medieval village feast days when groups would mock and mimic the nobility and the clergy. In daily life, the peasants may not have dared talk back to the bishops and landowners, yet during carnival the established order to social dynamics was reversed.

Heteroglossia

The anti-rite and presence of practices, like humor, enhance public participation because of a larger social force we can call *heteroglossia*. Heteroglossia works like a hurricane, which sweeps across warm waters, gathering power. If you take on the hurricane head on, you will break apart like the wooden pier at Gulfport, Mississippi during Hurricane Katrina, but if you understand that the hurricane moves by the intervention of the jet stream, high- and low-pressure zones and landmass features, when the storm makes landfall, then it becomes apparent that the storm's force is a liability. Barrier islands, for example, break up the storm surge. The cooler temperature and rough surface of the land weaken the whirlwind, and the prevailing winds across the region dictate the storm's direction. All the intervening climatic forces that operate in and outside of the hurricane are what we can call *heteroglossia*, which for us here includes the written, spoken, and performed word carried out in circumstances where speaking directly and singularly may be too daunting. Heteroglossia, as a set of ill-coordinated and variegated texts, artifacts, and social practices, may proliferate the face of much more powerful forces, but like the landforms that scour the winds of a storm, heteroglossia provides marked subversion. "[A]ll utterances are heteroglot in that they are functions of a matrix of forces practically impossible to recoup, and therefore impossible to resolve" (Holquist, 1981b, p. 428).

A common heteroglot practice in protests is street art, which *bombs* the surfaces of the non-protest street with stenciled grotesque faces, sober announcements, and playful graphics that would startle even the most experienced activists in 2006 (Nevaer & Sendyk, 2009). In the "spectral silence" of coming to Oaxaca City on November 1, recalls Claudio Albertani (2009), "the walls talked" with national heroes, sacred virgins, and reviled despots presented in radical imagery (p. 17). In my 2010–2011 observations, graffiti and murals, in schools and on streets, drew neighbors and office clerks to the sidewalks with cans of paint that matched the colors underneath the tags and stencils, which prolonged the heteroglossic turn. Chapter Five went in to greater depth on how a wall retains its unremarkable, load-bearing utility, until "getting up" (De La Rosa & Schadl, 2014) practices of street artists who bomb, tag, sticker and write on it into its shared, intertextual dimensions. This is not just about art, rather it is about power. For instance, in November 2006, after months of protesting in Oaxaca City, the feared federal police (PFP) had arrived removing tents, banners, and writing in the zócalo (Davies, 2007). Then, "while the PFP were scrubbing the walls … the spray-painting youngsters were adding slogans" (p. 157). The police wipe-down and the youthful writing form part of the heteroglossic clash of powers that, like a hurricane facing ground resistance, is impossible to resolve.[10] As for the Totopo, Shrimp, and Cheese Circus ad above, by playing it on the zócalo, the desalojo that occurred at the same spot four years earlier becomes an unfinished event for the teachers; as humor is only funny now, the text becomes present for the struggling teachers.[11]

For over a century, humor has been connected with Mexican politics (Barajas, 2000). Executive politicians in Mexico who repress or stand aloof from the public risk facing heteroglossic mocking assaults like the circus ad against the governor. Such politicians deserve special mention here, given how elite provincial politicians since 2000 have become quasi-sovereign (Martínez Vásquez, 2007a, p. 16) when the ruling PRI lost the presidency to the PAN opposition for two consecutive terms (2000–2012), and PRI governors had no higher executive to answer to. Governor Ruiz Ortiz, for example, decided to use force against the teachers in 2006 and ended up illegally relocating his government outside the city when the disturbances in town had escalated. Such brash executive conduct extends beyond provincial state governors, according to Mexico City storyteller María Antonia, who recalled how even low-level operatives in the capital city tended to disdain others. She recollected how one day the chief of staff of the spouse of a minister in the federal government called her seeking training in her oral craft. The staffer—the employee of someone married to someone who was appointed by someone who won an election—underscored that the training opportunity would bolster her career. Indignant, María Antonia never returned the call, pointing out the audacious level of entitlement that elite politicians and their coteries seem to feel toward other professionals. This detachment, however, leaves the politicians open to humorous barbs.

Such humor is most apparent in the political cartoon, which can provide both graphic and language-based content. Mexican cartooning makes executive power less distant, working to "disrobe (*desnudar*)" the politicians (Schmidt, 1996, p. 49) by shining a light on the backroom dealings (p. 59) without convincing or establishing dialog (p. 54). Additionally, Mexican Spanish involves a verbal art of joking whereby vocal and printed humor, in lowbrow fashion, relates to the experiences of everyday life. In teacher marches and encampments during my research, humor was juxtaposed with pointed statements for direct change. For example, as recent labor reforms have reduced the benefits public employees, like the teachers, may enjoy, cartoons have mediated how actors see the reforms relating to them and the direction of the nation. At the Mexico City, May 2010 plantón, I picked up a flyer that was printed by teachers' union pension advocates (Coordinadora Nacional de Jubilados y Pensionados Democráticos SNTE-CNTE 1989, 2010) that asked for a halt in the privatization of state worker benefits. These advocates focused specifically on the ISSSTE, the Institute for Social Security and Services for State Workers, which had recently been targeted for reform to minimize the federal government's contribution to state employee benefits like health care, retirement, and loans. The flyer summoned the working class and the "people" in general to fight for: "* The dignity of working conditions (*Empleo digno*) * Follow through on worker social protection * Suitable retirement circumstances for all * [and] Comprehensive and accessible health services." At the same time, below these bullet-point demands, the flyer reprinted the ISSSTE logo with the familiar safeguarding hands embracing a couple holding a child. Overhead, however, danger lurked, through the opaque gaze of a skull. Targeted for reform, the ISSSTE no longer enjoys ritual connection to the well-being of workers and their families. The flyer plainly states this in the bullet-point demands and then heteroglossically calls out through the skeletal specter of death that overshadows the ISSSTE's embrace.

In a graphic image, the words and the skull circulate in logical and heteroglossic textuality. Linking a serious message with a cartoon-based one, along established Mexican political cartoon tactic, can also embolden participants to speak up in unfamiliar or unsympathetic contexts. Political humor to command one's right to speak often begins with the wordplay and the human body. For example, in Mexican markets and squares we see a character called a *merolico* (Haviland, 2011), a clown-like performer who through vulgar wordplay can secure conversational freedom to peddle products and garner tips.[12] The merolico engages with the public via the *albur*, a practice that reinterprets others' words using common phrases. The albur utterance playfully carries nuances the listeners may not have anticipated, often with a sexual or vulgar intonation. Using alburs, not reserved to merolicos on the streets, allows someone to speak when it may not be their turn to speak. For example, when I began teaching in Mexico in the early 1990s, I was severe about classroom management. Lacking self-confidence, I scolded my students for tardiness and speaking out of turn. One day I immodestly stated I was going to "*enseñar*" a given concept to the class. A teenage student turned this statement into an albur, asking what part of me I was going to enseñar. Enseñar can mean to teach or to display, so an edgy and prepossessing teacher who promises to enseñar runs the risk of students rendering enseñar as exhibitionism, that is, to flash. Snickering laughter in the classroom! Just like the merolico who garners public attention using vulgarity in a community where politeness may be the norm, the student appropriated the right to albur his teacher because, rather than an overtly hostile prod, his utterance cleverly reworked my own. Further still, as teaching and learning involve knowledge exchanges, a responsive teacher cannot easily ignore a cunning upstart's response.[13] Hearing the enseñar response, however, I became embarrassed and vexed, which showed all that he had bested me in this duel. Had I stayed silent or countered on my virile enseñar ability, I might have won the standoff, but my albur response comes twenty years too late to have heteroglossic bearing; I can only make over-stewed theoretical points on what had once been open and ongoing.

In addition to the student alburing the teacher, teachers relate to one another using wordplay that similarly incorporates the vulgar and uncouth. In my literacy research, an embodied albur came up one day when the normally reserved elementary teacher, Raquel, presented at a storytelling workshop. I would observe many teachers placidly engaged in performances at storytelling workshops, like when I teamed up with Yolanda on the rigid cement of an elementary school basketball court to portray the storybook tree and a fountain. Raquel's workshop involved greater preparation and grit, and formed part of a statewide teacher professional development series led by professional Mexico City storytellers and novelists.[14] Her assignment one week involved presenting a recycled object to the group for which she found a Styrofoam cone and placed it upright on a sheet of paper. On the day she presented this cone, she opened with a written title: "*estetica posmoderna*," seemingly meaning, "postmodern aesthetics." As she had omitted the accent over the second "e" of estética, one workshop participant pointed out her orthographic lapse. "No," Raquel countered, challenging him to keep the accent off and sound it out as written. He did so, and following Spanish syllable stress rules, it came out as "es te TI ca pos mo DER na," or, "it's a little postmodern breast." This naughty-ish overture at the diploma course segued into Raquel's chronicle on the object with two possible titles. Her albur faithfully followed the way sex- or body-centered alburs[15] turn an otherwise sober statement into a speedy and witty one (Beniers, 2009). Thus, as a typically reserved person, Raquel told her story to storytellers.

In interpreting the corporeal playfulness of Raquel's entrée into her narrative, it would be shortsighted to underestimate how the albur sets up verbal combat. Beyond a student's jocularity or an opening move for storyteller, the albur is an ancient and textured way to emasculate someone else or to be self-deprecating.[16] Beristáin Díaz (1997) called the albur a highly symbolic and allegoric verbal variety of dialog "in which inventiveness (*ingenio*), imagination, opportunity, creativity and rapidness of response are calibrated. This is issued during the process of verbal interaction that transpires between experts that compete before witnesses. As an 'improvised fiesta'…[it is] an *interactive construction of a secret message*" (p. 39 emphasis in original).[17] While casting away social mores, the albur allows people to wreak vengeance on "applied social injustice" (p. 42). Only the adept can place the verbal wedge of the albur into the hostile yet fertile milieu of state repression and educational reform. Applied social injustice, as we will see below, has infused the albur into the battery of critical responses that actors levy on elite political leaders like 2010 PRI candidate for Oaxaca Governor, Eviel Pérez Megaña, President Felipe Calderón, Ulises Ruiz Ortiz, and SNTE President Elba Esther Gordillo. Analogous to how the skull symbolically introduces finite decay of the ISSSTE under the proposed reforms, in alburing the names of executive leaders, humorists create a space for presence in the face of bad governance and a repressive rule of force.

Beasts and Bodily Effluvia

In the summer of 2010, alburs and other mockery toward political aloofness would occur in Oaxacan gubernatorial elections, the results of which would eventually oust the PRI from an eighty-year run. This was the first election since the desalojo against the teachers and ensuing street protests against the governor, so curiosity arose over whether the PRI would get ousted by a vote of castigation.[18] Weeks before the elections, Oaxaca columnist Fouché (2010) could not resist introducing an albur as he discussed the gubernatorial hopefuls. When he assessed the PRI nominee, instead of calling him by his given name, Eviel Pérez Megaña, he penned Eviel Pérez *Me-engaña* (Deceives-me). Fouché then attacked the candidate's low intelligence: "Eviel Pérez Me-engaña. He wants to be or seem the standard bearer of honesty …[but] a moment always comes up when he shows what he lacks in terms of mental agility and political ability" (p. 9). The duel is on! Because the heteroglossic effort of the albur directs toward the wit of the albured-upon party, this overture awaits a comeback from the mocked candidate. Other political names have commonly faced alburs in the press and Oaxacan teachers' union documents. As discussed in Chapter Four, President Calderón has been dubbed "*FECAL*" for *FE*lipe *CAL*derón and *fecal,* the adjective for feces, which I saw in the banner carried in a May 2010 Mexico City teacher protest march saying: "*Fuera Elba Esther and FECAL,*" meaning "Down with [SNTE president] Elba Esther [Gordillo] and FECAL."

Politician alburs had become as common throughout the Oaxaca protests of 2006 as they would during my field visits from 2010 to 2011. During the marches that followed the desalojo in 2006, towering humanoid puppets and modified piñatas carried in marches had distorted the figure of Governor Ruiz Ortiz. As the marchers called for his removal, many of the million participants in the various marches portrayed the governor as absurd or as a non-governor. In one instance at a protest march, we see an image of Ruiz Ortiz with a sign: "Culises" (Law, 2008, min. 28). To approach the humor in the figure, in concert iconography from his illegitimate mandate, the name "Culises" alburs the governor as *culo* for the ass, *culero* for an asshole/jerk, and the first name, Ulises. The marchers carried the papier-mâché prisoner Ruiz Ortiz, an oversized male doll (*mono*) toted in the popular street processions (*calendas*), famous during feast days in Oaxacan towns and cities. Calenda processions and the figure of the mono in Oaxaca characteristically mediate joyful gatherings rather than struggle; the monos de calenda are accompanied by music and invite people out of their homes to join in with the open-air revelers. If the mono of the governor signaled playtime, the

Culises nameplate number 14062006—the fourteenth of June 2006—recalled the trauma of the desalojo. Recalling the desalojo might appear to trivialize the unwarranted assault the governor ordered against the teachers, unless we read the albur as an attempt to summon the elite politician to the crowded streets, the way that saints' day processions pass along streets in Oaxaca to draw neighbors out for the fun. The play on words invites the governor to a verbal duel; to win, the governor must leave behind his insulated life, beyond the stone balconies of the Palacio de Gobierno that the circus advertisement serenaded with derision. Here, besides the linguistic acts of alburs and carnival distortions of the governor's body, an allusion to the coarse social delights of street celebrations infuses into the story. Performance and remembrance walk hand-in-hand.

The year 2006 would become a banner year for repression, mockery, and memory on the streets of Oaxaca. Hernández Baca (2010) recalled the ways that protesters denounced Governor Ruiz Ortiz and SNTE President Elba Esther Gordillo:

> [T]hose famous works of graffiti began to cover the town showing: the face of Ulises Ruiz Ortiz with the body of a rat or donkey [and] of Elba Esther Gordillo, national director of the SNTE, with horns or embraced by Ruiz Ortiz; the stencils of Benito Juárez with the guerrilla cap; [and] the paint on the walls with consignas like "Ulises, brother of the pig and swine (*Ulises, hermano del puerco y del marrano*).[19] (p. 65)

As Ruiz Ortiz was a local mapache turned governor, Elba Esther Gordillo was a teacher from neighboring Chiapas who became one of Mexico's key powerbrokers, SNTE president, general secretary of the ruling PRI and consultant to the PAN opposition in their successful 2006 presidential campaign. As Ruiz Ortiz represents Oaxacan teachers as political constituents, Gordillo represents the teachers in the national apparatus of their trade union. The dissident teachers in Oaxaca and beyond, teachers who have remained in the SNTE but have joined the nonconformist Coordinadora Nacional de Trabajadores de la Educación (CNTE) caucus, have attacked Gordillo for being "the political face of manipulation in national politics," one teacher insisted. The union president is an "obscure figure" (Castro Sánchez, 2009) who was responsible for more than 150 teacher deaths, and although she had headed the PRI, she promoted Felipe Calderón of the PAN in his 2006 run for the presidency (p. 66). However, there is a political and economic purpose behind the union leader's repression. Ornelas (2008) indicated that Gordillo's rise to power marks a retreat from the state's nominal commitment for a broader social mission of the post-Revolutionary period and signals an expansion of a marketized system where individuals would need to take on more responsibility (p. 454). To date, Oaxacan teacher protest materials have targeted neoliberal restructuring of public education (Howell, 2009), that is, policy shifts that Gordillo has helped orchestrate, not the least of which is the ISSSTE reforms presented above.

Gordillo, who at present writing is incarcerated for fraud, has arguably stood as the most powerful political operator in Mexico, mixing with union and party politics and promoting the ISSSTE reforms that in effect reduce the benefits of the educational state workers she ostensibly represents. Two documents illustrate how the teachers disfigured her image and indexed her backroom political dealings. First, at the central table of the teachers' plantón in Oaxaca City, on the fourth anniversary of the desalojo, I found a graphic of Gordillo and the four presidents in the SNTE whose tenure corresponded to hers. The image displays inhuman portraits of two PRI chiefs from left to right: Carlos Salinas (1988–1994) and Ernesto Zedillo (1994–2000) as monkeys; then from the PAN opposition, Vicente Fox (2000–2006) as a snake and President Felipe Calderón (2006–2012). To the far right stands Gordillo crowning Calderón with the insignia of the mainstream news conglomerate, Televisa. On the bottom, a ghoulish-looking Gordillo speaks into a microphone. The quotation reads, "Four Presidents. A leader for Life: Elba Esther Gordillo Morales. 1989–2009 … and … how much longer?" In juxtaposition to the four presidents, Gordillo comes out with agency, for her mandate endured the longest of the lot. Salinas on the far left put her in office during his administration, and despite his power and wealth, exile, and later return, he retired from his formal role in politics. Each member of the bestiary followed suit until the squat Calderón cozies up to her. Without his bowing down, a standing the union president can still easily crown him with the Televisa emblem. She knows how to play politics and endure longer than other executives do. Due to this, the terrain of the trade union and public worker democratic battles becomes tangible to the reader: their official leader, Gordillo, has enjoyed so much influence in and outside the domain of education that the Sección 22 must fight all the harder for internal democracy.

Second, in addition to the leader for life image at the central tables, the teachers and other advocates for public employees have used playful distortions to names and images to make political points about labor reform issues. The Mexican section of la Coalición Trinacional en Defensa de la Educación Pública, a Canada-United States-Mexico-based organization to defend public education, publishes a bulletin and maintains several blogs and an online educational research journal. An article written by labor specialist Vital Galicia (2008) presents the process, outcomes, and magnitude of the neoliberal reforms to the ISSSTE and details Gordillo's leadership of SNTE, the chief body of Mexican public workers. The reforms, according to the article, have reduced state investment in worker pensions and the like. Elba Esther Gordillo, hardly mentioned in the article, stands as the keystone figure behind this retreat. The article displays this via the face of the union chief as the final frame in a series of images that chronicles political maneuverings that have gridlocked the ISSSTE, at the expense of the teachers and other state employees. Two layers of the story become clear: the lettered one of an expert and the heteroglossic one of absurdity.

The storyline of the three-framed visual begins with the iconic and unmodified insignia of the ISSSTE, with the two open hands embracing the woman, man, and small child and below it, "ISSSTE." Later in the article, the embracing hands of the welfare state's insignia turn up again, portraying the same man and woman with their arms raised, fists clenched, with the subtitle: "RESISSSTE," a play on the command form for the Spanish verb *resistir*. Finally, the ISSSTE hands caress Gordillo's face. The politician's face occupies the spot, displacing the man and woman. Below it reads "I$$$ThER," scripted to insinuate Gordillo penned in her own name with the Mexican Peso "$" over the ISSSTE logo (p. 10). The story of the ISSSTE reforms told through the article closes here, though the family of state workers in the image is walking away, and we do not know where they will end up without the ISSSTE's protection. Thus, as the article concludes, the graphic story remains undone, engaging the reader to consider what comes next.

Governability and the Anti-rite

In this chapter, good governance moves in political agencies like teachers' unions and state offices, playing out through the verbal games people play within earshot of elite power. Governability, "the capacity to institutionally process and apply political decisions via recognized channels and established rules of the game" (Hernández-Díaz, 2014, p. 55), exposes acts of misrule to ridicule. Movements over better governance play out in the verbal and spatial competitions between the serious and disdainful decisions of the power elite and the more numerous walking, sitting-in, and chanting public. In other words, friction over governability is an opportunity to take command over the field of possible meanings and shine a light on decisions made in meetings behind closed doors. In the previous chapter, the control over such fields often related to the geographic spaces taken by one group at the expense of another's. A plantón factors into governability by impeding easy passage through the avenues of the city where business owners and the governor hold sway and by the living presence of marching, shouting, and consuming. In this literacy-focused chapter, the joke is on the one unable to come down to the streets and answer back, for humor occupies space by displacing the commonsense, polite, and routine running of city life. Just as the zócalo during a plantón will have a warren of tents and tie-downs, the practice of humor will make claims that demand an answer. Just as the plantón tomorrow morning will obstruct foot traffic differently than it did today, the joke forces the interlocutor to ponder the present version of events and legitimacy of the comedic fool walking past. Humor obstructs by repulsing, reframing, or titillating; what is presented as fixed turns on its head.

When I approached Yolanda above, she seemed less enthusiastic about the playful ballad and the satirical circus. When she described it as the funny part of sending a political message, she was not dissuading me from pursuing the politics behind the joke, but instead the mockery and toilet language seemed too mundane and passing to her to merit much attention. Perhaps humor faces the nonchalance of the cultural insider, or perhaps its value stands in how humor is less a textual practice than a way of being, an ethos. For me as researcher, humor becomes more salient as these utterances may be drowned out in the louder, more radical voices in a struggle. Their story reveals a lot about the movement of governability in this literacy-focused chapter. Instead of reading it through the more familiar term of carnival (Bakhtin, 1984), humor as an ethos is perhaps better understood as heteroglossia, the turning of what is given as a single story into many, smaller and unfinished points of contestation (Holquist, 1981a, p. xix).

There is also a joy to wordplay and mockery, though I suggest that studying the words, sounds, and emotions involved in humor is less important that noticing the ways that non-serious, heteroglossic approaches encounter the all-too-serious and break ground for public space and counter-pedagogies. Indeed, humor need not be funny to serve the critical project of conversing with bad governance. Humor tells a story that is tellable best through humor, for you tell it at the level of the here-and-now without contradicting other stories related to the same topics. The teachers, for example, can shout their consignas about exploited workers and then bark out another that Ruiz Ortiz is the brother of a swine; one narrative does not make the other redundant. Still, humor has more tools than reasonable critiques into the causes and results of misrule, for as we see in these images, in a few pen strokes or uttered words, a whole context and innumerable texts come to life. Humor achieves this via popular devices that are understandable to more people than coherent credos. Contradicting or rationalizing against policy or a practice may be unfeasible; humor can best be enjoyed or answered back, as in the verbal dueling of the albur.

The humorous version of an event, shamelessly captivating the audience like the merolico in the park, becomes more urgent as in the case of 2006 where teachers' stories became cast simply as good or evil in the media. As Bautista Martínez (2008) has explained, the corporate media's representation of the 2006 crisis reduced the Movement to mere personality disputes (p. 37) and positioned the teachers and the more than 300 civic groups as duped into urban guerrilla warfare by a few bad apple ideologues. Then, as we have seen, paramilitaries shot at and shut down the independent media. Humor intercedes in this reduction; the story told through humor becomes more urgent, generative, and humanizing. Amplifying a joke on the zócalo, for example, unfinishes the ringing bullet that shot at the towers of the radio stations. Even if the joke bombs, the sound waves remain open.

Notes

1. The *corrido* or ballad enjoys popular success in protest circles. The Mexico City plantón during my research often had a corner where troubadours sang ballads. In Oaxaca, to find the author of central table music, I hummed tunes to two teachers until they identified it as one of José de Molina's, a regular musical presence at protest events.

2. Associating humans to animals comes off far more offensive to the humanity of the offended person in Mexican Spanish than in American English. For example, a common phrase issued in anger, "shut your *boca*," becomes overtly hostile with "shut your *hosico*," as the human mouth is boca and the animal muzzle, hosico.

3. The desalojo, and the teachers breaking the police line in 2006, would touch off months of street-level mobilization, which brought protesters from across the state and beyond and from diverse sectors of society to call for the governor's resignation (Osorno & Meyer, 2007). Ruiz held the governorship but became tainted for his human rights abuses, and his party, the PRI, would for the first time in generations lose the office in the next election cycle.

4. Franco became implicated in numerous repressive and antidemocratic practices such as hampering the freedom of the press (Beas Torres, 2007, p. 31) and forming part of Ruiz's inner circle, the *Bronx Oaxaqueño* (Martínez Vásquez, 2007b, p. 52).

5. Saldierna and Muñoz (2006) report how misrule existed in Oaxaca during the 2006 repression, but no major functionaries lost their jobs.

6. At a zócalo plantón in 1989, Martínez Vásquez (2005) has reported teachers using food from their region in humorous fashion, including those from the Isthmus of

Tehuantepec uttering political consignas starting with totopo, shrimp, and cheese (p. 129).

7. Since the 1930s, the public educator across Mexico has intervened in healthcare and community development projects, linking teaching with actual village conditions. Oaxacan teachers do not shy away from intellectual engagement with local, regional, and national political and pedagogical movements. Due to this grassroots teacher praxis, when I refer to Oaxacan educators engaging in political projects that involve humor, the reader should understand how teaching, politics, and the practices of quotidian community life enjoy a thick and rich history within which humor forms a part.

8. One teacher slated to teach a critical pedagogy workshop with more of liberal humanist than critical pedagogical training asked me how "critical" in critical pedagogy is different from critical thinking in mainstream schooling.

9. Historically nondominant individuals, following critical race and gender theorists (Douglas, 2015), face pressures to laugh, smile, and defer (p. 147), so not all laughter before authority is critical.

10. Heteroglossia hones a researcher's gaze down to a finer grain. Heteroglossia lowers the eyes, letting them fall on acts that may go unnoticed. Understanding heteroglossia, a researcher can pause at activism events that the activists themselves may not recognize as something intentional or noteworthy. To approach heteroglossic subversions, like the use of humor, notice how they take on friction with serious, singular, managerial, or absurd truths. A governor, who justifies the use of force as a first response against civil-servant activism, saying that he will do anything to defend society, opens the door to heteroglossias. As we see in this chapter, when presented as inevitable or responsible, using force against the peaceful becomes a fixed point plundered by heteroglossic call-outs like humor.

11. Heteroglossia, how small acts destabilize what people accept as natural, ordinary, or inexorable, turns into a battleground of meaning, understanding, and last words. Authoritarian practices like state-sponsored violence against teachers claim its victims, though. Via heteroglossia, there is little to do in order to get back the people killed, lifeworlds abandoned, funding squandered, and trees felled. Many of the teachers in this research maintain their own research agendas, though this is not to say they theorize the way I theorize. In the final writing of this book I am drawn to Joanne Rappaport's (2005) call for a "conscious and active commitment" on the part of researchers toward checking in with how actors on the ground know the way they know (p. 85) and to Ruth Trinidad Galván's (2015) approach to social worlds as an interlocutor first, researcher second (pp. 12–14).

12. Calling a public official *merolico* serves to label them a blabbermouth, a snake oil salesperson, one who manipulates the public with empty promises.

13. As a language teacher and teacher supervisor, I have tried to pause and consider what a student is saying and doing when they "misbehave," for those actions reveal

how students express their aggression, a component of attending to new learning (Larsen-Freeman, 1986) and where a teacher might scaffold student understanding. Humor, like the student's albur, might appear as misbehavior, but as I explore humor in use in this chapter, I marvel at my former student's nuanced eloquence—all rooted in the power of that classroom.

14. Raquel would later invite me to a workshop on narrative documentation of teaching, cofacilitated by an Oaxacan teacher and an Argentine pedagogue-storyteller (La Documentación Narrativa de Experiencias Pedagógicas, 2011). The training encompassed teacher storytelling as a relational research tool to reevaluate the knowledge, words, and images that go into classroom practice.

15. The body has been a vehicle for teacher humor. In a 1986 protest walk from Oaxaca to Mexico City, teachers with diarrhea from poorly cooked food and exposure to the burning sun humorously mocked the blisters on their feet (Martínez Vásquez, 2005). "Speaking about feet, how do blisters resemble us marchers? … I don't know.… Like marchers, blisters are "*en pie de lucha* (on foot and in the struggle)" (p. 113).

16. According to Johansson (2006), the practice dates to teasingly antagonistic pre-Columbian music. In the Istmo region of Oaxaca, for example, Campbell (2001) describes the mystique surrounding the double entendre-laced speeches of Polín, a legendary leader of the radical COCEI (p. 28).

17. Beristáin Díaz (1997) called the albur "boy humor" that influences political parody sketches, product marketing, and even highbrow literature. This all depends on speed and timing. The example Beristáin Díaz provides is the alburist turning the words of the other person against them: a motorist sees a passing car on the highway and in anger shouts, "*¡pendejo!* (You little shit!)." The passing driver becomes an alburist with "*¡te dejo!* (I'm leaving you behind)" (p. 39). The pendejo utterance issued soberly faces the te dejo one, which, similar in sound and rhythm, uses laughter rather than rage. This "penetrating" humor, following Beristáin Díaz (2001), shows witty strength at the expense of the other (p. 53).

18. For the elected leaders in the Oaxaca state government enjoying impunity for their actions and how this affected the 2010 elections, see Martínez (2010, p. 123).

19. *Puerco* and *marrano* offensively translate to pig.

References

Albertani, C. (2009). *Espejo de México: (Crónicas de barbarie y resistencia)*. San Pedro Cholula, Mexico: Altres Costa-Amic.

Bakhtin, M. M. (1984). *Rabelais and his world*. Bloomington, IN: Indiana University Press.

Balbuena Corro, H. H. (Ed.). (2009). *Matemáticas 6: Cuaderno de trabajo para el alumno. Sexto grado*. Mexico City: Secretaria de Educación Pública.

Barajas, R. (2000). The transformative power of art. *NACLA Report on the Americas, 33*(6), 6. Retrieved from EBSCO*host*.

Bautista Martínez, E. (2008). Oaxaca: La construcción mediática del vandalismo y la normalidad. *El Cotidiano, 23*(148), 37–44.

Beas Torres, C. (2007). La batalla por Oaxaca. In C. Beas Torres (Ed.), *La batalla por Oaxaca* (pp. 21–79). Oaxaca, Mexico: Ediciones Yope Power.

Beniers, E. (2009). Acerca de la inferencia en el intercambio verbal habitual y en la dilogía, el doble mensaje y la alusión. *Acta Poética, 30*(1), 295–321.

Beristáin Díaz, H. (1997). El albur: Retórica, política e ideología. *Desde la Antigüedad hasta Nuestros Días, 3*, 33–47.

Beristáin Díaz, H. (2001). La densidad figurada del lenguaje alburero. *Revista de Retórica y Teoría de Comunicación, 1*(1), 53–60.

Campbell, H. (2001). *Mexican Memoir: A personal account of anthropology and radical politics in Oaxaca.* Westport, CT: Bergin & Garvey.

Castro Sánchez, S. (2009). *Oaxaca más allá de la insurrección: Crónica de un movimiento de movimientos (2006–2007).* Oaxaca, Mexico: Ediciones ¡Basta!

CEDES 22. (2009). *Taller estatal de educación alternativa: TEEA 2009–2010* (Instructional material). Oaxaca, Mexico.

CEDES 22. (2010). *2010 Resolutivos del III congreso estatal de educación alternativa, 20–21 de mayo.* Oaxaca, Mexico: Sección 22, SNTE.

CNTE. (2010). *Convocatoria, IV Congreso Nacional de Educación Alternativa* (Ephemeral material). Mexico City.

CNTE. (2013). *Resolutivos, V Congreso Nacional de Educación Alternativa, 25–27 de abril de 2013* (Conference proceedings). Mexico City.

Comisión Civil Internacional de Observación por los Derechos Humanos. (2007). Informe sobre los hechos de Oaxaca. Quinta visita del 16 de diciembre de 2006 al 20 de enero de 2007. Barcelona: Comisión Civil Internacional de Observación de los Derechos Humanos (Human Rights Report).

Comber, B. (2001). Classroom explorations in critical literacy. In H. Fehring & P. Green (Eds.), *Critical literacy: A collection of articles from the Australian Literacy Educators' Association* (pp. 90–102). Newark, DE: International Reading Association.

Coordinadora Nacional de Jubilados y Pensionados Democráticos SNTE-CNTE 1989. (2010). Ephemeral material.

Critchley, S. (2002). *On humour.* New York, NY: Routledge.

Davies, N. (2007). *The people decide: Oaxaca's popular assembly.* Natick, MA: Narco News Books.

De La Rosa, M. G., & Schadl, S. M. (2014). *Getting up for the people: The visual revolution of ASAR-Oaxaca.* Oakland, CA: PM Press.

Douglas, E. R. (2015). Foucault, laughter, and gendered normalization. *Foucault Studies, 20*, 142–154.

el Fouché. (2010, June 7). Tequio y política. *El Correo de Oaxaca.*

Esteva, G. (2010). Beyond education. In L. Meyer & B. Maldonado (Eds.), *New world of Indigenous resistance: Noam Chomsky and voices from North, South and Central America.* San Francisco, CA: City Lights Books.

Foucault, M. (1998). The subject and power. In P. Rabinow & N. Rose (Eds.), *The essential Foucault: Selections from the essential works of Foucault 1954–1984* (pp. 126–144). New York, NY: The New Press.

Foweraker, J. (1993). *Popular mobilization in Mexico: The teachers' movement 1977–87*. New York, NY: Cambridge University Press.

García Canclini, N. (2001). *Hybrid cultures: Strategies for entering and leaving modernity* (Fourth printing). Minneapolis, MN: University of Minnesota Press.

Gee, J. P. (2004). *Situated language and learning: A critique of traditional schooling*. London: Routledge.

Goldstein, D. (2003). *Laughter out of place: Race, class, violence, and sexuality in a Rio shantytown*. Berkeley, CA: University of California Press.

Haviland, J. B. (2011). Who asked you, condom head? *Anthropological Quarterly, 84*(1), 235–264. Retrieved from EBSCO*host*.

Hernández, F. G. (2009). La educación alternativa y el movimiento pedagógico en el discurso de los maestros democráticos de Oaxaca, como contexto de la educación bilingüe e intercultural. In M. J. Bailón Corres (Ed.), *Ensayos sobre historia, política, educación y literatura de Oaxaca* (pp. 288–340). Oaxaca, Mexico: IIHUABJO.

Hernández Baca, L. T. (2010). *Toma la palabra, toma los medios, toma las calles: Oaxaca 2006. Los medios libres: Nuevas herramientas para los movimientos sociales*. Thesis for the Bachelor's in Social Anthropology, Escuela Nacional de Antropología e Historia, Mexico, City, Mexico. Retrieved from http://www.scribd.com/doc/51915322/TOMA-LA-PALABRA-TOMA-LOS-MEDIOS-TOMA-LAS-CALLES-OAXACA-2006

Hernández-Díaz, J. (2014). Reflexiones sobre los resultados electorales y la participación ciudadana en las elecciones federales de 2012. In E. Bautista Martínez & F. Díaz Montes (Eds.), *Oaxaca y la reconfiguración política nacional* (pp. 49–63). Oaxaca, Mexico: Instituto de Investigaciones Sociológicas de la Universidad Autónoma "Benito Juárez" de Oaxaca.

Hodges, D. C. (1995). *Mexican anarchism after the revolution*. Austin, TX: University of Texas Press.

Holquist, M. (1981a). Introduction. In M. M. Bakhtin & M. Holquist (Eds.), *The dialogic imagination: Four essays* (pp. xv–xxxiii). Austin, TX: University of Texas Press.

Holquist, M. (1981b). Glossary. In M. M. Bakhtin & M. Holquist (Eds.), *The dialogic imagination: Four essays* (pp. 423–434). Austin, TX: University of Texas Press.

Horton, M., & Freire, P. (1990). *We make the road by walking: Conversations on education and social change*. Philadelphia, PA: Temple University Press.

Howell, J. (2009). Vocation or vacation? Perspectives on teachers' union struggles in southern Mexico. *Anthropology of Work Review, 30*(3), 87–98.

Johansson, P. (2006). Dialogía, metáforas y albures en cantos eróticos nahuas. *Revista de Literaturas Populares, 6*(1), 63–95.

La Documentación Narrativa de Experiencias Pedagógicas. (2011). Doctor Daniel H. Suárez and Maestro Gabriel Roizman, facilitators. Oaxaca, Mexico, April 9, 2011 (workshop flyer). Universidad Pedagógica Nacional/Red Lee.

Larsen-Freeman, D. (1986). *Techniques and principles in language teaching*. New York, NY: Oxford University Press.

Lave, J., & Wenger, E. (1991). *Situated learning: Legitimate peripheral participation*. Cambridge: Cambridge University Press.

Law, Y. (2008). *Sígueme cantando: Sonidos de la lucha oaxaqueña* (DVD). Mal de ojo producciones.

Martínez, V. L. J. (2010). Y finalmente cayó. En I. Yescas Martínez & C. Sánchez Islas (Eds.), *Oaxaca 2010: Voces de la transición* (pp. 121-134). Oaxaca, Mexico: Carteles Editores.

Martínez Vásquez, V. R. (2005). ¡No que no, sí que sí!: Testimonios y crónicas del movimiento magisterial oaxaqueño. Oaxaca, Mexico: SNTE.

Martínez Vásquez, V. R. (2006). Movimiento magisterial y crisis política en Oaxaca. In J. V. Cortés (Ed.), *Educación sindicalismo y gobernabilidad en Oaxaca* (pp. 125–149). Oaxaca, Mexico: SNTE.

Martínez Vásquez, V. R. (2007a). *Autoritarismo, movimiento popular y crisis política: Oaxaca 2006*. Oaxaca, Mexico: UABJO.

Martínez Vásquez, V. R. (2007b). Crisis política en Oaxaca. *Cuadernos del Sur, 11*(24–25), 39–62.

Mayo, C. (2010). Incongruity and provisional safety: Thinking through humor. *Studies in Philosophy & Education, 29*(6), 509–521. doi:10.1007/s11217-010-9195-6

McLaren, P. (1999). *Schooling as a ritual performance: Toward a political economy of educational symbols and gestures*. Lanham, MD: Rowman & Littlefield.

Meyer, L. M., & Maldonado, B. (Eds.). (2004). *Entre la normatividad y la comunalidad: Experiencias innovadoras del Oaxaca indígena actual*. Oaxaca, Mexico: IEEPO/Colección Voces del Fondo; Serie Molinos de Viento.

Nevaer, L. E. V., & Sendyk, E. (2009). *Protest graffiti–Mexico: Oaxaca*. New York, NY: Mark Batty.

Olesen, T. (2007). The funny side of globalization: Humour and humanity in Zapatista framing. *International Review of Social History, 52*(15), 21–34.

Ornelas, C. (2008). El SNTE, Elba Esther Gordillo y el gobierno de Calderón. *RMIE, 13*(37), 445–469.

Osorno, D. E., & Meyer, L. (2007). *Oaxaca sitiada: La primera Insurrección del siglo XXI*. Mexico City: Random House Mondadori.

Rappaport, J. (2005). *Intercultural utopias: Public intellectuals, cultural experimentation, and ethnic pluralism in Colombia*. Durham, NC: Duke University Press.

Reed, T. V. (2005). *The art of protest: Culture and activism from the civil rights movement to the streets of Seattle*. Minneapolis, MN: University of Minnesota Press.

Romanienko, L. A. (2007). Antagonism, absurdity, and the avant-garde: Dismantling Soviet oppression through the use of theatrical devices by Poland's 'Orange' Solidarity Movement. *International Review of Social History, 52*(15), 133–151.

Saldierna, G., & Muñoz, A. E. (2006, October 19). Hay ingobernabilidad, pero no procede la desaparición de poderes. *La Jornada*. Retrieved from http://www.jornada.unam.mx/2006/10/19/index.php?section=politica&article=007n1pol

Sassen, S. (2002). The repositioning of citizenship: Emergent subjects and spaces for politics. *Berkeley Journal of Sociology, 46*, 4–26.

Schmidt, S. (1996). *Humor en serio: Análisis del chiste político en México*. Mexico City: Aguilar.

Stephen, L. (1996). The creation and recreation of ethnicity: Lessons from the Zapotec and Mixtec of Oaxaca. In H. Campbell (Ed.), *The politics of ethnicity in southern Mexico* (pp. 99–132). Nashville, TN: Vanderbilt University.

Stephen, L. (2013). *We are the face of Oaxaca: Testimony and social movements*. Durham, NC: Duke University Press.

Teune, S. (2007). Humour as a guerrilla tactic: The West German Student Movement's mockery of the establishment. *International Review of Social History*, *52*(15), 115–132.

Trinidad Galván, R. (2015). *Women who stay behind: Pedagogies of survival in rural transmigrant Mexico*. Tucson, AZ: University of Arizona Press.

Vich, V., Edwards, B. H., & Nicolini, N. (2004). Popular capitalism and subalternity: Street comedians in Lima. *Social Text*, *22*(4), 47–64.

Vital Galicia, J. A. (2008, June 15). La reforma a la Seguridad Social en México. *Punto de encuentro*: Órgano informativo de la *Coalición Trinacional en Defensa de la Educación P*ública, 8–10. Retrieved from http://www.trinational-usa.org/punto_de_encuentro.pdf\

Yescas Martínez, I., & Zafra, G. (1985). *La insurgencia magisterial en Oaxaca 1980*. Oaxaca, Mexico: IISUABJO.

8

Counter-pedagogies, Quality, Patrimony, and Governability

Closing Thoughts

This book showcases critical pedagogical practices through the construct of movement. I rendered the term movement from Tsing's (2005) friction of global connection, a device for the study of universally understood and locally engaged practices, products, and conceptions. Friction, one item in the social world generating inventive contact with another, embraces social and political contention not as a negater but rather as a point of departure. Friction is striking a matchstick against a rough surface to produce fire; friction is a group of parents and teachers organizing quality education after teacher absences for political functions, parental anger, and a locked school gate. Instead of extending friction as a methodological inroad into this research, however, I have opted for movement.

As a social and political concept, movement appeared in three ways in the twelve years it took to write up this story. First, Oaxacan teachers have used the term to describe a movement within the Sindicato Nacional de Trabajadores de la Educación trade union (SNTE), from 1980 to the present (Ornelas, 2008), to campaign for living wages and collective decision making (p. 63). Within the "Democratic Movement of Education Workers of Oaxaca" (Hernández Ruiz, 2006) movement, members stand against political patronage (p. 88), which over the years has the nationwide SNTE as a mechanism of state and business interests. Movement here means dissidence and democratic governance within a trade union that mainstream political insiders often direct.

Second, movement surfaces in the 2006 social uprising in Oaxaca, el Movimiento de 2006. If the dissident teachers' movement has struggled over salary and democracy (Yescas Martínez, 2008), the Movimiento emerged without a singular purpose or organizational structure. On June 14, 2006, 2,500 state police raided a teachers' movement encampment (Ortega, 2009, p. 18). Two days later, half a million Oaxacans marched in protest (p. 20). For the next five months of 2006 in Oaxaca City, the Movimiento protested a repressive system "embodied [by Governor] Ulises Ruiz [Ortiz]" (Esteva, 2007, p. 18), though, like many alter-globalization movements, 2006 in Oaxaca flourished more on self-management (Maeckelbergh, 2009) than of consensus. Teenagers walked the streets and tagged the walls, and artists who have exhibited internationally joined in and spoke out against repression. Lila Downs sang songs, and women banging pots and pans occupied radio stations. Committed teachers Andrea and Marcos met parents at the Iniciativa Ciudadana de Dialogo por la Paz, la Justicia y la Democracia en Oaxaca public encounters on restoring democracy and felt shame for the anger parents felt at the teachers' absenteeism. The Movimiento also included the deliberate mention of Oaxaca's *pueblos* in the naming of la Asamblea Popular de los Pueblos de Oaxaca, suggesting a local, aboriginal Oaxacan articulation of activism (Esteva, 2007, p. 16). However, a martyr of 2006 is US-based journalist, Bradley Will, and transnational documentary (Freidberg et al., 2007), religious iconography (Norget, 2009), human rights (CCIODH, 2007), and academic advocacy (LASA, 2007) contributed to the historical record. Movement, then, implies multiplicity and complexity, in both purpose and practice.

Third, the multiplicity and complexity of movement suggests a grounded, grassroots framework for social mobilization. With input from diverse individuals and organizations, activists and intellectuals have called the organization of 2006 a "movement of movements" (De Castro Sánchez, 2009, p. 165), that was carried out by peasant, youth, indigenous, religious, and trade union groups who had little in common save their resistance to official incorporation (p. 225). A movement of movements, however, is not a designation given to an ad hoc committee called for in extraordinary circumstances. Martínez Vásquez (2009), social commentator and participant in 2006, has explained how a "civic space" exists in Oaxaca, a network of diverse individuals and organizations (p. 344) where gossip and conversations on market prices circulate from house to house. A civic space reveals how a civil servant reported to me that a book-reading event she organized at the last minute could become standing room only, even without publicity. The civic space is also how thousands of roadblocks of burning tires and concrete rubble would proliferate when plainclothes police and paramilitaries menace the streets. When asked about their political leanings, as we have seen (el Alebrije, 2007), the roadblockers showed very little political consciousness at all. A movement of movements in 2006 may account for the organizational ethos of complexity and dynamism; however, movement also suggests a social compulsion, a reluctance to leave behind one's peers when there is danger.

These three uses of movement, the 1980s–present teachers' movement, the Movimiento's multiplicity and complexity and the civic-space-driven movement of movements, gave me cause to turn movement into a trope in this story. More specifically, from chapter to chapter, movement operates at once as a device for researching pedagogical and sociopolitical worlds; and second, movement is how the social spaces operate. Movement aptly captures an ethos of how to approach the lifeways of activist teachers.

What Is Teacher Resistance?

Final considerations come to us on the movement of quality, patrimony, and governability. Eight years have passed since the beginning of principal fieldwork for this story. Twelve years have passed since the governor of Oaxaca issued orders for the police to attack teachers at the annual protest encampment, an act of aggression that backfired when the teachers reorganized, and tens of thousands of others turned the trade union protest into a social movement. Today, dissident caucuses in the SNTE have proliferated, just as Oaxacan teachers remain active in the struggles against state repression and neoliberal educational reforms. President Peña Nieto's (2012) structural reforms have been met with opposition across Mexico. Arriaga Lemus (2014), a veteran of decades of teacher labor struggles in Mexico, rejected the reforms for making teaching less permanent work, destroying the unions, and eliminating collective hiring and standardized teacher assessment—all without consulting teachers (p. 30). Wendy explained that

in Mexico the [1917] Constitution is modified constantly … it makes adjustments per the interests of the market. In 2013, they began the modification of Article Three, on education, and Article 123, on labor. Afterwards they modified the laws governing education and labor. All this points toward modifying the labor situation for Mexican teachers (*docentes*); they got rid of the labor base (*base laboral*) and substituted the teacher induction and tenure processes (*el proceso de ingreso y permanencia*) with a competitive exam (*concurso*), using as their argument the primacy of the rights to childhood and the quest for quality education.

It is not only that the international development banks and all the left- and right-wing political parties in Mexico have backed the reforms,[1] Wendy said, but that the collective body of dissident teachers' movement may crumble.

There are structural reforms that teachers resist. Oaxacan teachers resist facing 4,000 federal police descending upon Oaxaca to break up the teachers' activism. Still, *why should the teachers resist,* queries López Aguilar (2016), a member of the teachers' movement, in a newspaper column. Labor governments worldwide have gone neoliberal—Tony Blair's England or Michelle Bachelet's Chile that have privatized, decentralized, reduced entitlements, and mandated standardized tests—placing Mexico's 2012 structural reforms into a mainstream of global educational policies. López Aguilar suggests the structural reforms lead to inferior instruction and incompetent leadership.

> The educational reform was designed by transnational financial organizations (International Monetary Fund, World Bank and Inter-American Development Bank), the [Organisation for Economic Co-operation and Development], that sells public policy recommendations, and by the impresarios from [the venture philanthropy foundation] Mexicanos Primero…. There was no diagnostic, follow-up or evaluation of the educational policies of earlier presidential administrations. They did not consider students, teachers, parents, researchers or specialists. For all this, they lack legitimacy. (para. 1)

The struggle in 2016, to López Aguilar, is a struggle over quality and governability, which is a struggle that the teachers, the rightful pedagogical agents of the state, must take up. Just as the streets and schools in 2016 have witnessed pedagogical movement, it is fitting to close with a reflection on the events happening in Mexican education after I completed fieldwork in 2011: the counter-pedagogies against the 2012 structural reforms, the swarm of support for the forty-three disappeared students in 2014, and the 2016 police violence against teachers in Nochixtlán, Oaxaca. In these, movement of quality, patrimony, and governability have shaped teacher resistance.

Quality: Some Observation Tower

Quality is our first political and pedagogical movement, and it represents complexity. Quality today is *a priori*, a matter-of-fact part of the deep structure of what teaching and learning across the globe must be; to argue against it would sound absurd or irresponsible, like a president saying airports can relax their security because of a low threat level. No teacher can imply that student learning does not matter, nor can school principal or zone supervisor legitimately oppose quality education even if nobody knows for sure what it is and looks like in theory and in practice. The commonsense of quality becomes more abstruse when introducing economic efficiency mechanisms in order to optimize teaching; fostering higher *performance (desempeño),*[2] *excellence,*[3] and greater *impact,*[4] which ring important, even imperative, despite their vagueness. A notion that is vague, contradictory even, can actually gain power in the complexity. National heroes work this way, with presidents celebrating Zapata as a state hero (Stephen, 1997) and the Ejército Zapatista de Liberación Nacional (Stephen, 2002) considering him revolutionary. In 2006, the Oaxaca governor's office ran a smear campaign to pressure teachers at the *plantones* back into the classrooms where their duties lay, while simultaneously casting the same protesting teachers as urban guerrilla fighters, an attribute that should disqualify them from classroom teaching. However, rendering quality pedagogical, through whichever techniques are in vogue or at hand, makes quality a friction of malleable substance, precisely because people make quality come to life in numerous, contradictory ways.

Just as quality maximization lacks specificity, teachers, parents, and students organize under it. There are opportunities for counter-pedagogies and interventions to redirect teaching and learning away from the centripetally of multiple-choice reading and instead toward reading in treehouses in Tecotitlán Elementary School. As administrators, supervisors, and donors call for quality maximization, they depend on committed and creative teachers to propose quality, deliver it, and photo-op it when children read aloud with exuberance at events like the Book Fair discussed in Chapter Three. Government, the conduct of conducts, leads to chances for counter-pedagogies, as high performance and excellence differentiate from bad teaching only when practiced by practice-oriented teachers. An articulate and creative teacher may conduct their work in ways that are unanticipated by funders and overseers. Quality is a movement that plays out on the streets and in schools, not in spite of the state that drafts educational reforms and deploys repressive force, but rather through these measures.

Quality remains workable when repression and reform menace those who carry quality out. Of primary value in this story is seeing pedagogies through movements and to appreciate the plurality of critical practices. Surely, however, quality is a construction drawn from capitalist techniques of optimization, from the ideological dominion of commercial efficiency and human resource flexibility. You will not hear many dissident teachers like those in Sección 22 mentioning the term *quality* except to call out culturally irrelevant curriculum, like the sixth-grade textbooks that use subway stations to teach math problems to students in villages without automobiles. Quality may be discursive, but police who are ordered to break up the protests of the state version of quality fire bullets that are not. Further, I recognize that teachers who protest reforms, such as the eight who were killed by police in Nochixtlán, Oaxaca, on June 22, 2016, face material consequences for acting on another kind of quality education. Still, multiple entry points for constructing opposing versions of quality can prevail, for the ideological dominance of neoliberal and neo-paternal versions of quality and the technocratic supremacy of standardized testing and commodified knowledge frameworks cannot foreclose on the chances for counter-pedagogies.

We know that multiplicity in quality education is possible due to the multiple versions of quality currently afoot. We can see it in two major left-leaning tendencies that are both autonomous and emancipatory. First, the teachers within the institutional structure of the Centro de Estudios y Desarrollo Educativo de Oaxaca (CEDES 22), the pedagogical wing of the Sección 22, push for quality education through claims that the state education system proletarianizes teaching and reduces freedom,[5] a departure point for the critical teaching López Aguilar describes above. While many teachers and their allies recognize that teaching and learning in terms of this brand of liberation from domination, others such as Esteva, Stuchul, and Prakash (2005), call liberation something difficult to opt out of, a repressive force. Perhaps it is overstated to label emancipatory education repressive, even if liberation pedagogies may lead teachers to settle for some assumptions of knowledge, action, and change at the expense of others. Educational autonomy advocates like Esteva, Stuchul, and Prakash reject the supplanting of the neoliberal efficiency of the state with the critical-dialectical problem posing of the radical left, that is, the swapping of one hegemony for another. Instead, supporters of autonomy (Figueroa Crespo, 2004; Maldonado, 2010) focus on teaching and learning through mutual aid, complementary work, and festival celebration practiced in rural life outside of schooling (Bonfil Batalla, 1996, p. 29). While radical-left teachers militate against the state-driven model for teaching and learning, autonomists favor teaching and learning that is de-schooled and detached from either privatized or quality-maximized teaching, each of which hinges on transformative learning writ large. Understood and carried out on its competing tendencies, quality education remains an unfinished project.

Left-wing or right, schooled or de-schooled, whichever mode of quality education is most worthy has not been a pivotal concern here. Instead, these chapters have sketched out situated practices, sheltered by a symbolic tarpaulin of quality education or sheltered by a literal tarpaulin that unites allies and adversaries in reading for pleasure. These practices move across pedagogical latitudes, from village schools, to parks in provincial capital cities and to global-city building facades of the power elite. These chapters have advanced the ways quality, patrimony, and governability, understood and enacted in abstract and concrete ways, have put social movements and education in motion through difference, antagonism, repression, and reform. A movement is perhaps no more than a point of contagion, where critical reactions are possible but not inevitable. Recent reforms to teacher induction and promotion mechanisms have shown how movements of quality education remain meaningful prisms for critical teaching and learning.

Chapter Two described quality rendered pedagogical through decades of teaching as technical instruction (of the scientific positivist tradition in late nineteenth century), anti-clerical, scientific, universal (of the Socialist 1930s), national unity (mid-twentieth century), teachers' union dissidence (post-1978), and neoliberal flexibility (1988 to present). In the five years since the opening vignette on the benefits and weaknesses of teaching through the popularity of *telenovelas*, quality has become an aperture where state educational policy and the teachers' movement have come into friction more acutely as the Mexican state is requiring further standardized tests for teacher placement and advancement. First, constitutional reforms (Peña Nieto, 2012) have mandated competitive civil service exams for becoming a teacher, which opposes the historic mission of rural normal schools drawing from lower socioeconomic candidates, primarily women, to enter into the *magisterio*. When a rural normal school in my research excluded candidates with too many electrical outlets, an indicator of affluence, now private technical college graduates can sit for the opposition exam and get a teaching placement. According to an email from Wendy, in this way, the state reforms conduct the profession away from an intellectual-of-the-poor teacher subjectivity in favor of an open competition and free-market ethos. She also believes that protecting the rights of children[6] to an excellent education drives these reforms. Quality as the right of all children would be too great a burden to place on teachers alone. Peña Nieto said that if "education is the policy of the state, the quality of educational processes requires the efforts of those obliged to be agents: the public powers, governmental agencies, authorities, institutions, teachers, trade organizations, experts, parents and society as a whole" (p. 2). Ensuring quality education, a right all children should enjoy, the president crowdsources public education, where the teachers, trained at rural normal schools and committed to socioeconomic transformation through public education, still play a role. As public schoolteachers, Wendy, Arriaga Lemus (2014), and López Aguilar (2016) critique the specifics of educational policy shifts, though their comments reveal how the policies, and the violence against teachers who protest them, mark a radical shift from the public good of teaching. Teaching from its collectivist, secular, and scientific pedagogical missionary work since the 1930s, to the individual-choice, capital-accumulation teaching of recent decades, now is so great that society must intervene.

Do the reforms to break the teachers' movement and the rule of force to secure compliance signal a death knell of quality education as an open and interpretable friction? Perhaps. Underwritten by the rights of childhood, quality has intertwined with neoliberal techniques of optimization, a neoconservative defense of the family, and criminalization of collective action. These are discourses a teacher cannot just simply ignore, for a teacher with their students who exit the classroom, play sports, or prolong recess cannot just do so on a whim when quality maximization and the rights of children are at stake. Teachers cannot just make up their own definition of quality out of nothing or speak out against addressing the achievement gaps in student learning during a faculty meeting. Furthermore, teachers who exercise their constitutional right to gather, face prosecution (Martínez Vásquez, 2007, p. 47) and character assassination (Sotelo Marbán, 2008) for letting down Oaxacan children and their families. Perhaps quality education has become a settled issue and not an open friction that teachers, parents, and families can bend toward their purposes. Perhaps quality is still in motion. Reiterating that teachers' responsibilities reside in the classroom and not in protests, the state seems vulnerable, even illegitimate, as arbiters of quality education and children's rights to it.

Serious doubts linger about the credibility of the state authorities on matters of education and children's rights. A 2009 deadly fire at ABC Daycare in the state of Sonora dogged President Felipe Calderón, whose party lost the presidency a year later in 2010. Calderón's successor, Peña Nieto, has seen his good governance blemished by the September 2014 disappearance of the forty-three Ayotzinapa students. The students were in transit to a memorial for students killed by the state on October 2, 1968, and *consignas* and graffiti say, "*fue el estado* (it was the state who did it)," below the presidential balcony. If the state is implicated in violence against children, the rights of a childhood as vindication for their version of quality education falls flat; complicity in killing children does not lay discursive terrain where contradictions can easily coexist. Indeed, harming children, or giving refuge to those who do, calls the state's child-advocating and quality education standing into suspicion. Correspondingly, positioning themselves as village intellectuals who are devoted to students and their families, when the police shoot them, the teachers can vindicate their actions alongside the Ayotzinapa forty-three who the state killed, too.

With such history unfolding, it is likely that differing versions of quality will remain in friction, the movement of quality enduring as arena of social movement, pedagogy, and education research. With live rounds shot at teachers and structural reforms thwarting their collective action, quality education proposals have hardly been muted or frayed. Discourses, as we have seen, thrive on incongruity rather than in spite of it. For example, a free market is nowadays part of the common sense of good governance, which, if the Coordinadora Nacional de Trabajadores de la Educación (CNTE) wing of the SNTE teachers' union question it, retains primacy despite statistics that show income disparity is widening and economic crises, like Mexico's peso devaluation in 1994, have intensified. The Oaxaca state government sows discontent against protesting teachers by classifying them as urban insurgents (Martínez, 2006), while at the same time, they bid teachers to return to the classroom and protect the rights of children. A free market as moral necessity, even as it widens the rich-poor gap, and sends teachers back to abandoned classrooms, though the same teachers threaten security, illustrates how discursive notions endure through contradiction. However, we should not overstate the creative potential of contradiction. The state, for example, cannot give refuge to people who abuse children and simultaneously claim the rights of children matter most. This mutual exclusivity will prove useful for social movement actors who discredit the state's ability to broker rural elementary classroom content because of the state's abuse of children. With the Mexico-USA-Canada-based Tri-National Coalition in Defense of Public Education, the Chilean student movements, and the education-focused corporate foundations, quality education remains a domain of freedom and action upon future action. Digital, print, and broadcast media have carried the contentious messages about quality education. López Aguilar (2016) asked why teachers fight in *La Jornada,* while head of the Secretaría de Educación Pública, Alonso Lujambio, is suggesting that the immense popularity of television soap operas made them teaching tools, a claim that public intellectuals in and out of education ridiculed him for in *La Jornada* and elsewhere. Finally, educational researcher Hugo Aboites (2012) published a critique of the paternalistic data-gathering process in the most recent educational reforms.

> For educational bureaucracy, evaluation is like holing up in some observation tower and observing thousands of teachers and students from on high. And it is to measure and grade them all as if they were a giant cluster of commodities, robotized and passive examples of human capital. With their baseline results they —once again *they*—can define what must be done, how it must be done ... in order to obtain that ever-so indefinite thing called "quality." (p. 13)

Print and broadcast media across Mexico will print front-page pieces on the teachers' movement and the state-sponsored reforms, including the ominous observation tower Aboites observes. The observation tower becomes the point of observation, too. Protestors, aware that they could be seen by the state authorities, painted signs that the state did Ayotzinapa just as protesters four years earlier painted President Calderón as a drunkard on the cement ground. The observation tower that observes, measures, promotes, and censures is an observation tower that is holding on in its vulnerability.

A facet of the movement of quality education that deserves further study is the social and emotional side of learning and activism in times of repression and reform. During the most violent period of the 2006 Movimiento, Andrea accepted prayer cards as a token of solidarity from a street vendor, and Marcos sought out street musicians and storytellers to feel safe. Solidarity and social interconnection, even among adversaries, became indispensable. Studies on concern for others (Lanas & Zembylas, 2015) and for the self (Gunzenhauser, 2008) have shown how pedagogies in conflict depend on the socio-affective. *Lower flying* (Ong, 2006) ethnographic approaches or *weak* conceptual frameworks (Gibson-Graham, 1996) that drive a research project at the outset might focus the eye on the interpersonal fine grain for affective pedagogical politics to shine more than it has here. The seemingly pointless banter with neighbors, colleagues, and strangers, the signature features of Oaxaca's civic space (Martínez Vásquez, 2009, p. 344), is a teachable and observable encounter. I might have represented them more fully had the louder voices of the consignas, the playfulness of wordplay and the ever-changing lifeworlds of the plantones not captured my interest so.

Patrimony—Latent Power Fund

Alongside quality, politics and pedagogies play out through the movement of patrimony on the streets and in schools. The teaching craft, which shapes behavioral dispositions and cognitive patterns, might appear too improvement-oriented and future-looking to engage in frictions of heritage. However, because public school teaching is under siege from the private, non-governmental and governmental sectors that are intent on supplanting the teachers who protest collectively with efficient and professional individual teachers, patrimonial claims figure prominently. The century-old collective of teachers has known discursive as well as violent attempts to prompt its disarticulation, such as the June 19, 2016, attack on teachers in Nochixtlán, Oaxaca, and the June 14, 2006, police raid on the protest plantón on the Oaxaca City *zócalo*. On the tenth anniversary of the 2006 police raid, Lourdes reported that thousands of federal police approached from the northwest to surround the teachers. While writing this in late June 2016, mainstream print media have reported violence between teachers and police. Social media posts from individual teachers, the Mexico-USA-Canada-based Tri-national Coalition to Defend Public Education, Desinformémonos and Grupo Etnografía y Educación-IMA exchange video and print testimonials of the clashes. Some say June 2016 has resembled June 2006, while others, Lourdes reports, call it police state fascism. Fascism in my research has come up only in satirical performances, such as the effigies of Governor Ruiz Ortiz as a storm trooper or the stencils of a diminutive President Felipe Calderón in oversized military dress, playing soldier on top of a tank. Fascist or not, the forces at play like the recent neoliberal reforms minimize the public rural normal schools and roll back the century of progress that public education has made in shaping Mexico into a modern, rational, and unified society. The threat against public school installations and individuals unsettles pedagogical patrimony, heritage, inheritance, wealth, and endowment, so that groups like small business owners who lose money when teachers occupy the streets can organize their protests around the defense of Oaxacan patrimony. The teachers turn to their collective movement and claim they shall remain a magisterio, a committed pedagogical movement with roots in the socialist 1930s and in the great social upheavals of the late 1960s and 1970s. Patrimony evokes heritage, though it moves politically and pedagogically toward a better future rather than in reverie for a vanished past.

As much as Oaxacan teachers mobilize on the streets, they mobilize in the classrooms through patrimony. This includes celebrating heroes and holidays. March 2011, Marcos met with his sixth-grade class outside on the esplanade before the *periódico* mural bulletin board of his school as his students read about the anniversary of President Lázaro Cárdenas nationalizing Mexico's subsoil oil deposits. At the same time, the class read about the March 21 celebration of the birth of Benito Juárez, Mexico's legendary Zapotec-speaking nineteenth-century liberal reformer. Embarking on a thematic and interdisciplinary unit on the life of Juárez, Marcos and his students on the esplanade developed an interdisciplinary and multimodal project on Oaxaca's most famous politician. Under the patrimonial shadow cast by a national hero, the formality and objective rationality of official textbook learning gave way to problem-solving, playfulness, and nonlinear thinking apropos, according to Carlos Lenkersdorf (2002, 2003), to the ways rural people of southeastern Mexico pose and resolve problems.

Patrimonial pedagogies do not only study heroes and holidays. The peer-based learning that is relevant to village life comes from the communalocratic (Martínez Luna, 2007) systems that govern play, work, signs of respect, and solidarity networks across rural Oaxaca. Students should learn this from their teachers, or so say the dissident teachers in the most recent in-service training manual for alternative education (CEDES 22, 2015). To the dissident teachers, public obligation and communalocratic inheritance may be in greater peril of demise today throughout the spaces of Oaxacan schooling, as free-market economic policies, international financial organization structural adjustments, and teacher evaluation innovations, justified as "quality improvements" eradicate the magisterio's prior progress, such as defending the right to public education (p. 3). On account of the threat to public education, it becomes incumbent on teachers, according to CEDES 22, to

> regenerate the necessary school culture through a reconnecting with culture itself, reframing all the latent power found in our state's communitarian knowledge (*saberes comunitarios*) [and] fortifying the link between educational actors in each school: the students, mothers, fathers, tutors, educational workers (*trabajadores de la educación*), and municipal [and] community authorities. (p. 3)

Proposing that pedagogies today revisit the mutual aid networks, the endowment of Oaxacan rural life is patrimony in friction. Teachers ought to shape teaching and learning around the lived ways in the villages and not force-feed urban, *Mestizo*, and assimilated epistemologies onto a terrain with a multimillennial cultural inheritance.

If they care to harvest it, patrimony is on the teachers' side. Repression and reform threaten Oaxacan heritage, which includes the role of the magisterio as the normal school-trained advocates for village welfare. Nowhere is there more palpable an assault on rural ways of life or a threat to the legacy of the magisterio than the case of the forty-three normal school students who were forcibly disappeared in 2014. The call for justice for the Ayotzinapa forty-three, the presumed-dead rural public educators from Guerrero, a state beset with indigenous cultural heritage, rural precarity, and social injustice akin to the conditions in Oaxaca, resonates across Guerrero, throughout Mexico, and at Mexican embassies and consulates worldwide. The waging of the struggle, however, is not restricted to the 2014 incidents that led to the disappearances. The Sección 9 of the CNTE dissident caucus of the SNTE posted flyers for a forum in Iztapalapa District of Mexico City, which reveals that the struggle over the forty-three is vindication of the role rural normal schools have played in training and placing classroom practitioners.[7] Similarly, the roadblock formed by teachers, discussed in Chapter Six, was designed to obstruct the governor's roofing project. Situating their *bloqueo* at the intersection where service trucks would need to pass, the teachers hoped to force the governor to open the Guelaguetza Festival beneath an unfinished roof, an insult to his executive stature. On the one hand, this action serves to shame the agent responsible for the violence of 2006; on the other hand, by forming a blockade, the teachers use their superior numbers to defend the integrity of the Guelaguetza Festival. In an attempt to build a unified nation, the state invented such cultural performances in 1932, though people from across the eight regions of the state have come to identify with the festival, which gets its name from the mutual aid customs still extant in villages. Governor Ruiz Ortiz would sit in the place of honor during the festival, so the teacher blockade of the site of an invented folkloric festival named for ancestral solidarity networks hampers the governor's ability to bring Oaxaca together under his authority and beneath his completed roof.

Patrimony, like quality, lives on ambiguity; nobody knows for certain what heritage, inheritance, or endowment means. Despite its vagueness, patrimony stimulates rival political views. Many teachers consider themselves the heirs of the socialist missionaries of the 1930s and defend their constitutional rights to protest so vehemently they break off the stony windowsills of historic buildings to launch at the police. Then, tourism industry advocates march and chant that Oaxaca wants peace and tourist revenue, so the delinquent teachers need to stop occupying the historic streets downtown and stop, for the love of god, destroying Oaxaca's patrimony. In this way, struggles over patrimony are those that interpret origin stories and view the world we live in now as having been granted valuable goods from those ancestries. Chartered by King Charles V, Holy Roman Emperor and located at a line-of-sight distance from Monte Albán, a 1,500-year-old hilltop city, Oaxaca City has no shortage of historical pedigree to draw upon. United Nations Educational, Scientific and Cultural Organization (UNESCO), a transnational cultural agency that originated in European postwar rubble, recognized Oaxaca City as significant enough to world patrimony for official protection, a distinction that correlates patrimony with vulnerability. The teacher, broker of community-based public health, science, hygiene, reading, and writing needs the teachers' movement because education reforms have disarticulated this brokerage.

In Oaxaca, of course, heritage saved from its destruction moves through multiple other frictions, such as indigenous language and cultural rights, Catholic family values, pan-Latin Americanism in the racial theories of José Vasconcelos, and revolutionary values of José Martí, just to name a few. For further study, the movement of patrimony could bear fruit in projects that examine course content and textbook topics. How stories of tradition and origins have remained contentiously motivating during the current turn of teaching and learning to bolster the knowledge society is a question I might have asked here. Or perhaps, how cultural groups and individuals are included or omitted from curricula might equally benefit from observing the movement of patrimony, by piecing together the notions that drive inclusion and exclusion from the wider social, textual, and historical worlds, rather than limiting the analysis to schools, families, and peers alone. Looking through the movement of patrimony would lend interesting insight into ability, nationalism, and group-identity refusal. As a reader of Antonio Gramsci's *traditional* schooling (Forgacs, 2000), especially his advocacy for curricula delivered through Latin and Greek to ensure historical and analytical rigor, over sterilized and mechanical learning of technical schooling (p. 316), I see tradition in friction today.

Governability—la Maestra Scolding You for What Is Not Your Fault

Quality education as a universal goal gives teachers footholds for quality counter-pedagogies, and Mexican and Oaxacan patrimony discourses enable a defense of the collective integrity of the magisterium. Teachers, furthermore, simply will not allow violent assaults against students and colleagues and insidious educational reforms to go unanswered. Governability, the tension generated by illegitimate use of force, engenders teaching practices in support of better governance. In a solemn act of protest, bad governance would arouse teachers to travel outside of their region to block traffic in Chapter Six. Governor Ruiz Ortiz wanted the traffic to flow because of his pet project to construct a roof over the open-air auditorium of the Guelaguetza Festival, an annual event where the sitting governor sits in a place of honor and provides a convocation. In addition, in a comical act of protest, the bad governance of the Mexican president motivated activists below the presidential balcony in Mexico City to throw shoes at a vinyl image of a distant, hapless, and illegitimate head of state in Chapter Seven. Activism and pedagogy center not just on political decisions the activists oppose but on the question of who has the basic competence to make them.

Movements of governability appear around the case of the student teachers from Ayotzinapa. Since the primary events of this research, the September 2014 disappearance of forty-three normal school students in Guerrero, Oaxaca's neighbor to the west, has a struggle over teaching and social movement that has turned into a translocal and transnational focal point for governability across Mexico and beyond. The forty-three, in transit to an anniversary commemoration for the 1968 student massacre and whose whereabouts or bodily remains continue to be unknown, are allegorical packages that point to a government beset with repressive incompetence. Protests, which have flourished worldwide, have involved the parents of the forty-three, showing the public that the state does not take care of their children, the future civil servant teachers.

Parenting, like teaching, demands basic competence. The purchase of the rights to a childhood discourse, seen above, carries within it the expectation that parents and teachers have the ability and commitment to ensure a quality childhood experience. Politicians, judges, and police officers also claim paternal and maternal power through their positions of authority. However, when the state's authority is illegitimate, the role of nurturing the next generation falls to someone more caring, responsive, and capable. A radio producer reads a letter on the case of Ayotzinapa to her child listeners, the *niñonautas* (child-explorers), explaining that

> Mexico, our country, is going through a complicated phase, as a few weeks ago 43 boys and girls (*muchachos*)—all students from a school in the countryside (*campo*) in a place called Ayotzinapa—disappeared. They were not much older than you, and they were treated unjustly. Imagine if your maestra scolds you for something that was not your fault and you are given extra work to do (*tarea*), or if a dog breaks a plate and you get blamed.... Well, something like this happened to these guys because someone very corrupt with power punished them for something they did not do. Maybe you have recently seen a lot of noise on the streets and people, citizens like us, out marching to demand the reappearance of the 43 young people, since their parents, friends and classmates miss them and want them back. We do not know these [43] guys personally, but we know their names and have seen their pictures in the newspaper and on TV. (Miret, 2014, para. 2–4)

This letter speaks directly to young people, appealing to their sense of right and wrong. We do not need to know the forty-three personally; suffice to say that they were like our classmates and friends. The letter continues:

> Today, niñonautas, it is important for us to ask the people who govern Mexico, our country, to help us find [the forty-three]. Today, niñonautas, it is the moment for you all to do whatever is possible in order to create a country that is responsible and free of corruption, robberies, violence, and mistreatment, because adults have done a lot of damage. We count on you guys, and we put ourselves in your hands. Remember that this country is yours, and now it is time to make things right. (Miret, 2014, para. 5–7)

The radio producer teaches the niñonautas about Ayotzinapa perhaps out of indignation or love; however, that she possesses the authority and mobilizes the transmission hardware to do so at all attests to the misinforming ineptitude of the president. For the sake of future good governance, Miret marshals the niñonautas into future public service because the state by itself, without the people of *our country*, cannot.

Governability motivates because of bad governance, not in spite of it. Using repressive force does not as much scatter people as it does anger them. Once the initial impact of fear subsides, as in the case of the June 14, 2006, police brutality against teachers on Oaxaca City, the corresponding indignation remains and inspires countermeasures. Surely, the mobilizations against the governor in Oaxaca in 2006 were not carefree, natural responses, when Church atria, thoroughfares, plazas, and urban parks became sites of dialogs, concerts, teach-ins, and solidarized encounters such as the teacher Andrea receiving a candy vendor's prayer cards to keep her safe from the police remain as trying episodes of teaching. There is something creative too, as struggles over governability take the misrule of the governors who cannot govern as a point of departure. The violent *desalojo* of Oaxaca City protests in 2006 emboldened teacher Rosa María Santiago Cruz (2010) to hamper the police, camaraderie that humanized her struggle (pp. 66–67). The violence of the helicopters and bazookas helped Santiago Cruz's colleague, Nazario Cuevas Martínez (2010), realize that the repressors had no recourse but to dispossess the teachers (p. 60) who reveled in what they knew as a collective body (p. 59). In 2006, angry parents would challenge teachers for absenteeism and authoritarianism toward the school communities, which motivated Andrea to return to her classes with greater tolerance for parental voices and democratic teaching practices. Bad governance motivates. López Aguilar (2016) says the teachers fight because of bad governance, the educational reforms carried out without "follow-up or evaluation of the educational policies of earlier presidential administrations" (para. 1). The reformers never "considered students, teachers, parents, researchers or specialists. For all this, they lack legitimacy" (para. 1).

Counter-pedagogy, Repression, and Reform

For education-based expressions of self-government or shaping the fields of possibilities where teaching, learning, and meaning play out I have used the term counter-pedagogy, a term I resist defining because critical practices once prescribed tend toward self-referencing. Right consciousness and correct action exist, established in prior ideological configuration, rather than a movement of forces that takes shape, inspires colleagueship, and remains standing. Movements on the streets and in schools take "movement" (Foucault, 1998a, p. 278) as watershed for critical thought and action, and the "labor of diverse inquiries" (1998b, p. 56) allows a gaze at multiple ways of critical teaching that might escape ordinary powers of observation. Teaching as a practice and subject position, in and out of schools, at times dislodges from the ordinary and identified modalities of what counts as teaching. However, the counter-pedagogies that materialize in social movement spaces where teachers confront repression and across schooling terrains, where teachers navigate the inapplicability of state reforms and rigidity of trade union alternative education, oxygenate a teacher practice within systemic norms but without falling prey to them.

The counter-pedagogy is a teacher-based counter-conduct, the critical response to power as government. Government is a practice of power that leads people to live in a given way; as intervention into the thoughts and actions of others, government works on those with the power to choose. Power as government, called "bourgeois outlawry" (McLaren, 2000, p. 209) or mere thinking about power rather than intervening (Said, 1986), may seem out of place in a critical ethnography where the intractability of poverty and violence shape fields of possibility. Withstanding police violence and culturally irrelevant educational reforms has not turned the teachers presented here into wholly radicalized trade unionists or formal education refusers but rather teachers who string up tarpaulins in schools to plan social events and on the streets to stand with their friends, bystanders, and even adversaries. Being with others helps social movement actors feel safe and cared for. For example, the 2006 *barricadas* were maintained by people without radical consciousness as paramilitaries drove around nighttime Oaxaca City and village teachers in this study organized reading events funded by their so-called antagonists in the state and business sector. A politics of affect may not adhere to what is official. Power as government works on individuals who can make choices on what they do and say, suggesting that social movement actors, or individuals without any collective membership, can also govern the way they socialize (eat, love, collectively bargain, play, and teach) in plural ways. The counter-conduct, or the education-based counter-pedagogy, starts here. When teachers obstruct traffic in visible public arteries, they provide physical resistance to the free flow of traffic and disrupt a repressive governor's roofing project over an auditorium, both acts of resistance. At the same time, shaming the governor by inhibiting his roofing project at the annual Guelaguetza Festival, a costly and corrupt event, the teachers ensure that if it rains, it will rain on the governor's seat of honor and poor person in the cheap seats alike. It says that Oaxaca public school classrooms for learning and public fora for cultural performance will each remain open air, plural, and publicly permeable rather than covered in privatized showpieces. It is the teachers who have to teach this; embodying a visible presence en masse on the streets. The teachers, as public intellectuals, furthermore force teaching out into the public eye of the avenue and sidewalk, placing teaching as an enactment beyond the bounded functionality of classroom instruction. The obstruction instructs; alternative public-functionary and public-school-teacher ways of being take hold and reshape what the state officials such as Governor Ruiz Ortiz would have the public believe.

Counter-pedagogies furthermore reshape through fear of violence. Violence plays a key role in governance, for example when police wearing riot gear wield shields and batons—and discharge live rounds into crowds on June 19, 2016, in Nochixtlán, Oaxaca—to direct their might at the few in order to provide deterrence for the many. As Lourdes revealed prior to the 2016 attacks, federal police traveling to Oaxaca by road extended their arrival time by days, and Andrea revealed how federal police in 2006 menaced the city so much that the candy vendor gifted her prayer cards, the rule of force renders fear into individual self-reliance and survival. This is not tolerable for the teachers. Gathering with others, adversaries as well as allies, becomes counter-pedagogical, for the teachers and others enact the solidarity, *convivencia*, and *respeto* long practiced in villages and urban *barrios*, forming an affective field of action faced with the chance of a breakdown of the collective into individualized disarray. More explicitly pedagogical is the practice of what Andrea called "democratic" schooling and what Marcos and his colleagues termed "self-governed pedagogies," each of which emerged out of the vulnerability felt on the streets of Oaxaca City in 2006. These are pedagogical practices that conduct schooling away from the highly teacher-centered toward a more inclusive and playful academic ethos.

Notes

1. Mexico's two principal opposition political parties, the Partido Acción Nacional and the Partido Revolucionario Democrático, have formed the Pact for Mexico with Partido Revolucionario Institucional President, Enrique Peña Nieto (Arriaga Lemus, 2016), an agreement that has legitimized and stabilized the president's mandate. Do to this, "the organized teachers' movement has become more relevant, and, consequently, the target of state violence and repression" (p. 112).

2. President Peña Nieto (2012) justified teacher performance evaluations, saying a teacher can only become a supervisor or director if "the qualities needed for the job" match the "performance (*desempeño*) and professional merit" of the teachers (p. 5).

3. Corporate foundation, Mexicanos Primero, rewards teachers for outstanding efforts in their own professional development and the enhancement of learning-centered and community-oriented schools (González Guajardo, 2010). The award, according to the same foundation, has become a national and international benchmark for teacher "excellence" (p. 19, emphasis added).

4. "Impact Three" in the Mexicanos Primero annual report reveals that the corporate foundation "bolstered (*impulsamos*) the participation of young people on Twitter and Facebook," with 650 million digital hits that indicate active learning (González Guajardo, 2010, p. 20). Quality is measured by the numbers of times a person was engaged in an activity, opening up chances for other calculations of student and community engagement, as we have seen.

5. Theoretically, alternative education training seminars instruct teachers that there are relationships in life that turn the human being into "a thing, something inanimate, losing [his or her] core essence of life: freedom" (CEDES 22, 2015, p. 21).

6. Inspired by the United Nations International Children's Emergency Fund, UNICEF, the rights to a childhood, as we saw in Chapter Two, have driven the Promajoven financial assistance program, which focuses on keeping pregnant girls in school (Secretaría de Educación Pública, 2007b).

7. The forty-three disappeared students stand for the besieged-by-reform normal schools, becoming activist packages for public education itself. It is not just a travesty levied against the forty-three and their families, for their disappearance signals a national desire for an education system that neither kills children nor eradicates rural normal schools, described by the teachers of Sección 9 (2014, para. 1).

References

Aboites, H. A. (2012, November-December). La disputa por la evaluación en México: Historia y futuro. *El Cotidiano*, (176), 5–17.

Arriaga Lemus, M. L. (2014, Fall). The struggle to democratize education in Mexico. *NACLA Report on the Americas, 47*(3), 30–33.

Arriaga Lemus, M. L. (2016). The Mexican teachers' movement: Thirty years of struggle for union democracy and the defense of public education. *Social Justice, 42*(3), 104–117. Retrieved from https://ezproxy.spscc.edu/login?url=http://search.proquest.com /docview/1802183693?accoun tid=1172

Bonfil Batalla, G. (1996). *México profundo: Reclaiming a civilization*. Austin, TX: University of Texas Press.

CCIODH. (2007). *Informe sobre los hechos de Oaxaca. Quinta visita del 16 de diciembre de 2006 al 20 de enero de 2007* (Report). Barcelona: CCIODH. Retrieved from http://cciodh.pangea.org/

CEDES 22. (2015). *Taller estatal de educación alternativa: TEEA 2015–2016* (Instructional material). Oaxaca, Mexico.

Cuevas Martínez, N. (2010). La barricada más grande lo llevo en el corazón. In M. A. Damián (Ed.), *Educación popular: Apuntes de una experiencia liberadora* (pp. 57–61). Oaxaca, Mexico: La Mano.

De Castro Sánchez, S. (2009). *Oaxaca, más allá de la insurrección: Crónica de un movimiento de movimientos (2006–2007)*. Ediciones¡ Basta!. Retrieved from https://www.insumisos.com/LecturasGratis/oaxaca%20mas%20alla%20de%20la%20insureccion%20–%20sergio%20de%20castro%20sanchez.pdf

el Alebrije. (2007). Las noches en la Ciudad de la Resistencia: Entrevista a "El Alebrije." In C. Beas Torres (Ed.), *La batalla por Oaxaca* (pp. 197–202). Oaxaca, Mexico: Ediciones Yope Power.

Esteva, G. (2007, November). La otra campaña, la APPO y la izquierda: Revindicar una alternativa. *Cuadernos del Sur, 12*(24/25), 5–37.

Esteva, G., Stuchul, D. L., & Prakash, M. (2005). From a pedagogy for liberation to liberation from pedagogy. In C. A. Bowers, F. Apffel-Marglin, C. A. Bowers, F. Apffel-Marglin (Eds.), *Rethinking Freire: Globalization and the environmental crisis* (pp. 13–30). Mahwah, NJ: Lawrence Erlbaum Associates Publishers. Retrieved from EBSCO*host*.

Figueroa Crespo, G. (2004). Programa Aula Abierta. In L. M. Meyer & B. Maldonado (Eds.), *Entre la normatividad y la comunalidad: Experiencias innovadoras del Oaxaca indígena actual* (pp. 234–276). Oaxaca, Mexico: IEEPO/Colección Voces del Fondo; Serie Molinos de viento.

Forgacs, D. (Ed.). (2000). *The Antonio Gramsci reader: Selected writings 1916–1935*. New York, NY: New York University Press.

Foucault, M. (1998a). What is critique? In P. Rabinow & N. Rose (Eds.), *The essential Foucault: Selections from the essential works of Foucault 1954–1984* (pp. 263–278). New York, NY: The New Press.

Foucault, M. (1998b). What is enlightenment? In P. Rabinow & N. Rose (Eds.), *The essential Foucault: Selections from the essential works of Foucault 1954–1984* (pp. 43–57). New York, NY: The New Press.

Freidberg, J., Van, L. J., Patterson, L., Alvarez, Q. F., Corrugated Films, & Mal de Ojo TV. (2007). *Un poquito de tanta verdad*. Seattle, WA: Corrugated Films.

Gibson-Graham, J. K. (1996). *The end of capitalism (as we knew it): A feminist critique of political economy*. Minneapolis, MN: University of Minnesota Press.

González Guajardo, C. (2010). *Mexicanos Primero: 2010 Annual report [informe anual]*. Mexico City: Mexicanos Primero. Retrieved from http://www.mexicanosprimero.org /images/stories/mp_recursos/mp_publicaciones_de_mexicanos_primero/Informe_Anual_2010_Mexicanos_Primero.pdf

Gunzenhauser, M. G. (2008). Care of the self in a context of accountability. *The Teachers College Record, 110*(10), 2224–2244.

Hernández Ruiz, S. (2006). Insurgencia magisterial y violencia gubernamental en Oaxaca. In J. V. Cortés (Ed.), *Educación, sindicalismo y gobernabilidad en Oaxaca* (pp. 87–123). Oaxaca, Mexico: SNTE.

Lanas, M., & Zembylas, M. (2015). Towards a transformational political concept of love in critical education. *Studies in Philosophy and Education, 34*(1), 31-44.

LASA. (2007). Violaciones contra la libertad académica y de expresión en Oaxaca de Juárez: Informe presentado por la delegación de la Asociación de Estudios Latinoamericanos (LASA) encargada de investigar los hechos relacionados con el impacto del conflicto social del año 2006. *Cuadernos del Sur, 11*(24–25), 155–171.

Lenkersdorf, C. (2002). Aspectos de educación desde la perspectiva maya-tojolabal. *Reencuentro, 33*, 66–74.

Lenkersdorf, C. (2003). Otra lengua, otra cultura, otro derecho: Un ejemplo de los maya-tojolabales. In J. E. Ordóñez Cifuentes (Ed.), *El derecho a la lengua de los pueblos indígenas:* Jornadas Lascasianas 11, No. 59 (pp. 17–29). Mexico City: Instituto de Investigaciones Jurídicas, Universidad Nacional Autónoma de México.

López Aguilar, M. D. (2016, June 16) ¿Por qué luchan los maestros? *La jornada.* Retrieved from http://www.jornada.unam.mx/2016/06/12/opinion/019a1pol 1/3

Maeckelbergh, M. (2009). *The will of the many: How the alterglobalization movement is changing the face of democracy.* London: Pluto Press.

Maldonado, B. (2010). *Comunidad, comunalidad y colonialismo en Oaxaca, México: La nueva educación comunitaria y su contexto* (Doctoral dissertation, Department of Mesoamerican and Andean Cultures, Faculty of Archaeology). Leiden University.

Martínez, N. (2006, August 22). Califica Procuraduría a APPO de guerrilla urbana. *El Universal.* Retrieved from http://www.eluniversal.com.mx/notas/370333.html

Martínez Luna, J. (2007). De Juárez a García. In G. Esteva, F. Gargallo, J. Martínez Luna, & J. Pech Casanova (Eds.), *Señor Juárez* (pp. 73–99). Oaxaca, Mexico: Archipiélago.

Martínez Vásquez, V. R. (2007). Crisis política en Oaxaca. *Cuadernos del Sur, 11*(24–25), 39–62.

Martínez Vásquez, V. R. (2009). Antinomias y perspectivas del movimiento popular en Oaxaca. In V. R. Martínez Vásquez (Ed.), *La APPO: ¿Rebelión o movimiento social?: Nuevas formas de expresión ante la crisis* (pp. 329–347). Oaxaca, Mexico: IISUABJO.

McLaren, P. (2000). *Che Guevara, Paulo Freire, and the pedagogy of revolution.* Lanham, MD: Rowman & Littlefield Publishers.

Miret, K. (2014, November 11). *Carta para los niños sobre Ayotzinapa.* Programa de Radio de Carmen Aristegui 102.5 FM (Radio program). Retrieved from https://cnteseccion9.wordpress.com/2014/11/page/2/

Norget, K. (2009). La Virgen de las barricadas: La Iglesia Católica, religiosidad popular y el movimiento de la Asamblea Popular de los Pueblos de Oaxaca. In V. R. Martínez Vásquez (Ed.), *La APPO: ¿Rebelión o movimiento social?: Nuevas formas de expresión ante la crisis* (pp. 301–328). Oaxaca, Mexico: IISUABJO.

Ong, A. (2006). *Neoliberalism as exception: Mutations in citizenship and sovereignty.* Durham, NC: Duke University Press.

Ornelas, C. (2008). El SNTE, Elba Esther Gordillo y el gobierno de Calderón. *RMIE, 13*(37), 445–469.

Ortega, J. (2009). La crisis de la hegemonía en Oaxaca: El conflicto político de 2006. In V. R. Martínez Vásquez (Ed.), *La APPO: ¿Rebelión o movimiento social?: Nuevas formas de expresión ante la crisis* (pp. 11–44). Oaxaca, Mexico: IISUABJO.

Peña Nieto, E. (2012, de diciembre de 10). *To the President of the board of the House of Representatives of the Congress of the Union [Presidente de la Mesa Directiva de La Cámara de Diputados de la Unión]* (Letter). Mexico City: Office of the President of United States of Mexico. Retrieved from http://pactopormexico.org/Reforma-Educativa.pdf

Said, E. (1986). Foucault and the imagination of power. In David Couzens Hoy (Ed.), *Foucault: A critical reader* (pp. 149–155). New York, NY: Basil Blackwell.

Santiago Cruz, R. M. (2010). 14 de junio: La unidad popular. In M. A. Damián (Ed.), *Educación popular: Apuntes de una experiencia liberadora* (pp. 62–67). Oaxaca, Mexico: La Mano.

Secretaría de Educación Pública. (2007b). *Estudiar es su derecho* (Handbook). Mexico City: Dirección General del Desarrollo Curricular de la Subsecretaría de Educación Básica de la Secretaría de Educación Pública.

Sección 9. (2014, October 30). *Foros Ayotzinapa: La defensa del normalismo y la educación pública* (Flyer from website). Retrieved from https://cnteseccion9.wordpress.com/2014/10/30/foros-ayotzinapa-la-defensa-del-normalismo-y-la-educacion-publica/

Sotelo Marbán, J. (2008). *Oaxaca: Insurgencia civil y terrorismo de estado*. Mexico City: Era.

Stephen, L. (1997). Pro-Zapatista and pro-PRI: Resolving the contradictions of Zapatismo in rural Oaxaca. *Latin American Research Review, 32*(2), 41–70.

Stephen, L. (2002). ¡Zapata *Lives!: Histories and cultural politics in Southern Mexico*. Berkeley, CA: University of California Press.

Tsing, A. L. (2005). *Friction: An ethnography of global connection*. Princeton, NJ: Princeton University Press.

Yescas Martínez, I. (2008). Movimiento magisterial y gobernabilidad en Oaxaca. *El Cotidiano, 23*(148), 63–72.

Index